How to Do *Everything* with Your

iPod & iTunes®
Third Edition

How to Do *Everything* with Your

iPod® & iTunes®
Third Edition

Guy Hart-Davis

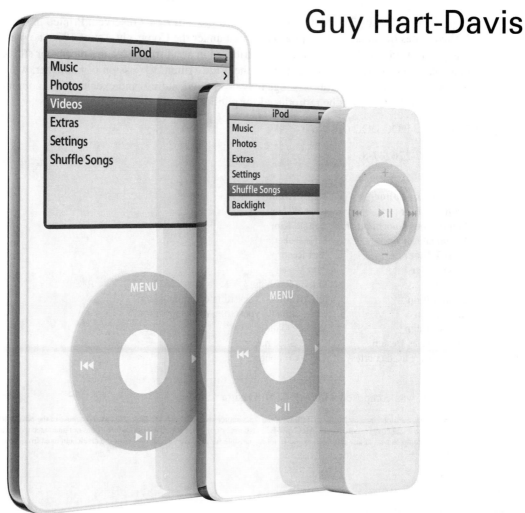

McGraw-Hill/Osborne

New York   Chicago   San Francisco   Lisbon
London   Madrid   Mexico City   Milan   New Delhi
San Juan   Seoul   Singapore   Sydney   Toronto

The McGraw·Hill Companies

McGraw-Hill/Osborne
2100 Powell Street, 10th Floor
Emeryville, California 94608
U.S.A.

To arrange bulk purchase discounts for sales promotions, premiums, or fund-raisers, please
contact **McGraw-Hill**/Osborne at the above address.

How to Do Everything with Your iPod® & iTunes®, Third Edition

234567890 DOC DOC 019876

ISBN 0-07-226247-8

Acquisitions Editor	Megg Morin
Project Editor	Janet Walden
Acquisitions Coordinator	Agatha Kim
Technical Editor	Clint Roberts
Copy Editor	Bart Reed
Proofreader	Pam Vevea
Indexer	Valerie Robbins
Composition	International Typesetting & Composition
Illustration	International Typesetting & Composition
Series Design	Mickey Galicia
Cover Series Design	Dodie Shoemaker

Cover image used courtesy of Apple Computer

This book was composed with Adobe® InDesign®

This book is dedicated to the people who gave us MP3,
AAC, Apple Lossless Encoding,
and the various iPods.

About the Author

Guy Hart-Davis is the author of three books on MP3 and digital audio, and 30 other computer books on subjects including Windows XP, Microsoft Office, Mac OS X, Adobe Creative Suite, and Visual Basic for Applications.

Contents at a Glance

Contents

Acknowledgments

I'd like to thank the following people for their help with this book:

- Megg Morin for developing the book and relaying hardware as necessary
- Agatha Kim for handling the acquisitions end of the book
- Clint Roberts for reviewing the manuscript for technical accuracy and contributing many helpful suggestions
- Bart Reed for editing the manuscript
- Janet Walden for coordinating the production of the book
- Pam Vevea for proofreading the book
- International Typesetting & Composition for laying out the pages
- Valerie Robbins for creating the index
- Sue Carroll, Bob Robinson, and Dimitri Proano at Apple for their help in getting the iPod images and permissions
- Pamela Roccabruna and Caroline Rubenstein at Altec Lansing Technologies, Inc.
- Aaron Roth at Arkon Resources, Inc.
- Jackie Romulo at Belkin
- Mike Jackle at Contour Design, Inc.
- Thomas Penberthy at Dr. Bott, LLC
- Starr Million Baker at INK Public Relations
- Jason Litchford at Griffin Technology
- Adrian Chan at Macally
- Carrie Baylor and Kelley Goethals at Marware, Inc.
- Vesna Vojnic at Matias Corporation
- David Gawlawski at Pressure Drop
- Amy Cesari at Speck Products Design
- Christine Taylor at Sonnet Technologies
- Jon Yokogawa at Ten Technology
- Roger Stewart for lurking in the background, pulling strings as required

Introduction

iPods are the best portable music players available at this writing. Small enough to fit easily into a hand or a pocket, a fifth-generation iPod can hold the contents of your entire CD collection in compressed audio files, your entire photo collection, and enough hours of video to keep you entertained for a week or more. An iPod nano holds much less (and doesn't hold video) but is correspondingly smaller and cuter. And an iPod shuffle, only the size of a packet of gum, not only holds enough music to keep you listening all day but also has enough battery life to play it all.

Whichever model of iPod you have, you can download a dozen CDs' worth of music from your computer to your iPod in less than a minute, and you can recharge your iPod quickly either from a power outlet or from your computer. And whether you use Windows or Mac OS X, you can enjoy music on your computer with iTunes, the best all-round jukebox and music-management application available.

But you know all this. (Those *are* iPod headphones you're wearing, aren't they?) If you're looking at this book in a bookstore, chances are you're wondering why anyone would need a 400-plus page book to use a simple music player.

Answer: They wouldn't. But the iPods aren't just portable audio players with terrific sound quality, huge capacity, and the ability to play video files (in some iPods). You can also load up your regular iPod or iPod nano with your calendars, and display your appointments on it. You can also copy to your iPod all your contact records and all your text notes—anything from a shopping list to a book. By using third-party utilities, you can transfer up-to-the-minute headlines, weather reports, stock quotes, driving directions, and other text from the Internet onto your iPod, swiftly and automatically. You can even transfer information from widely used organizers such as Microsoft Outlook (on Windows), Microsoft Entourage (on the Mac), and Palm Desktop (on both platforms).

So you can use your iPod to carry your essential information with you, and you can check your appointments or display driving directions even while the music keeps thundering. But that's not all. Because the iPod is based around a hard disk or flash memory and connects to your computer via USB, you can transfer to it any files that will fit on the disk or flash memory. So you can use your iPod to carry a backup of your vital documents with you, or even to transfer files from one computer to another. If your computer is a Mac, and you have the right kind of iPod, you can even install Mac OS X or System 9 on your iPod and boot your Mac from the iPod instead of from the Mac's hard disk.

What Does This Book Cover?

To help you get the maximum enjoyment and use from your iPod, this book covers just about every iPod topic you can think of and various related topics into the bargain.

 *This book shows you how to make the most of your iPod on Windows XP (on the PC) and Mac OS X. If you're using Windows 2000 rather than Windows XP, you should be able to follow along just fine, but you'll need to choose slightly different commands in the interface at some points. For example, Windows XP's default configuration is to use a different Start menu layout than Windows 2000. So if you're using Windows 2000, you'll need to make some different Start menu choices. You'll get used to this in next to no time.*

Chapter 1, "Choose an iPod and Get Your Computer Ready to Work with It," explains what an iPod is; how to distinguish the current iPod models from each other; and how their capabilities differ. The chapter then suggests how to choose the iPod that's best for you and shows you how to get your PC or Mac ready to work with your iPod.

Chapter 2, "Configure iTunes and Load Your iPod," runs you through the steps of charging your iPod, installing iTunes and the iPod software on your PC or Mac, and connecting the iPod for the first time. The chapter then shows you how to start creating your music library and how to load your iPod with music—and then disconnect it safely.

Chapter 3, "Listen to Music on Your iPod," shows you how to connect your speakers or headphones to your iPod, how to use your iPod's controls, and how to use the features on a regular iPod, an iPod nano, or an iPod shuffle.

Chapter 4, "Extend Your iPod's Capabilities with Accessories," discusses the various types of accessories available for the iPod, from mainstream accessories (such as cases and stands) to more esoteric accessories (wait and see).

Chapter 5, "Use Your iPod as Your Home Stereo or Car Stereo," discusses how to connect your iPod to your home stereo or car stereo.

Chapter 6, "Create Audio Files, Edit Them, and Tag Them," shows you how to use iTunes and other tools to build a music library packed with high-quality, accurately tagged song files. You'll learn how to choose the best location to store your music library, how to configure iTunes to get exactly the audio quality you need, and how to work with compressed audio in ways that iTunes itself can't manage. You'll also learn how to convert other audio file types to MP3, AAC, Apple Lossless Encoding, WAV, or AIFF so you can play them on your iPod, how to create audio files from cassettes or vinyl records, and how to save audio streams to disk so you can listen to them later.

Chapter 7, "Buy and Download Songs and Videos Online," explains your options for buying music and video files online. The chapter starts by covering what digital rights management (DRM) is and what it means for computer users. It then discusses what the iTunes Music Store is, how to set up an account, how to find music and videos by browsing and searching, and how to buy and download music and videos. The chapter also covers other online music stores that you may want to examine (although the song files most of the stores sell aren't directly compatible with iPods) and points you to sites where you can find free (and legal) songs online.

Chapter 8, "Burn CDs and DVDs from iTunes," shows you how to use the features built into iTunes to burn CDs and DVDs. You'll learn the basics of burning and the differences between audio CDs, MP3 CDs, and data CDs and data DVDs; learn to configure iTunes for burning CDs; and learn how to troubleshoot problems you encounter when burning CDs.

Chapter 9, "Enjoy Music with iTunes and Manage Your Music Library," shows you how to make the most of iTunes for playing back music (with or without graphical visual effects) and managing your music library. You'll learn how to use audio features such as the graphical equalizer, crossfading, and Sound Enhancer; how to control iTunes via keyboard shortcuts and via the iTunes widget on Mac OS X Tiger; how to browse, mix, and import and export music; how to share music with others and access the music others are sharing; and how to tune into podcasts.

Chapter 10, "Put Your Contacts and Calendars on Your iPod," covers how to put your contact information and calendars on your regular iPod or iPod nano so that you can carry them with you and view them whenever you need to. This chapter explains the vCard format, which is the key to putting contact information—or other text—onto the iPod manually, and it shows you how to create vCards using several widely used applications on both Windows and the Mac. The chapter also explains the two calendar file formats, iCalendar and vCalendar, and shows you how to create files in these formats manually when you need to do so.

Chapter 11, "Put Text and Books on Your iPod," shows you how to put text other than contacts and calendar information on your iPod. This chapter starts by discussing the limitations of the iPod as a text-display device and mentioning the types of text best suited to the iPod. Then it explains how to use the iPod's built-in Notes feature before going on to cover a variety of third-party utilities for putting text on your iPod.

Chapter 12, "Put Photos and Videos on Your iPod," shows you how to fine-tune the synchronization of photos and video files, view photos or videos on your iPod or on a connected TV, and configure and view a slide show. You'll also learn how to upload photos from a digital camera to a regular iPod, how to troubleshoot common photo-related problems, and how to create video files that will agree with your iPod.

Chapter 13, "Use Multiple iPods, Multiple Computers, or Both," explains how to synchronize several iPods with the same computer and shows you how to load your iPod from multiple computers. The chapter starts by walking you through the processes of moving an iPod from Mac OS X to Windows or the other direction. It also shows you how to change the computer to which your iPod is linked—a useful skill when you upgrade your computer.

Chapter 14, "Recover Your Songs and Videos from Your iPod," shows you how to transfer song files from your iPod's music library to your computer—for example, to recover songs from your iPod after the hard disk on your computer fails.

Chapter 15, "Use Your iPod with Software Other Than iTunes," explains why you might want to use software other than iTunes to control your iPod, and it gives examples of several Windows applications that are viable alternatives to iTunes. On the Mac, iTunes rules almost unchallenged, but Clutter provides a wonderful super-graphical interface that makes iTunes even easier to use.

Chapter 16, "Use Your iPod as an External Drive or Backup Device," shows you how to use your iPod as a hard drive for backup and portable storage. If your computer is a Mac, you can even boot from a regular iPod for security or to recover from disaster. Along the way, you'll learn how to enable disk mode on your iPod, transfer files to and from your iPod, and optimize your iPod's hard disk to improve performance if necessary.

Chapter 17, "Troubleshoot Your iPod," discusses how to troubleshoot your iPod when things go wrong. The chapter limbers up by discussing the components that make up your iPod, then walks you through things that make your iPod unhappy; how to keep your iPod's operating system up-to-date; and how to carry, store, and clean your iPod. You'll learn how to avoid voiding your warranty, approach the troubleshooting process in the right way, perform key troubleshooting maneuvers, and use your iPod's built-in diagnostic tools to identify suspected problems.

Chapter 18, "Troubleshoot iTunes," shows you how to solve specific problems with iTunes on Windows and the Mac. These problems include iTunes refusing to start, running very slowly, or starting but not appearing; iTunes failing to notice when you insert another CD; and iTunes running you out of hard-disk space by accident.

On the purple-shaded pages, you'll find a Special Project that explains how to maximize your iPod's battery life, discusses battery-replacement options, and provides graphical walkthroughs that show you how to replace the battery on first-, second-, third-, and fourth-generation regular iPod models and the iPod mini. The Special Project doesn't cover battery replacement on the iPod models that are currently under warranty and that will be under AppleCare extended coverage for a year longer than the warranty, because you'd be ill-advised to replace the battery on such iPods when you could have it done professionally for you.

TIP

Given the speed at which Apple introduces new iPods and new versions of iTunes, it's hard to keep this book up to date. For the latest news and extra tips, visit the How to Do Everything with Your iPod and iTunes *blog at http://ipoditunes .blogspot.com.*

Part I

Enjoy Audio with Your iPod and iTunes

Chapter 1

Choose an iPod and Get Your Computer Ready to Work with It

How to...

■ Understand what iPods are and what they do

■ Distinguish the different types of current iPods

■ Identify earlier iPod models (if you have one)

■ Choose the right iPod for your needs

■ Get your PC or Mac ready to work with your iPod

If you don't already have an iPod, you'll need to beg, borrow, or buy one before you can make the most of this book. This chapter tells you which different types of iPod are available at this writing, and shows you how to distinguish among earlier models in case you have one of those rather than a current model. The chapter then suggests how to choose the iPod—or iPods—that will best suit your needs. Finally, it shows you how to get your PC or Mac ready to work with your iPod.

If you're already the proud owner of an iPod, you may prefer to skip directly to Chapter 2, which shows you how to get up and running with it.

What Is an iPod?

The iPod is the umbrella term for the wildly popular portable music players built by Apple Computer. At this writing, there are three main families of iPod: regular, full-size iPods; the iPod nano; and the iPod shuffle. Figure 1-1 shows examples of the three.

In addition to these current models, Apple has also produced—and discontinued—four earlier generations of regular iPod and one generation of the iPod mini, a medium-size iPod built around a small hard disk. You'll meet these older models briefly later in this chapter.

All current iPods connect to your PC or Mac via USB, enabling you to transfer files quickly to the player. You can also use a FireWire connection to charge the regular video-capable iPod and the iPod nano, but not to transfer files to them. The early generations of iPods used FireWire connections only; more on this later in this chapter.

Apple has also collaborated with Motorola to produce mobile phones—the Motorola ROKR E1 and the Motorola RAZR V3i—that run a version of iTunes. Each holds up to 100 songs, and is available from Cingular in the U.S.A. See Chapter 2 for more information.

The Regular iPod with Video and What It Does

The fifth-generation regular iPod, also known as the "iPod with video," is a portable music and video player with a huge capacity, a rechargeable battery good for 8 to 15 hours of music playback (less if you watch a lot of video), and easy-to-use controls. The iPod is built around the type of hard drive used in small laptop computers and comes in two models—at this writing, 30GB and 60GB. (The capacity is engraved on the back of the iPod.) So far, Apple has continued to release higher-capacity iPods as miniature hard disks have increased in capacity, so the maximum capacity seems certain to rise. The more space on your iPod's hard disk, the more songs, video, or other data you can carry on it.

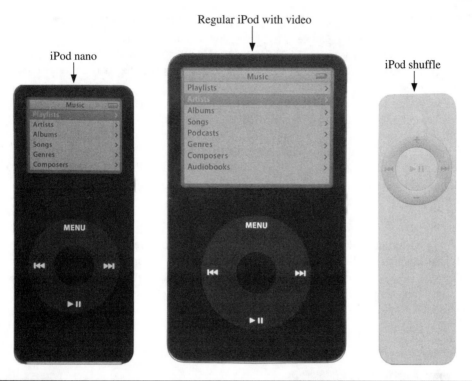

Regular iPod with video

iPod nano

iPod shuffle

FIGURE 1-1	iPods come in three basic types: regular iPods with video, the iPod nano, and the iPod shuffle.

Why Your iPod's Capacity Appears to Be Less Than Advertised

Sixty gigabytes is a huge amount of music—around 15,000 four-minute songs at the iPod's default audio quality, or enough for about 42 days' solid listening. It's also a decent amount of video: about 400 hours at the compression rate the iTunes Music Store uses. But unfortunately, you don't actually get the amount of hard-disk space that's written on the iPod.

There are two reasons for this. First, you lose some hard-disk space to the iPod's OS and the file allocation table that records which file is stored where on the disk. This happens on all hard disks that contain operating systems, and costs you only a few megabytes altogether.

(continued)

Second, the hard-drive capacities on iPods are measured in "marketing gigabytes" rather than in real gigabytes. A real gigabyte is 1024 megabytes, a megabyte is 1024 kilobytes, and a kilobyte is 1024 bytes. That makes 1,073,741,824 bytes (1024 × 1024 × 1024 bytes) in a real gigabyte. By contrast, a marketing gigabyte has a flat billion bytes (1000 × 1000 × 1000 bytes)—a difference of 7.4 percent.

So your iPod will actually hold 7.4 percent less data than its listed drive size suggests (and minus a bit more for the OS and file allocation table). You can see why marketing folks choose to use marketing megabytes and gigabytes rather than real megabytes and gigabytes—the numbers are more impressive. But customers tend to be disappointed when they discover that the real capacity of a device is substantially less than the device's packaging and literature promised.

The fifth-generation iPod (see Figure 1-2) has a 2.5-inch color screen with a resolution of 320×240 pixels, which is called Quarter VGA resolution, or QVGA for short. (VGA resolution is 640×480 pixels.) The screen can display videos, photos, and album covers as well as the iPod's menus, information about the song that's currently playing, and text-based items, such as your contacts, calendars, and notes.

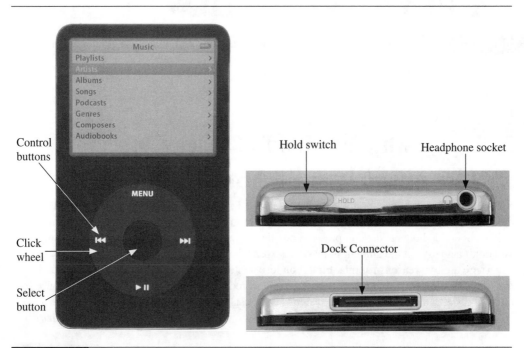

FIGURE 1-2   The front, top, and bottom of a fifth-generation, video-capable iPod.

Below the screen is a control device called the Click wheel or Scroll wheel. The Click wheel has four buttons built into it, which you click by pressing the wheel so that it tilts slightly in the required direction. You drag your finger around the surface of the Click wheel to scroll through items such as menus. You press the Select button, in the middle of the Click wheel, to access the item you've selected by scrolling.

At the bottom of the iPod is a narrow yet wide Dock Connector port, used for connecting the iPod to your computer or to accessories (such as a dock or a charger). At the top is a headphone socket and a Hold switch that you slide to put the iPod on hold (which locks all its controls) or to take it off hold again.

A regular iPod doubles as a contact database, calendar, and notebook, enabling you to carry around not only all your music but information as well. You can also put other textual information on your iPod and view it on the iPod's screen. With extra hardware, you can extend your iPod's capabilities even further. For example, with a custom media reader, you can transfer your digital photos to your iPod's hard disk directly from your digital camera without using a computer. This capability can make your iPod a great travel companion for your digital camera—especially a camera that takes high-resolution photos.

If music, contacts, calendar, notes, and other text aren't enough for you, you can also use your iPod as an external hard disk for your Mac or PC. Your iPod provides an easy and convenient means of backing up your data, storing files, and transporting files from one computer to another. And because your iPod is ultra-portable, you can take those files with you wherever you go, which can be great for school, work, and even play.

Your iPod supports various audio formats, including Advanced Audio Coding (AAC), MP3 (including Audible.com's Audible files), Apple Lossless Encoding, WAV, and AIFF. Although the iPod doesn't support other formats—such as Microsoft's Windows Media Audio (WMA), RealNetworks' RealAudio, and the open-source audio format Ogg Vorbis—at this writing, you can convert audio files in those formats to AAC, MP3, or another supported format easily enough so that you can put those files on your iPod.

Your iPod contains a relatively small operating system (OS) that lets it function on its own—for example, for playing back music and videos, displaying contact information, and so on. The OS also lets your iPod know when it's been connected to a computer, at which point the OS hands over control to the computer so you can manage it from there.

Your iPod is designed to communicate seamlessly with iTunes, which runs on both Mac OS X and Windows. If you prefer, you can use your iPod with other software as well on either operating system (Chapter 15 discusses some of the applications you can use). If you use your iPod with iTunes, you can buy songs or videos from the iTunes Music Store, download them to your Mac or PC, and play them either on your computer or iPod.

NOTE   *The iPod discussed in this section is the fifth generation of regular iPod. For brief details on the first four generations, see "Older iPods That Apple Has Now Discontinued," later in this chapter. Because you're most likely to have one of the current iPods if you're reading this book, the book concentrates on the latest iPod models and mentions the earlier models only at key points.*

The iPod nano and What It Does

The iPod nano is tiny—a little longer than a business card, quite a bit narrower, and barely as thick as a pencil. The iPod nano contains flash memory rather than a hard disk, and has a relatively modest capacity: at this writing, 2GB and 4GB models are available, but higher-capacity models are likely to be released before long. Flash memory is shockproof, so the iPod nano won't skip unless you damage it badly enough to prevent it from playing. And flash memory uses far less power than a hard disk—around 1/30 of the amount a hard drive takes—so the iPod nano requires only a tiny battery.

The iPod nano (see Figure 1-3) comes in either black or white and has a similar layout to the regular iPod, with a screen at the top of the front, the main control buttons built into the Click wheel, a Dock Connector port on the bottom, and a Hold switch on the top. The only major difference in layout is that the headphone socket is on the bottom of the iPod nano rather than on the top.

The iPod nano can display photos and album art on its screen. The iPod nano's capacity is engraved on the back.

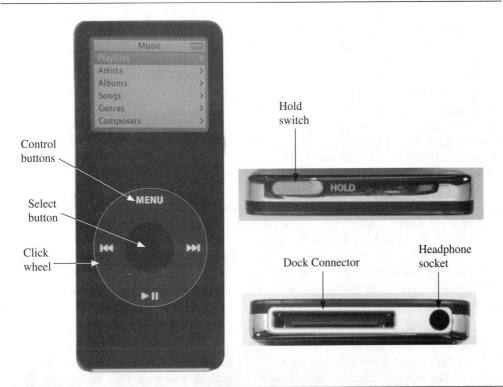

FIGURE 1-3   The iPod nano is very small and contains flash memory rather than a hard disk. Its controls and ports are similar to those on a regular iPod, but its headphone socket is on the bottom rather than the top.

The iPod shuffle and What It Does

First released in January 2005, the iPod shuffle is the smallest and least expensive iPod, costing $99 for the 512MB model and $129 for the 1GB model. At this writing, larger sizes seem imminent.

NOTE   *The iPod shuffle's capacity is written in a box on the front of its USB connector—for example, "512MB" or "1GB."*

The iPod shuffle uses flash memory rather than a hard disk and is about the same size as a pack of gum. It has no screen and two play modes, either playing back an existing playlist in order or "shuffling" the songs into a random order—hence its name. To change from playlist mode to random mode, you use the three-position switch on the back; its third position is Off, turning the iPod shuffle off.

The iPod shuffle (see Figure 1-4) has only five buttons: Play/Pause, Previous Track and Next Track, and Volume Up and Volume Down. The buttons are laid out in a circular arrangement similar to that of the regular iPod and the iPod nano. Though limited and small, the controls are easy to use.

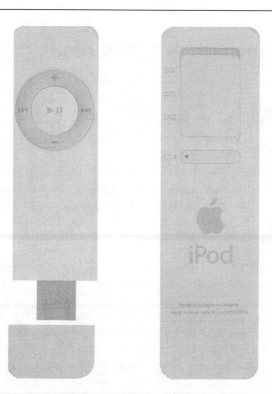

FIGURE 1-4   The iPod shuffle is small enough to slip in almost any pocket—or simply hang around your neck on its included lanyard.

The iPod shuffle's other features are two connectors: a standard headphone socket at the top, and a standard USB 2.0 connector at the bottom.

Without a screen, the only way you can navigate through your playlist is by using the Previous button and Next button and listening to the track that plays. The Shuffle mode makes a virtue out of this limitation by offering to mix up the music for you.

The iPod shuffle is great for exercise or extreme activities that would threaten a regular iPod or an iPod nano. But it's also great if you often get new music and want to focus your listening on it without being distracted by your existing collection, or if you want to force yourself to listen to artists or albums that you normally neglect.

Because of the iPod shuffle's limitations, much of what you'll read in the rest of this book doesn't apply to it. For example, you can't put your contacts, your calendar, or notes on the iPod shuffle, because it has no way to display them to you; nor can you import photos from a digital camera. The iPod shuffle doesn't offer equalizations, but it does support the Start Time and End Time options in iTunes, which let you tell iTunes and your iPod to skip part of the beginning or end of a track when playing it back.

Alternatives to the iPod

iPods are pretty wonderful. But if you're considering buying an iPod as a portable audio player, it's worth considering what it *doesn't* do and what some possible alternatives are.

Other Hard Drive-Based Players

The iPod is the market-leading portable music player at this writing, far outselling its many competitors, such as the Nomad series from Creative Labs, the Samsung Yepp players, and the iriver PMC players. These series include various players in similar capacities to the regular iPods and the iPod nano. The higher-capacity players use hard disks, as do some of the lower-capacity players. Other lower-capacity players use flash memory, like the iPod nano does.

The key difference is that most of the competitors are Windows-based players that work with Windows Media Player and its digital rights management (DRM) technologies rather than working with iTunes and its DRM. You can't use these players with iTunes; nor can you use an iPod with Windows Media Player.

Some Windows-based players have other features, such as radio tuners and the ability to record audio via a microphone or a line-in socket. The more expensive players allow you to play video files as well, either by downloading the video from a PC running Microsoft Windows XP Media Center Edition or by recording it directly onto the device.

All hard drive-based players can skip if you bump them hard enough. Regular iPods have a memory chip that acts as a buffer for the next few minutes of audio, so you won't hear skips unless you give the iPod severe bumps for minutes on end. If you need a player for extreme sports that won't skip, get an iPod nano, an iPod shuffle, or another flash memory-based player. These won't skip unless you destroy them—and they're much smaller than hard drive-based players.

Other Flash Memory-Based Players

The iPod nano and the iPod shuffle compete against other flash memory-based players, most of which include features such as these:

- A screen that displays the information for the song and lets you navigate the various songs on the player. The iPod nano outshines most of the competition on this front, but the iPod shuffle offers no screen at all.

- A microphone or line-in recording capability. This enables you to dictate notes, record live audio (for example, at a concert), or create compressed files (usually MP3 files) directly from an audio source (such as a CD player).

- A radio for when you tire of the songs you've loaded.

PDA

Many PDAs can play audio at decent quality; many contain enough storage, either built in or on an add-in card, to carry enough music for a day or more. Playing music on a PDA is usually more clumsy than doing so on an iPod—for example, you may have to use a stylus to issue commands—but a music-capable PDA can be an acceptable audio solution.

Regular iPods and the iPod nano can carry your phone book, calendars, and text notes, but they don't have any text-entry capabilities. iPod fans and pundits have long predicted an iPod keyboard that will let you type text onto your iPod, but Apple hasn't obliged yet.

Mobile Phone

Mobile phones have become constant companions for many people—so what could be more natural than having them play music as well? Newer models of mobile phones include enough memory to store several days' worth of music, and they provide basic PDA capabilities too.

Many iPod aficionados reckon that if you crossed a mobile phone with an iPod, you'd have the ultimate device. The ROKR from Motorola, a mobile phone that can synchronize with iTunes, was Apple's first step in this direction. The ROKR is limited to using the AAC format (rather than, say, being able to play MP3 files as well) and can contain a maximum of 100 songs. In addition to being able to play back music through headphones and pause it automatically when you receive an incoming call, the ROKR contains a stereo speaker powerful enough to enable you to share your music with those in your immediate circle. A subsequent model, the Motorola RAZR V3i, introduced a sleeker design, but is also limited to a maximum of 100 songs.

But the iPod shuffle isn't only for playing music. You can also use the iPod shuffle as an external disk, and because of its diminutive size, the iPod shuffle is a great way to take your key documents with you.

The chip in the iPod shuffle includes an FM tuner and an analog-to-digital converter (ANDAC) for voice recording. The iPod shuffle doesn't use these capabilities, nor does it use the chip's capability to drive an LCD screen.

Troubleshooting the iPod shuffle is usually more straightforward than troubleshooting the regular iPods and the iPod nano because there are fewer things to go wrong with the iPod shuffle. There's also no screen for displaying diagnostic information.

The iPod shuffle plays AAC, MP3, WAV, and Audible.com files, but it can't play AIFF files or Apple Lossless Encoder files.

Older iPods That Apple Has Now Discontinued

This book concentrates on the current iPod models so as to be as useful as possible to current buyers. But much of what is in the book also applies to many of the earlier iPod models that Apple has now discontinued.

Figure 1-5 shows a second-generation regular iPod, a third-generation regular iPod, a fourth-generation regular iPod, and the late lamented iPod mini.

- The first-generation and second-generation regular iPods have the control buttons arranged in a circle around the Click wheel. The iPod has a monochrome screen and connects to a computer via a FireWire port on the iPod's top.

- The third-generation regular iPod has the control buttons arranged in a line across the iPod under the screen. The iPod has a monochrome screen and connects to a computer via a Dock Connector port on the bottom.

- The fourth-generation regular iPod has a Click wheel with the control buttons integrated into it. Most fourth-generation iPods have a color screen, although some early models have monochrome screens. All connect to a computer via a Dock Connector port on the bottom.

- The iPod mini has a Click wheel with the control buttons integrated into it. The iPod mini has a monochrome screen, contains a tiny hard disk, and connects to a computer via a Dock Connector port on the bottom.

Apple has also released—and discontinued—a special-edition iPod called the iPod U2. This is a regular fourth-generation iPod with a black case, a red Scroll wheel, laser-engraved signatures of the members of U2 on the back, and a special discount for buying The Complete U2 *from the iTunes Music Store.*

Fourth-generation regular iPod

iPod mini

Third-generation regular iPod

Second-generation regular iPod

FIGURE 1-5   Some of the iPod models that have been discontinued.

Choose the iPod That's Best for You

By ruthlessly discontinuing earlier iPod models even when they were selling strongly, Apple has made the process of choosing among the different iPods pretty straightforward:

- If you need the smallest player possible, or a player for active pursuits, get an iPod shuffle.

- If you want the cutest medium-capacity player, get an iPod nano. The iPod nano is great for smaller music libraries, or for carrying only the newest or most exciting songs in your colossal library with you, but its lower capacity can make it seem a poor value alongside the regular iPod.

- If you want a mobile phone that can play AAC files, get a Motorola ROKR E1 or RAZR V3i.

- If you want to watch videos as well as listen to songs, get a fifth-generation regular iPod. If you want to carry as many songs and videos as possible with you, get the highest-capacity model available.

iPod Nominal Capacity	iPod Real Capacity	128 Kbps		160 Kbps		320 Kbps		Apple Lossless Encoder[1]	
		Hours	Songs	Hours	Songs	Hours	Songs	Hours	Songs
512MB	512MB	8	125	7	100	4	50	n/a[2]	n/a
1GB	1GB	17	250	14	200	8	100	n/a	n/a
2GB	2GB	34	500	28	400	15	200	5	72
4GB	3.7GB	67	1,000	54	800	27	400	10	143
30GB	27.9GB	500	7,500	400	6,000	200	3,000	71	1,075
60GB	55.8GB	1,000	15,000	800	12,000	400	6,000	143	2,140

[1]Apple Lossless Encoder encoding rates vary; these figures are approximations.
[2]The iPod shuffle cannot play Apple Lossless Encoder files.

TABLE 1-1   iPod Capacities at Widely Used Compression Ratios

Table 1-1 (above) shows you how much music you can fit onto the current iPod models at widely used compression ratios for music. For spoken audio (such as audio books, plays, or talk radio), you can use lower compression ratios (such as 64 Kbps or even 32 Kbps) and still get acceptable sound with much smaller file sizes. The table assumes a "song" to be about four minutes long and rounds the figures to the nearest sensible point. The table doesn't show less widely used compression ratios such as 224 Kbps or 256 Kbps. (For 256 Kbps, halve the 128 Kbps numbers.)

The iPod refers to tracks as "songs," so this book does the same. Even if the tracks you're listening to aren't music, the iPod considers them to be songs. Similarly, the iPod and this book refer to "artists" rather than "singers," "bands," or other terms.

Audio Formats That the iPods Support

At this writing, the regular iPod and the iPod nano support five audio formats: AAC, MP3 (including Audible.com's AA format), WAV, AIFF, and Apple Lossless Encoder. iPods don't support some major formats, such as the following:

■ Windows Media Audio (WMA), Microsoft's proprietary format. WMA has built-in digital rights management (DRM) capabilities and is used by several of the largest online music stores (such as Napster 2.0). iTunes can convert unprotected WMA files into your music library, turning them to AAC files or MP3 files.

- RealAudio, the RealNetworks format in which much audio is streamed across the Internet and other networks.
- Ogg Vorbis, the new open-source audio format intended to provide royalty-free competition to MP3.

Because you can convert audio files from one format to another, and because the MP3 format is very widely used, this limitation isn't too painful. But if your entire music library is in, say, WMA or Ogg format, you'll have to do some work before you can use it on your iPod. Worse, if your songs are in another compressed format, you'll lose some audio quality when you convert them to AAC or MP3.

The iPod shuffle supports AAC, MP3 (including AA), and WAV, but not Apple Lossless Encoder or AIFF. The Motorola ROKR and RAZR support only AAC.

Get Your PC or Mac Ready to Work with Your iPod

If your PC or Mac is a recent model, it probably is ready to work with whichever new iPod you choose. If it's older, or if it's a budget model, or if you've picked up an older iPod, you may need to add new components.

Here are the requirements for a fifth-generation iPod, an iPod nano, or an iPod shuffle:

- A PC running Windows XP Home Edition or Windows XP Professional with Service Pack 2 or later, or Windows 2000 with Service Pack 4 or later, or a Mac running Mac OS X 10.2.8 (Jaguar), Mac OS X 10.3.4 (Panther), Mac OS X 10.4 (Tiger) or later.

- A USB port. For fast transfers, you need a USB 2.0 port, although you can scrape by with a USB 1.x port if you're patient. The USB port must deliver enough power to recharge your iPod. If your keyboard has a built-in USB port (as many Apple keyboards do), chances are that it doesn't deliver enough power for your iPod.

- An optical drive (a CD drive or a DVD drive).

- A CD recorder if you want to burn CDs from iTunes.

NOTE   *First- and second-generation regular iPods connect only via FireWire. (This is because USB 2.0 hadn't been implemented when Apple introduced the iPod, and FireWire was about 35 times faster than USB 1.x. Apple had also built FireWire into all Macs for several years.) Third- and fourth-generation iPods and the iPod mini can use either USB or FireWire for connecting to a computer.*

How Much Faster USB 2.0 Is Than USB 1.*x*

The terms USB 1.*x* and USB 2.0 don't suggest a great difference, but USB 2.0 is up to 40 times faster than USB 1.*x*. USB 1.*x* has a top speed of 12 megabits per second (Mbps), which translates to a maximum transfer of about 1.5MB of data per second; USB 2.0 has a top speed of 400 Mbps, which gives a data transfer rate of about 60MB per second. So loading your iPod via a USB 2.0 port will go far faster than via a USB 1.*x* port. The difference is most painful when you're loading a regular iPod, but you'll feel the pinch of USB 1.*x* even with the lower capacity of an iPod shuffle or an iPod nano.

Get Your PC Ready to Work with Your iPod

If you bought your PC in 2003 or later, it most likely has everything you need to start using your iPod and iTunes:

- A USB 2.0 port
- Windows XP (either Home Edition or Professional) or Windows 2000 (either Professional or Server)
- A 500 MHz or faster processor (you can get away with a slower processor, but it won't be much fun)
- 128MB RAM (for Windows XP) or 96MB RAM for Windows 2000. Much more RAM is much better
- Enough hard-disk space to contain your media library, on either an internal hard disk or an external hard disk
- A CD burner

If your PC can't meet those specifications, read the following sections to learn about possible upgrades.

Add USB 2.0 if Necessary

Most PCs manufactured in 2003 or later include one or more USB 2.0 ports—some have a half-dozen or more USB ports. If your PC has one or more, you're all set.

The Motorola ROKR uses only USB 1.x, so if you're using a ROKR, you don't need to upgrade to USB 2.0.

1

How to ...   Check the Speed of Your PC's USB Ports

Windows doesn't provide an easy way to check whether your PC's USB ports are USB 1.*x* or USB 2.0. To find out, check your PC's manual. Failing that, try the following:

- Open the System Properties dialog box: On Windows XP, press WINDOWS KEY–BREAK or choose Start | Control Panel, click the Performance And Maintenance item, and then click the System item. On Windows 2000 choose Start | Settings | Control Panel, and then double-click the System item. In the System Properties dialog box, click the Hardware tab and then click the Device Manager button. Expand the Universal Serial Bus Controllers item and see if the USB controllers include "USB 2.0" in their names.

- On Windows XP, plug a known USB 2.0 device (such as your iPod) into a port whose speed you want to test. If Windows displays a notification-area pop-up saying "HI-SPEED USB Device Plugged into non-HI-SPEED USB Hub" or "This USB device can perform faster if you connect it to a Hi-Speed USB 2.0 port," the port is USB 1.*x* rather than USB 2.0. If Windows doesn't display the pop-up, the port is USB 2.0.

Check Your Operating System Version

Make sure your PC is running Windows XP or Windows 2000. If you're in doubt about which of the many versions of Windows your computer is running, display the System Properties dialog box (press WINDOWS KEY–BREAK or choose Start | Control Panel | System) and check the readout on the General tab (see Figure 1-6). If you don't have one of these versions of Windows, upgrade to one of them—preferably to Windows XP.

> NOTE
>
> *Apple doesn't support using versions of Windows other than Windows XP and Windows 2000 with the iPod, but you can use an iPod with Windows 98 Second Edition or Windows Me if you get third-party software such as Anapod Explorer (www.redchairsoftware.com). Chapter 15 discusses Anapod Explorer and other third-party software for controlling iPods.*

Check Memory and Disk Space

If you don't know how much memory your computer has, check it. The easiest place to check is the General tab of the System Properties dialog box (Start | Control Panel | System).

To check disk space, open a Windows Explorer window to display all the drives on your computer (for example, on Windows XP, choose Start | My Computer). Right-click the drive in question and choose Properties from the shortcut menu to display the Properties dialog box for the drive. The General tab of this dialog box shows the amount of free space and used space on the drive.

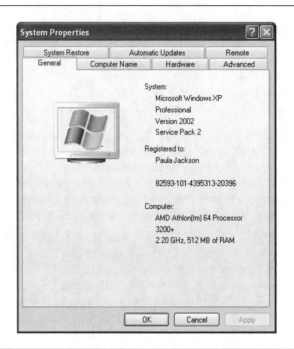

FIGURE 1-6   The readouts on the General tab of the System Properties dialog box include the version of Windows and the amount of RAM in your PC.

Add a CD-R Drive if Necessary

If you want to be able to burn audio CDs from iTunes, add a recordable CD drive to your computer. Which drive technology is most appropriate depends on your computer type and configuration:

- For a desktop PC that has an open 5.25" bay and a spare connector on an EIDE channel, an internal EIDE CD drive is easiest. (If your desktop PC has SCSI, use SCSI instead, because SCSI requires fewer processor cycles than EIDE.)

- For a desktop PC that has no open 5.25" bay or no spare EIDE connector, or for a portable PC, consider either a USB 2.0 CD drive or a FireWire CD drive (if your PC has a FireWire port).

NOTE   *Because USB 1.x is relatively slow, USB 1.x CD recorders can manage only 4× burning speeds. Therefore, you'll probably want to use USB 1.x only when you must—for example, if you have a USB 1.x drive available and can't afford to upgrade.*

Get Your Mac Ready to Work with Your iPod

If you bought your Mac in 2004 or later, chances are it's already all set to work with your iPod: It has one or more FireWire ports or USB 2.0 ports, Mac OS X (Tiger or Panther) with iTunes, plenty of disk space and memory, and a recordable CD drive or a DVD burner as well. But if you have an earlier Mac, it may lack USB 2.0 ports, which means you'll need to add them. And if your Mac has a plain CD-ROM drive, you may need to add a recordable drive to get the best out of iTunes.

Add USB 2.0 if Necessary

If your Mac lacks a USB 2.0 port, you should be able to add one. You can add USB 2.0 ports to a desktop Mac by inserting a PCI card in a vacant slot. You can add USB 2.0 ports to a PowerBook or iBook by inserting a PC Card.

If you have an iPod shuffle and your Mac has only a USB 1.x port, you probably don't need to upgrade, because the USB 1.x port will fill an iPod shuffle in a tolerably short time. If you have a Motorola ROKR, you need only USB 1.x.

Check Your Operating System Version

Make sure your version of Mac OS is advanced enough to work with your iPod. The fifth-generation regular iPod requires Mac OS X 10.3.9 or later, so if you have an earlier version, you'll need to update. The iPod nano and iPod shuffle require Mac OS X 10.3.4 or later, but even so, it's a good idea to apply the latest updates available to the version of Mac OS X (Tiger or Panther) that you're using. Upgrade if necessary, or use Software Update (choose Apple | Software Update) to download the latest point releases. If you're not sure which version of Mac OS X you have, choose Apple | About This Mac to display the About This Mac window. Then look at the Version readout.

NOTE *Apple frequently adds new features to iTunes and the iPods. To get the latest features and to make sure that iTunes and your iPod work as well as possible, keep Mac OS X, iTunes, and the iPod software up to date. To check for updates, choose Apple | Software Update.*

Check Disk Space and Memory

Make sure your Mac has enough disk space and memory to serve your iPod adequately.

In most cases, memory shouldn't be an issue: If your Mac can run Mac OS X and conventional applications at a speed you can tolerate without sedation, it should be able to handle your iPod. Technically, Panther requires an absolute minimum of 128MB of RAM, but most users reckon 256MB a practical minimum, 512MB a good idea, and 1GB or more the best for heavy use. Tiger requires a minimum of 256MB; again, more is better, and much more is much better.

Disk space is more likely to be an issue if you will want to keep many thousands of songs and many hours of video in your media library. The best situation is to have enough space on your hard drive to contain your entire media library, both at its current size and at whatever size you expect it to grow to within the lifetime of your Mac. That way, you can easily synchronize your entire library easily with your iPod (if your library fits on your iPod) or just whichever part of your library you want to take around with you for the time being.

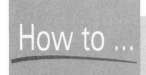

Check the Speed of Your Mac's USB Ports

If you're not sure of the speed of your Mac's USB ports, check them like this:

1. Choose Apple | About This Mac to display the About This Mac dialog box.

2. Click the More Info button to display the System Profile window.

3. Expand the Hardware entry in the Contents pane if it's collapsed. Then click the USB item to display its contents.

4. Select one of the USB Bus items in the USB Device Tree pane and check the Speed readout in the lower pane, as shown here. If the readout says "Up to 12 Mb/sec," it's USB 1.*x*. If the readout says "Up to 480 Mb/sec," it's USB 2.0.

5. Press ⌘-Q or choose System Profiler | Quit System Profiler to close System Profiler.

For example, to fill a 60GB iPod with music and video, you'll need 60GB of hard-disk space to devote to your media library. Recent desktop Macs have hard disks large enough to spare 60GB without serious hardship, but if you have an older desktop Mac, a PowerBook, or an iBook, you may not be able to spare that much space. For example, the G4 1.33 GHz iBook comes with a 60GB hard disk, the same size as the iPod's disk. (You can upgrade the iBook's hard disk to 100GB when you buy it.)

If you have a PowerMac, you should be able to add another hard drive without undue effort. Typically, the least expensive option will be to add another EIDE hard drive or SCSI drive (depending on the configuration of your Mac) to the inside of your Mac. Alternatively, you can go for an external FireWire, USB, or SCSI drive (if your Mac has SCSI).

If you have a PowerBook, an iBook, an iMac, an eMac, or a Mac mini, your best bet is probably to add an external FireWire or USB hard drive. Upgrading the internal hard drive on these Macs tends to be prohibitively expensive—and you have to transfer or reinstall the operating system, your applications, and all your data after the upgrade.

Add a CD-R Drive if Necessary

If your Mac doesn't have a CD burner, you may want to add one so you can burn CDs from iTunes and other applications.

For a desktop Mac that has a full-size drive bay free, an internal CD-R drive is the least expensive option. Alternatively, turn to one of the alternatives that suit both desktop Macs and portables: external FireWire, USB, or SCSI recordable CD drives.

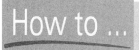

If you add an internal SuperDrive to a desktop Mac, you can burn playlists to DVD as well, which can be useful for archiving your music.

How to ...   Connect an Older iPod via FireWire

If you have first- or second-generation iPod, you'll need to connect it to your computer via FireWire rather than via USB.

If your computer is a Mac, this shouldn't be a problem, because all Macs for the last several years include one or more FireWire ports. If you have an older Mac that doesn't have FireWire, add a PCI card (for a desktop Mac) or a PC Card (for a PowerBook). Make sure the card is compatible with the version of Mac OS X you're using, and then install the card and any drivers needed to make it work.

If your computer is a PC, it's less likely to have a FireWire port, because FireWire isn't part of the standard PC specification. But you can add one or more FireWire ports easily enough by inserting a PCI card (in a desktop PC) or a PC Card (in a laptop PC).

On a PC that has built-in FireWire, there's one more thing to watch out for. FireWire ports and cables come in two basic types: four-pin and six-pin. Four-pin ports are more compact than six-pin ports, so they're easier to build into laptops. Six-pin cables supply power to the FireWire devices, but four-pin cables do not supply power. Six-pin cables can recharge your iPod, but four-pin cables cannot.

If your PC or Mac does have a FireWire port, you can use the port to charge your fifth-generation regular iPod or your iPod nano, but not to transfer data to the iPod.

Chapter 2

Configure iTunes and Load Your iPod

How to...

- Identify the different components included with your iPod
- Perform a full initial charge (if needed)
- Set up your iPod and connect it to your PC or Mac
- Install iTunes and the iPod Software
- Start creating your music library from existing files and CDs
- Load music onto your iPod or ROKR

In this chapter, you'll unpack your iPod (if you haven't already done so), give it an initial full charge if it needs one, and connect it to your PC or Mac. You'll install iTunes and the iPod Software if you don't already have them installed. Then you'll start creating your music library from any existing digital audio files you have and from your audio CDs. Finally, you'll load your music library—or part of it—onto your iPod.

This chapter discusses how to proceed on both Windows and the Mac. Most of the way, the process is the same for both operating systems. Where they differ, the chapter presents Windows first and then the Mac, so you can skip to the sections that cover the operating system that you're using.

What's in the Box?

Over the five generations and several models, the iPod's box has grown smaller and smaller and its contents fewer. The fifth-generation iPod, the iPod nano, and the iPod shuffle ship with the following:

- The iPod itself.
- A pair of white ear-bud headphones.
- A USB cable for connecting your iPod to your computer. The iPod shuffle doesn't come with a cable because it connects directly via a built-in USB jack, but it does come with a lanyard for hanging it around your neck.
- An iPod Dock Adapter, a plastic insert that fits into an iPod Universal Dock to adapt the dock to your iPod's contours. The iPod shuffle doesn't have this item either.
- A CD containing iTunes and the iPod Software (for the Mac and Windows) and several booklets containing instructions, the license agreement for the iPod, and so on.
- A slip case to protect the iPod against scratches. The iPod shuffle doesn't include this case, and the earliest iPod nanos didn't either.

NOTE   *Earlier iPod models included more accessories, such as a dock for parking the iPod on your desk, a case for carrying it, a power adapter for charging it, and a wired remote control for controlling the music while the iPod was stowed in its case or your pocket. You can buy Apple accessories for the iPod, as well as a bewildering array of third-party accessories, from the Apple Store (http://store.apple.com). See Chapter 4 for a discussion of the main categories of accessories and some of the most interesting items.*

Install the iPod Software and iTunes

Before you connect the iPod to your PC or Mac, install the iPod Software and iTunes on your computer. Insert the CD in the optical drive and follow the prompts. The process is a little different for Windows and the Mac, so the operating systems are discussed separately.

Install the iPod Software and iTunes in Windows

Before you connect your iPod to your PC, install the iPod Software, iTunes, and QuickTime (which provides some of the encoding and playback functionality to iTunes):

> *If you've lost the iPod CD, or if you'd like to have the very latest version of the software, download the iTunes installer and the iPod Software installer from the iTunes area of the Apple website: www.apple.com/iTunes. When installing the downloaded version of iTunes, you may see an Open File—Security Warning dialog box. Click the link on the Publisher line to check that the digital certificate for the file is okay (the Digital Signature Information readout on the General tab of the Digital Signature dialog box should read, "This digital signature is OK") and then click the Run button to continue the installation.*

1. Close all other applications before running the installer, because you'll need to reboot your PC afterwards.

2. Insert the iPod CD in your PC and let AutoRun launch the installation routine. If it doesn't run automatically, choose Start | My Computer, right-click the icon for your CD drive, and choose AutoPlay from the shortcut menu.

3. Select the language to use and accept the license agreement.

4. For a regular iPod or an iPod nano, enter the serial number, which is engraved on the back of the iPod below the box that gives the iPod's capacity. The iPod shuffle doesn't have a serial number. Select your country, and then fill in the required registration information.

5. On the Choose Destination Location screen, choose the folder in which to install the iPod Software (the default location, an iPod folder in your Program Files folder, is usually best). The installation routine then launches the iTunes + QuickTime installation, for which you have to accept another license agreement.

6. On the Setup Type screen, you need to make three decisions:

   ■ **Whether to install shortcuts for iTunes and QuickTime on your desktop**   The installation routine creates shortcuts on your Start menu anyway, so you may decide you don't need the shortcuts on the desktop.

   ■ **Whether to use iTunes as the default player for audio files**   This is a good idea if you plan to use iTunes as your main audio player. If you plan to use iTunes only for iPod synchronization and use another player (for example, Windows Media Player) for music, don't make iTunes the default player. iTunes associates itself with the AAC, MP3, and WAV file extensions.

■ **Whether to make QuickTime the default player for media files (such as video files)**   This option is selected by default, but you may prefer to use Windows Media Player instead, which has better integration with Windows than QuickTime does.

7. On the Choose Destination Location screen, choose the destination folder for iTunes. Again, the default location (an iTunes folder in your Program Files folder) is usually best.

8. Restart your computer when prompted.

After your computer has restarted and you've logged in, connect your iPod to the computer using the USB cable. Wait for Windows to detect the iPod. This usually happens in a few seconds, but it may take a minute or two. You'll see a series of pop-up messages in the notification area (the area at the opposite end of the taskbar from the Start button) as the Found New Hardware Wizard works out what the iPod is: a "USB storage device," an "Apple iPod," and then a "disk drive."

The Found New Hardware Wizard then tells you that your new hardware is ready for use. But if the iPod is a regular iPod or an iPod nano, you'll then see the iPod Not Readable dialog box (shown here), which tells you that the iPod must be reformatted before you can use it with your PC. This is because the iPods ship formatted with the Mac file system, which Windows cannot read. So you must reformat the iPod before Windows can read it.

To reformat the iPod, click the Update button. In the iPod Updater dialog box (Figure 2-1), click the Restore button, and then click the blue Restore button in the confirmation dialog box. Wait for the update process to complete and then click the Close button (the X button) to close the iPod Updater dialog box.

If Windows can't detect your iPod, see "iTunes Won't Recognize Your iPod" in Chapter 18 for solutions.

Launch iTunes in Windows

Double-click the iTunes icon on the desktop (if you let the installer add it) or choose Start | All Programs | iTunes | iTunes to start iTunes. Accept the license agreement, and then follow the steps of the iTunes Setup Assistant:

FIGURE 2-1   When you first connect a new regular iPod or iPod nano to your PC, you'll need to reformat it so that the PC can read it.

1. On the Find Music Files page (see Figure 2-2), choose which music files to add to your music library. Then click the Next button. Here are some points to keep in mind:

   ■ iTunes searches your My Music folder and its subfolders. You can search other folders manually later.

   ■ If you leave the Add MP3 and AAC Files check box selected, iTunes adds MP3 files and AAC files directly to the library.

   ■ If you leave the Add WMA Files check box selected, iTunes finds unprotected WMA files and converts them to AAC files, leaving the WMA files untouched. If you have many WMA files, this conversion may take several hours—in which case you might prefer to perform it later.

   NOTE   *WMA files can be protected with digital rights management (DRM) restrictions that control which computers can play the files. iTunes can't convert protected WMA files to AAC files.*

2. On the Keep iTunes Music Folder Organized page (see Figure 2-3), choose whether you want iTunes to automatically change the names of song files, as well as the names of the folders that contain them, when you edit the tag information in the songs.

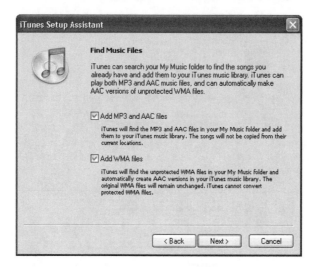

FIGURE 2-2 The easiest way to add your music files to your music library is to let iTunes add them automatically from your My Music folder. If your files are stored in another folder, you can add them manually later.

FIGURE 2-3 The Keep iTunes Music Folder Organized page offers a crucial choice: whether iTunes automatically changes file and folder names to match a song's tags or leaves the file and folder names alone. In most cases, it's best to manage file and folder names yourself.

The default setting is No, I'll Change The File And Folder Names Myself, but you can select the Yes, Keep My iTunes Music Folder Organized option button if you want to have iTunes change the names of the files and folders automatically for you. See the "Decide Whether to Let iTunes Organize Your Music Folder" upcoming sidebar for advice on choosing between these settings.

After you click the Finish button on the iTunes Setup Assistant, the iTunes window appears. If your computer is connected to the Internet, iTunes checks to see if an updated version is available. If one is available, iTunes prompts you to download it (which may take a few minutes, depending on the speed of your Internet connection) and install it. Usually, after updating iTunes, you'll need to run through the iTunes Setup Assistant again. You may also need to restart your PC.

Install the iPod Software and iTunes on the Mac

This section discusses how to install the iPod Software and iTunes on the Mac. iTunes may already be installed, but you must install the iPod Software so that your Mac can recognize your iPod.

How to ...   Decide Whether to Let iTunes Organize Your Music Folder

Take a moment to think about the Keep iTunes Music Folder Organized setting, because it decides whether you or iTunes controls the organization of your music library.

If you turn this feature on, iTunes stores a song in a file named after the track number (if you choose to include it) and name. iTunes places the song in a folder named after the album; this folder is stored within a folder named after the artist, which is placed in your iTunes Music folder.

For example, if you rip the album *No Wow* by The Kills, iTunes stores the second song as \The Kills\No Wow\02 Love Is a Deserter.aac on Windows or as /The Kills/No Wow/02 Love Is a Deserter.aac on Mac OS X. If you then edit the artist field in the tag to "Kills" instead of "The Kills," iTunes changes the name of the artist folder to "Kills" as well.

This automatic renaming is nice and logical for iTunes, but you may dislike the way folder and file names change when you edit the tags. If so, turn off the Keep iTunes Music Folder Organized feature. You can change this setting at any time on the Advanced tab of the iTunes dialog box (Windows) or the Preferences dialog box (Mac), but it's least confusing to make a choice at the beginning and stick with it.

Install the iPod Software on the Mac

First, install the iPod Software on your Mac. Here's how to do so:

1. Insert the iPod CD in your Mac's optical drive. If your Mac doesn't display a Finder window showing the CD's contents, double-click the CD's icon on the desktop.

2. Double-click the Install iPod Software item, and then follow through the installation process, accepting the license agreement and choosing the hard disk on which to install the software. (In fact, you must install the software onto the startup volume, so you don't actually get a choice.)

3. When you finish the installation, the iPod Updater launches automatically. Unless your iPod needs updating, choose iPod Updater | Quit iPod Updater or press ⌘-Q to quit the iPod Updater.

Install iTunes on the Mac (if It's Not Already Installed)

If you have a Mac running Mac OS X, you most likely have iTunes installed already. iTunes is included in a default installation of Mac OS X. Even if you explicitly exclude iTunes from the installation, Software Update offers you each updated version of iTunes that becomes available, so you need to refuse the updates manually or tell Software Update to ignore them (select the iTunes item in the list and press ⌘-BACKSPACE or choose Update | Ignore Update) if you're determined to keep iTunes off your Mac.

You can also install iTunes from the iPod CD (insert the iPod CD and double-click the iTunes installer). But unless your iPod has just been manufactured, chances are good that a new version of iTunes is available via Software Update—so you might as well start with the latest version.

If you've managed to refuse all these updates, the easiest way to install the latest version of iTunes is to use Software Update:

1. Choose Apple | Software Update to launch Software Update, which checks automatically for updates. (If an Internet connection isn't available, you may need to establish one.)

2. If Software Update doesn't turn up a version of iTunes that you can install, choose Software Update | Reset Ignored Updates. Software Update then checks automatically for the latest versions of updates you've ignored and presents the list.

3. Make sure the iTunes check box is selected and then click the Install Items button. Follow through the update process, entering your password in the Authenticate dialog box and accepting the license agreements.

4. Restart your Mac when Software Update prompts you to do so. iTunes Setup then runs automatically (see the next section).

Set Up iTunes if You Haven't Already Done So

If you haven't used iTunes before, or if you've just installed it, follow the steps in the iTunes Setup Assistant to configure iTunes.

If the iTunes Setup Assistant isn't running yet, click the iTunes icon on the Dock or (if the Dock doesn't include an iTunes icon) choose Go | Applications from the Finder menu (or press ⌘-SHIFT-A) and double-click the iTunes icon in your Applications folder.

During the setup process, you make the following decisions:

- **Whether to use iTunes for Internet audio content**   If you accept the default setting (leaving the Yes, Use iTunes For Internet Audio Content option button selected), iTunes becomes the helper application for audio you access through your web browser (for example, Safari).

- **Whether to have iTunes scan your hard disk for any music files so that it can add them to your music library**   Scanning now is usually a good idea (see Figure 2-4), but you may prefer to add files manually later (see "Add Existing Song and Video Files to Your Music Library," later in this chapter).

- **Whether to have iTunes take you directly to the iTunes Music Store so that you can start spending money there**   Select the No, Take Me To My iTunes Library option button if you'd rather build up your library from your CDs and existing audio files first.

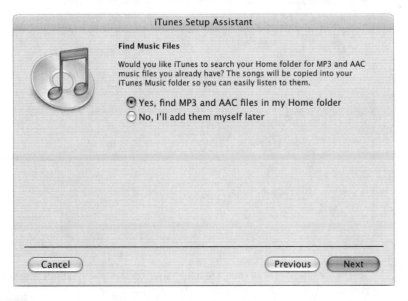

| FIGURE 2-4 | iTunes offers to scan your Home folder for AAC and MP3 files. If your files are in other folders, you can add them manually later. |

iTunes requires QuickTime for some of its features to work. The iTunes Setup Assistant may prompt you to use Software Update (choose Apple | Software Update) to install the latest version of QuickTime so that all the iTunes features work.

Complete the iPod Setup Assistant

After you install iTunes and the iPod Software and connect your iPod, iTunes displays the iPod Setup Assistant (see Figure 2-5). Change the name in the The Name Of My iPod Is text box if you like. Clear the Automatically Update Songs On My iPod check box if you want to update your iPod manually from the start.

For a fifth-generation iPod or an iPod nano, you can select the Automatically Copy Photos To My iPod check box and choose the appropriate folder in the Synchronize Photos From drop-down list. For an iPod shuffle, which cannot display photos, this check box and drop-down list do not appear.

If you want to register your iPod, click the Register My iPod button on the second screen and follow through the registration procedure. (You can also register later at www.apple.com/register.) Otherwise, just click the Finish button to close the iPod Setup Assistant and apply your choices to your iPod.

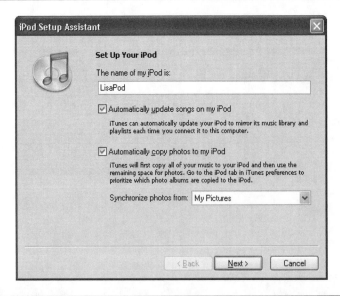

FIGURE 2-5   The iPod Setup Assistant lets you name your iPod, choose whether to update it automatically from the start, and register it with Apple.

Start Your iPod

When your iPod is fully charged (if it needed charging before use), turn it on, and then choose the display language it should use for communicating with you. (Depending on where you bought your iPod, it may be set to display a different language at first than the language you want.) Your choices range from English, German, French, Italian, and Spanish through Norwegian and Finnish to Japanese, Korean, and Simplified and Traditional Chinese.

NOTE *For instructions on setting up an iPod shuffle, see "Connect and Load Your iPod shuffle," toward the end of this chapter.*

To turn on your iPod, press any button; the Select button (in the middle of the Scroll wheel) is usually the most convenient. Your iPod displays the Apple logo for a few seconds and then displays the Language Settings screen. Use the Scroll wheel to scroll to the language you want to use and then press the Select button.

To turn off your iPod, press and hold the Play/Pause button for a couple of seconds until the display goes blank.

If your iPod is on but it's not playing any music or video, it automatically goes to sleep after a few minutes if you don't press any buttons.

Start Creating Your Music Library

Before you can add any songs to your iPod, you normally add them to your music library. This section gets you started with the basics of adding songs to your music library either from CDs or from existing digital audio files. Chapter 9 covers this topic in far greater depth, discussing how to plan, create, and manage an effective music library for iTunes, your iPod or iPods, and your household.

Add Existing Song and Video Files to Your Music Library

While setting up iTunes, you probably let iTunes add song files automatically to your music library from your My Music folder (Windows) or your Home folder (Mac). You can quickly add further songs to your music library from other folders—but before you do, check whether iTunes is set to copy the songs to your music folder.

Decide Whether to Copy All Song and Video Files to Your Music Library

The ideal setup is to store all your songs and video files within your My Music folder (Windows) or your Home folder (Mac). Typically, your My Music folder or your Home folder is on your computer's hard drive, or on its primary hard drive, if it has more than one. That means your hard drive must have enough space for all your songs and videos, not to mention the operating system, your applications, and all your other files (for example, documents, pictures, and e-mail messages). For a modest-size music library, this is easy enough. But for the kind of music library that most music enthusiasts accumulate over the years, it means your computer must have a huge hard drive. The same applies if your library contains many video files.

 **Recover from the Wrong Language: Reset All Settings**

If you choose the wrong language on your iPod, or if a helpful friend changes the language for you, you may find it difficult to navigate the menus to change the language back to your usual language. You can recover by resetting all settings. This option isn't as drastic as it sounds: It turns off Repeat, Shuffle, EQ, Sleep Timer, and Backlight Timer; it puts Startup Volume and Contrast to their midpoints; and it sets the language to its local default. For example, if you bought your iPod in the United States, resetting all settings should return the language to English.

To reset all settings, follow these steps:

1. Press the Menu button as many times as is necessary to return to the main screen. (Five times is the most you should need to press the Menu button to get back to the main screen, even from the deepest recesses of the menus.) You'll see the iPod text at the top of the menu, no matter which language your iPod is using.

2. Scroll down three clicks to select the fourth item on the main menu. This is the Settings item, but you may not be able to recognize the name in another language.

3. Press the Select button to display that menu.

4. Scroll down to the last item on the menu, the Reset All Settings item. This item appears in English, no matter which language your iPod is currently using.

5. Press the Select button to display that menu.

6. Scroll down to the second item. This is the Reset item; again, it appears in English, no matter which language your iPod is using.

7. Press the Select button. Your iPod resets and then displays the Language selection menu startup screen.

8. Choose your preferred language.

 Another possibility is to store your entire music library on a server or on an external disk. See Chapter 9 for a discussion of this option.

If your computer does have a huge hard drive, all is well. But if it doesn't, you'll have to either make do with only some of the songs you want or store some of the files on other drives or other computers. You can tell iTunes to store references to where song files are located rather than store a copy of each file in the music library folder on your hard drive.

Even if your computer has enough hard drive space for all your songs, you may prefer not to store them in your My Music folder or your Home folder so that you can more easily share them through the file system with other members of your household. iTunes' Sharing features (discussed in Chapter 9) enable you to share even files stored in your private folders, but they limit other users to playing the songs (rather than adding them to their music libraries) and work only when iTunes is running. For more flexibility, you may prefer to store shared songs on a server or in a folder that all members of your household can access.

To control whether iTunes copies song files or merely stores references to where the song files are, follow these steps:

1. In Windows, choose Edit | Preferences to display the iTunes dialog box and then click the Advanced tab. On the Mac, choose iTunes | Preferences to display the Preferences dialog box and then click the Advanced button. For either OS, make sure the General subtab is selected.

2. Select the Copy Files To iTunes Music Folder When Adding To Library check box if you want to copy the files (see Figure 2-6). Otherwise, clear this check box.

3. Click the OK button to close the dialog box.

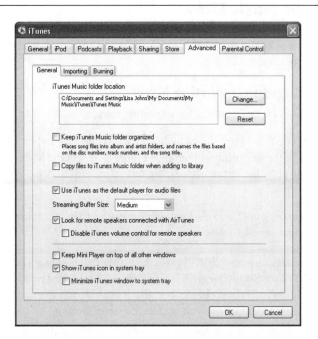

FIGURE 2-6   Clear the Copy Files To iTunes Music Folder When Adding To Library check box if you don't want to store a copy of each song file on your hard disk.

Storing references is great when you have too little space free on your hard disk to accommodate your colossal music library. For example, if you have an iBook whose hard disk is bulging at the seams, you might choose to store in your music library references to music located on an external hard disk rather than trying to import a copy of each song. However, you won't be able to play any song stored on the external hard disk when your iBook isn't connected to it.

Add Songs to Your Music Library

To add songs to your music library, follow these steps:

- ■ In Windows, to add a folder of songs, choose File | Add Folder To Library. In the Browse For Folder dialog box, navigate to and select the folder you want to add. Click the OK button, and iTunes either copies the song files to your library or adds references to the song files.

- ■ In Windows, to add a single file, choose File | Add File To Library or press CTRL-O. In the Add To Library dialog box, navigate to and select the file you want to add. Click the OK button, and iTunes adds it.

- ■ On the Mac, choose File | Add To Library or press ⌘-O. In the Add To Library dialog box, navigate to and select the folder or the file you want to add and then click the Choose button to add the folder or file.

Copy CDs to Your Music Library

The other way to add your existing digital music to your music library is to copy it from CDs. iTunes makes the process as straightforward as can be, but you should first verify that the iTunes settings for importing music are suitable.

Check iTunes' Settings for Importing Music

Follow these steps to check iTunes' settings for importing music:

1. In Windows, choose Edit | Preferences to display the iTunes dialog box, click the Advanced tab, and then click the Importing subtab (see Figure 2-7). On the Mac, choose iTunes | Preferences to display the Preferences dialog box, click the Advanced button, and then click the Importing subtab.

You can also display the iTunes dialog box by pressing CTRL-COMMA and the Preferences dialog box by pressing ⌘-COMMA.

2. In the On CD Insert drop-down list, choose the action that you want iTunes to take when you insert a CD: Show Songs, Begin Playing, Import Songs, or Import Songs And Eject. Usually Show Songs is the best choice, because it enables you to check that iTunes has correctly identified the CD before you import the songs from it.

3. Verify that AAC Encoder is selected in the Import Using drop-down list.

4. Verify that High Quality (128 Kbps) is selected in the Setting drop-down list.

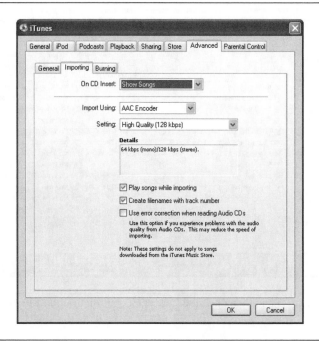

FIGURE 2-7   Before importing music, make sure that iTunes is configured with suitable settings.

5. Clear the Play Songs While Importing check box if you want to import the songs from your CDs as quickly as possible.

6. Click the OK button to close the dialog box.

iTunes can store the music extracted from CDs in several different formats, including Advanced Audio Coding (AAC, the default), MP3, and Apple Lossless Encoder. Chapter 6 discusses the pros and cons of the various formats and how to choose between them. For the moment, this book assumes that you are using AAC.

Add a CD to Your Music Library

To add a CD to your music library, follow these steps:

1. Start iTunes if it's not already running.

2. Insert the CD in your computer's optical drive (CD drive or DVD drive). iTunes loads the CD and displays an entry for it in the Source pane. If an Internet connection is available, iTunes retrieves the CD's information and displays it (see Figure 2-8).

3. Click the Import CD button. iTunes extracts the audio from the CD, converts it to the format you chose, and saves the files to your music library.

FIGURE 2-8 Load a CD and then click the Import CD button to import its songs into your music library.

> **NOTE** *If you've chosen the Import Songs setting in the On CD Insert drop-down list on the Importing subtab of the Advanced tab of the iTunes dialog box or the Preferences dialog box, you don't need to click the Import CD button, as iTunes automatically starts importing the songs from the CD. If you've chosen the Import Songs And Eject setting, iTunes imports the songs and ejects the CD as soon as it has finished.*

After adding the first CD, click the Library item in the Source pane, double-click the first song you imported from the CD to start it playing, and listen to it to make sure there are no obvious defects (such as clicks or pauses) in the sound. If you have time, listen to several songs, or even the entire CD. If the songs sound fine, you probably don't need to use error correction on your CD drive. But if you do hear defects, turn on error correction and copy the CD again. Here's how:

1. In Windows, choose Edit | Preferences to display the iTunes dialog box, click the Advanced tab, and then click the Importing subtab. On the Mac, choose iTunes | Preferences to display the Preferences dialog box, click the Advanced button, and then click the Importing subtab.

2. Select the Use Error Correction When Reading Audio CDs check box.

3. Click the OK button to close the dialog box.

How to ... Connect Older iPod Models

The fifth-generation iPod, the iPod nano, and the iPod shuffle connect to your computer via USB—preferably USB 2.0, but USB 1.x also works if you can tolerate the slow transfer speeds. You can connect the fifth-generation iPod and the iPod nano via FireWire only to charge them, not to synchronize or transfer data.

Older iPods mostly prefer FireWire connections:

- First- and second-generation regular iPods connect only via FireWire. These iPods have a regular FireWire port on the top.

- Third-generation iPods prefer FireWire but can connect via USB for synchronization and data transfer. The iPod mini can connect either via USB or FireWire. Fourth-generation iPods prefer a USB 2.0 connection, but can also use FireWire. These iPods connect to the USB cable or FireWire cable via the Dock Connector rather than a standard FireWire port.

4. In your music library, click the first song on the CD, hold down SHIFT, and click the last song to select all the songs. Press DELETE or BACKSPACE on your keyboard, click the Yes button in the confirmation dialog box, and then click the Yes button in the dialog box that asks whether you want to move the files from your music folder to the Recycle Bin (Windows) or the Trash (Mac).

5. Click the CD's entry in the Source pane and then click the Import CD button to import the songs again. Check the results and make sure they're satisfactory before importing any more CDs.

Connect Your iPod to Your Computer

To connect a fifth-generation iPod or iPod nano to your computer, plug the wider end of the USB cable that came with your iPod into the Dock Connector port on the iPod's bottom. Then plug the other end into a USB port on your computer or on a USB hub attached to your computer.

NOTE
If you have an iPod Dock, plug the wider end of the cable into the connector on the back of the iPod Dock. The symbol side of the connector goes upward, facing the matching symbol on the iPod Dock. Slide the iPod, facing forward, onto the connector in the iPod Dock to complete the connection. If you have a pair of amplified speakers or a stereo input on a receiver available, you can connect it to the Line Out port on the back of the iPod Dock so that you can play music from the iPod through the speakers. If you have a photo-capable iPod and Dock, you can connect an S-video cable to the S-video Out port on the back of the iPod Dock to play a slideshow of photos on your TV.

To connect an iPod shuffle, plug it directly into a USB port, into a USB hub, or into a USB extension cable.

Load Your iPod with Music

If you chose in the iTunes Setup Assistant to let iTunes update your regular iPod or iPod nano automatically, iTunes performs the first update after you connect your iPod. If your music library (and videos, for a fifth-generation iPod) will fit on the iPod, iTunes copies all the songs (and videos) to the iPod (see Figure 2-9). All you need to do is wait until the copying is complete and then disconnect the iPod (see "Eject and Disconnect Your iPod," later in this chapter).

FIGURE 2-9   iTunes copies the songs in your music library to your iPod.

NOTE   *USB 2.0 connections are fast, but your first-ever synchronization of a regular iPod may take an hour or two if your music library contains a large number of songs and videos. This is because iTunes copies each song and video to the iPod. Subsequent synchronizations will be much quicker, because iTunes will need only to transfer new songs and videos you've added to your music library, remove those you've deleted, and update the data on songs whose tags (information such as the artist name and song name) you've changed. If you're using USB 1.x rather than USB 2.0 to synchronize an iPod, the first synchronization will take several hours if your music library contains many songs and videos. You might plan to perform the first synchronization sometime when you can leave your computer and your iPod to get on with it—for example, overnight, or when you head out to work.*

If Your Music Library Won't Fit on Your iPod...

If your music library is bigger than your iPod's capacity, iTunes warns you of the problem (see Figure 2-10). Click the Yes button to let iTunes put an automatic selection of songs on your iPod; iTunes creates a playlist named *iPod's name* Selection, assigns a selection of songs to it, and copies them to the iPod. Click the No button if you want to make the selection yourself. Either way, select the Do Not Ask Me Again check box if you want iTunes to remember your choice.

Configure How Your iPod Is Loaded

If you decide against having iTunes load your iPod automatically, change your iPod's settings as follows:

1. Right-click your iPod's entry in the Source pane and then choose iPod Options from the shortcut menu to display the iPod tab of the iTunes dialog box (Windows) or the Preferences dialog box (Mac).

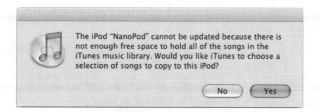

FIGURE 2-10   If your music library is too large to fit on your iPod, decide whether to let iTunes choose a selection of songs for it automatically.

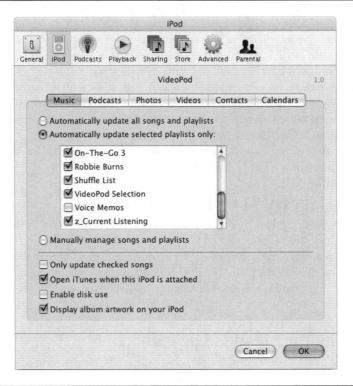

FIGURE 2-11 You can configure automatic or manual updating on the iPod tab of the iTunes dialog box or Preferences dialog box.

2. Click the Music subtab (see Figure 2-11, above) if its contents aren't already displayed, then select the appropriate option button:

■ Select the Automatically Update All Songs And Playlists option button to synchronize your entire music library.

■ Select the Automatically Update Selected Playlists Only option button to synchronize your iPod with the playlists whose check boxes you select in the list box.

■ Select the Manually Manage Songs And Playlists option button if you prefer to add songs to, and remove songs from, your iPod manually.

3. For a fifth-generation iPod, click the Videos subtab and choose the appropriate option button:

■ Select the Automatically Update All Videos option button to synchronize all your videos.

- Select the Automatically Update Selected Playlists Only option button to synchronize the playlists whose check boxes you select in the list box.
- Select the Do Not Update Videos option button to prevent iTunes from putting any videos on your iPod.

NOTE

iTunes disables the controls on the Videos subtab if you select the Manually Manage Songs And Playlists option button on the Music subtab. However, you can add videos to the iPod by dragging them to it, as described in the next section.

4. Click the OK button to close the dialog box.

Load Music on Your iPod Manually

If you decided against automatic updating of either your entire music library or iTunes' automatic selection from it, you need to load your iPod manually. You can perform either of the following actions:

- Connect your iPod to your computer, wait until its entry appears in the Source pane, and then drag songs, artists, albums, playlists, or videos to its entry. When you drop the items, iTunes copies the songs to the iPod, which takes a few seconds.

TIP

To force iTunes to copy to your iPod any AAC files and MP3 files that lack the tag information your iPod normally requires, add the songs to a playlist. Doing so can save you time over retagging many files manually and can be useful in a pinch. (In the long term, you'll probably want to make sure all your AAC files and MP3 files are tagged properly.)

- Create a playlist for your iPod by choosing File | New Playlist, typing the name in the text box, and then pressing ENTER (Windows) or RETURN (Mac). Drag songs, albums, or artists to the playlist to add them. When you're ready to load the playlist, connect the iPod to your computer, wait until its entry appears in the Source pane, and then drag the playlist to the entry. iTunes then copies the songs to the iPod all at once.

TIP

If you create many playlists, organize them into folders to make them easier to access. To create a folder, click the existing folder in which you want to place the new folder. To create a top-level folder, click the Library item in the Source pane. Choose File | New Folder, type the name for the folder, and then press ENTER (Windows) or RETURN (Mac). You can then move existing playlists to the folder by dragging them to it.

Connect and Load Your iPod shuffle

Because the iPod shuffle is so different from the regular iPod and the iPod nano, connecting it and loading it is different too.

To connect your iPod shuffle, plug it into a high-power USB port on your computer. If your computer's configuration doesn't let you plug the iPod shuffle directly into a USB port, attach a USB 2.0 cable and plug the iPod shuffle into the cable instead. Alternatively, you can pay $29 for an iPod shuffle Dock from the Apple Store (http://store.apple.com), but most people find this accessory overpriced.

The iPod shuffle is formatted with the FAT32 file system for use with both PCs and Macs, so the iPod Software doesn't need to reformat it the first time you connect it to a PC. (By contrast, regular iPods and the iPod nano come formatted with the Mac file system.)

Load Your iPod shuffle

Unlike the regular iPod (and even the iPod nano), the iPod shuffle doesn't have enough capacity to hold any but the most modest music library. To get around this limitation, Apple added a feature called Autofill to iTunes for the iPod shuffle. Autofill lets you tell iTunes to fill your iPod shuffle to capacity with songs from either your music library or from a specified playlist. You can also load your iPod shuffle manually if you prefer.

You can also use Autofill with the Motorola ROKR.

Configure Your iPod shuffle

Before loading your iPod shuffle for the first time, check that it is correctly configured:

1. Right-click the iPod shuffle's entry in the Source pane and then choose iPod Options to display the iPod tab of the iTunes dialog box (Windows) or the Preferences dialog box (Mac; see Figure 2-12).

2. Select the Convert Higher Bitrate Songs To 128 Kbps AAC For This iPod check box if you want to get as many songs as possible on the iPod shuffle.

Converting songs to 128 Kbps has two benefits: It prevents higher-bitrate songs from sneaking onto the iPod shuffle and hogging its limited space, and it enables you to load songs in formats that the iPod shuffle doesn't support (for example, Apple Lossless Encoder). The drawbacks are that the conversion slows down the loading process a bit and reduces sound quality somewhat.

3. If you want to be able to store data on your iPod shuffle as well as songs, select the Enable Disk Use check box and then drag the slider so that it shows the amount of space you want to reserve for data.

4. Click the OK button to close the dialog box.

Load Your iPod shuffle Using Autofill

The easiest way to load your iPod shuffle is to use Autofill:

1. Connect your iPod shuffle to your computer and wait for iTunes to add its entry to the Source pane.

2. Click the iPod shuffle's entry in the Source pane to display the iPod shuffle's contents (see Figure 2-13).

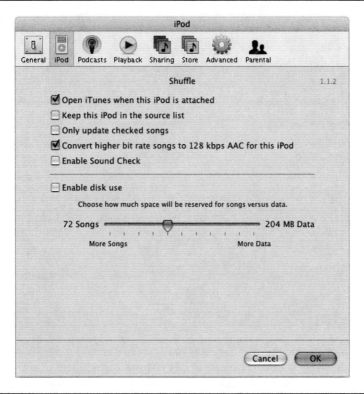

FIGURE 2-12   On the iPod shuffle, you can make iTunes convert higher-bitrate songs to 128 Kbps, and you can specify the amount of space you want to reserve for data.

The first time you use Autofill, configure it:

1. In the Autofill From drop-down list, select the Library entry if you want iTunes to choose songs from your entire music library. Choose a playlist if you want to confine the selection to just that playlist.

2. Select the Choose Songs Randomly check box if you want a random selection on your iPod shuffle. Clear this check box if you want iTunes to choose from your chosen playlist (or your music library) in order, starting from the first song and using all the available space.

3. Select the Replace All Songs When Autofilling check box if you want iTunes to remove the songs that are currently on your iPod shuffle. Clear this check box if you want to keep the existing songs.

4. Select the Choose Higher Rated Songs More Often check box if you want iTunes to prefer the songs you've given a higher rating.

FIGURE 2-13   Autofill is the fast-and-easy way to fill your iPod with songs chosen by iTunes either from your entire music library or from a specific playlist.

Once you've configured Autofill, follow these steps to load songs on your iPod shuffle:

1. Click the iPod shuffle's entry in the Source pane.

2. Click the Autofill button to load a new selection of songs. Wait until the display shows that the update is complete and then check the list for songs you don't want to hear. If you find any, select them, and press the Delete button to remove them. You can then either add replacement songs manually or clear the Replace All Songs When Autofilling check box and click the Autofill button again to fill up the remaining space with other songs.

3. When you're satisfied with the selection iTunes has loaded, disconnect the iPod shuffle. (See "Eject and Disconnect Your iPod," later in this chapter, for more detail.)

TIP   *With its limited capacity, the iPod shuffle is a great target for a well-thought-out Smart Playlist. See "Automatically Create Smart Playlists Based on Your Ratings and Preferences" in Chapter 9 for details on Smart Playlists. See also the upcoming sidebar, "Keep Your iPod shuffle Loaded with Your New Music," for a way to use Smart Playlists to put the latest songs you've acquired onto your iPod shuffle.*

How to ... Keep Your iPod shuffle Loaded with Your New Music

2

If you want to load your iPod shuffle with the latest music you've added to your music library, use the Recently Added Smart Playlist that iTunes prompts you to create when you set up an iPod shuffle on your computer.

Check that your iPod shuffle is set up to use the Recently Added Smart Playlist by following these steps:

1. Connect your iPod shuffle to your computer.

2. Click the iPod shuffle's entry in the Source pane to display the iPod shuffle's contents. The Autofill pane appears at the bottom of the contents area.

3. Make sure that Recently Added is selected in the Autofill From drop-down list.

Next, check that the Recently Added Smart Playlist is set to track songs added during a suitably long period of time. The default setting is two weeks. If you add music frequently, you may need to specify a shorter interval; if you seldom add music, you may need a longer interval. You can choose among days, weeks, and months.

Right-click the Recently Added item in the Source pane and choose Edit Smart Playlist from the shortcut menu to display the Smart Playlist dialog box. Check the condition, change it if necessary, and then click the OK button to close the dialog box.

If you chose not to allow iTunes to create the Recently Added Smart Playlist, create it manually:

1. Choose File | New Smart Playlist (or press CTRL-ALT-N in Windows or ⌘-OPTION-N on the Mac) to display the Smart Playlist dialog box.

2. Select the Match The Following Condition check box and specify the condition shown here. (Again, change the length of time if necessary.)

   ```
   Date Added   Is in the last   2   weeks
   ```

3. Select the Live Updating check box.

4. Click the OK button to close the dialog box, type the name for the playlist, and then press ENTER (Windows) or RETURN (Mac).

Load Your iPod shuffle Manually

Instead of using Autofill, you can load your iPod shuffle manually. The most direct way is to connect the iPod shuffle to your computer, wait until the iPod shuffle's entry appears in the Source pane, and then drag songs, artists, albums, or playlists to its entry. iTunes copies the songs to the iPod shuffle when you drop them.

A way that's usually more convenient is to select the Keep This iPod in the Source List check box on the iPod tab of the iTunes dialog box (Windows) or the Preferences dialog box (Mac). Selecting this check box makes iTunes always display an entry for your iPod shuffle in the Source pane, even when it's not connected. You can drag songs to the iPod's entry whenever is convenient, and then connect your iPod shuffle at your leisure so that you can update it with all the songs you've added.

Another option is to create a playlist for the iPod shuffle and then drag songs to the playlist. When you're ready to load the playlist, connect the iPod shuffle to your computer, wait until the iPod shuffle's entry appears in the Source pane, and then drag the playlist to the entry. iTunes then copies the songs to the iPod shuffle all at once.

Load Your Motorola ROKR

The Motorola ROKR is the first mobile phone that runs a version of iTunes and can synchronize with iTunes on the PC or Mac. The Motorola RAZR V3i (which has been announced but is not yet available at this writing) also runs iTunes and has similar capabilities to the ROKR, so it is likely to behave in the same way.

NOTE *The first ROKR model, the E1, was widely viewed as disappointing by critics—and compared to an iPod, it perhaps is. But if you consider the ROKR as a phone that can also play music well, it has more than enough appeal to be worth evaluating. Subsequent models may well be more compelling.*

The ROKR includes a 512MB memory card for storing music and other data. Presumably to prevent the ROKR from cutting too deeply into the sales of iPods, Apple has limited the ROKR's music database to holding 100 songs. This is one of the critics' main disappointments—but 100 songs are enough to last many listeners for several days.

To get started with the ROKR, install iTunes and the iPod Software as described earlier in this chapter, and then connect the ROKR to your PC or Mac via the supplied cable. The cable has a custom end for the ROKR and a standard USB end for your computer. On detecting the ROKR the first time you connect it, iTunes displays the Mobile Phone Setup Assistant dialog box (shown here).

In the The Name Of My Mobile Phone Is text box, type the name you want to give your ROKR. Clear the Automatically Choose Songs For My Mobile Phone check box (which is selected by default) if you want to load your ROKR manually, then click the Done button. iTunes then appears, and the ROKR appears in the Source pane, identified by the name you just assigned it.

If you left the Automatically Choose Songs For My Mobile Phone check box selected, iTunes chooses 100 songs (assuming your music library contains that many or more) and copies them to your ROKR. Because the ROKR uses USB 1.*x* rather than USB 2.0, the copying process will take a while—USB 1.*x* transfers a few songs a minute rather than the song-a-second that USB 2.0 usually manages. Wait patiently, and disconnect your ROKR when iTunes and the ROKR tell you it is safe to do so.

If you cleared the Automatically Choose Songs For My Mobile Phone check box, load songs on to your ROKR manually. You can also use Autofill (see "Load Your iPod shuffle Using Autofill" earlier in the chapter for details).

To configure your ROKR, right-click its item in the Source pane and choose Options from the shortcut menu. On the Phone tab of the iTunes dialog box or the Preferences dialog box (shown here), you can make the following choices:

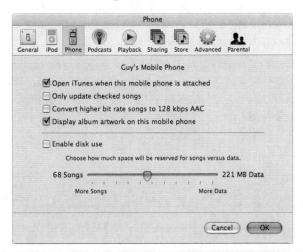

- Leave the Open iTunes When This Mobile Phone Is Attached check box selected (as it is by default) if you want iTunes to spring to life when you connect the ROKR.

- Select the Only Update Checked Songs check box if you want iTunes to skip any songs whose check boxes you've cleared when it's deciding what to put on the ROKR.

- Select the Convert Higher Bit Rate Songs to 128 Kbps AAC check box if you want to pack as many songs as possible onto the ROKR. (Quality may suffer a bit when you downsample songs to 128 Kbps—but this bitrate is usually adequate for mobile listening.)

- Leave the Display Album Artwork On This Mobile Phone check box selected (as it is by default) unless you don't want the ROKR to display album artwork for the songs you're listening to.

■ If you want to use the ROKR as an external disk, select the Enable Disk Use check box and drag the slider along the More Songs-More Data axis to specify how much space you want to devote to songs and how much to data.

Click the OK button to close the dialog box.

Eject and Disconnect Your iPod

When iTunes has finished loading songs and video onto your iPod, you can disconnect your iPod unless you're using it in disk mode (or you need to continue recharging its battery). iTunes displays the message "iPod update is complete. OK to disconnect." The iPod displays the message "OK to disconnect." When you see this message, you can unplug the iPod from the cable or from your computer.

If you're using disk mode, however, iTunes doesn't prepare the iPod for disconnection after it finishes loading songs. Instead, it leaves the iPod mounted on your computer as a disk so that you can transfer files to and from it manually. When your iPod is in disk mode like this, it displays the "Do not disconnect" message. In Mac OS X, an icon for the iPod appears on the desktop unless you have specifically chosen to exclude it (see the upcoming sidebar, "Prevent Your iPod from Appearing on the Desktop in Mac OS X").

If you forget to eject your iPod before you log out of Mac OS X, you shouldn't need to log back in to eject the iPod. If it's a regular iPod or an iPod nano, make sure that the screen is displaying the "OK to disconnect" message and then disconnect the iPod. If it's an iPod shuffle, make sure that the amber light isn't blinking.

How to ... Prevent Your iPod from Appearing on the Desktop in Mac OS X

When your iPod is mounted in disk mode, it appears on the Mac OS X desktop by default. You can prevent it from appearing, but doing so also prevents CDs and DVDs from appearing. Here's how:

1. Click the Finder button on the toolbar, or click the desktop.
2. Choose Finder | Preferences to display the Finder Preferences window.
3. Click the General tab if it isn't already displayed.
4. Clear the CDs, DVDs, And iPods check box.
5. Click the Close button on the window, or choose File | Close Window or press ⌘-w, to close the window.

You can eject your iPod in any of the following ways (see Figure 2-14):

- Click the Eject button that appears next to the iPod's entry in the Source pane.

- Right-click the iPod's entry in the Source pane and then click the Eject item on the shortcut menu.

- Click the iPod's entry in the Source pane and then click the Eject iPod button in the lower-right corner of the iTunes window.

- Click the iPod's entry in the Source pane and then choose Controls | Eject *iPod's name* or press CTRL-E (Windows) or ⌘-E (Mac).

Click the Eject button for the iPod.

Right-click the iPod's entry and choose Eject.   Select the iPod and then click the Eject iPod button.

FIGURE 2-14   The three easiest ways to eject your iPod are to click its Eject button, right-click its Source pane entry and choose Eject, or click the Eject iPod button.

Chapter 3

Listen to Music on Your iPod

How to...

- Connect your headphones or speakers to your iPod
- Use your iPod's controls
- Navigate through your iPod's screens
- Customize the settings on your iPod
- Play music on the iPod shuffle
- Play music on the Motorola ROKR

This chapter shows you how to get started using your iPod, whether it's a regular iPod, an iPod nano, or an iPod shuffle. You'll start by connecting your headphones or speakers, using your iPod's controls to play music, and navigating through the screens of its graphical user interface. After that, you'll learn how to customize the settings to make your iPod easier and faster to use and how to make the most of the iPod's features (other than playing music).

Much of this chapter applies to the regular iPod, the iPod nano, and the iPod mini, so this chapter treats them together as much as possible. Where the iPod nano behaves differently, this chapter tells you. The iPod shuffle is substantially different, so this chapter discusses it separately.

Connect Your Headphones or Speakers

To get sound out of your iPod, connect your headphones or speakers to the headphones port. The headphones port is on the top of the regular iPod and the iPod mini, and on the bottom of the iPod nano and iPod shuffle: a 1/8" (3.5mm) round hole, into which you slide a miniplug of the corresponding size.

There's nothing to connecting the miniplug and the port, but a couple of things are worth mentioning:

- The iPod headphone port delivers up to 60 milliwatts (mW) altogether—30 mW per channel. To avoid distortion or damage, turn down the volume when connecting your iPod to a different pair of headphones, powered speakers, or an amplifier. Make the connection, set the volume to low on the speakers or amplifier, and then start playing the audio.

- If you have an iPod Dock, you can play music from your iPod when it's docked. Plug a cable with a stereo miniplug into the Line Out port on the iPod Dock and connect the other end of the cable to your powered speakers or your stereo. Use your iPod's controls to navigate to the music, play it, pause it, and so on. Use the volume control on the speakers or the receiver to control the volume at which the songs play.

- The headphones port on the first- and second-generation regular iPods is surrounded by a recessed ring that contains connectors for the remote controls. When you connect a remote control to one of these iPods, push it in firmly. Otherwise, the remote connection may not be made, even if the sound comes through okay.

Use Headphones with Your iPod

At this writing, all iPods come with a pair of ear-bud headphones—the kind that fit in your ear rather than sit on your ear or over your ear. The headphones come with foam covers that soften the impact of the headphones on your ears, help clean your ears, and are almost impossible to wash without losing.

The iPod headphones are designed to look good with the iPod—and in fact their distinctive white has helped muggers in many countries target victims with iPods rather than those with less desirable audio players. They're good-quality headphones with a wide range of frequency response: from 20 Hz (hertz) to 20 kHz (kilohertz; thousand hertz), which is enough to cover most of the average human's hearing spectrum. Apple emphasizes that the iPod headphones have drivers (technically, *transducers*) made of neodymium, a rare earth magnet that provides better frequency response and higher sound quality than alternative materials (such as cobalt, aluminum, or ceramics).

A wide range of frequency response and high sound quality are desirable, but what's more important to most people is that their headphones be comfortable and that they meet any other requirements, such as shutting out ambient sound or enhancing the wearer's charisma. See the sidebar "Choose Headphones to Suit You" for suggestions on evaluating and choosing headphones.

How to ...   Choose Headphones to Suit You

If you don't like the sound your iPod's headphones deliver, or if you just don't find them comfortable, use another pair of headphones with your iPod. Any headphones with a standard miniplug will work; if your headphones have a quarter-inch jack, get a good-quality miniplug converter to make the connection to your iPod.

Headphones largely break down into three main types, although you can find plenty of exceptions:

- *Ear-bud* headphones are the most discreet type of headphones and the easiest to fit in a pocket. Most ear buds wedge in your ears like the iPod's ear buds do, but others sit on a headband and poke in sideways.

- *Supra-aural* headphones sit on your ears but don't fully cover them. Supra-aural headphones don't block out all ambient noise, which makes them good for situations in which you need to remain aware of the sounds happening around you. They also tend not to get as hot as circumaural headphones, because more air can get to your ears.

(continued)

■ *Circumaural* headphones sit over your ears, usually enclosing them fully. *Open* circumaural headphones allow external sounds to reach your ears, whereas *sealed* circumaural headphones block as much external sound as possible. Sealed headphones are good for noisy environments, but even better are noise-canceling circumaural headphones such as Bose's QuietComfort headphones, which use electronics to reduce the amount of ambient noise that you hear.

Headphones can cost anywhere from a handful of dollars to many hundred dollars. Even ear buds can be impressively expensive: Shure's top-of-the-line set, the E5c ear buds, cost $499 (www.shure.com), and Etymotic Research, Inc.'s ER-4 Micro-Pro earphones go for $330 (www.etymotic.com). When choosing headphones, always try them on for comfort and listen to them for as long as possible, using a variety of your favorite music on your iPod, to evaluate their sound as fully as you can.

Whichever type of headphones you choose to use, don't turn the volume up high enough to cause hearing damage. Instead, if you use your iPod often with a high-end pair of headphones, get a headphone amplifier to improve the sound. A headphone amplifier plugs in between the sound source (in this case, your iPod) and your headphones to boost and condition the signal. You don't necessarily have to listen to music *louder* through a headphone amplifier—the amplifier can also improve the sound at a lower volume. Many headphone amplifiers are available from various manufacturers, but HeadRoom's BitHead and Total BitHead seem especially well regarded (www.headphone.com). You can also find plans on the Web for building your own headphone amplifier.

Use Speakers with Your iPod

Instead of using headphones, you can also connect your iPod to a pair of powered speakers, a receiver, or an amplifier, or your car stereo. To make such a connection, use a standard cable with a 1/8" stereo headphone connector at the iPod end and the appropriate type of connector at the other end. For example, to connect your iPod to a conventional amplifier, you need two phono plugs on the other end of the cable.

NOTE *Powered speakers are speakers that contain an amplifier, so you don't need to use an external amplifier. Many speaker sets designed for use with portable CD players, MP3 players, and computers are powered speakers. Usually, only one of the speakers contains an amplifier, making one speaker far heavier than the other. Sometimes the amplifier is hidden in the subwoofer, which lets you put the weight on the floor rather than on the furniture.*

The iPod will work with any pair of speakers or stereo that can accept input, but you can also get various speakers designed specifically for the iPod. Chapter 4 discusses some of the options and suggests how to choose among them.

Get Familiar with the Controls on a Click-Wheel iPod

To keep the various iPod models as streamlined as possible, Apple has reduced the number of controls to a minimum by making each control fulfill more than one purpose. You'll get the hang of the controls' basic functions easily, but you also need to know how to use the controls' secondary functions to get the most out of your iPod—so keep reading.

> **NOTE** *This section discusses the controls on the iPods that have Click wheels—that's fifth-generation and fourth-generation regular iPods, the iPod nano, and the iPod mini. For instructions on the iPod shuffle's controls, see "Play Music on the iPod shuffle," near the end of this chapter.*

Read Your iPod's Display

Your iPod has an LCD display that shows a handful of lines of text (exactly how many depends on the model of iPod) and multiple icons. Figure 3-1 shows the display with labels.

The title bar at the top of the display shows the title of the current screen—for example, "iPod" for the main menu (the top-level menu), "Now Playing" when your iPod's playing a song, or "Artist" when you're browsing by artist.

To turn on the display's backlight, hold down the Menu button for a moment. The backlight uses far more power than the LCD screen, so don't use the backlight unnecessarily when you're trying to extract the maximum amount of playing time from a single battery charge. You can configure how long your iPod keeps the backlight on after you press a button (see "Set the Backlight Timer," later in this chapter).

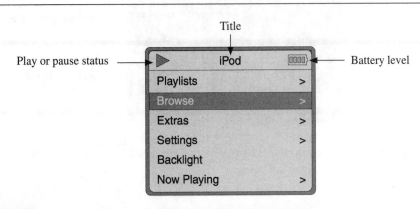

Title

Play or pause status ⟶ iPod ⟵ Battery level

Playlists	>
Browse	>
Extras	>
Settings	>
Backlight	
Now Playing	>

FIGURE 3-1   The iPod's LCD display contains around six lines of text and key icons.

Use Your iPod's Controls

Below the iPod's display are the iPod's main controls, which you use for accessing songs and playing them back. The fifth-generation iPod and the iPod nano have the control buttons integrated into the Click wheel, as do the fourth-generation iPod and the iPod mini. Figure 3-2 shows a fifth-generation iPod.

NOTE   *Earlier iPods have different arrangements of controls. On third-generation iPods, the controls are arranged as a line of four buttons below the screen. On second- and first-generation iPods, the controls are arranged as a ring of four buttons around the Scroll wheel and the Select button.*

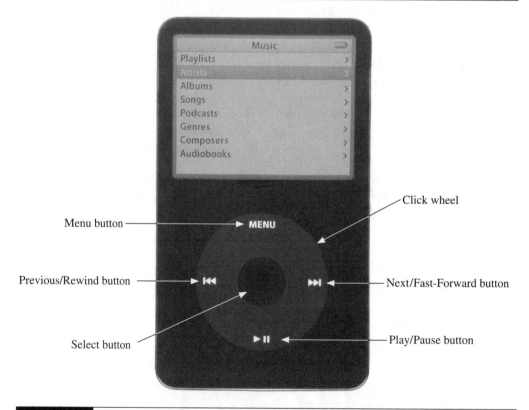

FIGURE 3-2   The control buttons on all current and recent iPods except the iPod shuffle are integrated into the Click wheel.

Use the Buttons and the Click Wheel

Use the buttons and the Click wheel as follows:

- Press any button to switch on your iPod.

- Press the Menu button to move up to the next level of menus. Hold down the Menu button for a second to turn the backlight on or off.

- Press the Previous/Rewind button or the Next/Fast-Forward button to navigate from one song to another and to rewind or fast-forward the playing song. Press one of these buttons once (and release it immediately) to issue the Previous command or the Next command. Hold the button down to issue the Rewind command or the Fast-Forward command. Your iPod rewinds or fast-forwards slowly at first, but then speeds up if you keep holding down the button.

- Press the Play/Pause button to start playback or to pause it. Hold down the Play/Pause button for three seconds or so to switch off your iPod.

- Press the Select button to select the current menu item.

- Scroll your finger around the Click wheel to move up and down menus, change the volume, or change the place in a song.

The Click wheel adjusts the scrolling speed in response to your finger movements on the Click wheel and the length of time you scroll for: When you're scrolling a long list, it speeds up the scrolling as you continue the scroll, then slows down as you ease back on the scroll. This behavior makes scrolling even long lists (such as the Songs list, which lists every song on your iPod) swift and comfortable once you get used to it.

Browse and Access Your Music

The iPod's menu-driven interface makes browsing and accessing your music as easy as possible on the device's compact display.

Once you've accessed a list of songs—a playlist, an album, or a listing of all songs by an artist or composer—you can press the Play button to play the list from the start. Alternatively, you can scroll down to another song and then press the Play button to start playing from that song.

You can customize the main menu on your iPod (see "Customize the Main Menu for Quick Access to Items," later in this chapter, for details). This chapter assumes you're using the default menu layout.

Play a Playlist

To access your playlists, choose the Music item and press the Select button, then scroll to the Playlists item and press the Select button again. On the resulting screen, scroll down to the playlist you want to play and then press the Select button.

Browse Your Music

To browse your music, select the Music item on the main menu. Your iPod displays the Music menu, contents of which may vary depending on the model of iPod. The fifth-generation iPod contains entries for Playlists, Artists, Albums, Songs, Podcasts, Genres, Composers, and Audiobooks, while the iPod nano contains entries for Playlists, Artists, Albums, Songs, Genres, and Composers. The iPod nano displays entries for Podcasts and Audiobooks only when you have these items loaded on the iPod.

> TIP *You can also make your iPod display a Compilations entry on the Music menu. To do so, choose Settings | Compilations | On. (To turn Compilations off again, choose Settings | Compilations | Off.) You can control what iTunes considers a compilation by selecting or clearing the Part Of A Compilation check box on the Info tab of the Song Information dialog box, or choosing Yes or No in the Part Of A Compilation drop-down list in the Multiple Song Information dialog box. You'll learn about both these dialog boxes in detail in Chapter 6.*

Scroll to the browse category you want to use, and then press the Select button to access that category. Here are some points to keep in mind:

- The Artists category displays an alphabetical list of all the music on your iPod sorted by artist. The first entry, All, displays an alphabetical list of all the albums on your iPod. Otherwise, scroll down to the artist and press the Select button to display a list of the albums by the artist. This menu also has a first entry called All. This entry displays an alphabetical list of all songs by the artist.

> NOTE *At this writing, the fifth-generation iPod handles an artist's albums differently than the iPod nano and the earlier iPods. If the iPod contains songs from only one album by the artist you display, the fifth-generation iPod shows you a list of those songs immediately. By contrast, when you access an artist on the iPod nano and earlier iPods, the iPod always shows you a list of albums, even if there is only one album on the list. The iPod also displays an All item on the albums list, but this is redundant when there is only one album by the artist.*

- The Albums category displays an alphabetical list of all the albums on your iPod. Scroll down to the album you want and then press the Select button to display the songs it contains.

> NOTE *The data for the artist, album, song title, genre, composer, and so on comes from the tag information in the song file. An album shows up in the Artists category, the Albums category, the Genres category, or the Composers category because one or more files on your iPod has that album entered in the Album field on its tag. So, the entry for an album doesn't necessarily mean that you have that entire album on your iPod—you may have only one song from that album.*

■ The Songs category displays an alphabetical list of every song on your iPod. Scroll down to the song you want to play and then press the Select button to start playing the song.

■ The Podcasts category displays an alphabetical list of all the podcasts on your iPod. Scroll down to the podcast you want, and then press the Select button to view the episodes available.

■ The Genres category displays a list of the genres you've assigned to the music on your iPod. (Your iPod builds the list of genres from the Genre field in the tags in AAC files, Apple Lossless Encoding files, and MP3 files.) Scroll to a genre and then press the Select button to display the artists whose albums are tagged with that genre. You can then navigate to albums and songs by an artist.

■ The Composers category displays a list of the composers for the songs on your iPod. (Your iPod builds the list of composers from the Composer field in the tags in the song files.) Scroll to a composer and press the Select button to display a list of the songs by that composer.

■ The Audiobooks category displays a list of the audiobooks on your iPod. Scroll down to the audiobook you want, and then press the Select button to start it playing.

How to ... **Use the Composers Category Effectively to Find Music**

The Composers category is primarily useful for classical music, because these songs may be tagged with the name of the recording artist rather than that of the composer. For example, an album of The Fargo Philharmonic playing Beethoven's *Ninth Symphony* might list The Fargo Philharmonic as the artist and Beethoven as the composer. By using the Composers category, you can access the works by composer: Bach, Beethoven, Brahms, and so on.

However, there's no reason why you shouldn't use the Composers category to access nonclassical songs as well. For example, you could use the Composers category to quickly access all your Nick Drake cover versions as well as Drake's own recordings of his songs. The only disadvantage to doing so is that the tag information for many CDs in the CD Database (CDDB) doesn't include an entry in the Composer field, so you'll need to add this information if you want to use it. In this case, you may be better off using iTunes to create a playlist that contains the tracks you want in the order you prefer.

There's also no reason why you should confine the contents of the Composers field to information about composers. By editing the tags manually, you can add to the Composer field any information by which you want to be able to sort songs on your iPod.

Play Songs

Playing songs on your iPod is largely intuitive.

Start and Pause Play

To start playing a song, take either of the following actions:

- Navigate to the song and press the Play/Pause button or the Select button.
- Navigate to a playlist or an album and press the Play/Pause button or the Select button.

To pause play, press the Play/Pause button.

Change the Volume

To change the volume, scroll counterclockwise (to reduce the volume) or clockwise (to increase it) from the Now Playing screen (see Figure 3-3). The volume bar at the bottom of the screen shows the volume setting as it changes.

Change the Place in a Song

As well as fast-forwarding through a song by using the Fast-Forward button, or rewinding through a song by using the Rewind button, you can *scrub* through a song to quickly change the location.

Scrubbing can be easier than fast-forwarding or rewinding because your iPod displays a readout of how far through the song the playing location currently is. Scrubbing is also more peaceful, because whereas Fast Forward and Rewind play blips of the parts of the song you're passing through (to help you locate the passage you want), scrubbing keeps the song playing until you indicate you've reached the part you're interested in.

FIGURE 3-3   Scroll counterclockwise or clockwise to change the volume from the Now Playing screen.

3

To scrub through a song, follow these steps:

1. Display the Now Playing screen.

2. Press the Select button to display the scroll bar (see Figure 3-4).

3. Scroll counterclockwise to move backward through the song or clockwise to move forward through the song.

4. Press the Select button to cancel the display of the scroll bar, or wait a few seconds for your iPod to cancel its display automatically.

To display the lyrics for the currently playing song on a fifth-generation iPod or an iPod nano, press the Select button twice from the Now Playing screen. Scroll down to see more lyrics (if there are more). Press the Select button again to access the Ratings screen, and press it once more to return to the Now Playing screen. Earlier iPods can't display lyrics.

Use the Hold Switch

The Hold switch, located on the top of your iPod, locks your iPod controls in their current configuration. The Hold switch helps protect your iPod controls against being bumped in active environments—for example, when you're exercising at the gym or barging your way onto a packed bus or subway train. When the Hold switch is pushed to the Hold side so that the red underlay shows, your iPod is on hold.

The Hold switch is equally useful for keeping music playing without unintended interruptions and for keeping your iPod locked in the Off position, which prevents the battery from being drained by the iPod being switched on accidentally when you're carrying it.

If your iPod seems to stop responding to its other controls, check first that the Hold switch isn't on. If you're using a remote that includes a Hold switch, check that one too.

FIGURE 3-4   To "scrub" forward or backward through the current song, press the Select button and then scroll clockwise (to go forward) or counterclockwise (to go backward).

Attach and Use the Remote Control for Easy Operation

If you have a remote control for your iPod, plug it into the headphone port and then plug your headphones (or speakers) into the port on the remote control's cable.

The remote control is largely self-explanatory, but two points are worth mentioning:

- The remote control in second-generation iPods connects via a recessed ring around the headphone socket. With these models, you need to push the jack of the remote-control unit firmly into its socket for it to engage. If the remote control seems to stop working, check first that it's plugged in properly. If the problem persists, check the Hold switch on the remote.

- The remote control in third- and fourth-generation iPods and the iPod mini uses a separate connection socket next to the headphone socket. This connection seems to work better than the second-generation connection, but the different socket means that the remote controls for second-generation iPods and later models aren't compatible; nor are the remote controls with this separate connection compatible with fifth-generation iPods and the iPod nano, which don't have the socket. So if you're shopping for a remote control, make sure you get the right type for your iPod.

Recharge Your iPod's Battery to Keep the Songs Coming

The battery icon on your iPod's display shows you how your iPod is doing for battery power. Four bars is a full charge; one bar means the battery is nearly empty.

You can recharge your iPod by plugging it into your computer or into an iPod Power Adapter (if you have one; Apple used to include an iPod Power Adapter with each iPod, but now it's an optional accessory). To recharge your iPod, your computer must have a high-power USB port. The easiest way to tell whether your USB connection can recharge the iPod is to plug in the iPod and see if it starts to charge. Keep the following points in mind:

- The advantage to using the computer is that you don't need to lug around the AC adapter around with you; the disadvantage is that if your computer is a portable, you'll need to lug the computer's AC adapter, because the iPod draws power from the computer's battery when the computer is running on the battery.

- The advantage to using the AC adapter is that you can run the iPod from the adapter even while the battery is charging.

The battery in an iPod nano is designed to recharge in about three hours, the battery in an iPod shuffle in about four hours, and the battery in a fifth-generation iPod in about five hours. After about half that time, the battery should be at about 80 percent of its charge capacity—enough for you to use the iPod for a while.

When recharging from a computer, your iPod displays each of the four bars in the battery icon in sequence. When your iPod displays all four bars together, the charging is complete.

When recharging from the AC adapter, your iPod flashes a large battery icon and displays the word *Charging* at the top of the screen. When charging is complete, your iPod displays the battery icon without flashing it as well as the word *Charged* at the top of the screen.

NOTE   *See the Special Project insert to this book for advice on how to get the longest life possible from your iPod's battery.*

Navigate the Extras Menu

The Extras menu provides access to your iPod's Clock, Games, Contacts, Calendar, Notes, Stopwatch, and Screen Lock features:

■ To use your iPod's clock features, scroll to the Clock item on the Extras menu and then press the Select button. On the first Clock screen, which lists the clocks already configured, select the clock you want, or use the New Clock option to add a new clock to the list. (For each clock, you choose the city and time zone.) The second Clock screen gives you access to the Alarm Clock and Sleep Timer settings, as well as options for changing the city with which the clock is associated, deleting the clock, and turning Daylight Savings Time on and off.

NOTE   *Fourth-generation and earlier iPods and the iPod mini have only a single clock.*

■ To play the games included with the iPod, scroll to the Games item on the Extras menu and then press the Select button. From the Games menu, scroll to Brick, Music Quiz, Parachute, or Solitaire, and then press the Select button.

■ To access a contact, scroll to the Contacts item on the Extras menu and then press the Select button. On the Contacts screen, scroll to the contact and then press the Select button. See Chapter 10 for details on how to put contacts onto your iPod.

■ To use the calendars, scroll to the Calendar item on the Extras menu and then press the Select button. The iPod displays the list of calendars. Scroll to the calendar you want and press the Select button to display the calendar in month view. Scroll to access the day you're interested in and then press the Select button to display the events listed for that day. The one-month display shows empty squares for days that have no events scheduled and dots for days that have one or more events. If the day contains more appointments than will fit on the iPod's display, scroll up and down. See Chapter 10 for a discussion of how to transfer your calendars to the iPod.

■ To access your text notes, scroll to the Notes item on the Extras menu and then press the Select button. Chapter 11 discusses how to put notes on your iPod.

Choose Settings for Your iPod

To choose settings for your iPod, scroll to the Settings item on the main menu and then press the Select button. Work through those of the following sections that interest you.

Check the "About" Information for Your iPod

To see the details of your iPod, display the About screen by choosing Settings | About. The About screen includes the following information:

- Your iPod's name, serial number, and model
- Your iPod's hard-disk capacity and the amount of space free right now
- The iPod Software version number of your iPod's software
- On some iPod models, whether the iPod is formatted for Windows or for the Mac

 In most cases, it's worth updating your software to the latest version available. To do so, download the latest version of the iPod Software Updater from the Apple Software Downloads website (www.apple.com/swupdates/), run the iPod Software Updater, and follow through its screens.

Customize the Main Menu for Quick Access to Items

You can customize your iPod's main menu by controlling which items appear on it. By removing items you don't want, and adding items you do want, you can give yourself quicker access to the items you use most. For example, you might want to promote the Playlists item from the Music menu to the main menu, or you might want to put the Screen Lock item on the main menu so that you could lock your iPod's screen more easily.

To customize the main menu, follow these steps:

1. Choose Settings | Main Menu to display the Main Menu screen.

2. Scroll to the item you want to affect.

3. Press the Select button to toggle the item's setting between On and Off.

4. Make further changes as necessary. Then press the Menu button twice to return to the main menu and see the effect of the changes you made.

To reset your main menu to its default settings, choose the Reset Main Menu item at the bottom of the Main Menu screen and then choose Reset from the Menus screen. (Another way of resetting your main menu is to reset all settings on your iPod, as described in "Recover from the Wrong Language: Reset All Settings" in Chapter 2—all settings includes the main menu.)

Apply Shuffle Settings to Randomize Songs or Albums

Instead of playing the songs in the current list in their usual order, you can tell your iPod to shuffle them into a randomized order by changing the Shuffle setting to Songs. Similarly, you can have your iPod shuffle the albums by a particular artist or composer into a random order by changing the Shuffle setting to Albums.

To change the Shuffle setting, scroll up to the Shuffle item on the Settings menu and press the Select button to choose the Shuffle setting you want. The settings are Off (the default), Songs, and Albums.

To shuffle songs on an iPod shuffle, move the slider on the back to the Shuffle position.

Repeat One Track or All Tracks

The Repeat item on the Settings menu lets you choose between repeating the current song (choose the One setting), all the songs in the current list (the All setting), or not repeating any songs (Off, the default setting). Scroll to the Repeat item and then press the Select button one or more times to change the setting.

Set the Backlight Timer

To customize the length of time that the display backlight stays on after you press one of the iPod's controls, scroll to the Backlight Timer option and press the Select button. Then you can choose from the following settings:

- Choose the Off setting to keep the backlight off until you turn it on manually by holding down the Menu button for a second. You can then let the backlight go off automatically after the set delay or hold down the Menu button again for a couple of seconds to turn it off.
- Specify the number of seconds for the backlight to stay on after you press a control.
- Choose the Always On setting to keep the backlight on until you choose a new setting from this screen. (Even holding down the Menu button doesn't turn off the backlight when you choose Always On.) This setting is useful when you're using your iPod as a sound source in a place that's too dark to see the display without the backlight and when you need to change the music frequently. Be warned that Always On gets through battery power surprisingly quickly.

Change the Speed at Which Audiobooks Play

If you listen to audiobooks on your iPod, you may want to make them play faster or slower. To do so, choose the Audiobooks item on the Settings menu and choose Slower, Normal, or Faster from the Audiobooks screen.

Choose Equalizations to Make Your Music Sound Better

Your iPod contains a graphical equalizer—a device that alters the sound of music by changing the level of different frequency bands. For example, a typical equalization for rock music boosts the lowest bass frequencies and most of the treble frequencies, while reducing some of the midrange frequencies. The normal effect of this arrangement is to punch up the drums, bass, and vocals, making the music sound more dynamic. A typical equalization for classical music leaves the bass frequencies and midrange frequencies at their normal levels while reducing the treble frequencies, producing a mellow effect overall and helping avoid having the brass section blast the top off of your head.

NOTE   *The iPod shuffle doesn't include a graphical equalizer.*

Your iPod should include the following equalizations: Acoustic, Bass Booster, Bass Reducer, Classical, Dance, Deep, Electronic, Flat, Hip Hop, Jazz, Latin, Loudness, Lounge, Piano, Pop, R & B, Rock, Small Speakers, Spoken Word, Treble Booster, Treble Reducer, and Vocal Booster. You might long for a Vocal Reducer setting for some artists or for karaoke, but the iPod doesn't provide one.

The names of most of these equalizations indicate their intended usage clearly, but Flat and Small Speakers deserve a word of explanation:

- Flat is an equalization with all the sliders at their midpoints—an equalization that applies no filtering to any of the frequency bands. If you don't usually use an equalization, there's no point in applying Flat to a song, because the effect is the same as not using an equalization. But if you *do* use an equalization for most of your tracks, you can apply Flat to individual tracks to turn off the equalization while they play.

- Small Speakers is for use with small loudspeakers. This equalization boosts the frequency bands that are typically lost by smaller loudspeakers. If you listen to your iPod through portable speakers, you may want to try this equalization for general listening. Its effect is to reduce the treble and enhance the bass.

TIP   *Don't take the names of the equalizations too literally, because those you find best will depend on your ears, your earphones or speakers, and the type of music you listen to. For example, if you find crunk sounds best played with the Classical equalization, don't scorn the Classical equalization because of its name.*

To apply an equalization, scroll to the EQ item on the Settings menu. The EQ item shows the current equalization—for example, EQ – Rock. To change the equalization, press the Select button. On the EQ screen, scroll to the equalization you want and then press the Select button to apply it. Choose the Off "equalization" at the top of the list if you want to turn equalizations off.

Specifying an equalization from the Settings menu works well enough when you need to adjust the sound balance for the music you're playing during a listening session. But if you want to use different equalizations for the different songs in a playlist, you should use the iPod's other method of applying an equalization—by using iTunes to specify the equalization for the song, as described in "Specify an Equalization for an Individual Song" in Chapter 9. Your iPod then applies this equalization when you play back the track on the iPod. The equalization also applies when you play the track in iTunes.

Choose Whether to Include a Compilations Item in the Music Menu

If you want to be able to access compilation albums directly from the Music menu, scroll to the Compilations item on the Settings menu and then press the Select button to change the setting from the default Off to On.

Use Sound Check to Standardize the Volume

Sound Check is a feature for normalizing the volume of different songs so you don't have to crank up the volume to hear a song encoded at a low volume and then suffer ear damage because the next song was recorded at a far higher volume. Scroll to the Sound Check item on the Settings menu and then press the Select button to toggle Sound Check on or off.

> **NOTE** *For Sound Check to work on your iPod, you must also turn on the Sound Check feature in iTunes. Press CTRL-COMMA or choose Edit | Preferences to display the iTunes dialog box in Windows, or press ⌘-COMMA or choose iTunes | Preferences on the Mac to display the Preferences dialog box. Click the Playback tab to display its controls. Select the Sound Check check box and then click the OK button to close the dialog box.*

Turn the Clicker Off or Redirect the Clicks

By default, your iPod plays a clicking sound as you move the Click wheel to give you feedback. You can turn off this clicking sound by choosing Settings | Clicker | Off. On the iPod nano, you can also choose to direct the clicking sound to the headphones, the iPod's tiny built-in (and hidden) speaker, or both, instead of turning it off: choose Settings | Clicker | Headphones; Settings | Clicker | Speaker; or Settings | Clicker | Both.

Set the Date and Time

To set the date and time on your iPod, choose Extras | Date & Time to display the Date & Time screen. From here, you can use the Set Time Zone item to access the Time Zone screen, on which you can set the time zone (for example, U.S. Mountain). Use the Set Date & Time item on the Date & Time screen to access a screen that presents a simple interface for setting the time and date. Scroll to adjust each value in turn. Press the Select button to move to the next value.

To make your iPod display the time in the title bar, set the Time In Title item on the Date & Time screen to On.

Choose How to Sort and Display Your Contacts

To specify how your iPod should sort your contacts' names and display them onscreen, scroll to the Contacts item on the Settings screen and then press the Select button to display the Contacts screen.

To change the sort order, scroll to the Sort item and then press the Select button to toggle between the First Last setting (for example, "Joe Public") and the Last, First setting (for example, "Public, Joe").

To change the display format, scroll to the Display item and then press the Select button to toggle between the First Last setting and the Last, First setting.

Most people find using the same sort order and display format best, but you may prefer otherwise. For example, you might sort by Last, First but display by First Last.

Make the Most of Your iPod's Extra Features

The regular iPod and the iPod nano include a sleep timer for putting you to sleep, an alarm clock for waking you up, and alerts to help you avoid missing Calendar appointments. You can even create playlists and rate songs on the iPod and have those playlists and ratings transferred back to iTunes when you synchronize your iPod.

Use the Sleep Timer to Lull You to Sleep

Your iPod's Sleep Timer is like the Sleep button on a clock radio or boom box: It lets you determine how long to continue playing music, presumably to lull you to sleep. You can set a value of 15, 30, 60, 90, or 120 minutes.

Choose Extras | Clock, select the clock, and then choose Sleep Timer. Scroll to the number of minutes, and then press the Select button. When you move to the Now Playing screen, your iPod displays a clock icon and the number of minutes remaining on the Now Playing screen so you can see the Sleep Timer is running. To turn off the Sleep Timer, access the Sleep screen again and select the Off setting.

Use Your iPod's Alarm Clock to Wake You Up

Your iPod's Alarm Clock feature lets you blast yourself awake either with a beep or with one of your existing playlists. To use the Alarm Clock, follow these steps:

1. Create a custom playlist for waking up if you like (or create several—one for each day of the week, maybe). If you don't have your computer at hand, and your iPod doesn't contain a suitable playlist, create an On-the-Go playlist on your iPod.

2. Choose Extras | Clock, select the appropriate clock, and then choose Alarm Clock to display the Alarm Clock screen.

3. Scroll to the Alarm item and press the Select button to toggle the alarm on or off, as appropriate.

4. Scroll to the Time item and press the Select button to access the Alarm Time screen. Scroll to the appropriate time and then press the Select button to return to the Alarm Clock screen.

5. Scroll to the Sound item and press the Select button to display the Alarm Clock listing of playlists available. Select the playlist (or select Beep to go with a simple beeping alarm) and press the Select button to return to the Alarm Clock screen.

6. Connect your iPod to your speakers or stereo (unless you sleep with headphones on).

7. Go to sleep.

When the appointed time arrives, your iPod wakes itself (if it's sleeping) and then wakes you.

Get Alerts for Your Calendar Appointments

Your iPod can remind you of appointments in your Calendar when their times arrive. Choose Extras | Calendar, scroll down to the Alarms item, and then press the Select button. Choose the On setting for Alarms to receive a beep and a message on the screen. Choose the Silent setting to receive only the message. Choose the Off setting to receive neither the beep nor the message.

Create a Playlist on Your iPod

One of the features that iPod users pressed Apple for was the ability to create playlists on the fly on their iPods rather than having to create all playlists through iTunes ahead of time. Apple obliged, enabling you to create a new playlist called On-the-Go. You can even save this playlist under a different name, so you can keep it for later enjoyment and also create another On-the-Go playlist.

To create your On-the-Go playlist, follow these steps:

1. If you've previously created an On-the-Go playlist, decide whether to clear it or add to it. To clear it, choose Music | Playlists | On-the-Go | Clear Playlist | Clear Playlist.

2. Navigate to the first song, album, artist, or playlist you want to add to the playlist.

3. Press the Select button and hold it down until the item's name starts flashing.

Repeat steps 2 and 3 for each additional item to the On-the-Go playlist.

To play your On-the-Go playlist, choose Playlists | On-the-Go. (Until you create your first On-the-Go playlist, selecting this item displays an explanation of what the On-the-Go playlist does.)

To save your On-the-Go playlist under a different name, choose Playlists | On-the-Go | Save Playlist | Save Playlist. The iPod saves the playlist under the name *New Playlist 1* (or *New Playlist 2*, or the next available number). After synchronizing your iPod with iTunes, click the playlist in the Source pane, wait a moment and click it again, type the new name, and then press ENTER (Windows) or RETURN (Mac).

Rate Songs on Your iPod

To assign a rating to the song that's currently playing, follow these steps:

1. Display the Now Playing screen if it's not currently displayed.

2. Press the Select button three times in quick succession. Your iPod displays five hollow dots under the song's name on the Now Playing screen.

3. Scroll to the right to display the appropriate number of stars in place of the five dots. Then press the Select button to apply the rating.

Use Your iPod as a Stopwatch

The fifth-generation iPod and the iPod nano include stopwatch functionality. To use it, choose Extras | Stop | Timer.

Lock the Screen on Your iPod

You can lock the screen to protect the iPod's contents.

1. Choose Extras | Screen Lock | Set Combination and set the four-digit code you want, scrolling each number to the appropriate digit and then pressing the Select button to move to the next digit.

2. Press the Select button to apply the combination.

To lock the screen:

1. Choose Extras | Screen Lock | Turn Screen Lock On.

2. Verify the number displayed on the Screen Lock screen, and then scroll to the Lock item and press the Select button. You'll then need to enter the code on the Enter Code screen to unlock the iPod.

If you forget your combination, all shouldn't be lost: Just connect your iPod to its home computer, and it unlocks. But if this doesn't work (don't ask why not), you'll need to restore the iPod's software to unlock it. See Chapter 17 for instructions on restoring the iPod's software.

Play Music on the iPod shuffle

With no screen, the iPod shuffle needs only a limited set of controls for playing music (see Figure 3-5). These are largely intuitive but have a couple of hidden tricks:

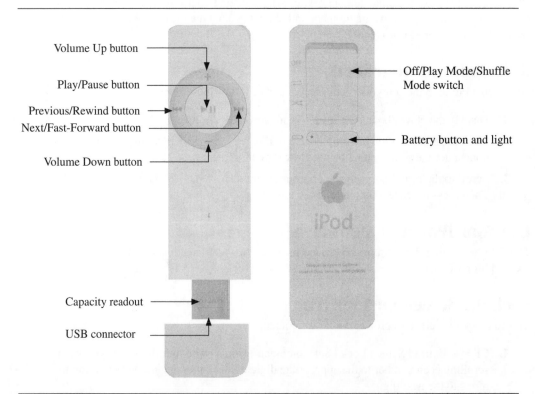

FIGURE 3-5 The iPod shuffle's limited set of controls includes a couple of hidden tricks.

- To start playing the songs on the iPod shuffle in the order of the playlist, move the switch on the back of the iPod shuffle to Play mode and then press the Play/Pause button.

> **NOTE** *If the iPod shuffle blinks green and amber several times in succession when you press the Play/Pause button, your iPod shuffle probably has no songs on it. Move the switch to the Off position, wait for five seconds or more, move the switch back to the Play mode position, and press the Play/Pause button again. If you see green and amber blinking again, connect your iPod shuffle to your computer and make sure that some songs are loaded on it.*

- To start playing the songs in random order, move the switch to Shuffle mode and then press the Play/Pause button. When you hit a part of the playlist that you want to hear in sequence, move the switch to Play mode to continue in sequence.

- Press the Play/Pause button three times in immediate succession to move to the start of the playlist. To get to the end of the playlist, press the Play/Pause button three times and then press the Previous/Rewind button once.

> **NOTE** *When your iPod shuffle is in Shuffle mode and you move to the beginning of the playlist, it shuffles the playlist again.*

- Press the Next/Fast-Forward button to skip to the next song. Hold it down to fast-forward through the song.

> **NOTE** *When the iPod shuffle is paused, you can press the Next/Fast-Forward button to start the next song playing, or press the Previous/Rewind button to start the previous song playing. The iPod shuffle doesn't remain paused when you press the Next/Fast-Forward button or the Previous/Rewind button, unlike other iPod models.*

- Press the Previous/Rewind button to return to the start of the current song; press it again to go to the start of the previous track. Hold the button down to rewind through the current song.

- Press the Volume Up button to increase the volume, or press the Volume Down button to decrease the volume.

- To put the iPod shuffle on hold, hold down the Play/Pause button for several seconds. The status light gives three orange blinks to indicate that hold is applied. To remove hold, press the Play/Pause button for several seconds again until the status light blinks green.

- To reset the iPod shuffle, slide the switch on the back to the Off position, wait five seconds or more, and then slide the switch to Play mode or Shuffle mode.

> **NOTE** *If, when you press a button on the iPod shuffle, you see only the orange light on the front, it means that the iPod shuffle is on hold. Hold down the Play/Pause button for several seconds until the green light blinks three times to take it off hold.*

Below the mode switch on the back of the iPod shuffle is a battery status button containing an LED that lights up when you turn on the iPod shuffle. You can also press the status button to check the battery's current status:

Battery Light Color	Battery Status
Green	Plenty of charge for several hours' playing
Amber	Low—around an hour or less
Red	Critically low—recharge at once
No light	No charge

Play Music on the Motorola ROKR

To play music on the Motorola ROKR mobile phone, press the iTunes key on the front of the phone. You can also access iTunes by selecting the iTunes item from the phone's main screen, but using the iTunes key is quicker and easier.

You can then navigate the iTunes menu system by pressing the joystick button up and down and by using the soft keys to access the selected item (the equivalent of pressing the Select button on an iPod) or go up one menu (the equivalent of pressing the Menu button on an iPod).

Chapter 4

Extend Your iPod's Capabilities with Accessories

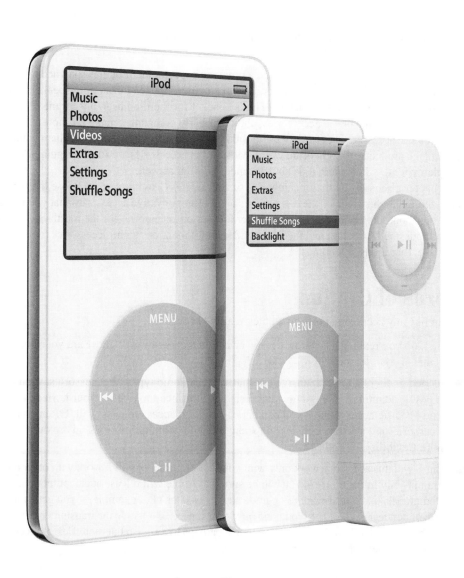

How to...

- ■ Approach buying iPod accessories the right way
- ■ Select cases for your iPods
- ■ Learn about power adapters and car adapters for your iPod
- ■ Investigate headphone accessories for your iPod
- ■ Choose iPod stands and docks
- ■ Choose a radio transmitter
- ■ Learn about strange accessories you might possibly want

Like many a consumer product that's been a runaway success, the iPod has spawned a huge market for accessories—from cases to stands, from microphones for input to speakers for output, from handbags to a custom jacket. (That's a jacket for the iPod user, not for the iPod itself.) Apple makes some of the accessories, and third-party companies make far more.

Some of these accessories are widely useful (although you may not need any of them yourself). Others are niche products. Yet others are weird. Most of the accessories are for the regular iPod, but there are plenty for the iPod nano, iPod shuffle, and iPod mini as well.

This chapter discusses the major categories of accessories (leaving you to choose the types you need) and highlights some of the less obvious and more innovative accessories that you might want to know about for special needs. The chapter focuses on accessories for the fourth- and fifth-generation iPods, the iPod nano, and the iPod shuffle, but it mentions some accessories for the iPod mini and the earlier iPods as well.

A Few Words of Caution

Before you buy any accessory, perform a quick reality check:

- ■ First, do you really need the accessory, or is it just cool or cute? These are your dollars, so this is your decision.

- ■ Second, is there a less expensive alternative? For some types of accessories, such as power adapters and cassette adapters, you don't need to restrict your horizons to iPod-specific accessories—you can choose generic accessories as well. Often, generic accessories are substantially less expensive than custom accessories, give you much more flexibility, or both.

- ■ Third, will this accessory work only with your current iPod, or will it work with other iPods you may buy in the future? (You can be sure that Apple will release such compelling new iPod models that you'll want to upgrade sooner or later.) For example, if you get a radio transmitter designed for the iPod nano only, you'll need to upgrade the transmitter as well if you buy a regular iPod. In this case, buying a perhaps less stylish but more flexible accessory might make better financial sense.

Cases

Your iPod is built to be carried, so it's hardly surprising that a wide variety of cases has been developed for iPods—everything from bifold cases to armband cases to armored cases and waterproof cases.

> TIP
>
> *Many stores sell iPod cases, but at this writing, the prime sources are the Apple Store (http://store.apple.com), the Everything iPod store (www.everythingipod.com), and the Think Different Store (http://thinkdifferentstore.com).*

4

The Apple Store has user ratings for all third-party cases (but not for Apple cases), which can help you weed out superficially attractive losers.

Early iPod models included a case, and the iPod mini included a plastic belt-clip. At this writing, the fifth-generation iPod includes a slip case, the iPod nano also has a slip case (although the first iPod nanos didn't), and the iPod shuffle includes a lanyard designed for hanging the iPod around your neck.

Choosing a Case

When choosing a case, first make sure that it will fit your iPod. As you can see at a glance, the regular iPod, iPod nano, and iPod shuffle are very different sizes. What's perhaps less obvious is that each different generation of regular iPod has somewhat different dimensions—and even within a generation, iPods with higher-capacity disks can be thicker than their lower-capacity siblings.

Beyond getting the size right, the remaining choices are yours. The following paragraphs summarize the key ways in which the cases differ. You get to decide which points are important for you:

■ **How the case attaches to you (if at all)**   Many cases attach to your belt, whereas some hook on to a lanyard that goes around your neck or a strap that goes over your shoulder. Still others attach to an armband, which some people find better for performing vigorous activities. (Most people find the iPod shuffle and iPod nano ideal for an armband, the iPod mini tolerable, and the regular iPod uncomfortable.) Some cases come with a variety of attachments—for example, a belt clip and an armband, or a mounting for sticking your iPod to a flat surface. Other cases are simply protective, designed to be carried in a pocket or a bag.

> NOTE
>
> *Examples of armband cases include the Action Jacket from Netalogic, Inc. ($29.99; www .everythingipod.com). The Action Jacket is made of thick neoprene with holes that let you see the screen and access the front-panel controls. It attaches to either a belt clip or an armband.*

■ **The amount of protection the case provides**   In general, the more protection a case provides, the larger and uglier it is, the more it weighs, and the more it costs. Balance your need for style against your iPod's need for protection for when gravity gets the better of your grip.

■ **Whether or not the case is waterproof**   If you plan to take your iPod outdoors for exercise, you may want to get a case that's water-resistant or waterproof. Alternatively, carry a sturdy plastic bag in your pocket for weather emergencies. Either way, if your iPod has a Dock Connector port, it's a good idea to protect it.

■ **Whether or not the case lets you access your iPod's controls**   On the face of it, access to the controls might seem a compelling feature in a case—and sometimes it is. But if you have a remote control for your iPod, your need to access your iPod's controls once you've set the music playing will be much less. Generally speaking, the more waterproof the case, the less access it offers to your iPod's controls.

■ **Whether or not the case can hold your iPod's headphones and remote control**   If you'll be toting your iPod in a bag or pocket, a case that can hold your iPod's ear-bud headphones and remote control (if you have one) as well as the player itself may be a boon. You may even want a case that can accommodate the iPod's cable and power adapter (again, if you have one) for traveling. But if you're more interested in a case that straps firmly to your body and holds your iPod secure, you probably won't want the case to devote extra space to store other objects.

TIP   *If you're looking for a case that'll take your iPod's complete entourage, consider the type of case designed for portable CD players and built into a padded belt.*

■ **Whether or not you need to take your iPod out of the case to dock or recharge it**   Some cases are designed to give you access to your iPod's Dock Connector port and front panel controls, so you can leave your iPod in the case unless you need to admire it. With more protective cases, usually you need to remove your iPod more often.

■ **What the case is made of and how much it costs**   Snug cases tend to be made of neoprene. Impressive cases tend to be made of leather. Leather and armor cost more than lesser materials.

■ **Whether the case is single-purpose or multipurpose**   Most cases are designed for carrying, either in your pocket or attached to your belt or clothing. Others, such as the Xtremity Protective iPod Case ($29.95; http://thinkdifferentstore.com and other retailers), convert to mount the iPod in your car or home.

TIP   *When shopping for a case, look for special-value bundles that include other iPod accessories you need—for example, a car cassette adapter or cables for connecting the iPod to a stereo.*

Cases for Regular iPods

There are too many cases available for the regular iPod models to round up here—and new cases are being released every month, if not every week. But here are some standout cases popular with the iPoderati:

■ If you have a rugged lifestyle and want your iPod to share it, consider the iPod Armor case from Matias Corporation ($39.95; http://matias.ca/ipodarmor/index.php).

The iPod Armor cradles your iPod in a full metal jacket made of anodized aluminum padded with open-cell EVA foam. If you land on this case, you're more likely to damage yourself than your iPod. There's also an iPod Armor mini for the iPod mini.

- The ToughSkin from Speck Products ($34.95; www.speckproducts.com) is a ruggedized cover for fourth- and fifth-generation iPods. The ToughSkin (see Figure 4-1) is a polymer case with rubber bumpers, providing protection, a good grip, and easy access to your iPod's controls.

- The Sleevz for iPod from RadTech ($20.95; www.radtech.us) is a thin, form-fitting case made of a soft-but-tough material through which you can press the buttons. It has a window for the iPod's screen and a die-cut knockout for cable access to iPods with the Dock Connector.

- Peter Kinne Design (www.peterkinne.com) makes wooden cases for the regular iPod, iPod nano, and iPod mini. Prices range from $35 to $45.

FIGURE 4-1   The ToughSkin provides a stylish way to protect your iPod from moderate harm.

Cases for the iPod nano

At this writing, the iPod nano has just been released, but already a promising variety of cases is available:

- iPod nano Tubes, slim silicone cases that your iPod nano can snuggle into. $29 for a set of five different colors (http://store.apple.com).
- Incase nano Wallet ($19.95) and Incase Leather Folio for iPod nano ($24.95), both from the Apple Store.
- DecalGirl iPod nano Skin ($5.99; www.everythingipod.com) in various flashy designs. Figure 4-2 shows some examples.
- invisibleSHIELD ($19.99; http://thinkdifferentstore.com), a full-body wrap of protective film.
- eXo Xskn ($18.99; http://thinkdifferentstore.com), a thin case with a two-tone touch wheel.

The Apple Store also offers iPod nano Armbands ($29), and the iPod nano Lanyard Headphones ($39) that offer a means of carrying your iPod nano.

Cases for the iPod shuffle

The iPod shuffle has less need of cases than other iPods, not only because it comes with its own lanyard for carrying, but also because its plastic case is adequate protection for all but the meanest of pockets.

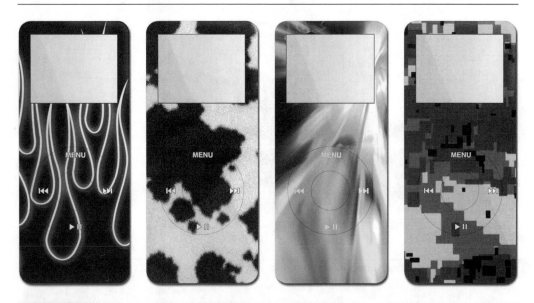

FIGURE 4-2   The DecalGirl iPod nano Skins come in a variety of striking designs.

If you do decide you need a case, however, you won't have any trouble finding one. Here are some of the possibilities:

- The Apple iPod shuffle Sport Case from the Apple Store ($29; http://store.apple.com) is a waterproof case with an integrated lanyard. You can access the iPod shuffle's controls through the case.

- The Apple iPod shuffle Armband from the Apple Store ($29; http://store.apple.com) is an armband onto which the iPod shuffle clips. The iPod shuffle is still exposed to the elements; you take care of the consequences.

- The iPod shuffle Gel Shield from Pacific Rim Technologies ($24.99 for a three-pack of Gel Shields; www.pacrimtechnologies.com) is a silicone shield that stretches over the iPod shuffle; a separate piece stretches over the cap. The Gel Shield comes in several colors, and you can mix colors in your three-pack.

- The iPod shuffle Leather Case with Front Side Flap and Leather Case with Back Side Flap from PodsPlus ($19.99 each; www.podsplus.com) are snug leather cases that expose the iPod shuffle's controls and ports. Each comes in a variety of colors and works with either the regular USB cap or the lanyard cap.

- The PodsPlus Silicone Skin for iPod shuffle from PodsPlus ($14.99 for two; www.podsplus .com) is a silicone shield, somewhat like the iPod shuffle Gel Shield, that you stretch over the iPod shuffle, with a separate piece for covering the cap. The PodsPlus Silicone Skin for iPod shuffle comes in several colors.

- The Exotica iPodica "shuffle muffles" from HotRomz.com ($14.95; www.hotromz.com/ ipod_shuffle.html) let you disguise your iPod shuffle as a furry beast. Various hues and color combinations are available.

- The PodBrix ($28.99; http://podbrix.com) is a T-shirt designed for wearing with the iPod shuffle. A built-in magnetic clasp on the chest lets you stick your iPod shuffle right onto the shirt (the iPod shuffle's Flash memory is magnetic) without needing to use the iPod shuffle's lanyard.

Stands and Docks

Cases can be great, but you won't always want to carry your iPod. Sometimes, you'll want to park it securely so you can use it without worrying about knocking it down, or so you can contemplate its lustrous beauty.

If your iPod came with a dock, you're all set. Otherwise, you can get an iPod Dock from Apple or a third-party stand or dock.

The fifth-generation iPod and the iPod nano include iPod Dock Adapter inserts that let you use docks built to Apple's Universal Dock standard, so if you've got one of these iPods, the Apple iPod Universal Dock ($39; http://store.apple.com) should be a strong contender for your dollars.

The Universal Dock includes a line-out port that delivers a standard volume rather than a variable volume. The standard volume means that you're less likely to damage your receiver or speakers by putting too great a volume through them. (It also means that you can't adjust the volume on the iPod, only on the receiver or speakers.) You can also connect a regular iPod to a TV via the port on the iPod Dock so that you can display slideshows and videos on the TV.

TIP *Another option for docking your iPod is to get a set of portable speakers designed to include an iPod stand. See "Portable Speakers for the iPod," later in this chapter, for examples.*

Stands and Docks for Regular iPods

Here are some of the stands and docks available for the regular iPod models:

- **iCradle**   The iCradle from Pacific Rim Technologies ($25.99; www.pacrimtechnologies .com) is a dock for third-generation and later iPods that use a Dock Connector. Aside from being less expensive than Apple's iPod Dock, the iCradle provides regular USB 2.0 and FireWire ports at the back, allowing you to connect the iCradle to your computer via a regular cable rather than needing a cable with the Dock Connector at one end. Like the iPod Dock, the iCradle provides a line-out port for playing audio back from your iPod at a high quality and a fixed volume.

- **FlipStand**   The FlipStand from Speck Products ($29.95; www.speckproducts.com) is a protective hard case for your iPod that also acts as a stand when you flip the door fully open. The FlipStand fits the third-generation and later regular iPods.

- **Podholder**   The PodHolder ($15; http://thinkdifferentstore.com) is a clear acrylic stand for supporting your iPod at an angle on a flat surface.

Stands and Docks for the iPod nano

Here are a couple of the docks available for the iPod nano:

- **Apple iPod nano Dock**   The Apple iPod nano Dock ($29; http://store.apple.com) is a dock specifically tailored for the iPod nano. This dock is less expensive than the Apple iPod Universal Dock, but you won't be able to use it with any other iPod models you own.

- **mTUNE-N with iPod nano Dock**   The mTUNE-N with iPod nano Dock from Macally ($49.99; www.macally.com) is a pair of cordless headphones that have a dock pocket for the iPod nano built in, so that the iPod nano sits just above your ear. If you can stand oversized circumaural headphones and can't stand headphone cords, this might be just what you need.

TIP *If you already have another iPod Dock with a Dock Connector (for example, from a regular iPod you own), you will probably be able to use it with your iPod nano. If the iPod nano's iPod Dock Adapter doesn't fit the dock, try connecting the iPod nano using only the Dock Connector. Because the iPod nano is so light, the Dock Connector usually provides enough support.*

Stands and Docks for the iPod shuffle

You might think the iPod shuffle too small to need a dock—but others disagree:

- The Apple iPod shuffle Dock ($29; http://store.apple.com) is Apple's own dock for the iPod shuffle—a straightforward base with a cap-like USB connection standing up. The iPod shuffle Dock simplifies the process of connecting your iPod shuffle to your computer, especially if your computer's USB ports are hard to reach, but it seems a poor value.

4

CAUTION *Unlike the Apple Docks for regular iPods, the iPod nano, and the iPod mini, the iPod shuffle Dock doesn't have a line-out connector, so you can't play music directly from your iPod shuffle.*

- The DecoDock ($24.99; www.pdrop.com/products/decodock_index.html) is an art-techno-styled dock that works only with the iPod shuffle. The DecoDock (see Figure 4-3) makes a pleasant alternative to scrabbling for a free USB port on your computer, but it's much more expensive than a USB extension cable, which can offer much of the same convenience.

Car and Bike Mounting Kits

The iPod on your body or desk gets you only so far. To get further, you'll probably want to use your iPod in your car or on your bike. To prevent it from shifting around as you shift gears, you'll probably want to secure it.

FIGURE 4-3   The DecoDock is designed to recharge your iPod shuffle in style—and even includes an integrated holder for the iPod shuffle's cap.

Car Mounts

If you want to secure your iPod in your car, you can choose between many types of holders and mounts, including the following:

- **Gripmatic**   The Gripmatic from Netalog, Inc. ($29.99; www.everythingipod.com) is a multiangle mount designed for use in the car. You can mount the Gripmatic either with screws or with adhesive (both of which are provided).

- **TuneDok Car Holder**   The TuneDok Car Holder for iPod from Belkin ($29.99; www .belkin.com) lets you mount any regular iPod in your car's cup holder. The TuneDok includes large and small bases to fit securely in any cup holder.

- **iGrip**   The iGrip ($8.99; http://thinkdifferentstore.com) is an adhesive pad that you can use to secure your iPod to your car dashboard or another convenient location. Refreshingly low-tech, the iGrip will also stick to other objects, such as your mobile phone or the case for your shades.

- **iSqueez**   The iSqueez from Griffin Technology ($9.99; www.griffintechnology.com) is a flexible iPod nest that mounts in your cupholder (see Figure 4-4).

All-in-One Adapters for the Car

Securing your iPod in your car tends to be only half the problem. The other half is playing the sound from the iPod through the car's stereo system. Chapter 5 discusses this problem

FIGURE 4-4   The Griffin iSqueez is an inexpensive solution to persuading your iPod to stay in place during emergency stops.

in more detail, but one solution is to use an all-in-one gadget. Most of these combine three main components:

■ A power adapter that connects to your car's 12-volt accessory outlet or cigarette-lighter socket.

■ A means of piping the iPod's output to your stereo. This can use a direct cable connection, a cassette adapter, or a radio transmitter.

■ A cradle or other device for holding the iPod, either built onto the power adapter (using the power adapter as its support) or fitting into a cup holder or onto the dash.

Many different all-in-one gadgets are available. Here are a couple of examples:

■ **TransPod**   The TransPod from Digital Lifestyle Outfitters (www.dlodirect.com) comes in several different models designed for the different generations of regular iPods and the iPod nano, offering different ways of transferring the audio to the car stereo. For example, the TransPod for the fifth-generation iPod costs $99.99 and includes a digital FM transmitter with a range of frequencies, as well as a line-out socket that lets you connect the iPod directly to the car stereo.

■ **Belkin TuneBase FM for iPod mini**   The Belkin TuneBase FM for iPod mini ($79.99; www.belkin.com) is a car adapter, a charger, and an FM transmitter for the iPod mini, all built into a single unit. The TuneBase FM (see Figure 4-5) consists of a cigarette-lighter adapter, a flexible neck, and an FM transmitter that forms the base of a stand for the iPod mini. The TuneBase FM lets you choose any of multiple channels between 88.1 and 107.9 MHz.

FIGURE 4-5   The Belkin TuneBase FM for iPod mini is an all-in-one car radio transmitter and car holder for the iPod mini.

If you already have a mounting device for the car (or are prepared to leave your iPod loose in the glove box or on the passenger seat), you can get two-in-one gadgets that don't include a mounting device:

- **SoundFeeder**   The SoundFeeder from Arkon ($27.99; www.everythingipod.com) is a radio transmitter and power adapter without a mounting kit.

- **Monster iCarPlay Wireless Plus**   The Monster iCarPlay Wireless Plus ($79.95; http://thinkdifferentstore.com) combines a digital radio transmitter with a power adapter. The iCarPlay Wireless Plus offers a full range of radio frequencies, including three presets that you can program for frequencies that are normally free in your area, and it works with all iPods that have the Dock Connector—third-generation and later regular iPods, the iPod nano, and the iPod mini.

Bike Mounts

If you want to mount your iPod on your bike, your options are more limited:

- **Bike Holder Accessory**   The Bike Holder Accessory ($7.95; http://thinkdifferentstore .com) from Marware works with cases such as the iPod SportSuit Convertible, iPod SportSuit Basic, and the iPod Leather C.E.O. The Bike Holder Accessory lets you strap your iPod to your bike's handlebars so that you can manipulate the music when you have a hand free.

Power Adapters and Battery Packs

Your iPod may have come with a power adapter for recharging from an electrical socket instead of recharging via USB or FireWire from your Mac or PC. But you may want to supplement the standard adapter with a more specialized adapter. You may also want to prolong your AC-free playing time by using a backup battery pack.

You may also need to replace your iPod's internal battery. The Special Project insert to this book discusses where to buy replacement batteries and shows you how to install them in the first four generations of regular iPod and in the iPod mini.

iCharge Battery Pack

The iCharge ($12.99; http://thinkdifferentstore.com) is a small recharger for all iPod models that use the Dock Connector. The iCharge plugs into the Dock Connector, takes its power from a 9V battery (the brick-shaped battery with both terminals at one end), and includes an LED indicator that lets you monitor the charge status.

Backup Battery Pack for iPod

The Battery Backup Pack for iPod from Belkin ($69.99; www.belkin.com) is a clip-on battery pack for third-generation and later iPods. The Backup Battery Pack runs off four AA batteries, connects through the Dock Connector, and provides up to 20 hours of additional playing time.

TunePower Rechargeable Battery Pack

The TunePower Rechargeable Battery Pack from Belkin ($99.99; www.belkin.com) is a rechargeable lithium-ion external battery for all iPod models that use the Dock Connector. The TunePower clips on to the back of the iPod, using any of several included sleeves to make a good fit, and connects via the Dock Connector. Belkin claims 8–10 hours of play time for the TunePower.

BTI iPod Battery

The iPod Battery from Battery Technology, Inc. ($99; www.batterytech.com) is a rechargeable lithium-ion external battery for iPods with the Dock Connector but not for the iPod nano. The iPod Battery clips on to the back of the iPod, connects to the Dock Connector, and provides up to 40 hours of playback—enough for a long trip away from a regular power source for your iPod.

TuneJuice

The TuneJuice ($19.99; http://thinkdifferentstore.com) is an external battery pack for iPods with the Dock Connector. The TuneJuice is built around a 9V battery, connects via the Dock Connector, and provides up to eight hours of playing time.

Apple iPod Shuffle External Battery Pack

The Apple iPod shuffle External Battery Pack ($29; http://store.apple.com) takes two AAA batteries, delivers up to 20 hours of battery life, and replaces the iPod shuffle's cap. The iPod shuffle connects to the External Battery Pack through its USB connector. The battery cap includes a lanyard so that you can still hang the iPod shuffle around your neck.

Basic AC Power Adapters

Apple used to include an iPod Power Adapter with early iPod models, which gave you two ways to recharge your iPod: from your computer or from the iPod Power Adapter. Now that Apple no longer includes the adapter, you may want to buy one to give yourself more flexibility.

For a fourth- or fifth-generation iPod or an iPod nano, you'll probably want to get the iPod USB Power Adapter ($29; http://store.apple.com). For an iPod that prefers FireWire, get the iPod FireWire Power Adapter (also $29).

Car Adapters

If you drive extensively (or live in a vehicle), you may find even your iPod's impressive battery life isn't enough for your lifestyle. To recharge your iPod in your car, you need a power adapter that'll run from your car's 12-volt accessory outlet or cigarette-lighter socket. Technically, such an adapter is an *inverter*, a device that converts DC into AC, but we'll stick with the term *adapter* here.

You can choose between a generic car adapter, a FireWire car adapter, and a custom car adapter for the iPod. Another option is an all-in-one device that combines a power adapter with a radio transmitter and (in some cases) a mounting kit, as discussed in "All-in-One Adapters for the Car," earlier in this chapter.

Generic Car Adapter

If you have an iPod Power Adapter, the simplest and most versatile option is to get a generic car adapter that plugs into your car's 12-volt accessory outlet or cigarette-lighter socket. Models vary, but the most effective types give you one or more conventional AC sockets. You plug your iPod's cable into the iPod Power Adapter, and then plug that into one of these AC sockets, just as you would any other AC socket.

The advantage to these adapters is that you can run any electrical equipment off them that doesn't draw too heavy a load—a portable computer, your cell phone charger, a portable TV, or whatever. The disadvantage is that such adapters can be large and clumsy compared with custom adapters.

Cost usually depends on the wattage the adapter can handle; you can get 50-watt adapters from around $20 and 140-watt adapters for around $50, whereas 300-watt adapters cost more like $80. A 50-watt adapter will take care of your iPod and portable computer easily enough.

USB or FireWire Car Adapters

Your next option is to get a car adapter that provides a USB port or FireWire port into which you can plug your iPod's cable. The adapter draws power through the 12-volt accessory socket or cigarette-lighter socket and provides power to the USB port or FireWire port.

An example of such an adapter is the FirePod charger from CompuCable Manufacturing Group ($19.95; www.compucable.com). The FirePod provides one FireWire port and one USB port, so you can power two devices at once.

iPod-Specific Adapters

If the only thing you want to power from your car is your iPod, you can get a car adapter designed specially for the iPod. You'll find an impressive number of different models available, including the following:

- Belkin iPod Car Charger ($19.95; www.belkin.com) is a charger for iPods with the Dock Connector.

- Griffin PowerPod ($24.99; www.griffintechnology.com) is an adapter with a FireWire socket into which you plug your FireWire cable. Griffin makes a PowerPod (see Figure 4-6) that works with most iPods.

- XtremeMac Premium iPod Car Charger ($19.95; www.xtrememac.com/foripod/car_charger .shtml) is an adapter with a springy coil of cable built in. You plug the Dock Connector at the other end of the cable into your iPod, and you're in business.

- The AutoPod charger from Netalog, Inc. ($29.99; www.everythingipod.com) is similar to the iPod Car Charger—an adapter with a built-in, coiled cable that leads to a Dock Connector. You can choose between black and white models. Netalog also makes other AutoPod models that include mounts.

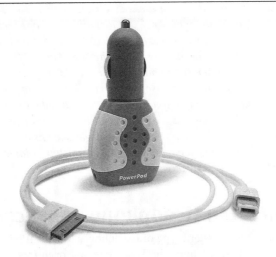

| FIGURE 4-6 | You can power your iPod from a car's cigarette-lighter socket or 12-volt accessory outlet with an adapter such as the PowerPod. |

World Travel Adapters

If you travel abroad with your iPod, the lightest and easiest way to recharge it is from your PowerBook, iBook, or portable PC. You have to have your computer with you, and you need a way to plug your computer into an electrical socket so you don't deplete its battery by charging your iPod. But even that tends to be better than having to plug in your iPod separately.

If you need to recharge your iPod directly from the electric socket, get an adapter that lets you plug your iPod's power adapter into electric sockets in different countries. The adapter can handle multiple voltages, so you can plug it safely in even in countries that think 240 volts is just a refreshing tingle.

For such adapters, you have the choice between a set of cheap and ugly adapters and a set of stylish and sophisticated adapters. The cheap and ugly adapters you can get from any competent electrical-supply shop; they consist of an assortment of prong-converter receptacles into which you plug your iPod's U.S. prongs. The resulting piggyback arrangement is clumsy, and sometimes you have to jiggle the adapters to get a good connection. But these adapters are inexpensive (usually from $5 to $10) and functional, and they work for any electrical gear that can handle the different voltages.

The stylish and sophisticated adapters are designed by Apple and are (collectively) called the World Travel Adapter Kit. The kit costs $39 from the Apple Store (http://store.apple.com) or an authorized reseller. You slide the U.S. prongs off your iPod adapter and replace them with a set of prongs suited to the country you're in. The kit includes six prongs that'll juice up your iPod in continental Europe, the United Kingdom, Australia, Hong Kong, South Korea, China, and Japan, as well as in the United States. These adapters also work with the white power adapters that come with the PowerBook G4 and the iBook, but they won't help you plug in any of your other electrical equipment.

TIP *If you're going somewhere sunny that lacks electricity, or you live somewhere sunny that suffers frequent power outages, or if you lost all your money investing in Enron and will do anything to reduce your next electric bill, one option for powering your laptop is a portable folding solar panel such as the Note Power 20 ($230; www.cetsolar .com/notepower20.htm). Compared to batteries and an AC adapter, a solar panel is an unwieldy form of power, but it can be useful when a electrical supply isn't available and batteries won't last you long enough. Your iPod can take its power from your laptop—again, provided the laptop has a suitable USB or FireWire port. If you need power only for your iPod, look at a lower-power solar charger such as the X & Y Solar Powered iPod Charger from the Coldplay.com Shop (£74.99; http://uk.coldplayshop.com/mall/ productpage.cfm/Coldplay/200135/64003).*

Special Headphones and Headphone Enhancers

You can connect pretty much any standard type of headphones to your iPod—over-the-ear (circumaural) headphones, on-the-ear (supra-aural) headphones, or in-the-ear headphones (ear buds), such as Apple's iPod In-Ear Headphones ($39). If the headphones have a quarter-inch jack rather than a miniplug, you'll need a miniplug converter; make sure its quality is high enough for your headphones, or it will degrade the audio. And if you want to enhance sound quality, you might want to try a headphone amplifier (see Chapter 3).

Choosing headphones should be a straightforward matter of balancing sound quality, comfort, cost, style, and special needs, such as excluding other noises or keeping your ears warm. I'll let you make the choice on your own; but in the next few sections, I'll quickly mention three headphone-related products that may be of interest. Okay, the first product is actually a pair of headphones, but it's an unusual pair that you might care to know about.

Zip Cord Retractable Earbuds

Getting the headphone cord tangled is a perennial problem with ear-bud headphones, particularly when you need to stuff them into your pocket or pack quickly. The Zip Cord Retractable Earbuds from Netalog, Inc. ($26.95; www.everythingipod.com) feature an integrated spool onto which you can quickly retract the cord when you need to stow them.

Speaker and Headphone Splitters

Headphones are great for solitary listening, but if you find there are times when you want to share your music without using speakers, you need a headphone splitter. A typical splitter is a Y-shaped cable or device with a stereo miniplug at one end and two stereo jacks on the other end. The miniplug goes into your iPod or other audio source, and then each set of headphones plugs into one of the stereo jacks.

You can find splitters at RadioShack and most other electronics stores at prices starting from a few bucks. When buying a splitter, make sure it has high-quality contacts so that it won't degrade the audio signal. It's also a good idea to check that the splitter balances the sound between the jacks so that each listener receives the same signal level. Different signal levels tend to be more of a problem when you daisy-chain splitters to share the signal with two or more people. Some splitters, such as the iShare Earbud Splitter ($12.95; www.xtrememac .com), are explicitly designed for daisy-chaining, but most aren't. Some splitters, such as the Audio Splitter for iPod shuffle ($12.95; www.xtrememac.com) are designed to fit properly on only one model (or some models) of iPod, which means they're convenient (and often stylish) in the short term but may be limiting when you want to upgrade to a new iPod.

4

> TIP *If you use a basic splitter, use two sets of headphones that have the same impedance to help avoid problems with audio quality. You'll usually need to check the headphones' instructions to find out their impedance, which is measured in ohms (Ω). Two sets of iPod ear buds will do the trick nicely.*

Splitters are best used in static situations such as on a plane, in a car, or on the sofa reacquainting yourself with the baser parts of heavy metal after your sensitive neighbors have twitched their way to bed. (On the street, splitter users run the risk of garroting children, lassoing lampposts, and suffering unexpected sharp tugs at their ears.) You can also use a splitter to connect an iPod or other sound source to multiple receivers or speakers instead of headphones, or to a mixture of output devices. For example, when DJing, you might run one pair of headphones and a receiver.

Koss eq50 Three-Band Equalizer

If your iPod's graphic equalizer settings don't always suit you, or you want to be able to change the equalizer settings manually while you're playing music, try a portable graphic equalizer such as the Koss eq50 ($19.99, various retailers). You plug the eq50 into your iPod and then plug your headphones or other listening gear into the eq50.

The eq50 is a pocket-size unit that runs on two AAA batteries. It offers three frequency sliders, giving you reasonable, but not fine, control over the equalization of your music. For best effect, use the eq50 in concert with your iPod's built-in equalizations.

Remote Controls

If you connect your iPod to your stereo (as discussed in "Connect Your iPod to Your Stereo" in Chapter 5), you'd probably appreciate being able to control your iPod from across the room. You can do so by using a wireless remote control.

Apart from price and looks, consider the following points when evaluating a remote control:

- Does it use infrared (IR) or radio frequency (RF)? RF typically gives better range and works around corners. But IR has the advantage that universal remote controls can learn from some IR remote controls.

- Do you need features for the latest iPods, such as the ability to control your iPod's picture features, or do you simply want to play back music?

naviPod and naviPro eX

The naviPod wireless remote control from Ten Technologies ($49.95; available from http://store
.apple.com and other retailers) uses an infrared signal transmitted from its remote control to the
receiver that connects to the iPod. Current models of the naviPod work with third-generation and
later iPods and the iPod mini.

The naviPro eX ($49.95; http://store.apple.com and other retailers) works only with fourth-
generation iPods (including the iPod U2) and the iPod mini. As well as playing back your music,
the naviPro eX (see Figure 4-7) can navigate the iPod's photo features, enabling you to give
a remote-controlled slideshow when your iPod is connected to a TV or a projector.

AirClick

The AirClick from Griffin Technology ($39.99; www.griffintechnology.com) is a family of remote
controls with models for third-, fourth-, and fifth-generation regular iPods, the iPod mini, and Macs
and PCs. Each AirClick package consists of a receiver module that connects to the iPod or iPod
mini (or the computer) and a remote control that you use to send signals to the receiver.

iDirect

The iDirect Remote Control from Digital Lifestyle Outfitters ($49.99; www.dlodirect.com) is
a remote-control kit that works with third- and fourth-generation regular iPods and the iPod mini.
The receiver unit is designed for the regular iPod but also works with the iPod mini, even though
it looks oversized on the iPod mini because it overlaps the sides.

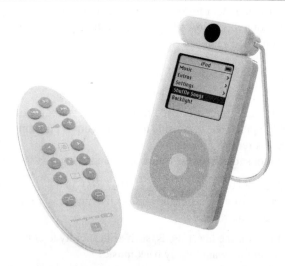

FIGURE 4-7   The naviPro eX from Ten Technologies provides infrared remote control of
your iPod.

The iDirect uses standard infrared signals, which give a good range (up to 100 feet, depending on how many walls, ceilings, and neighbors are in the way) and can be learned by universal remote controls. This means that you can use your universal remote control to control your iPod as well as your TV, DVD, and other misconnected electronic debris.

RemoteRemote

The RemoteRemote family of remote controls from Engineered Audio, LLC ($40 each; www .engineeredaudio.com) are radio-frequency (RF) remotes designed for the various latest iPod models. The RemoteRemote 2 works with third- and fourth-generation iPods and with the iPod mini; it even has a black model to go with the iPod U2. The RemoteRemote mini works with the iPod mini.

Flashlight and Laser Pointer

The iPod's backlight can save you in a pinch if you get stuck in near-total darkness, but it's nothing like a real flashlight. But you can turn a third- or fourth-generation iPod or an iPod mini into a flashlight—or a laser pointer—with the Griffin iBeam set ($19.99; www.griffintechnology .com). These lights (see Figure 4-8) plug into the headphone jack and the remote-control jack on the iPod and shine at the press of a button.

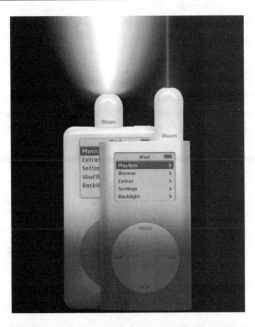

FIGURE 4-8   The iBeam set from Griffin Technology can turn your iPod into a flashlight or a laser pointer.

Input Devices for the iPod

In its original incarnation, the iPod's only input device was the computer, which fed it data along the FireWire cable. But with the iPod's tearaway success have come demands for additional input devices for the iPod—and the market has supplied them in the form of iPod microphones and a media-card reader.

 *At this writing, the iPod's firmware is limited to recording in mono at 8 KHz, which is low quality suitable only for spoken audio. You can't record high-quality audio on an iPod unless you install Linux on it.*

iPod Voice Recorder

The Belkin Voice Recorder for iPod ($49.99, www.belkin.com) is a microphone with an integrated tiny speaker that plugs into the headphone socket and remote-control socket of third- and fourth-generation iPods. (The Voice Recorder doesn't work with the fifth-generation iPod or with the iPod mini.)

Plugging in the Voice Recorder switches your iPod to its Voice Memo screen—which you can also access manually by choosing Extras | Voice Memos | Record Now—from which you can start recording by pressing the Select button with the Record item selected. Once the recording is running, you can pause it by using the Pause command, or you can stop the recording and save it by using the Stop And Save command. Your iPod saves the recording under a name that consists of the date and time—for example, 6/25 4:45 P.M.

You can play back and delete the memos from the Extras | Voice Memos screen. When you synchronize your iPod with iTunes, your voice memos are transferred to your computer and added to the Voice Memos playlist.

Universal Microphone Adapter

The Universal Microphone Adapter from Belkin ($29.99; www.belkin.com) lets you connect an external microphone to third- and fourth-generation iPods. The iPod Microphone Adapter connects to the headphone port and remote-control port on the top of the iPod and includes a headphone port to allow you to listen to the audio.

iTalk

The Griffin iTalk ($39.99; www.griffintechnology.com) is similar to the Voice Recorder for iPod, but it outdoes the Voice Recorder in two important ways. First, the iTalk (see Figure 4-9) lets you connect an external microphone, whereas the Voice Recorder doesn't. Second, the iTalk has a built-in speaker that lets you listen to audio at low volumes.

iPod Camera Connector

The iPod Camera Connector from Apple ($29; http://store.apple.com) is a device for transferring photos from a USB-equipped digital camera to your iPod. The iPod Camera Connector works with photo-capable fourth-generation iPods and with all fifth-generation iPods.

FIGURE 4-9   The Griffin iTalk lets you record audio directly onto your regular iPod.

Digital Camera Link for iPod

The Digital Camera Link for iPod from Belkin ($49.99; www.belkin.com) is a device that enables you to transfer photos from a USB-equipped digital camera to a third- or fourth-generation iPod. You connect the Digital Camera Link to the iPod via the Dock Connector and to the camera via the camera's USB cable, and then you press a button to transfer the photos. The Digital Camera Link runs off two AA batteries.

Portable Speakers for the iPod

You can use your iPod as the sound source for just about any stereo system, as you'll see in "Connect Your iPod to Your Stereo" in the next chapter. But if you travel with your iPod, or simply prefer a compact lifestyle, you may want portable speakers that will treat your iPod as the center of their universe. A variety of iPod-specific speakers are available to meet most constraints of budgets and portability.

> **NOTE**   *Apart from speakers mentioned here, another possibility is the Groove Bag Tote Speaker Purse, discussed in the "Weird Stuff" section, near the end of this chapter.*

Choosing Portable Speakers for the iPod

If you've decided that you need portable speakers specifically for your iPod, you've already narrowed down your choices considerably. Bear the following in mind when choosing portable speakers:

- *How much sound do the speakers make?* The best design in the world is useless if the speakers deliver sound too puny for your listening needs.

- *Do the speakers recharge the iPod?* Some speakers recharge the iPod as it plays. Others just wear down the battery.

■ *Do the speakers work with all iPods?* Some speakers are designed only to work with a particular iPod model. Others can recharge various iPods (for example, all iPods with the Dock Connector) but can accept input from other players via a line-in port.

■ *How are the speakers powered?* Some speakers are powered by replaceable batteries; others by rechargeable batteries; and others by AC power.

SoundDock

The SoundDock from Bose ($299; www.bose.com) is one of the larger and more powerful speaker systems designed for the iPod. The SoundDock works with all iPod models that have the Dock Connector port, but it requires an adapter for some models. The SoundDock runs on AC power and recharges your iPod as it plays.

On Stage

The JBL On Stage ($159; http://store.apple.com) is a round speaker unit that runs off AC power and delivers up to 6W per channel. The On Stage is designed for iPods with the Dock Connector, but you should check before buying to ensure that it's compatible with the iPod you have.

Despite running on AC power, the On Stage weighs only 1 lb. and is quite portable, which makes it a fair travel solution.

inMotion Series

The inMotion series from Altec Lansing (various prices; www.alteclansing.com) are stereo systems designed for various iPod models. In most inMotion models, the iPod connects through a Dock Connector that enables you to recharge it from the inMotion. You can play back audio from the iPod shuffle (but not recharge it) by connecting it via a cable.

Figure 4-10 shows the inMotion iM3, which runs off four AA batteries, giving up to 24 hours of playback, and is the size of a paperback book when folded. It delivers up to 4W RMS.

PodWave

If you need only a low volume of sound from your iPod's speakers, try the PodWave from MacAlly ($39.99; www.macally.com). The PodWave (see Figure 4-11) is a small tube that connects to any iPod via the headphone port, runs off a single AA battery, and produces 500 mW of power per channel. The PodWave doesn't recharge the iPod.

Sharper Image Travel Soother

The iPod Compatible Travel Soother 20 Radio/Alarm Clock ($99.95; www.sharperimage.com) is a portable stereo radio with an alarm clock built in. So far, so normal—but the Travel Soother also features an input that allows you to play your iPod (or any other sound source) through its speaker, making for an interesting travel solution for iPod enthusiasts. A little over twice the size

4

FIGURE 4-10   The inMotion iM3 balances portability and power, and it works with most iPods. Altec Lansing also makes other models of inMotion speakers.

and heft of a regular iPod, the Travel Soother also features 20 different soundscapes (including "Summer Night" and "Fireside") for white-noising your brain when you don't have suitable music. The Travel Soother runs off its own batteries (or off AC power if you buy an adapter) and doesn't recharge the iPod.

FIGURE 4-11   The PodWave is a miniature set of speakers that plays audio from any device with a headphone port.

Radio Transmitters

Portable speakers are a great way of getting a decent amount of audio out of your iPod when you're at home or traveling with a moderate amount of kit. But where portable speakers aren't practical, or when you need to travel light, you can use a radio transmitter to play audio from your iPod through a handy radio. This is useful in hotels, in cars, in friends' houses—and even in your own home.

Choosing a Radio Transmitter

Many models of radio transmitters are available. Apart from price and esthetics, consider the following when choosing between them:

- *Does the transmitter fit only one model of iPod, or will it work for any device?* You may find that the choice is between a transmitter designed to fit only your current model of iPod or a less stylish transmitter that will work with any iPod—or indeed any sound source.

- *Is the transmitter powered by the iPod, or does it have its own power source?* Drawing power from the iPod's battery is a neater arrangement, because you don't have to worry about keeping the battery in the transmitter charged (or putting in new batteries) or connecting an external power supply. But drawing power from the iPod tends to limit the transmitter to working with certain iPod models only.

- *Is the transmitter powerful enough for your needs?* Even among low-power transmitters that are legal for unlicensed use, power and range vary widely.

- *How many frequencies can the transmitter use?* Some transmitters are set to broadcast on a single frequency, which means you're out of luck if a more powerful local station happens to be using that frequency. Many transmitters offer several preset frequencies among which you can switch. Some transmitters provide a wide range of frequencies.

- *Does the transmitter have other tricks?* Some transmitters are designed for use in your car or another vehicle, whereas others are general purpose.

Low-power radio transmitters are legal in the United States, but some other countries don't permit them. If you don't know whether your country permits radio transmitters, check before buying one.

Podfreq

The Podfreq from Sonnet Technologies ($99.95; www.podfreq.com) is a relatively powerful radio transmitter that's built in the shape of an iPod case. The iPod slips inside the Podfreq (see Figure 4-12), and the Podfreq's aerial extends past the top of the iPod. The Podfreq offers a full range of digital tuning from 88.3 to 107.7 MHz, enabling you to avoid other stations even if the airwaves are jammed.

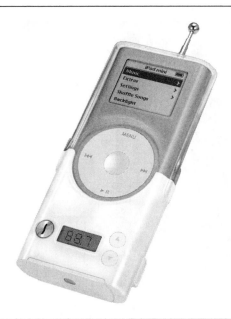

FIGURE 4-12   The Podfreq is one of the larger radio transmitters built for the iPod—and one
of the most powerful.

Instead of taking the audio from the iPod's headphone port, the Podfreq takes the audio from
the Dock Connector, which gives a line-out signal at a standard volume that should be cleaner than
the audio from the headphone port. The bottom of the Podfreq includes FireWire and mini-USB 2.0
ports, enabling you to synchronize and recharge your iPod even when it's installed in the Podfreq.

iTrip Family and iFM

The iTrip family from Griffin Technology ($39.99 each; www.griffintechnology.com) consists of
compact radio transmitters designed for the third- and fourth-generation iPods, the iPod nano, and
the iPod mini. The iFM ($49.99; www.griffintechnology.com) is a compact radio transmitter and
remote control that works for any Click-wheel iPod, including the fifth-generation iPod, the iPod
nano, the fourth-generation iPod, and the iPod mini. The iTrip models and iFM draw power from
the iPod's battery rather than using batteries of their own. The iTrip for iPod nano (see Figure 4-13)
attaches to the bottom of the iPod nano and lets you set it to broadcast on any frequency between
87.7 and 107.9 FM, so you should be able to get the signal through even in a busy urban area. The
iFM (also shown in Figure 4-13) connects to the Dock Connector port via a cable, offers multiple
presets, and even lets you toggle equalizations on and off remotely.

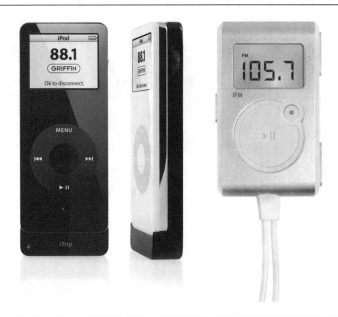

FIGURE 4-13 The iTrip family includes a version for the iPod nano. The iFM works with any Click-wheel iPod, including the fifth-generation iPod, connecting via a cable to the Dock Connector port.

Weird Stuff

This section mentions a small handful of oddball accessories determined not to fit into the previous categories.

Burton Amp Jacket

A while back, Burton Snowboards and Apple teamed up to produce the Burton Amp, a limited-edition waterproof snowboarding jacket designed to house an iPod. The iPod fits into a secure chest pocket from which wires run to a remote control built into a fabric data strip on the left forearm. From the remote control, wires run to the neck of the jacket, where you plug in your headset. Burton subsequently produced the Burton Shield ($379.95) with similar features, and also difficult to find.

If you're a fanatical snowboarder, you own an iPod, you're short a waterproof jacket, and you happen to have several hundred dollars burning a hole in your wallet, the Burton jacket may seem an opportunity that can't be missed. For most of the rest of the world, though, it is a fair illustration of the triumph of style over sense.

Most boarders will either go for an iPod shuffle (ideal for stunts) or iPod nano, or will achieve the same effect at no cost by attaching their iPod's own remote control to their torso or sleeve, padding or reinforcing an internal pocket, and perhaps running the wires under the fabric (or taping them down) to avoid tangling in aerial maneuvers.

Burton Amp Pack

The Burton Amp Pack ($199; http://store.apple.com or www.burton.com) is a laptop backpack with a special storage pocket for the iPod and a remote control pad built into the shoulder strap. The Amp Pack is designed for iPods with the Dock Connector.

Groove Bag Tote Speaker Purse

The Groove Bag Tote Speaker Purse from Felicidade ($199; www.drbott.com) is a bizarre anti-fashion accessory—a soft, faux-leather bag containing amplified speakers and a pocket for your iPod. The iPod pocket is see-through (see Figure 4-14), giving you access to your iPod's controls and enabling you to flash your iPod at passersby.

FIGURE 4-14   The Groove Bag Tote Speaker Purse is a dramatic way to carry your iPod.

Chapter 5

Use Your iPod as Your Home Stereo or Car Stereo

How to...

- Equip your iPod with speakers
- Connect your iPod to your stereo
- Play music throughout your house from your iPod
- Play music through an AirPort Express network
- Connect your iPod to your car stereo

By the time you've loaded a few thousand songs onto your iPod, you'll probably have decided that headphones only get you so far. To enjoy your music the rest of the time, chances are that you'll want to play it from your iPod through your home stereo or your car stereo. This chapter shows you the various ways of doing so, from using cables to using radio waves.

Equip Your iPod with Speakers

The simplest way to get a decent volume of sound from your iPod is to connect it to a pair of powered speakers (speakers that include their own amplifier). You can buy speakers designed especially for the iPod (see "Portable Speakers for the iPod" in Chapter 4 for some examples), but you can also use any iPod with any powered speakers that accept input via a miniplug connector (the size of connector used for the iPod's headphones). Speakers designed for the iPod tend to be smaller and more stylish than general-purpose speakers, but also considerably more expensive.

To get the highest sound quality possible from your iPod, get an iPod Dock and connect its line-out port to the speakers or receiver rather than using the output from the iPod's headphone port.

Connect Your iPod to Your Stereo

If you already have a stereo that produces good-quality sound, you can play songs from your iPod through the stereo. There are three main ways of doing this:

- Connect the iPod directly to the stereo with a cable.
- Use a radio transmitter to send the music from the iPod to your radio, which plays it.
- Use your computer to play the music from your iPod through an AirPort Express wireless access point that's connected to your stereo.

Connect Your iPod to Your Stereo with a Cable

The most direct way to connect your iPod to your stereo system is with a cable. For a typical receiver, you'll need a cable that has a miniplug at one end and two RCA plugs at the other end. Figure 5-1 shows an example of an iPod connected to a stereo via the amplifier.

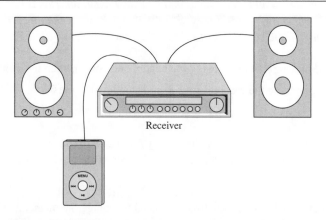

Receiver

FIGURE 5-1   A miniplug-to-RCA-plugs cable is the most direct way of connecting your iPod to your stereo system.

Some receivers and boom boxes use a single stereo miniplug input rather than two RCA ports. To connect your iPod to such devices, you'll need a stereo miniplug-to-miniplug cable. Make sure the cable is stereo, because mono miniplug-to-miniplug cables are common. A stereo cable has two bands around the miniplug (as on your iPod's headphones), whereas a mono cable has only one band.

NOTE

If you have a high-quality receiver and speakers, get a high-quality cable to connect your iPod to them. After the amount you've presumably spent on your iPod and your stereo, it'd be a mistake to degrade the signal between them by sparing a few bucks on the cable.

You can find various home-audio connection kits that contain a variety of cables likely to cover your needs. These kits are usually a safe buy, but unless your needs are peculiar, you'll end up with one or more cables you don't need. So if you do know which cables you need, make sure a kit offers a cost savings before buying it instead of the individual cables.

TIP

Connect your iPod to your receiver as follows:

1. Connect the miniplug to your iPod's headphone port. If you have an iPod Dock, connect the miniplug to the dock's line-out port instead, because this gives better sound quality than the headphone port.

2. If you're using the headphone port, turn down the volume on the iPod all the way.

3. Whichever port you're using, turn down the volume on the amplifier as well.

4. Connect the RCA plugs to the left and right ports of one of the inputs on your amplifier or boom box—for example, the AUX input or the Cassette input (if you're not using a cassette deck).

Don't connect your iPod to the Phono input on your amplifier. This is because the Phono input is built with a higher sensitivity to make up for the weak output of a record player. Putting a full-strength signal into the Phono input will probably blow it.

5. Start the iPod playing. If you're using the headphone port, turn up the volume a little.

6. Turn up the volume on the receiver so that you can hear the music.

7. Increase the volume on the two controls in tandem until you reach a satisfactory sound level.

Too low a level of output from your iPod may produce noise as your amplifier boosts the signal. Too high a level of output from your iPod may cause distortion.

If you plug your iPod directly into your stereo, get a remote control for the iPod so that you don't need to march over to the iPod each time you need to change the music. See "Remote Controls" in Chapter 4 for details of some of the remote controls available for the iPod.

Use a Radio Transmitter Between Your iPod and Your Stereo

If you don't want to connect your iPod directly to your stereo system, you can use a radio transmitter to send the audio from the iPod to the radio on your stereo. See "Radio Transmitters" in Chapter 4 for examples of radio transmitters designed for the iPod.

The sound you get from this arrangement typically will be lower in quality than the sound from a wired connection, but it should be at least as good as listening to a conventional radio station in stereo. If that's good enough for you, a radio transmitter can be a neat solution to playing music from your iPod throughout your house.

Using a radio transmitter has another advantage: You can play the music on several radios at the same time, giving yourself music throughout your dwelling without complex and expensive rewiring.

Use an AirPort Express and Your Computer

If you have an AirPort Express (a wireless access point that Apple makes), you can use it not only to network your home but also to play music from your computer or your iPod through your stereo system. (Figure 5-2 shows a typical setup.) To do so, follow these general steps:

1. Connect your AirPort Express to your receiver via a cable. The line-out port on the AirPort Express combines an analog port and an optical output, so you can connect the AirPort Express to the receiver in either of two ways:

    ■ Connect an optical cable to the AirPort Express's line-out socket and to an optical digital-audio input port on the receiver. If your receiver has an optical input, use this arrangement to get the best sound quality possible.

    ■ Connect an analog audio cable to the AirPort Express's line-out socket and to the RCA ports on your receiver.

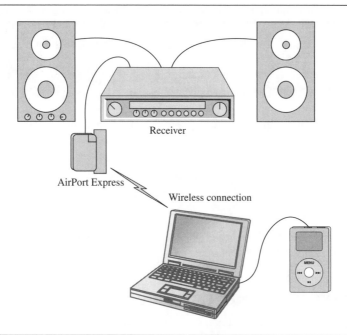

5

FIGURE 5-2   If you have an AirPort Express, you can play music on your computer or your iPod through your stereo system across the wireless network.

2. If your network has a wired portion, connect the Ethernet port on the AirPort Express to the switch or hub using an Ethernet cable. If you have a DSL that you will share through the AirPort Express, connect the DSL via the Ethernet cable.

3. Plug the AirPort Express into an electric socket.

4. Install the software that accompanies the AirPort Express on your computer. Then use the AirPort Admin Utility for Windows or the AirPort Express Assistant (on the Mac only) to configure the network.

5. Connect your iPod to your computer.

6. Launch iTunes if it isn't already running.

7. If your iPod is set for automatic updating of songs and playlists, right-click its entry in the Source pane and choose iPod Options to display the iPod tab of the iTunes dialog box (on Windows) or the Preferences dialog box (on the Mac). Select the Manually Manage Songs And Playlists option button, click the Yes button in the confirmation dialog box, and then click the OK button to close the dialog box.

8. Click the Choose Speakers button (the large button at the bottom of the iTunes window) and choose the entry for your AirPort Express from the drop-down list. (This button appears only if iTunes has detected an AirPort Express within striking distance.)

9. Click your iPod's entry in the Source pane to display its contents. You can then play the songs on the iPod back via your computer to the speakers connected to the AirPort Express.

10. To switch back to playing through your computer's speakers, click the Choose Speakers button at the bottom of the iTunes window again. This time, choose the Computer entry from the drop-down list.

If you changed your iPod's updating preferences in step 7, remember to change updating back to your preferred setting before you disconnect your iPod.

Connect Your iPod to Your Car Stereo

You can connect your iPod to your car stereo in any of the following ways:

■ Use a cassette adapter to connect your iPod to your car's cassette player.

■ Use a radio-frequency device to play your iPod's output through your car's radio.

■ Wire your iPod directly to your car stereo and use it as an auxiliary input device.

■ Get a car with a built-in iPod connection.

Each of these methods has its pros and cons. The following sections tell you what you need to know to choose the best option for your car stereo.

Use a Cassette Adapter

If your car stereo has a cassette player, your easiest option is to use a cassette adapter to play audio from your iPod through the cassette deck. You can buy such adapters for between $10 and $20 from most electronics stores or from an iPod specialist.

The adapter is shaped like a cassette and uses a playback head to input analog audio via the head that normally reads the tape as it passes. A wire runs from the adapter to your iPod.

A cassette adapter can be an easy and inexpensive solution, but it has a couple of disadvantages. First, the audio quality tends to be poor, because the means of transferring the audio to the cassette player's mechanism is less than optimal. If the cassette player's playback head is dirty from playing cassettes, audio quality will be that much worse. To keep the audio quality as high as possible, clean the cassette player regularly using a cleaning cassette.

Second, many autoreverse cassette players can't play input from a cassette adapter for more than 30 minutes or so without deciding they need to change directions and look for more music on the other side of the adapter—which can't supply it. So if you use a cassette adapter, you may have to reset the direction of play every once in a while. This isn't difficult, but it gets tedious fast.

> **TIP**
>
> *If you're considering using a cassette adapter, check out the SmartDeck from Griffin Technology ($29.95, www.griffintechnology.com). The SmartDeck connects to your iPod via the Dock Connector and lets you control your iPod by using the cassette deck's controls.*

Use a Radio Transmitter

5

If your car stereo doesn't have a cassette deck, your easiest option for playing music from your iPod may be to get a radio transmitter. This device plugs into your iPod and broadcasts a signal on an FM frequency to which you then tune your radio to play the music. Better radio transmitters offer a choice of frequencies to allow you easy access to both the device and your favorite radio stations.

> **NOTE**
>
> *See the section "Radio Transmitters" in Chapter 4 for a discussion of how to choose among the many radio transmitters offered and examples of transmitters designed for the iPod.*

Radio transmitters can deliver reasonable audio quality. If possible, try before you buy by asking for a demonstration in the store (take a portable radio with you, if necessary).

The main advantages of these devices are that they're relatively inexpensive (usually between $15 and $50) and they're easy to use. They also have the advantage that you can put your iPod out of sight (for example, in the glove compartment—provided it's not too hot) without any telltale wires to help the light-fingered locate it.

On the downside, most of these devices need batteries (others can run off the 12-volt accessory outlet or cigarette-lighter socket), and less expensive units tend not to deliver the highest sound quality. The range of these devices is minimal, but at close quarters, other radios nearby may be able to pick up the signal. If you use the radio transmitter in an area where the airwaves are busy, you may need to keep switching the frequency to avoid having the transmitter swamped by the full-strength radio stations.

If you decide to get a radio transmitter, you'll need to choose between getting a model designed specifically for the iPod and getting one that works with any audio source. Radio transmitters designed for the iPod typically mount on the iPod, making them a neater solution than general-purpose ones that dangle from the headphone socket.

> **TIP**
>
> *A radio-frequency adapter works with radios other than car radios, so you can use one to play music through your stereo system (or someone else's). You may also want to connect a radio-frequency adapter to your PC or Mac and use it to broadcast audio to a portable radio. This is a great way of getting streaming radio from the Internet to play on a conventional radio.*

Wire Your iPod Directly to Your Car Stereo

If neither the cassette adapter nor the radio-frequency adapter provides a suitable solution, or if you simply want the best audio quality you can get, connect your iPod directly to your car stereo. How easily you can do this depends on how the stereo is designed:

- If your car stereo is one of the few that has a miniplug input built in, get a miniplug-to-miniplug cable and you'll be in business.

- If your stereo is built to take multiple inputs—for example, a CD player (or changer) and an auxiliary input—you may be able to simply run a wire from unused existing connectors. Plug your iPod into the other end, press the correct buttons, and you'll be ready to rock-and-roll down the freeway.

- If no unused connectors are available, you or your local friendly electronics technician may need to get busy with a soldering iron.

If you're buying a new car stereo, look for an auxiliary input that you can use with your iPod.

Use a Built-in iPod Connection

If your car has a special provision for an iPod hookup, you need only get this feature or adapter installed, and you'll be away. At this writing, manufacturers such as BMW (vehicles including the Z4, the 3 Series, the X3 and X5, and the MINI Cooper and Cooper S), Mercedes (some 2005 and later models), and Volvo (S40, S60, S80, V50, V70, XC70, and XC90) offer either built-in iPod adapters or optional integration kits. Acura, Audi, Ferrari, Honda, Infiniti, Nissan, and Volkswagen have announced models with iPod connections. And Harley-Davidson has started putting iPod connectors on some of its newer models of motorcycles.

If your car manufacturer hasn't yet provided its own means of integrating an iPod, look for a third-party solution. For example, VAIS Technology (www.vaistech.com) sells input adapters with an iPod interface for Toyota and Lexus navigation systems. These adapters not only let you play back music from the iPod through the car's stereo and control the iPod using the stereo system's controls, they let you display the song information from the iPod on the stereo's display, making it easier to see what you're listening to.

Part II

Create and Manage Your Media Library

Chapter 6

Create Audio Files, Edit Them, and Tag Them

How to...

- Choose where to store your music library
- Choose suitable audio-quality settings in iTunes
- Convert audio files from other audio formats to AAC or MP3
- Create AAC files or MP3 files from cassettes, vinyl, or other sources
- Remove scratches, hiss, and hum from audio files
- Trim, sever, and otherwise abbreviate MP3 files
- Rename MP3 files efficiently
- Save audio streams to disk

In Chapter 2, you learned how to start creating your music library by copying music from your CDs and importing your existing music files. This is a great way to put songs on your iPod quickly, but to get the most enjoyment out of your music, you'll probably want to customize iTunes' settings rather than use the defaults.

You may also want to do things with AAC files and MP3 files that iTunes doesn't support. For example, you may receive (or acquire) files in formats your iPod can't handle, so you'll need to convert the files before you can use them on your iPod. You may want to create AAC files or MP3 files from cassettes, LPs, or other media you own, and you may need to remove clicks, pops, and other extraneous noises from such recordings you make. You may want to trim intros or outros off audio files, split files into smaller files, or retag batches of files in ways iTunes can't handle. Last, you may want to record streaming audio to your hard disk.

Although iTunes now prefers AAC to MP3, most of the world is still using MP3. For this reason, at this writing there are many more—and more capable—MP3 applications than AAC applications. You'll find that the coverage in this chapter reflects this situation. But unless you've been creating AAC files with an application other than iTunes, you'll probably need to edit and tag MP3 files rather than AAC files, so the slight bias toward MP3 shouldn't be a problem.

Where many applications offer similar functionality, this book mentions freeware applications and applications that offer functional evaluation versions in preference to applications that insist you buy them outright without giving you a chance to try them.

Choose Where to Store Your Music Library

Because your music library can contain dozens—or even hundreds—of gigabytes of music files, you must store it in a suitable location if you choose to keep all your music files in it.

6

The alternative to keeping all your music files in your music library is to instead store references to where the files are located in other folders. Doing so enables you to minimize the size of your music library. But for maximum flexibility and to make sure you can access all the tracks in your music library all the time, keeping all your music files in your music library folder is best—if you can do so.

To change the location of your music library, follow these steps:

1. Display the iTunes dialog box or the Preferences dialog box:

   ■ In Windows, choose Edit | Preferences or press CTRL-COMMA or CTRL-Y to display the iTunes dialog box.

   ■ On the Mac, choose iTunes | Preferences or press either ⌘-COMMA or ⌘-F to display the Preferences dialog box.

2. Click the Advanced tab to display its contents, and then click the General subtab. Figure 6-1 shows the Advanced tab of the iTunes dialog box in Windows. The Preferences dialog box for iTunes on the Mac has the same controls except for the Show iTunes Icon In System Tray check box and the Minimize iTunes Window To System Tray check box, which are Windows-only items.

FIGURE 6-1   You may need to move your music folder from its default location to a folder that has more disk space available.

3. Click the Change button to display the Browse For Folder dialog box (Windows) or Change Music Folder Location dialog box (Mac).

4. Navigate to the folder that will contain your music library, select the folder, and then click the Open button. iTunes returns you to the Advanced tab.

5. Click the OK button to close the iTunes dialog box or the Preferences dialog box. iTunes displays the following dialog box, asking if you want iTunes to move your existing music library files to the folder you specified.

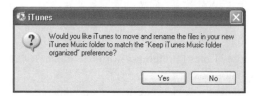

6. To keep all your music library files together in the new location, click the Yes button. You'll see the Organizing Files dialog box as iTunes organizes the files into the new location. To keep your existing music library files in their current locations but put any new files in the new location, click the No button.

To reset your music library folder to its default location (the iTunes\iTunes Music folder in Windows or the iTunes/iTunes Music folder on the Mac), click the Reset button on the Advanced tab of the iTunes dialog box or the Preferences dialog box. Again, iTunes asks if you want to move your existing files to the new location. Click the Yes button or the No button as appropriate.

Configure iTunes for the Audio Quality You Want

Before you rip and encode your entire CD collection, check that the settings in iTunes are suitable for your needs. iTunes' default is to encode to AAC files at 128 Kbps in stereo: a fair choice for defaults, but you may well want to change them. It's worth investing a little time in choosing the right settings for ripping and encoding, because ripping tracks more than once quickly becomes a severe waste of time.

First, decide which music format and audio quality you want. Then choose the appropriate settings in iTunes.

Choose the Best Audio Format for Your Needs

At this writing, iTunes can encode audio in five formats: AAC, MP3, Apple Lossless Encoding, WAV, and AIFF. AAC, MP3, and Apple Lossless Encoding are compressed audio formats, whereas WAV and AIFF are not compressed.

How to ... Understand CD-Quality Audio and Lossy and Lossless Compression

CD-quality audio samples audio 44,100 times per second (a sampling rate of 44.1 KHz) to provide coverage across most of the human hearing range. Each sample contains 16 bits (2 bytes) of data, which is enough information to convey the full range of frequencies. There are two tracks (for stereo), doubling the amount of data. CD-quality audio consumes around 9MB (megabytes) of storage space per minute of audio, which means that around 74 minutes of music fits on a standard 650MB CD and 80 minutes on a 700MB CD. The data on audio CDs is stored in *pulse code modulation (PCM)*, a standard format for uncompressed audio.

To make more music fit on a device with a limited capacity (for example, your iPod), you need to compress it so that it takes up less space. AAC and MP3 use *lossy compression*, compression that discards the parts of the audio data that your ears won't be able to hear or that your brain won't be able to pick out even though your ears hear it. Lossy audio codecs use *psychoacoustics*, the science of how the human brain processes sound, to select which data to keep and which to discard. As a crude example, when one part of the sound is masked by another part of the sound, the encoder discards the masked part, because you wouldn't hear it.

How much data the encoder keeps depends on a setting called the *bitrate*. Almost all encoders let you choose a wide range of bitrates. In addition, most MP3 encoders can encode either at a constant bitrate (CBR) or a variable bitrate (VBR). The pros and cons of CBR and VBR are discussed in the sidebar "Choose Between CBR and VBR, and a Suitable Stereo Setting, for MP3," later in this chapter.

The advantage of lossy compression is that a well-designed codec can produce good-sounding audio at a fraction of the file size of uncompressed audio. For example, AAC and MP3 sound good to most people at a bitrate of 128 Kbps, which produces files around a tenth of the size of the uncompressed audio. The disadvantage of lossy compression is that the audio can never sound perfect, because some data has been discarded.

Better than lossy compression is *lossless compression*, which reduces the file size without discarding any of the audio data. Apple Lossless Encoding is lossless compression and produces extremely high-quality results.

The advantage of lossless compression is that it produces audio that is as high in quality as the uncompressed audio. The disadvantage is that lossless compression reduces the file size by much less than lossy compression, because it doesn't discard audio data.

AAC

AAC is the abbreviation for Advanced Audio Coding, a *codec* (*co*der/*dec*oder) for compressing and playing back digital audio. AAC was put together by a group of heavy hitters in the audio and digital-audio fields, including Fraunhofer IIS-A (the German company that developed MP3), Sony Corporation, Dolby Laboratories, AT&T, Nokia, and Lucent.

AAC is newer than MP3 (which is discussed in the next section), is generally agreed to deliver better sound than MP3, and is more tightly controlled than MP3. It is one of the key audio components of the MPEG-4 specification, which covers digital audio and video.

AAC files can be either protected with digital rights management (DRM) technology or unprotected.

NOTE *The iTunes Music Store (discussed in Chapter 7) uses AAC for its songs, so if you buy songs from it, you won't have any choice about using AAC. If necessary, you can convert the songs to other formats. For example, you might convert a song from AAC to MP3 so that you can use it with an MP3 player that can't handle AAC.*

QuickTime 6 and later versions include an AAC codec. If your Mac has QuickTime 6.2 or a later version installed, iTunes uses MPEG-4 AAC as its default encoding format. (If your Mac has an earlier version of QuickTime installed, iTunes uses MP3 as its default encoding format.)

NOTE *AAC can work with up to 48 full-frequency audio channels. This gives it a huge advantage over MP3, which can work with only two channels (in stereo) or a single channel (in mono). If you're used to listening to music in stereo, 48 channels seems an absurd number. But typically, only a small subset of those channels would be used at the same time. For example, conventional surround-sound rigs use 5.1 or 7.1 setups, using six channels or eight channels, respectively. Other channels can be used for different languages, so that an AAC player can play a different vocal track for differently configured players. Other tracks yet can be used for synchronizing and controlling the audio.*

Advantages of AAC For music lovers, AAC offers higher music quality than MP3 at the same file sizes, or similar music quality at smaller file sizes. Apple reckons that 128 Kbps AAC files sound as good as 160 Kbps MP3 files—so you can either save a fair amount of space and enjoy the same quality or enjoy even higher quality at the same bitrate. Around 24 Kbps, AAC streams provide quite listenable sound, whereas MP3 streams sound quite rough. (*Streaming* is the method of transmission used by Internet radio, in which you can listen to a file as your computer downloads it.)

Small file sizes are especially welcome for streaming audio over slow connections, such as modem connections. AAC streamed around 56 Kbps sounds pretty good (though not perfect), whereas MP3 sounds a bit flawed.

The main advantage of AAC for the music industry is that the format supports digital rights management (DRM). This means that AAC files can be created in a protected format with custom limitations built in. For example, the song files you can buy from the iTunes Music Store are authorized to be played on up to three different computers at the same time. If you try to play a song on a computer that's not authorized, the song won't play.

NOTE *To tell whether an AAC file is protected, choose File | Get Info and check the Kind readout on the Summary tab of the Song Information dialog box. If the file is protected, the Kind readout reads "Protected AAC Audio File." If not, Kind reads "AAC Audio File." Alternatively, check the file extension: The .m4p extension indicates a protected file, whereas the .m4a extension indicates an unprotected file.*

Disadvantages of AAC   AAC's disadvantages are largely acceptable to most users of iTunes and the iPod:

- At the time of writing, AAC files aren't widely used. One reason is that, because AAC is relatively new and hasn't been very widely implemented, few AAC encoders and decoders are available. However, in iTunes (and QuickTime) and the iPod, Apple has provided AAC encoding and decoding for the Mac and for Windows. Because AAC is the default format for audio encoding in iTunes, its usage is growing rapidly.

- Encoding AAC files takes more processor cycles than encoding MP3 files. But as processors continue to increase in speed and power by the month if not by the week, this becomes less and less of a problem. Even relatively antiquated Macs (such as my PowerBook G3/333) and PCs (for example, a Celeron 600) have plenty of power to encode and decode AAC—they just do so more slowly than faster computers.

- For consumers, the largest potential disadvantage of AAC is the extent to which DRM can limit their use of the files. At the time of writing, Apple has delivered a relatively flexible implementation of DRM in the music sold by the iTunes Music Store. However, if Apple and the record companies tighten the licensing terms of the files in the future, consumers may have cause for concern. In this sense, AAC could act as a Trojan horse to wean customers off MP3 and onto AAC, then gradually lock them in to a format that the music industry can control.

MP3

Like AAC, MP3 is a file format for compressed audio. MP3 became popular in the late 1990s and largely sparked the digital music revolution by making it possible to carry a large amount of high-quality audio with you on a small device and enjoy it at the cost of nothing but the device, battery power, and time.

Among Mac users, MP3 has been overshadowed recently by AAC since Apple incorporated the AAC codec in iTunes, QuickTime, and the iPod. But MP3 remains the dominant format for compressed audio on computers running Windows (where its major competition comes from WMA, Microsoft's proprietary Windows Media Audio format) and computers running Linux.

MP3's name comes from the Motion Picture Experts Group (MPEG; www.chiariglione.org/mpeg/—*not* www.mpeg.org), which oversaw the development of the MP3 format. MP3 is both the extension used by the files and the name commonly used for them. More correctly, MP3 is the file format for MPEG-1 Layer 3—but most people who listen to MP3 files neither know that nor care to know such details.

MP3 can deliver high-quality music in files that take up as little as a tenth as much space as uncompressed CD-quality files. For speech, which typically requires less fidelity than music, you can create even smaller files that still sound good, enabling you to pack that much more audio in the same amount of disk space.

Apple Lossless Encoding

Apple Lossless Encoding is an encoder that gives results that are mathematically lossless—there is no degradation of audio quality in the compressed files. The amount that Apple Lossless

Encoding compresses audio depends on how complex the audio is. Some songs compress to around 40 percent of the uncompressed file size, whereas others compress to only 60–70 percent of the uncompressed file size.

Apple Lossless Encoding is a great way to keep full-quality audio on your computer—at least, if it has a large hard disk (or several large hard disks). Apple Lossless Encoding gives great audio quality on the iPod as well, of course, but it's not such a great solution for most people. This is for two reasons: First, the large amount of space that Apple Lossless Encoding files consume means that you can't fit nearly as many songs on your iPod as you can using AAC or MP3. Second, the Apple Lossless Encoding files are too large for the iPod's memory chip to buffer effectively. As a result, the iPod has to read the hard drive more frequently, which reduces battery life.

The iPod shuffle doesn't play Apple Lossless Encoding files at all, mostly because of its low capacity. The Motorola ROKR plays only AAC files—not MP3 files or Apple Lossless Encoding files.

WAV and AIFF

WAV files and AIFF files are basically the same thing—uncompressed PCM audio, which is also referred to as "raw" audio. WAV files are PCM files with a WAV header, whereas AIFF files are PCM files with an AIFF header. The *header* is a section of identification information contained at the start of the file.

AIFF tends to be more widely used on the Mac than in Windows, which favors WAV. However, iTunes can create and play both AIFF files and WAV files on both Windows and Mac OS X.

If you want the ultimate in audio quality, you can create AIFF files or WAV files from your CDs and store them on your computer and iPod. However, there are three reasons why you shouldn't do this:

- Each full-length CD will take up between 500MB and 800MB of disk space, compared to the 50MB to 80MB it would take up compressed at 128 Kbps. Apple Lossless Encoding gives a better balance of full audio quality with somewhat reduced file size.

- Your iPod won't be able to buffer the audio effectively, will need to access the hard drive more frequently, and will deliver poor battery life. This is a consideration only for iPods that have hard drives, not for the iPod nano (whose storage is memory chips).

- Neither AIFF files nor WAV files have containers for storing tag information, such as the names of the artist, the CD, and the song. iTunes does its best to help by maintaining the tag information for AIFF files or WAV files in its database, but if you move the files (for example, if you copy them to a different computer), the tag information doesn't go with them. By contrast, Apple Lossless Encoding files have containers for their tag information.

The iPod shuffle doesn't play WAV or AIFF files at all. As with Apple Lossless Encoding files, this is mostly because of the iPod shuffle's low capacity.

How to Choose the Best Format for iTunes and Your iPod

Choosing the best audio format for iTunes and your iPod can be tough. You'll probably be torn between having the highest-quality audio possible when playing audio on your computer and packing the largest possible number of good-sounding songs on your iPod—and making sure it has enough battery life for you to listen to plenty of those songs each day.

For the highest possible audio quality on your computer, use Apple Lossless Encoding. (WAV and AIFF are also possible, but they use more space, have no tag containers, and offer no advantage over Apple Lossless Encoding.) For the largest possible number of songs on your iPod, use AAC.

Unless you're one of the very few people who find it practicable to keep two copies of each song in your music library (or at least two copies of each song that you want to be able to play both on your computer and on your iPod), you'll probably be best off going with AAC at a high enough bitrate that you don't notice the difference in quality between the AAC files and Apple Lossless Encoding files.

6

Did you know?

Digital Audio Formats the iPod Can't Play

For most of the music you store on your computer and enjoy via iTunes or your iPod, you'll want to use AAC, MP3, or whichever combination of the two you find most convenient. Both iTunes and the iPod can also use WAV files and AIFF files.

For you as a digital-audio enthusiast, other formats that may be of interest include the following:

- WMA is an audio format developed by Microsoft. It's the preferred format of Windows Media Player, the Microsoft audio and video player included with all desktop versions of Windows. WMA supports DRM, but its DRM is incompatible with iTunes and the iPod.

- mp3PRO is designed to be a successor to MP3. It delivers higher audio quality than MP3 at the same bitrates. For example, mp3PRO files encoded at the 64 Kbps bitrate are similar in quality to MP3 files encoded at the 128 Kbps bitrate. Like MP3, mp3PRO requires hardware and software manufacturers to pay royalties to Thomson Corporation. At this writing, mp3PRO products are available but not widespread. For more information, start at mp3PROzone (www.mp3prozone.com).

- Ogg Vorbis is an open-source format that's patent free but not yet widely used. You can get an Ogg Vorbis plug-in for QuickTime (from www.illadvised.com/~jordy) that enables iTunes to play Ogg Vorbis songs or to convert them to another iTunes format (such as AAC or MP3). To play Ogg Vorbis files on your iPod, you'll need to convert them to AAC or MP3. (You can also convert them to Apple Lossless Encoding, WAV, or AIFF, but doing so makes little sense, because Ogg Vorbis is a lossy format.)

NOTE   *AAC delivers high-quality audio, small file size, and enough flexibility for most purposes. But if you want to use the files you rip from a CD on a portable player that doesn't support AAC, or you need to play them using a software player that doesn't support AAC, choose MP3 instead. Similarly, if you want to share your music files with other people in any way other than sharing your music library via iTunes, MP3 is the way to go—but remember that you need the copyright holder's explicit authorization to copy and distribute music.*

Check or Change Your Importing Settings

To check or change the importing settings, follow these steps:

1. Display the iTunes dialog box or the Preferences dialog box:
   - In Windows, choose Edit | Preferences or press CTRL-COMMA or CTRL-Y to display the iTunes dialog box.
   - On the Mac, choose iTunes | Preferences or press either ⌘-COMMA or ⌘-Y to display the Preferences dialog box.

2. Click the Advanced tab, then click the Importing subtab to display its contents. Figure 6-2 shows the Importing subtab on iTunes for the Mac. The Importing tab on iTunes for Windows has the same controls.

3. In the On CD Insert drop-down list, choose the action you want iTunes to perform when you insert a CD: Show Songs, Begin Playing, Import Songs, or Import Songs And Eject. These settings are easy to understand, but bear in mind that Show Songs, Import Songs, and Import Songs And Eject all involve looking up the song names in the CD database (unless you've already played the CD and thus caused iTunes to look up the names), so iTunes will need to use your Internet connection.

4. In the Import Using drop-down list, specify the file format you want to use by choosing the appropriate encoder:
   - The default setting is AAC Encoder, which creates compressed files in AAC format. AAC files combine high audio quality with compact size, making AAC a good format for both iTunes and your iPod.
   - The other setting you're likely to want to try is MP3 Encoder, which creates compressed files in the MP3 format. MP3 files have slightly lower audio quality than AAC files for the same file size, but you can use them with a wider variety of software applications and hardware players than AAC files.
   - Apple Lossless Encoding files have full audio quality but a relatively large file size. They're good for iTunes but typically too large for the iPod.
   - AIFF files and WAV files are uncompressed audio files, so they have full audio quality but take up a huge amount of space. You'll seldom need to use either of these formats.

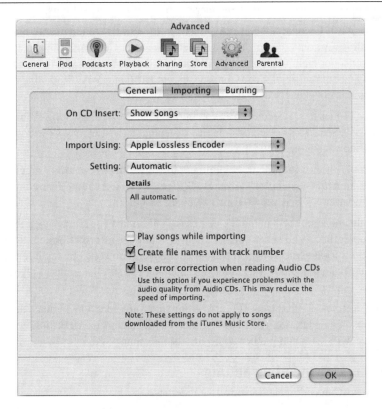

6

FIGURE 6-2   Configure your audio quality settings on the Importing subtab of the Advanced tab of the iTunes dialog box or the Preferences dialog box.

5. In the Setting drop-down list, choose the setting you want to use:

■ For the AAC Encoder, the Setting drop-down list offers the settings High Quality (128 Kbps), Podcast, and Custom. When you select Custom, iTunes displays the AAC Encoder dialog box so you can specify custom settings. See the next section, "Choose Custom AAC Encoding Settings," for a discussion of these options.

■ For the MP3 Encoder, the Configuration drop-down list offers the settings Good Quality (128 Kbps), High Quality (160 Kbps), Higher Quality (192 Kbps), and Custom. When you select Custom, iTunes displays the MP3 Encoder dialog box so you can specify custom settings. See "Choose Custom MP3 Encoding Settings," later in this chapter, for a discussion of these options.

- The Apple Lossless Encoding encoder has no configurable settings.
- For the AIFF Encoder and the WAV Encoder, the Configuration drop-down list offers the settings Automatic and Custom. When you select Custom, iTunes displays the AIFF Encoder dialog box or the WAV Encoder dialog box (as appropriate) so you can specify custom settings. See "Choose Custom AIFF and WAV Encoding Settings," later in this chapter, for a discussion of these options.

6. If you want iTunes to play each CD as you import it, leave the Play Songs While Importing check box selected (it's selected by default). Listening to the CD may slow down the rate of ripping and encoding, so you may prefer not to use this option.

7. If you want iTunes to include track numbers in song names (creating names such as *01 Cortez the Killer* instead of *Cortez the Killer*), leave the Create File Names With Track Number check box selected (it's selected by default).

   Including the track numbers in the file names isn't necessary for iTunes itself to keep the tracks in order, because iTunes can use the track-number information in a track's tag. (Some utilities for downloading songs from an iPod can sort songs by tag information, too.) But you may want to include the numbers so that you can sort the songs easily into album order in the Finder.

   Including the track number is useful for keeping tracks in order when you create MP3 CDs. This is only a consideration when you're encoding the songs as MP3 files, because you can't create MP3 CDs using other audio file formats than MP3.

Choose Custom AAC Encoding Settings

To choose custom AAC encoding settings, follow these steps:

1. On the Importing subtab of the Advanced tab of the iTunes dialog box or the Preferences dialog box, choose AAC Encoder in the Import Using drop-down list.

2. In the Setting drop-down list, choose the Custom item to display the AAC Encoder dialog box:

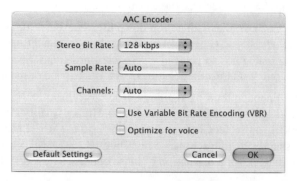

3. In the Stereo Bit Rate drop-down list, specify the bitrate. You can use from 16 Kbps to 320 Kbps. The default is 128 Kbps.

The 128 Kbps setting provides high-quality audio suitable for general music listening. You may want to experiment with higher bitrates to see if you can detect a difference. If not, stick with 128 Kbps so as to get the largest possible amount of quality music on your iPod.

If you listen to spoken-word audio, experiment with the bitrates below 64 Kbps to see which bitrate delivers suitable quality for the material you listen to, and select the Optimize For Voice check box.

4. In the Sample Rate drop-down list, specify the sample rate by choosing Auto, 44.100kHz, or 48.000kHz. 44.100 KHz is the sample rate used by CD audio; unless you have a data source that uses a 48.000 KHz sampling rate, there's no point in choosing this option. For most purposes, you'll get best results by using the Auto setting (the default setting), which makes iTunes use a sampling rate that matches the input quality. For example, for CD-quality audio, iTunes uses the 44.100 KHz sampling rate.

5. In the Channels drop-down list, select Auto, Stereo, or Mono, as appropriate. In most cases, Auto (the default setting) is the best bet, because it makes iTunes choose stereo or mono as appropriate to the sound source. However, you may occasionally need to produce mono files from stereo sources.

6. If you want to use variable bit rate encoding (VBR) rather than constant bit rate encoding (CBR), select the Use Variable Bit Rate Encoding (VBR) check box. If you want to optimize the encoding for voice instead of music, select the Optimize For Voice check box.

7. Click the OK button to close the AAC Encoder dialog box.

How to ... Choose an Appropriate Compression Rate, Bitrate, and Stereo Settings

To get suitable audio quality, you must use an appropriate compression rate for the audio files you encode with iTunes.

iTunes' default settings are to encode AAC files in stereo at the 128 Kbps bitrate using automatic sample-rate detection. iTunes calls those settings High Quality, and they deliver great results for most purposes. If they don't suit you, you can either choose the Podcast setting to create files suitable for podcasting (in other words, with lower quality and a smaller file size) or specify custom AAC settings for the files you create. With AAC you can change the bitrate, the sample rate, and the channels.

iTunes' MP3 encoder gives you more flexibility. The default settings for MP3 are to encode MP3 files in stereo at the 160 Kbps bitrate, using CBR and automatic sample-rate detection. iTunes calls those settings High Quality, and they deliver results almost as good as the High Quality settings with the AAC encoder, although they produce significantly larger files because the bitrate is higher.

(continued)

For encoding MP3 files, iTunes also offers preset settings for Good Quality (128 Kbps) and Higher Quality (192 Kbps). Beyond these choices, you can choose the Custom setting and specify exactly the settings you want: bitrates from 16 Kbps to 230 Kbps, CBR or VBR, sample rate, channels, the stereo mode, whether to use Smart Encoding Adjustments, and whether to filter frequencies lower than 10 Hz. If possible, invest a few days in choosing a compression rate for your music library. Choosing an unsuitable compression rate can cost you disk space (if you record at too high a bitrate), audio quality (too low a bitrate), and the time it takes to rip your entire collection again at a more suitable bitrate.

Choose a representative selection of the types of music you plan to listen to using your computer and your iPod. Encode several copies of each test track at different bitrates and then listen to them over several days to see which provides the best balance of file size and audio quality.

Make sure some of the songs test the different aspects of music that are important to you. For example, if your musical tastes lean to female vocalists, listen to plenty of those types of songs. If you prefer bass-heavy, bludgeoning rock, listen to that. If you go for classical music as well, add that to the mix. You may find that you need to use different compression rates for different types of music to achieve satisfactory results and keep the file size down.

Choose Custom MP3 Encoding Settings

To choose custom MP3 encoding settings, follow these steps:

1. On the Importing tab of the iTunes dialog box or the Preferences dialog box, choose MP3 Encoder in the Import Using drop-down list.

2. In the Setting drop-down list, choose the Custom item to display the MP3 Encoder dialog box:

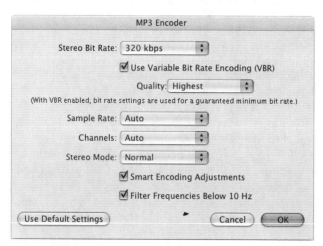

3. In the Stereo Bit Rate drop-down list, select the bitrate you want to use.

The choices range from 16 Kbps to 320 Kbps. 16 Kbps produces shoddy-sounding audio even for the spoken word, but it may be useful when you need to get long passages of low-quality audio into a small file. At the other extreme, 320 Kbps produces audio high enough in quality that most people can't distinguish it from CD-quality audio.

iTunes uses the bitrate you select as the exact bitrate for CBR encoding and as the minimum bitrate for VBR encoding.

See the section "Understand CD-Quality Audio and Lossy and Lossless Compression" earlier in this chapter for a discussion of CD-quality audio. "Choose an Appropriate Compression Rate, Bitrate, and Stereo Settings," also earlier in this chapter, offers advice on choosing a compression rate that matches your needs.

4. Select the Use Variable Bit Rate Encoding check box if you want to create VBR-encoded files instead of CBR-encoded files.

See the sidebar "Choose Between CBR and VBR, and a Suitable Stereo Setting, for MP3" later in this chapter, for a discussion of CBR and VBR.

If you select this check box, choose a suitable setting in the Quality drop-down list. The choices are Lowest, Low, Medium Low, Medium, Medium High, High, and Highest. iTunes uses the bitrates specified in the Stereo Bit Rate drop-down list as the guaranteed minimum bitrates. The Quality setting controls the amount of processing iTunes applies to making the file sound as close to the original as possible. More processing requires more processor cycles, which will make your computer work harder. If your computer is already working at full throttle, encoding will take longer.

5. In the Sample Rate drop-down list, set a sample rate manually only if you're convinced you need to do so.

You might want to use a lower sample rate if you're encoding spoken-word audio rather than music and don't need such high fidelity.

Choices range from 8 KHz to 48 KHz (higher than CD-quality audio, which uses 44.1 KHz).

The default setting is Auto, which uses the same sample rate as does the music you're encoding. Using the same sample rate usually delivers optimal results.

6. In the Channels drop-down list, select Auto, Mono, or Stereo. The default setting is Auto, which uses mono for encoding mono sources and stereo for stereo sources.

7. In the Stereo Mode drop-down list, choose Normal Stereo or Joint Stereo. See the sidebar "Choose Between CBR and VBR, and a Suitable Stereo Setting, for MP3," later in this chapter, for a discussion of the difference between normal stereo and joint stereo. If you select Mono in the Channels drop-down list, the Stereo Mode drop-down list becomes unavailable because its options don't apply to mono.

8. Select or clear the Smart Encoding Adjustments check box and the Filter Frequencies Below 10 Hz check box, as appropriate. These check boxes are selected by default. In most cases, you'll do best to leave them selected.

Smart Encoding Adjustments allows iTunes to tweak your custom settings to improve them if you've chosen an inappropriate combination.

As mentioned earlier, frequencies below 10 Hz are infrasound and are of interest only to animals such as elephants, so filtering them out makes sense for humans.

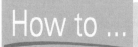

To restore iTunes to using its default settings for encoding MP3 files, click the Use Default Settings button in the MP3 Encoder dialog box.

9. Click the OK button to close the MP3 Encoder dialog box.

10. Click the OK button to close the iTunes dialog box or the Preferences dialog box.

How to ... Choose Between CBR and VBR, and a Suitable Stereo Setting, for MP3

After choosing the bitrate at which to encode your MP3 files, you must choose between constant bitrate (CBR) and variable bitrate (VBR). You must also choose whether to use joint stereo or normal stereo.

CBR simply records each part of the file at the specified bitrate. CBR files can sound great, particularly at higher bitrates, but generally VBR delivers better quality than CBR. This is because VBR can allocate space more intelligently as the audio needs it. For example, a complex passage of a song will require more data to represent it accurately than will a simple passage, which in turn will require more data than the two seconds of silence before the massed guitars come crashing back in.

The disadvantage to VBR, and the reason why most MP3 encoders are set to use CBR by default, is that many older decoders and hardware devices can't play it. If you're using iTunes and an iPod, you won't need to worry about this. But if you're using an older decoder or hardware device, you may need to check that it can manage VBR.

So VBR is probably a better bet. A harder choice is between the two different types of stereo that iTunes offers: joint stereo and normal stereo. (iTunes also offers mono—a single channel that gives no separation among the sounds. The only reason to use mono is if your sound source is mono; for example, a live recording that used a single mono microphone.)

Stereo delivers two channels: a left channel and a right channel. These two channels provide positional audio, enabling recording and mixing engineers to separate the audio so that different sounds appear to be coming from different places. For example, the engineer can make one guitar sound as though it's positioned on the left and another guitar sound as though it's positioned on the right. Or the engineer might fade a sound from left to right so it seems to go across the listener.

Normal stereo (sometimes called *plain stereo*) uses two tracks: one for the left stereo channel and another for the right stereo channel. As its name suggests, normal stereo is the normal form of stereo. For example, if you buy a CD that's recorded in stereo and play it back through your boom box, you're using normal stereo.

Joint stereo (sometimes called *mid/side stereo*) divides the channel data differently to make better use of a small amount of space. The encoder averages out the two original channels (assuming the sound source is normal stereo) to a mid channel. It then encodes this channel, devoting to it the bulk of the available space assigned by the bitrate. One channel contains the data that's the same on both channels. The second channel contains the data that's different on one of the channels. By reducing the channel data to the common data (which takes the bulk of the available space) and the data that's different on one of the channels (which takes much less space), joint stereo can deliver higher audio quality at the same bitrate as normal stereo.

Use joint stereo to produce better-sounding audio when encoding at lower bitrates, and use normal stereo for all your recordings at your preferred bitrate. Where the threshold for lower-bitrate recording falls depends on you. Many people recommend using normal stereo for encoding at bitrates of 160 Kbps and above, and using joint stereo for lower bitrates (128 Kbps and below). Others recommend not using normal stereo below 192 Kbps. Experiment to establish what works for you.

The results you get with joint stereo depend on the quality of the MP3 encoder you use. Some of the less-capable MP3 encoders produce joint-stereo tracks that sound more like mono tracks than like normal-stereo tracks. Better encoders produce joint-stereo tracks that sound very close to normal-stereo tracks. iTunes produces pretty good joint-stereo tracks.

Using the same MP3 encoder, normal stereo delivers better sound quality than joint stereo—at high bitrates. At lower bitrates, joint stereo delivers better sound quality than normal stereo, because joint stereo can retain more data about the basic sound (in the mid channel) than normal stereo can retain about the sound in its two separate channels. However, joint stereo provides less separation between the left and right channels than normal stereo provides. (The lack of separation is what produces the mono-like effect.)

Choose Custom AIFF and WAV Encoding Settings

The AIFF Encoder dialog box (shown on the left in Figure 6-3) and the WAV Encoder dialog box (shown on the right in Figure 6-3) offer similar settings. AIFFs and WAVs are essentially the same apart from the file header, which distinguishes the file formats from each other.

In either of these dialog boxes, you can choose the following settings:

- ■ **Sample Rate**   Choose Auto (the default setting) to encode at the same sample rate as the original you're ripping. Otherwise, choose a value from the range available (8 KHz to 48 KHz).

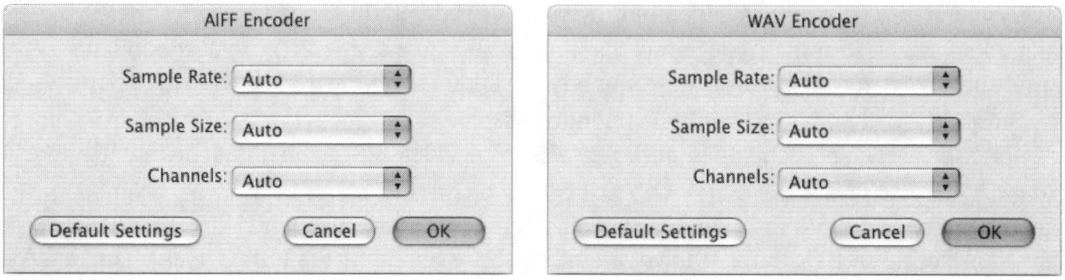

AIFF Encoder		WAV Encoder	
Sample Rate: Auto		Sample Rate: Auto	
Sample Size: Auto		Sample Size: Auto	
Channels: Auto		Channels: Auto	
Default Settings Cancel OK		Default Settings Cancel OK	

FIGURE 6-3   If you choose to encode to AIFF or WAV files, you can set encoding options in the AIFF Encoder dialog box (left) or the WAV Encoder dialog box (right).

- **Sample Size**   Select Auto to have iTunes automatically match the sample size to that of the source. Otherwise, select 8 Bit or 16 Bit, as appropriate. PCM audio uses 16 bits, so if you're encoding files from CDs, iTunes automatically uses a 16-bit sample size.

- **Channels**   Select Auto (the default setting) to encode mono files from mono sources and stereo files from stereo sources. Otherwise, select Mono or Stereo, as appropriate.

Deal with CDs That Your Computer Can't Rip

This book's discussion of importing audio from CDs so far has assumed that you're dealing with regular audio CDs: CDs that comply with the Red Book format, the basic format for putting audio data on a CD without any anti-copying protection or digital rights management (DRM). Some unprotected CDs use the CD Extra format (a subset of Red Book) to put non-audio data on the CD as well.

Philips and Sony defined the Red Book format in 1980. (The standard was published in a red binder—hence the name. Subsequent standards include Orange Book and Yellow Book, named for similar reasons.) Red Book ensures the disc will work with all drives that bear the Compact Disc logo and entitles the disc to bear the Compact Disc Digital Audio logo.

You can import audio from any Red Book or CD Extra CD without a problem using iTunes (or another application) on Windows, Mac OS X, or Linux. But because many music enthusiasts have shared the music they've ripped from CDs with other people over the Internet, the music industry has taken to including protection on some of the CDs they release.

Understand Current Copy-Protection Techniques on the CDs You Buy

At this writing, the music industry is using several copy-protection solutions to prevent customers from ripping or burning copies of the CDs they buy. These solutions include:

- **CDS from Macrovision Corporation (www.macrovision.com)**   CDS, originally called Cactus Data Shield and developed by the Israel-based company Midbar Tech, comes in several types, including CDS-100 and CDS-300. CDS-100 "restricts" (read: "largely prevents") playback on computers while allowing playback on audio players and DVD players. CDS-300 is a combined hardware and software solution that dynamically encodes the CD's audio to DRM-protected WMA files so that PC users can use the files with Windows Media Player and portable devices that support Windows Media DRM.

6

> NOTE   *CDS-100 is typically used for prerelease copies of music in the aim of discouraging reviewers from creating digital copies of the songs and putting them into circulation on the P2P networks. CDS-300 is typically used on commercial CDs.*

- **key2audioXS from Sony DADC (www.key2audio.com)**   key2audioXS places a special signature on the disc that prevents it from being played and copied on computers. Disc publishers can choose whether to allow customers to burn any copies of the discs.

> NOTE   *By mid 2005, key2audio protection had been used on tens of millions of CDs. Anecdotal evidence suggests that most of these protected audio discs have been sold in Europe, with smaller numbers having been sold in the U.S. and the U.K., which are two markets that have historically been more sensitive to crippled audio discs. key2audio-protected discs have generated bad publicity by making computers hang.*

- **MediaMax from SunnComm (www.sunncomm.com)**   MediaMax is a copy-protection technology that supposedly works on both PCs and Macs. MediaMax requires you to install software from the disc onto your computer before you can play the music. MediaMax uses digital keys downloaded from the SunnComm website to verify that you are the owner of the CD. MediaMax was the copy-protection mechanism used on the first No. 1 audio disc to use protection, "Contraband," from Velvet Revolver, in 2004.

> NOTE   *MediaMax uses protected WMA files for PC playback. These files don't work with iTunes and the iPod, but you can use Windows Media Player to burn the WMA files to a CD and then rip that CD with iTunes. Doing so involves more effort and a loss of audio quality, but if you're desperate, it can be an acceptable solution.*

Some copy-protection solutions add deliberate errors to the data on the disc to make it harder for optical drives to read while allowing audio-only CD players (which have more effective error-correction mechanisms) to read the discs successfully. Other copy-protection solutions include compressed audio in a separate session on the disc, usually with a player that is intended to spring into action when the disc is loaded on a computer.

Who Benefits from Copy-Protected Audio Discs?

The companies that make copy-protection for audio discs present the copy protection as being good for all parties concerned: the record companies, the artists, and the customers. Most customers—and even some artists—disagree.

For record companies, copy-protected audio discs are mostly positive, because they help to reduce the amount of piracy they suffer. However, copy-protected audio discs have drawn many complaints from customers unable to play the discs on their computers or specialized optical-disc players (for example, DVD players). Artists also benefit from reduced piracy of their music but suffer from negative feedback from fans who can't play the discs as they expect to.

Customers benefit little or not at all from copy-protected audio discs:

- Protected discs can cause computers to hang (freeze) or crash.

- Those discs that do not play on computers severely restrict the customers' ability to enjoy the music, preventing them from putting the songs on their computers or portable devices.

- Those discs that permit playback only of lower-quality audio files included in a separate session on the disc, or that create DRM-restricted WMA files on the fly, also limit the customers' choice, and are useless for anyone wanting to play the music with iTunes or put it on an iPod.

- Those discs that include deliberate errors on the discs to make them harder or impossible for CD drives to play make the error-correction mechanisms on the players work harder to compensate. Using the error-correction mechanism on the player like this makes the disc less resistant to real damage (for example, scratches), because the player will be unable to correct many damage-related errors on top of the deliberate copy-protection errors. The discs may also degrade more quickly than unprotected CDs.

CAUTION *In November 2005, computer security experts discovered that various audio discs released by Sony-BMG that used a copy-protection method called XCP were compromising the security of PCs that played them. XCP surreptitiously installed what's known as a "rootkit"—tools commonly used by malevolent hackers to subvert Windows' standard functionality. A media firestorm ensued, and Sony-BMG announced that it would cease production of XCP-protected discs for the time being. At this writing, the issue is not fully resolved, and Windows users should beware audio discs that use such aggressive and dangerous copy-protection mechanisms.*

Most of the CD-protection solutions are aimed at Windows users and work only with Windows Media Player. These solutions don't work for iTunes on either Windows or the Mac, nor for Windows Media Player on the Mac.

How to Recognize Copy-Protected Discs

Copy-protected discs won't play on all CD drives. This means that they don't conform to the Red Book CD standard, so they are technically and legally *not* CDs. You should be able to recognize them as follows:

- The discs shouldn't bear the Compact Disc Digital Audio logo (because they're not CDs), but some do. And in any case, many Red Book CDs don't bear this logo, usually for reasons of label design or laziness. So the presence or lack of the CDDA logo isn't a good way to distinguish a copy-protected disc.

- The disc may carry a disclaimer, warning, or notice such as "Will *not* play on PC or Mac," "This CD [*sic*] cannot be played on a PC/Mac," "Copy Control," or "Copy Protected."

- The disc may attempt to install on your computer software that you must use to access the music on the disc. In extreme cases, the disc may install software that compromises your computer's functionality and that opens it to attack from malware.

- The disc won't play on your computer, or it will play but won't rip.

What Happens When You Try to Use a Copy-Protected Disc on a Computer

When you try to use a copy-protected disc on a computer, any of the following may happen:

- The disc may play back without problems. You may even be able to rip it by using a conventional audio program (such as iTunes) or a specialized, heavy-duty ripper (such as Exact Audio Copy). If you can rip the disc, the copy protection has failed (or your drive has defeated it).

NOTE

Exact Audio Copy is a free application that you can download from www.exactaudiocopy.de. Exact Audio Copy is postcard-ware—if you like it, you send a postcard to register.

- The disc may not play at all.
- The disc may cause your computer's operating system to hang.
- You may be unable to eject the disc on some PCs and many Macs. (If this happens to you, see the upcoming sidebar "Eject Stuck Audio Discs.")

NOTE

If your Mac has a SuperDrive, download the Apple SuperDrive Update from www.apple .com/hardware/superdrive/ before attempting to use any copy-protected audio discs in the drive. Once you've installed this update, you'll be able to eject copy-protected audio discs.

Learn about Ways to Get Around Copy Protection

Customers annoyed by copy-protected audio discs quickly found ways to circumvent the copy protection. In many cases, the most effective solution is to experiment with different drives. Some drives can play audio discs protected with some technologies; others can't.

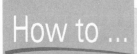

Eject Stuck Audio Discs

If you insert a non-CD audio disc into your CD drive and your PC or Mac can't handle it, you may be unable to eject the disc. The PC or Mac may hang. If your computer is a Mac, and you restart it with the disc in the CD drive, your Mac may start up to a gray screen.

On PCs and some Macs, you can use the manual eject hole on the CD drive to eject the disc. Straighten one end of a sturdy paper clip and push it into the hole to eject the disc.

If your Mac doesn't have a manual eject hole, don't go prodding the wrong hole. Instead, follow as many of these steps as necessary to fix the problem:

1. Restart your Mac. If it's too hung to restart by conventional means, press the Reset button (if it has one) or press ⌘-CTRL-POWER. At the system startup sound, hold down the mouse button until your Mac finishes booting. This action may eject the disc.

2. If you're using System 9 and have Mac OS X installed, restart your Mac and boot Mac OS X. Again, if your Mac is too hung to restart by conventional means, press the Reset button or press ⌘-CTRL-POWER. At the system startup sound, hold down X to boot Mac OS X. Open iTunes from the dock or the Applications folder and then click the Eject button.

3. Restart your Mac. Once again, if it's too hung to restart by conventional means, press the Reset button or press ⌘-CTRL-POWER. At the system startup sound, hold down ⌘-OPTION-O-F to boot to the Open Firmware mode. You'll see a prompt screen that contains something like the text shown here (the exact text varies depending on the model of Mac):

```
Apple PowerBook3, 5 4.5.3f2 BootROM built on 10/25/02 at 10:31:30
Copyright 1994-2002 Apple Computer, Inc.
All Rights Reserved

Welcome to Open Firmware, the system time and date is:  10:27:06 02/03/2003

To continue booting, type "mac-boot" and press return.
To shut down, type "shut-down" and press return.

 ok
0> _
```

4. Type **eject cd** and press RETURN. If all is well, the CD drive will open. If not, you may see the message "read of block0 failed. can't OPEN the EJECT device." Either way, type **mac-boot** and press RETURN to reboot your Mac.

If Open Firmware mode won't fix the problem, you'll need to take your Mac to a service shop.

> **CAUTION** *Title I of the Digital Millennium Copyright Act (DMCA), which was passed in 1998, states that it's illegal to circumvent "effective technological measures" protecting a copyrighted work. There are various ifs and buts (for example, you can circumvent such measures to make another program interoperate with a copyrighted work), but essentially Title I says if someone has protected a copyrighted work with a technological measure that could be argued to be "effective" (whatever that means), it's illegal to crack that measure. There are heavy penalties if you do so deliberately and for "commercial advantage" or private gain—fines of up to $500,000 and five years' imprisonment for a first offense, and double those for a second offense.*

If you don't have multiple CD or DVD drives to experiment with, you might be interested to hear of two crude solutions that have proved successful with some copy-protected audio discs:

- Stick a strip of tape on the disc to mask the outermost track. This track contains extra information intended to confuse computer CD drives. By masking the track, people have managed to obviate the confusion.

- Use a marker to color the outermost track on the disc dark so the laser of the drive won't read it.

> **TIP** *Many DVD drives are better at playing copy-protected discs than many plain CD-ROM drives. This is because the DVD drives are designed to work with multiple types of discs— DVDs, CDs, recordable CDs (CD-Rs), rewritable CDs (CD-RWs), and (for DVD recorders) various types of recordable DVDs, depending on the capabilities of the drive. These extra capabilities include greater tolerance for faults on the discs.*

Both of these techniques require a steady hand—and both constitute willful circumvention of the copy protection, possibly exposing those performing them to retribution under the DMCA.

Unlike early versions of SunnComm's MediaMax copy-protection mechanism, later versions of MediaMax cannot be disabled by holding down SHIFT while loading the CD on a Windows PC for the first time. Holding down SHIFT prevents the CD from automatically loading a driver used to protect the music.

Holding down SHIFT might be interpreted as an active attempt to bypass the copy-protection mechanism. But you can also turn off the AutoPlay feature for an optical drive permanently by following these steps:

1. Choose Start | My Computer to open a My Computer window.

2. Right-click the optical drive and choose Properties from the shortcut menu to display the Properties dialog box.

3. Click the AutoPlay tab to display its contents (see Figure 6-4).

4. In the Select A Content Type drop-down list, select the Music CD item.

5. If the Prompt Me Each Time To Choose An Action option button is selected, select the Select An Action To Perform option button.

6. Select the Take No Action item in the list box.

FIGURE 6-4 Turning off AutoPlay on your optical drive can help you avoid installing CD copy-protection software unintentionally on your PC.

7. In the Select A Content Type drop-down list, select the Mixed Content item.

8. If the Prompt Me Each Time To Choose An Action option button is selected, select the Select An Action To Perform option button.

9. Select the Take No Action item in the list box.

10. Click the OK button to close the Properties dialog box.

11. Choose File | Close or press ALT-F4 to close the My Computer window.

What Happens When You Convert a File from One Compressed Format to Another

Don't convert a song from one compressed format to another compressed format unless you absolutely must, because such a conversion gives you the worst of both worlds.

For example, say you have a WMA file. The audio is already compressed with lossy compression, so some parts of the audio have been lost. When you convert this file to an

MP3 file, the conversion utility expands the compressed WMA audio to uncompressed audio—essentially, to a PCM file (such as WAV or AIFF)—and then recompresses it to the MP3 format, again using lossy compression.

The uncompressed audio contains a faithful rendering of all the defects in the WMA file. So the MP3 file contains as faithful a rendering of this defective audio as the MP3 encoder can provide at that compression rate, plus any defects the MP3 encoding introduces. But you'll be able to play the file on your iPod—which may be your main concern.

So if you still have the CD from which you imported the song, import the song again using the other compressed format rather than converting the song from one compressed format to another. Doing so will give you significantly higher quality. But if you don't have the CD—for example, because you bought the song in the compressed format—converting to the other format will produce usable results.

Convert Other File Types to Formats Your iPod Can Play

Regular iPods, the iPod nano, and the iPod mini can play AAC files, MP3 files (including Audible files), Apple Lossless Encoding files, AIFF files, and WAV files. The iPod shuffle can play AAC files and MP3 files. These common formats should take care of all your regular listening in iTunes and on the iPod.

But if you receive files from others, or download audio from the Internet (as described in Chapter 7), you'll encounter many other digital-audio formats. This section describes a couple of utilities for converting files from one format to another—preferably to a format your iPod can use, or to a format from which you can encode a format that your iPod can manage.

Convert a Song from AAC to MP3 (or Vice Versa)

Sometimes, you may need to convert a song from the format in which you imported it, or (more likely) in which you bought it, to a different format. For example, you may need to convert a song in AAC format to MP3 so that you can use it on an MP3 player other than your iPod.

NOTE   *If the AAC is a protected song you bought from the iTunes Music Store, you cannot convert it directly. Instead, you must burn it to a CD and then rip that CD to the format you need.*

To convert a song from one compressed format to another, follow these steps:

1. In iTunes, display the Advanced menu and see which format is listed in the Convert Selection To command (for example, Convert Selection To AAC or Convert Selection To MP3). If this is the format you want, you're all set, but you might want to double-check the settings used for the format.

2. Display the iTunes dialog box or the Preferences dialog box:

   ■ In Windows, choose Edit | Preferences or press CTRL-COMMA or CTRL-Y to display the iTunes dialog box.

   ■ On the Mac, choose iTunes | Preferences or press either ⌘-COMMA or ⌘-Y to display the Preferences dialog box.

3. Click the Advanced tab, and then click the Importing subtab to display its contents.

4. In the Import Using drop-down list, specify the encoder you want to use. For example, choose MP3 Encoder if you want to convert an existing file to an MP3 file; choose AAC Encoder if you want to create an AAC file; or choose Apple Lossless Encoding if you want to create an Apple Lossless Encoding file.

NOTE *Unless the song file is currently in WAV or AIFF format, it's usually not worth converting it to Apple Lossless Encoding.*

5. If necessary, use the Setting drop-down list to specify the details of the format. (See "Check or Change Your Importing Settings," earlier in this chapter for details.)

6. Click the OK button to close the dialog box.

7. In your music library, select the song or songs you want to convert.

8. Choose Advanced | Convert Selection To *Format*. (The Convert Selection To item on the Advanced menu changes to reflect the encoder you chose in Step 4.) iTunes converts the file or files, saves it or them in the folder that contains the original file or files, and adds it or them to your music library.

NOTE *Because iTunes automatically applies tag information to converted files, you may find it hard to tell in iTunes which file is in AAC format and which is in MP3 format. The easiest way to find out is to issue a Get Info command for the song (for example, right-click the song and choose Get Info from the shortcut menu) and check the Kind readout on the Summary tab of the Song Information dialog box.*

After converting the song or songs to the other format, remember to restore your normal import setting on the Importing tab of the iTunes dialog box or the Preferences dialog box before you import any more songs from CD.

Convert WMA Files to MP3 or AAC

If you buy music from any of the online music stores that focus on Windows rather than on the Mac, chances are that the songs will be in WMA format. WMA is the stores' preferred format for selling online music because it offers digital rights management (DRM) features for protecting the music against being stolen.

If you buy WMA files protected with DRM, you'll be limited in what you can do with them. In most cases, you'll be restricted to playing the songs with Windows Media Player (which is one of the underpinnings of the WMA DRM scheme), which won't let you convert the songs directly to another format. But most online music stores allow you to burn the songs you buy to CD.

In this case, you can convert the WMA files to MP3 files or AAC files by burning them to CD and then use iTunes to rip and encode the CD as usual.

Windows: GoldWave

GoldWave, from GoldWave, Inc. (www.goldwave.com), is a powerful audio editor that lets you convert files from various audio formats to other formats. GoldWave's Batch Processing feature (File | Batch Processing) is great for converting a slew of files at once.

You can download a 15-day evaluation version of GoldWave from the GoldWave, Inc., website or from various Internet locations, including C|net's www.download.com. The registered version of GoldWave costs $40.

Mac: SoundApp

You can get various audio-conversion utilities for the Mac. Most of them cost money, but one of the best is free. That utility is called SoundApp, and you can download it from many Internet archives. At this writing, the current version has a minimalist interface and runs in Classic, but it works fine.

6

Create Audio Files from Cassettes or Vinyl Records

If you have audio on analog media such as cassette tapes, vinyl records, or other waning technologies, you may want to transfer that audio to your computer so you can listen to it using iTunes or your iPod. Dust off your gramophone, cassette deck, or other audio source, and then work your way through the following sections.

You may need permission to create audio files that contain copyrighted content. If you hold the copyright to the audio, you can copy it as much as you want. If not, you need specific permission to copy it, unless it falls under a specific copyright exemption. For example, the Audio Home Recording Act (AHRA) personal use provision lets you copy a copyrighted work (for example, an LP) onto a different medium so you can listen to it—provided that you use a "digital audio recording device," a term that doesn't cover computers.

Connect the Audio Source to Your Computer

Start by connecting the audio source to your computer with a cable that has the right kinds of connectors for the audio source and your sound card. For example, to connect a typical cassette player to a typical sound card, you'll need a cable with two RCA plugs at the cassette player's end (or at the receiver's end) and a male-end stereo miniplug at the other end to plug into your sound card. If the audio source has only a headphone socket or line-out socket for output, you'll need a miniplug at the source end too.

Because record players produce a low volume of sound, you'll almost always need to put a record player's output through the Phono input of an amplifier before you can record it on your computer.

If your sound card has a Line In port and a Mic port, use the Line In port. If your sound card has only a Mic port, turn the source volume down to a minimum for the initial connection, because Mic ports tend to be sensitive.

If you have a Mac that doesn't have an audio input, consider a solution such as the Griffin iMic (www.griffintech.com), which lets you record via USB.

Record on Windows

To record audio on Windows, you can use the minimalist sound-recording application, Sound Recorder, or add (and usually pay for) a more powerful application. This section discusses how to use Sound Recorder and how to use two other applications: Musicmatch Jukebox Plus and GoldWave.

One of the best cross-platform solutions for recording and editing audio files is Audacity (freeware; http://audacity.sourceforge.net). Audacity runs on Windows, Mac OS X, and Linux, using very nearly the same interface on each platform.

First, whichever application you choose, you'll need to specify the audio source.

If you have a lot of records and tapes that you want to copy to digital audio files, consider buying an audio-cleanup application that includes recording capabilities instead of an application whose strengths lie mainly in recording. For example, applications such as Magix's Audio Cleaning Lab and Steinberg's Clean Plus focus mainly on audio cleanup (removing crackle, pops, hiss, and other defects) but include more-than-adequate recording capabilities.

Specify the Audio Source for Recording in Windows

To set Windows to accept input from the source so you can record from it, follow these steps:

1. If the notification area includes a Volume icon, double-click this icon to display the Volume Control window. Otherwise, choose Start | Control Panel to display the Control Panel and then open the Volume Control window from there. For example, in Windows XP, click the Advanced button in the Device Volume group box on the Volume tab of the Sounds And Audio Devices Properties dialog box.

Depending on your audio hardware and its drivers, the Volume Control window may have a different name (for example, Play Control).

2. Choose Options | Properties to display the Properties dialog box. Then select the Recording option button to display the list of devices for recording (as opposed to the devices for playback). The left screen in Figure 6-5 shows this list.

3. Select the check box for the input device you want to use—for example, select the Line-In check box or the Microphone check box, depending on which you're using.

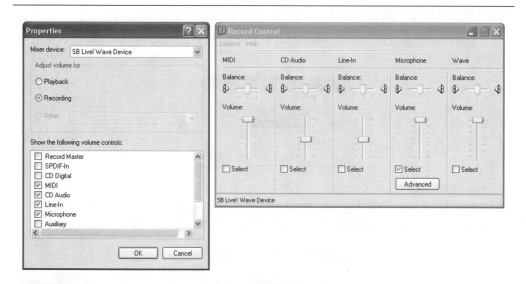

FIGURE 6-5   Click the Recording option button in the Properties dialog box (left) to display the Record Control window (right) instead of Volume Control.

4. Click the OK button to close the Properties dialog box. Windows displays the Record Control window, an example of which is shown on the right in Figure 6-5. (Like the Volume Control window, this window may have a different name—for example, Recording Control.)

5. Select the Select check box for the source you want to use.

6. Leave the Record Control window open for the time being so you can adjust the input volume on the device if necessary.

Record with Sound Recorder

Sound Recorder is one of the applets that comes built into Windows. To run Sound Recorder, choose Start | All Programs | Accessories | Entertainment | Sound Recorder.

Sound Recorder works fine except that it can't record files longer than 60 seconds, which makes it next to useless for recording music. But you can sidestep around this limitation by creating a blank file longer than the longest item you want to record and then recording over this blank file. This takes a little effort but is worth the trouble.

There are two parts to making Sound Recorder record files longer than 60 seconds. The first part, which is compulsory, is to create a blank dummy file long enough to contain whatever you want to record. The second part, which is optional, is to make Sound Recorder open this file automatically when you start it so that you don't have to open it manually.

Create the Dummy File   To create the blank dummy file, follow these steps:

1. Choose Start | All Programs | Accessories | Entertainment | Sound Recorder to launch Sound Recorder:

2. Mute your sound source.

3. Click the Record button (the button with the red dot) to start recording a blank file. Sound Recorder makes the file 60 seconds long, its default maximum:

4. Let the recording run until it stops automatically at 60 seconds.

5. Choose File | Save to display the Save As dialog box.

6. Save the file under a descriptive name such as Dummy.wav.

7. Choose Edit | Insert File to display the Insert File dialog box.

8. Select the file you saved and click the Open button to insert it in the open version of the file. This adds another 60 seconds to the file's length, doubling it.

9. Repeat the procedure of inserting the saved file in the open file until the open file reaches the length you need.

To increase the file's size more quickly, save the open file after inserting another one or two minutes in it. You can then insert the saved file, adding two or three minutes to the open file at a time.

10. When the file reaches the length you need, choose File | Save to save it.

11. Press ALT-F4 or choose File | Exit to close Sound Recorder.

Make Sound Recorder Open the Dummy File Automatically   To make Sound Recorder open the dummy file automatically, follow these steps:

1. Right-click the Sound Recorder entry on your Start menu and choose Properties from the shortcut menu to display its Properties dialog box (see Figure 6-6).

FIGURE 6-6   Use the Properties dialog box to configure Sound Recorder to open your dummy file automatically.

2. In the Target text box, enter the path and file name to the file you recorded, inside double quotation marks, after the path name and file name of the executable, so that it looks something like this:

```
%SystemRoot%\System32\sndrec32.exe "C:\Documents and Settings\
Your Name\My Documents\Dummy.wav"
```

3. Click the OK button to close the Properties dialog box.

Now, when you start Sound Recorder, it automatically opens the dummy file. You can then record audio up to the length of the dummy file.

Record a Sound File   To record a file with Sound Recorder, follow these steps:

1. Choose Start | All Programs | Accessories | Entertainment | Sound Recorder to launch Sound Recorder and make it open the dummy file.

If you didn't change the Sound Recorder shortcut, open your dummy file manually.

2. Get the audio source ready to play.

3. Click the Record button to start recording.

4. Start the audio playing.

5. To stop recording, click the Stop button.

6. Choose File | Save As to display the Save As dialog box:

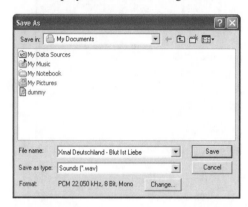

7. Specify the location and name for the file. (Don't overwrite your dummy file.)

8. Make sure the Format field, at the bottom of the Save As dialog box, is displaying the format in which you want to save the file. This field gives brief details of the format—for example, "PCM 22 050 KHz, 8 Bit, Mono" or "Windows Media Audio V2, 160 Kbps, 48 KHz, Stereo." To set a different format, click the Change button and work in the Sound Selection dialog box:

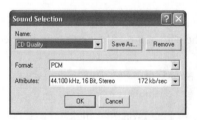

- To select a predefined set of attributes, select CD Quality, Radio Quality, or Telephone Quality in the Name drop-down list. If you're recording music you want to turn into an AAC file or MP3 file, choose the CD Quality item. You can define your own named formats by choosing appropriate settings in the Format drop-down list and Attributes drop-down list and then clicking the Save As button. You can then reuse these formats more quickly the next time you need the same settings.

- Otherwise, choose the format in the Format drop-down list and then select the appropriate attributes in the Attributes drop-down list. For example, you might choose PCM in the Format drop-down list and the 44.100kHz, 16 Bit, Stereo setting in the Attributes drop-down list to record pulse code modulation audio at the highest quality that Sound Recorder supports.

9. Click the OK button to close the Sound Selection dialog box.

10. Click the Save button in the Save As dialog box to save the file.

6

> **TIP** *The Format drop-down list in Sound Recorder includes an MPEG Layer-3 item, which creates MP3 files. Unfortunately, owing to a licensing issue, the encoder included with Windows can encode only up to 56 Kbps at 24 KHz, which makes it useless for high-quality audio. So you'll get much better results from creating WAV files with Sound Recorder and then using iTunes to encode them to MP3 files or AAC files.*

Record with Musicmatch Jukebox Plus

One of the best solutions for recording audio files on Windows is Musicmatch Jukebox Plus, which you can download from the Musicmatch website (www.musicmatch.com) and activate for $19.99. Musicmatch Jukebox Plus includes ripping and encoding to MP3, mp3PRO, and other formats; music library management; CD burning; and legitimate music downloads from its online music service. When recording audio input, Musicmatch Jukebox Plus can automatically detect the end of songs, which can make recording from cassettes or records much simpler.

> **NOTE** *Apple included Musicmatch Jukebox Plus as the Windows application for managing second- and third-generation iPods until Apple released iTunes for Windows. You can still use Musicmatch Jukebox Plus to manage your iPod on Windows if you choose.*

To record audio in Windows using Musicmatch Jukebox Plus, work through the steps in the following sections.

Set Musicmatch Jukebox Plus to Record from the Source   First, set Musicmatch Jukebox Plus to accept input from the same device. To do so, choose Options | Recorder | Source | Line In or Options | Recorder | Source | Mic In, as appropriate. Alternatively, choose Options | Recorder | Settings to display the Recorder tab of the Settings dialog box and then select Line In or Mic in the Recording Source drop-down list.

> **TIP** *If you're recording several tracks' worth of material from an external source, consider using the Auto Song Detect feature. To use it, select the Active check box in the Advanced Recorder Options dialog box and then use the Gap Length and Gap Level text boxes to specify the amount and level, respectively, of silence that represent a break between tracks. The default is 2000 ms (two seconds) at 10 percent volume. These settings work well for many types of music, but if you're recording music that includes dramatic pauses, you may need to increase the gap length to avoid truncating songs just before the music starts up again.*

Start Recording   To start recording in Musicmatch Jukebox Plus, follow these steps:

1. Get the sound source ready to play.

2. In the Recorder window, enter the artist name, album name, and track name. (Otherwise, Musicmatch Jukebox Plus uses the default data: Artist, Album, and "line in track *NN*"— so if you're using the default naming convention, you'll find the tracks in the Artist\ Album folder.)

3. Click the Record button in the Recorder window in Musicmatch Jukebox Plus to start recording from the source.

4. Click the Stop button to stop recording the current track. Musicmatch Jukebox Plus adds the track to your music library and sets you up to record another track.

Record Audio with GoldWave

To record audio with GoldWave (mentioned earlier in this chapter), follow these steps:

1. Click the New button to display the New Sound dialog box:

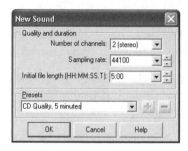

2. Specify the quality settings you want to use:

   ■ You can choose a preset in the Presets drop-down list. For example, to record audio at CD quality, select the CD Audio item.

   ■ Alternatively, use the Manual Quality Settings controls to specify exactly what you want. Select the number of channels (1 or 2) in the Channels drop-down list and then select the sampling rate in the Sampling Rate drop-down list.

3. In the Initial File Length drop-down list, select an initial file length longer than the audio you want to record. The default length is one minute, which is too short for most songs.

4. Click the OK button to close the New Sound dialog box. GoldWave creates a new sound file named Untitled*N*, where *N* is the next unused number (for example, Untitled1), and displays the Control window.

5. Click the Record button in the Control window to start recording the sound.

6. Click the Stop Recording button in the Control window to stop the recording.

Import the Sound File into iTunes and Convert It

After saving the sound file in an audio format that iTunes can handle (preferably the WAV format), import the sound file into iTunes and then use the Advanced | Convert Selection To command to convert the sound file to an AAC file or an MP3 file. Once you've done that, tag the compressed file with the appropriate information so that you can access it easily in iTunes and copy it to your iPod.

Record Audio on the Mac

To record audio on the Mac, work through this section and then choose which of the following two sections to work through.

Specify the Audio Source for Recording on the Mac

To specify the source on the Mac, follow these steps:

1. Choose Apple | System Preferences to display the System Preferences window.

2. Click the Sound item to display the Sound preferences sheet.

3. Click the Input tab to display it (see Figure 6-7).

4. In the Choose A Device For Sound Input list box, select the device to use (for example, Line In).

5. Start some audio playing on the sound source. Make sure that it's representative of the loudest part of the audio you will record.

6. Watch the Input Level readout as you drag the Input Volume slider to a suitable level.

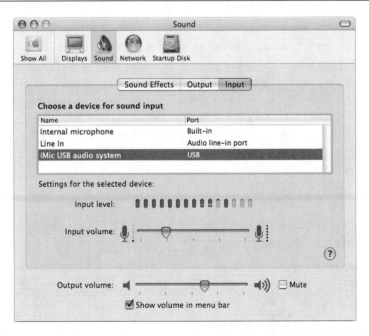

FIGURE 6-7   Configure your sound source on the Input tab of the Sound window.

Mac: Record Audio with iMovie

If you don't have a custom audio-recording application (we'll examine a couple in a moment), you can record audio into a blank iMovie movie and export it as a sound file. Follow these steps:

1. Click the iMovie icon in the Dock to launch iMovie. (Alternatively, choose Go | Applications and double-click the iMovie icon.)

2. Press ⌘-N (or choose File | New Project) to start a new project.

3. In the resulting dialog box, enter the file name, choose where to save it, and then click the Save button.

4. In iMovie, click the Audio button to display the audio controls.

5. Click the Record Audio button to start recording the audio. iMovie displays the progress on the timeline.

6. Click the Stop button (which replaces the Record Audio button) to stop recording the audio.

7. Manipulate the audio if necessary.

8. Choose File | Share (or press ⌘-SHIFT-E) to display the Share sheet.

9. Click the QuickTime button to display the QuickTime sheet.

10. In the Compress Movie For drop-down list, select the Expert Settings item.

11. Click the Share button to display the Save Exported File As dialog box (see Figure 6-8).

12. Specify the name and location for the exported file.

13. In the Export drop-down list, select the Sound To AIFF item or the Sound To Wave item, as appropriate. (If you have other QuickTime plug-ins installed, other choices may be available, such as Sound To Ogg Vorbis.) If appropriate, click the Options button to display a dialog box for setting any options available in the format.

14. In the Use drop-down list, select the quality setting—for example, 44.1 KHz 16 Bit Stereo.

15. Click the Save button to save the audio file.

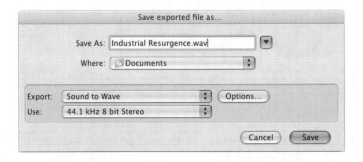

FIGURE 6-8   Choose the Sound To Wave export option in the Save Exported File As dialog box.

From here, you can import the AIFF file or WAV file into iTunes and convert it to another format (such as AAC, MP3, or Apple Lossless Encoding) if necessary, as described in the next section.

Mac: Two Other Options for Recording Audio

iMovie is a workable tool for recording audio, and it comes free with every Mac. But if you're prepared to spend a few fistfuls of dollars, you can have sound-recording and -editing software that's much easier to use and that offers far greater capabilities. Better yet, if you choose the right application, you'll get audio-cleanup features into the bargain.

Two such applications you may want to try are Amadeus II and Sound Studio for OS X.

Amadeus II

Amadeus II from HairerSoft (www.hairersoft.com/Amadeus.html) is a powerful application for recording and editing audio. You can download a 15-day trial version of Amadeus II. The full version costs $30 for a single-user license.

TIP   *Amadeus II includes repair functions you can use to eliminate hiss and crackles from recordings.*

Sound Studio for OS X

Sound Studio for OS X from Felt Tip Software (www.felttip.com) is a digital audio editor with a wide range of features. You can download an evaluation version of the software from the Felt Tip Software website. The full version costs $49.99. Figure 6-9 shows Sound Studio for OS X recording audio.

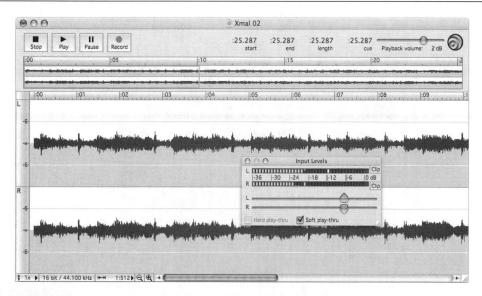

FIGURE 6-9   Recording audio with Sound Studio for OS X.

Sound Studio for OS X also includes repair features for eliminating noise from recordings.

Remove Scratches and Hiss from Audio Files

If you record tracks from vinyl records, audio cassettes, or other analog sources, you may well get some clicks or pops, hiss, or background hum in the file. Scratches on a record can cause clicks and pops, audio cassettes tend to hiss (even with noise-reduction such as Dolby), and record players or other machinery can add hum.

All these noises—very much part of the analog audio experience, and actually appreciated as such by some enthusiasts—tend to annoy people accustomed to digital audio. The good news is that you can remove many such noises by using the right software.

If you chose to use Audacity (mentioned earlier in this chapter as a cross-platform audio solution), you'll be glad to know you can use it to remove noise from a recording as well. Select the part of the recording that you want to affect (for example, choose Edit | Select | All, or drag through the noisy part of the recording) and then choose Effect | Noise Removal. Follow through the steps in the Noise Removal dialog box to remove the noise.

Windows: GoldWave

Earlier in this chapter you met GoldWave, an audio editor you can use to convert audio files from one format to another. GoldWave also includes features for filtering audio and eliminating unwanted sounds. Figure 6-10 shows GoldWave working on eliminating the pops and clicks from a WAV file.

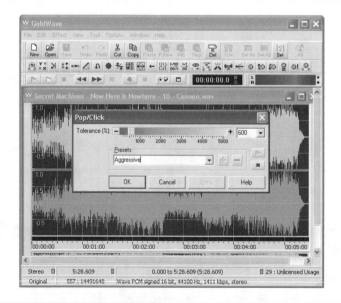

FIGURE 6-10   GoldWave can also remove pops and clicks from an audio file.

Windows: Audio Cleaning Lab

Audio Cleaning Lab from Magix (www.magix.com) provides strong features for cleaning up audio, together with features for recording audio into several formats, including WAV, MP3, and Ogg Vorbis.

Depending on where you shop, you can find various different versions of Audio Cleaning Lab, starting at around $29.99. Figure 6-11 shows Audio Cleaning Lab Deluxe, which features an idiosyncratic and loud interface (I find shades help), but it's relatively easy to use.

Mac: Amadeus II

Amadeus II, introduced a bit earlier in this chapter, offers the following strong features for cleaning up audio files:

- Use the Repair Centre (Effects | Sound Repair | Open Repair Centre) to hunt down and eliminate clicks and pops in a sound file.

- The Effects | Denoising submenu contains options for suppressing various types of noise (for example, white noise).

- The Filter window (Effects | Filter) lets you apply specific filtering to a channel.

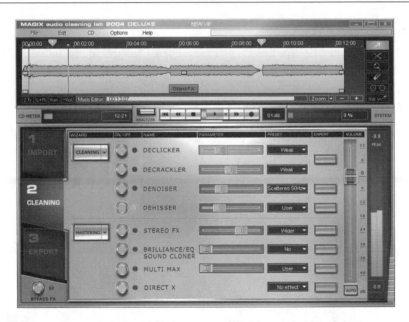

FIGURE 6-11   Audio Cleaning Lab comes in a variety of versions, including Deluxe.

Trim Audio Files to Get Rid of Intros and Outros You Don't Like

The Start Time and Stop Time features on the Options tab of the Song Information dialog box in iTunes let you suppress the beginning and end of a file if you don't want to hear them: The file remains unchanged, but you tell iTunes to omit the parts you don't want to hear. But you may want to go further and actually remove the introduction or the end of the file—or you may want to split a file into two or more separate files. This section presents a Windows utility and a Mac utility for doing that with MP3 files.

Crop with iTunes

iTunes enables you to crop audio files, but only by subterfuge. To do so, specify the Start Time and Stop Time parameters on the Options tab of the Song Information dialog box and then choose Advanced | Convert Selection To *Format*. iTunes creates an audio file in the specified format that contains only that part of the song that appears between the start time and the stop time.

Windows: MP3 TrackMaker

MP3 TrackMaker, from Heathco Software (www.heathcosoft.com), is a small utility for dividing MP3 files into smaller files and for joining two or more MP3 files into a single MP3 file. You can download an almost fully functional demo version (it's limited to joining three tracks or splitting a file into three tracks) for free, or you can pay $13 for the full version.

MP3 TrackMaker needs little explanation. Use the controls on its Split tab (shown on the left in Figure 6-12) to divide an MP3 file into smaller files. Use the controls on its Join tab (shown on the right in Figure 6-12) to join two or more MP3 files into a single MP3 file.

Mac: mEdit

mEdit is a freeware tool for cropping MP3 files on the Mac. You can download it from various software archives on the Internet. It runs in Classic mode but still functions well.

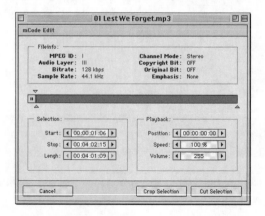

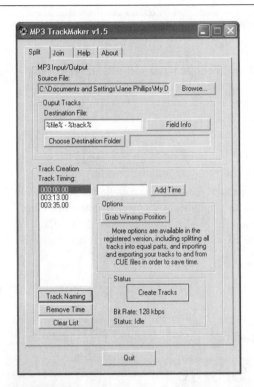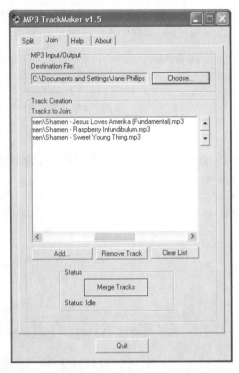

FIGURE 6-12   Use MP3 TrackMaker to divide MP3 files into smaller MP3 files or to join multiple MP3 files into a single MP3 file.

mEdit is straightforward to use. You open the file you want to crop, specify cropping options, execute the crop, and then save the file. You can also use mEdit to cut a section out of the middle of a file. By cropping the same source file twice (or more times) to different destination files, you can effectively use mEdit to split MP3 tracks into multiple files as well.

Tag Your Compressed Files with the Correct Information for Sorting

The best thing about compressed audio formats such as AAC, MP3, and Apple Lossless Encoding—apart from their being compressed and still giving high-quality audio—is that each file format can store a full set of tag information about the song the file contains. The tag information lets you sort, organize, and search for songs on iTunes. Your iPod needs correct artist, album, and track name information in tags to be able to organize your AAC files and MP3 files correctly. If a song lacks this minimum of information, iTunes doesn't transfer it to your iPod.

You can force iTunes to load untagged songs on your iPod by assigning them to a playlist and loading the playlist. But in most cases it's best to tag all the songs in your music library—or at least tag as many as is practicable.

Your main tool for tagging song files should be iTunes, because it provides solid if basic features for tagging one or more files at once manually. But if your music library contains many untagged or mistagged files, you may need a heavier-duty application. This section shows you how to tag most effectively in iTunes and then presents two more powerful applications—Tag&Rename for Windows, and MP3 Rage for the Mac.

Tag Songs Effectively with iTunes

The easiest way to add tag information to an AAC file or MP3 file is by downloading the information from CDDB (the CD database) when you rip the CD. But sometimes you'll need to enter (or change) tag information manually to make iTunes sort the files correctly—for example, when the CDDB data is wrong or not available, or for existing song files created with software other than iTunes, such as song files you've created yourself.

Tag Song Files after Encoding when Offline

Even if you rip CDs when your computer has no Internet connection, you can usually apply the CD information to the song files once you've reestablished an Internet connection. To do so, select the album or the songs in your music library and then choose Advanced | Get CD Track Names. If the CD's details are in CDDB, iTunes should then be able to download the information.

If you imported the songs by using software other than iTunes, or if you imported the songs using iTunes on another computer and then copied them to this computer, iTunes objects with the "iTunes cannot get CD track names" dialog box shown here. In this case, you'll need to either reimport the songs on this computer or tag the songs manually.

NOTE *Often, MP3 files distributed illegally on the Internet lack tag information or include incorrect tags.*

If you need to change the tag information for a whole CD's worth of songs, proceed as follows:

1. In iTunes, select all the song files you want to affect.

2. Right-click (or CTRL-click on the Mac) the selection and choose Get Info from the shortcut menu to display the Multiple Song Information dialog box. Alternatively, choose File | Get Info or press CTRL-I (Windows) or ⌘-M (Mac). Figure 6-13 shows the Windows version of the Multiple Song Information dialog box.

NOTE *By default, when you issue a Get Info command with multiple songs selected, iTunes displays a dialog box to check that you want to edit the information for multiple songs. Click the Yes button to proceed; click the Cancel button to cancel. If you frequently want to edit tag information for multiple songs, select the Do Not Ask Me Again check box in the confirmation dialog box to turn off confirmations in the future.*

3. Enter as much common information as you can: the artist, year, album, total number of tracks, disc number, composer, comments, and so on. If you have the artwork for the CD available, drag it to the Artwork pane.

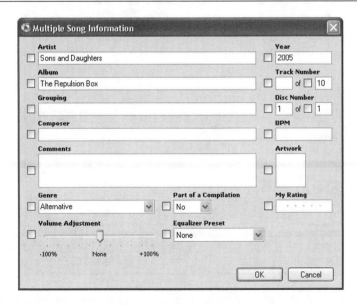

FIGURE 6-13   Use the Multiple Song Information dialog box to enter common tag information for all the songs on a CD or album at once.

4. Click the OK button to apply the information to the songs.

5. Click the first song to clear the current selection. Right-click (or CTRL-click on the Mac) the song and choose Get Info from the shortcut menu to display the Song Information dialog box for the song. Click the Info tab to display it if iTunes doesn't display it automatically. Figure 6-14 shows the Windows version of the Song Information dialog box for the song "Rama Llama." The song's title appears in the title bar of the dialog box.

6. Add any song-specific information here: the song name, the track number, and so on.

7. If you need to change the song's relative volume, equalizer preset, rating, start time, or stop time, work on the Options tab.

8. If you want to add lyrics to the song (either by typing them in or by pasting them from a lyrics site), work on the Lyrics tab.

9. Click the Previous button or the Next button to display the information for the previous song or next song.

10. Click the OK button to close the Song Information dialog box when you've finished adding song information.

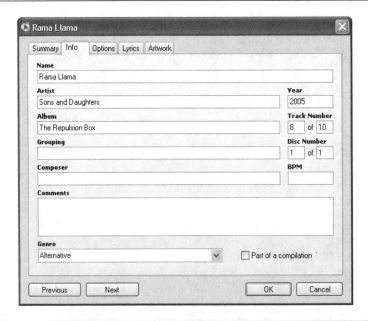

FIGURE 6-14   Use the Song Information dialog box (whose title bar shows the song's name) to add song-specific information.

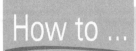

Submit CD Information to CDDB Using iTunes

If a CD you want to rip turns out not to have an entry in CDDB (as indicated by the dialog box shown here), you can submit an entry yourself. Users submitting entries like this have added many of the entries in CDDB for older or less widely known CDs. Mainstream entries are submitted by the record companies themselves: They submit a listing to CDDB (and other online CD-information services, such as WindowsMedia.com) as a matter of course when they release a new CD.

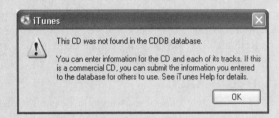

At this writing, CDDB contains entries for an enormous number of CDs—so unless you have an unusual CD, chances are any CD you want to rip already has an entry in CDDB. You may find that your CD is listed under a slightly different title or artist name than you're expecting—for example, the artist might be listed as "Sixpack, Joe" rather than "Joe Sixpack." Check carefully for any close matches before submitting an entry so you don't waste your time. You may also find CDDB contains two or more entries for the same CD.

When submitting an entry to CDDB, type the CD title, artist name, and song titles carefully using standard capitalization, and double-check all the information before you submit it. Otherwise, if your entry is accepted and entered in CDDB, anyone who looks up that CD will get the misspellings or wrong information you entered.

Here's how to submit an entry to CDDB:

1. Enter the tag information for the CD.

2. Choose Advanced | Submit CD Track Names to display the CD Info dialog box and then check the information in the Artist, Composer, Album, Disc Number, Genre, and Year fields. Select the Compilation CD check box if the CD is a compilation rather than a work by an individual artist.

3. Establish an Internet connection if you need to do so manually.

4. Click the OK button. iTunes connects to CDDB and submits the information.

A Windows Tag Editor: Tag&Rename

Tag&Rename, from SOFTPOINTER, Ltd., is a terrific tag-editing application for various types of files, including AAC and MP3. You can download a free 30-day evaluation version from www .softpointer.com/tr.htm and from various other sites on the Internet. The full version costs $29.95.

Tag&Rename can derive tag information by breaking down a file's name into its constituents. For example, if you set Tag&Rename on the file Aimee Mann - Lost in Space - 06 - Pavlov's Bell. mp3, Tag&Rename can derive the artist name (Aimee Mann), the album name (*Lost in Space*), the track number (06), and the song name ("Pavlov's Bell") from the file and then apply that information to the tag fields.

It can also derive tag information from the folder structure that contains an MP3 file that needs tagging. For example, if you have the file 06 - Pavlov's Bell.mp3 stored in the folder Aimee Mann\Lost in Space, Tag&Rename will be able to tag the file with the artist name, album name, track name, and track number.

Figure 6-15 shows Tag&Rename in action, working on the ID3 tags of some MP3 files.

A Mac Tag Editor: Media Rage

Media Rage, from Chaotic Software (www.chaoticsoftware.com), is an impressive bundle of utilities for tagging, organizing, and improving your MP3 files. The tagging features in Media

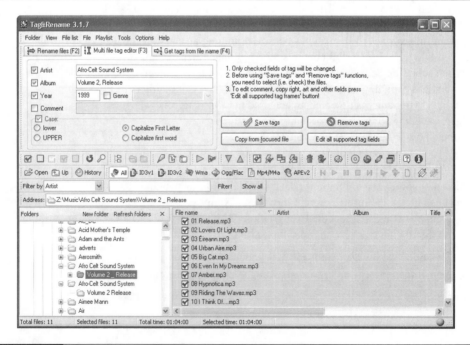

FIGURE 6-15   Tag&Rename can edit multiple ID3 tags at once.

Rage include deriving tag information from file names and folder paths and changing the tags on multiple files at once.

You can download a fully functional evaluation version of Media Rage from the Chaotic Software website. The registered version of Media Rage costs $29.95.

Save Audio Streams to Disk So You Can Listen to Them Later

If you get into listening to Internet radio, you'll probably want to record it so that you can play it back later. iTunes doesn't let you save streaming audio to disk because recording streaming audio typically violates copyright. So you need to use either a hardware solution or a third-party application to record streams.

To solve the problem via hardware, use a standard audio cable to pipe the output from your computer's sound card to its Line In socket. You can then record the audio stream as you would any other external input by using an audio-recording application such as those discussed earlier in this chapter—for example, Sound Recorder, GoldWave, or Musicmatch Jukebox Plus on Windows, or iMovie, Amadeus II, or Sound Studio on Mac OS X.

The only problem with using a standard audio cable is that you won't be able to hear the audio stream you're recording via external speakers. To solve this problem, get a stereo Y-connector. Connect one of the outputs to your external speakers and the other to your Line In socket. Converting the audio from digital to analog and then back to digital like this degrades its quality, but unless you're listening to the highest-bitrate Internet radio stations around, you'll most likely find the quality you lose a fair tradeoff for the convenience you gain.

To solve the problem via software, get an application that can record the audio stream directly. This section discusses some possibilities for Windows and Mac OS X.

Windows: Zinf

For Windows, the easiest option for recording MP3 streams is Zinf, a freeware open-source music player available from www.zinf.org. Zinf (shown on the left in Figure 6-16) can handle various formats, including MP3 and Ogg Vorbis files, and it can record streams to files.

 Zinf is the latest incarnation of the FreeAmp open-source player. You can still find FreeAmp in many online archives. FreeAmp has a similar interface to Zinf and offers many of the same features, including the ability to record streams to files.

To record MP3 streams with Zinf, follow these steps:

1. Click the Options button to display the Zinf Preferences dialog box (shown on the right in Figure 6-16).

2. Click the Streaming category to display it.

3. Select the Save SHOUTcast/icecast Streams Locally check box.

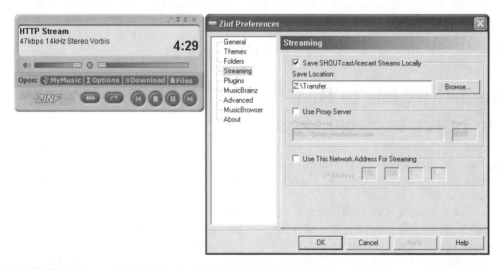

Zinf is an open-source freeware music player that can record audio streams to files so that you can listen to them later.

4. Use the Browse button and the resulting Browse For Folder dialog box to specify the folder in which to save the streamed files. Make sure the drive on which the folder is located contains plenty of free space.

5. Click the OK button to close the Zinf Preferences dialog box.

6. Tune into the audio stream. Zinf records the stream automatically under an autonamed file.

7. You may find that Windows XP Service Pack 2 tries to block Zinf, as shown here. Click the Unblock button to allow Zinf to connect to the Internet.

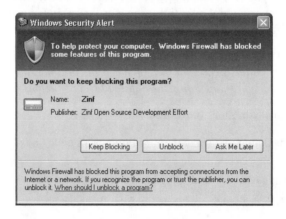

Windows: Total Recorder

If you want to record stream types that Zinf or FreeAmp can't record, try Total Recorder, from High Criteria, Inc. (www.highcriteria.com):

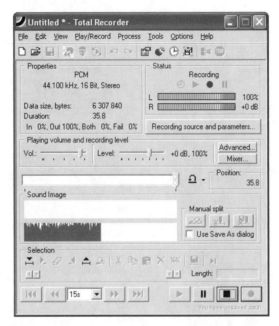

Total Recorder comes in a Standard Edition ($11.95 for a license), a Professional Edition ($35.95), and a Developer Edition ($64, but you probably won't want this unless you're developing software). Both Standard and Professional can save MP3 streams. High Criteria provides trial versions of Total Recorder, but they're so thoroughly crippled you'll need to open your wallet to actually get anything done.

Mac: RadioLover

For the Mac, perhaps the most promising option at the time of writing for recording streams from iTunes or other sources is RadioLover, which you can download from VersionTracker.com (www.versiontracker.com). RadioLover, formerly known as StreamRipperX, is $15 shareware that can tap into and record iTunes' Internet radio streams.

Mac: Audio Hijack

Audio Hijack, from Rogue Amoeba Software ($16; www.rogueamoeba.com/audiohijack/), is a full-featured application for recording the audio output of applications and manipulating that output.

Audio Hijack (see Figure 6-17) includes timers that you can set ahead of time to record the shows you're interested in. It can also apply equalization to applications that don't have equalizers themselves. For example, you can use Audio Hijack to equalize the output of Apple's DVD player.

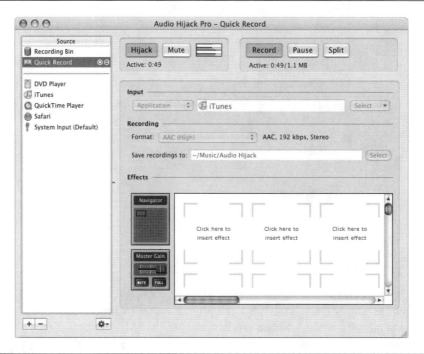

FIGURE 6-17   Audio Hijack can record the audio output of various applications and apply effects to that output.

Chapter 7

Buy and Download Songs and Videos Online

How to...

- Understand what the iTunes Music Store is
- Understand digital rights management (DRM)
- Set up an account with the iTunes Music Store
- Configure iTunes Music Store settings
- Access the iTunes Music Store
- Buy songs and videos from the iTunes Music Store
- Listen to songs and watch videos you've purchased
- Authorize and deauthorize computers for the iTunes Music Store
- Buy and download music from other online music stores
- Download music from other online sources

Ripping your own CDs, tapes, and records can produce an impressive library of song files, but the lengthy process may make you wonder if you couldn't just get the song files directly without needing to mess with the physical media. And of course you can, by downloading them via the Internet in a variety of ways—some legal and some not.

If you use your iPod with iTunes on Mac OS X or Windows, you can buy music from the iTunes Music Store, Apple's online music service. This chapter discusses what the iTunes Music Store is, how it works, and how to use it. Because the iTunes Music Store works in almost exactly the same way on Mac OS X and Windows, this chapter discusses both operating systems and, for balance, shows some screens from each. The iTunes Music Store also sells music videos, Pixar films, and some TV shows at this writing, with the promise of more to come once Apple has put the necessary licensing arrangements in place.

The early part of this chapter also discusses digital rights management (DRM), because you should understand a little about it before using the store. The end of the chapter discusses other online sources of music, from online music stores other than the iTunes Music Store to free sources of songs.

Understand Digital Rights Management

Currently, the music industry and consumers are engaged in a vigorous struggle over how music is sold (or stolen) and distributed:

- The record companies are aggressively rolling out copy-protection mechanisms on audio discs (see "Understand Current Copy-Protection Techniques on the CDs You Buy" in Chapter 6) to prevent their customers from making unauthorized pure-digital copies of music.

- Some consumers are trying to protect their freedom to enjoy the music they buy in the variety of ways that law and case law have established to be either definitely legal or sort-of legal. For example, legal precedents that permit the use of VCRs, personal video recorders (PVRs), and home audio taping suggest that it's probably legal to create compressed audio files from a CD, record, or cassette, as long as they're for your personal use.

- Other people—"consumers" in a sense other than the usual, perhaps—are deliberately infringing the record companies' copyrights by copying, distributing, and stealing music via peer-to-peer (P2P) networks, recordable CDs and DVDs, and other means.

Also participating in this struggle is the movie industry, which suffers similar piracy problems. VCRs and PVRs provide plenty of precedent for making copies of copyrighted works for personal use and sharing them with other people (for example, on videotape or DVD), but widespread distribution of digital video files on P2P networks is another matter entirely.

Behind this struggle lies digital rights management (DRM), technologies for defining which actions a user may take with a particular work and restricting the user to those actions, preferably without preventing them from using or enjoying the work in the ways they expect to.

Understand That DRM Is Neither "Good" nor "Bad"

DRM is often portrayed by consumer activists as being the quintessence of the Recording Industry Association of America's and Motion Picture Association of America's dreams and of consumers' nightmares. The publisher of a work can use DRM to impose a wide variety of restrictions on the ways in which a consumer can use the work.

For example, some digital books are delivered in an encrypted format that requires a special certificate to decrypt, which effectively means that the consumer can read them only on one authorized computer. DRM also prevents the consumer from printing any of the book or copying any of it directly from the reader application. As you'd imagine, these restrictions are unpopular with most consumers, and such books haven't exactly made a splash in the marketplace: Consumers prefer traditional physical books that they can read wherever they want to, lend to a friend, photocopy, rip pages out of, drop in the bath, and so on.

But how good or bad DRM is in practice depends on the implementation. When both publishers and consumers stand to gain from DRM being implemented effectively, compromise of the kind that Apple has achieved with the iTunes Music Store makes sense.

Music is almost ideal for digital distribution, and the record companies are sitting on colossal archives of songs that are out of print but still well within copyright. It's not economically viable for the record companies to sell pressed CDs of these songs, because demand for any given CD is likely to be relatively low. But demand is there, as has been demonstrated by the millions of illegal copies of such songs that have been downloaded from P2P services. If the record companies can make these songs available online with acceptable DRM, they'll almost certainly find buyers.

NOTE

In passing, it's worth mentioning that some enterprising smaller operators have managed to make an economic proposition out of selling pressed CDs or recorded CDs of out-of-print music to which they've acquired the rights. By cutting out middlemen and selling directly via websites and mail order, and in some cases by charging a premium price for a hard-to-get product, such operators have proved that making such music available isn't impossible. But doing so certainly requires a different business model than the lowest-common-denominator, pack-'em-high-and-hope-they-fly model that the major record companies so doggedly pursue.

Historically, video has not been a good candidate for digital distribution, because the files have been too big to transfer easily across the Internet. But now that faster broadband connections are becoming increasingly widespread, distributing even full-quality video files is workable.

Know a Store's DRM Terms Before You Buy Any Protected Material

Before you buy any song (or video) that is protected by DRM, make sure you understand what the DRM involves, what restrictions it places on you, and what changes the implementer of the DRM is allowed to make. In most cases, when you "buy" a song that is protected by DRM, you buy not the song but a license to listen to the song in limited circumstances—for example, on a single computer or several computers, or for a limited length of time. You may or may not be permitted to burn the song to CD for storage or so that you can play it in conventional audio players (rather than on computers). In most cases, you are not permitted to give or sell the song to anyone else, nor can you return the song to the store for a refund or exchange.

The store that sells you the license to the song usually retains the right to change the limitations on how you can use the song. For example, the store can change the number of computers on which you can play the song, prevent you from burning it to CD, or even prevent you from playing it anymore. Any restrictions added may not take place immediately if your computer isn't connected to the Internet, but most online music stores require periodic authentication checks to make sure the music is still licensed for playing.

In general, "buying" songs online compares poorly to buying a physical CD, even though you have the option of buying individual songs rather than having to buy the entire contents of the CD. Even though you don't own the music on the CD, you own the CD itself, and can dispose of it as you want. For example, you can create digital copies of its contents (assuming that the CD is not copy-protected), lend the CD to a friend, or sell the CD to an individual or a store.

The sections in this chapter about the iTunes Music Store and other online music stores explain the current DRM the stores impose on the songs they sell. You should check the terms and conditions of each store for changes to the DRM before buying from that store.

Similar restrictions and considerations apply to video files you buy from the iTunes Music Store. In most cases, if the same content is available on a conventional medium (such as a DVD or a video cassette), buying it on that medium will give you more flexibility than buying a digital file.

Buy Songs and Videos from the iTunes Music Store

So far, the iTunes Music Store is one of the largest and most successful attempts to sell music online. (The latter part of this chapter discusses other online music services, including Wal-Mart and Napster 2.0.) The iTunes Music Store is far from perfect, and its selection is still very limited compared to what many users would like to be able to buy, but it's an extremely promising start. At the time of this writing, the iTunes Music Store is available to users of iTunes on the Mac and Windows (but not to users of other music players).

These are the basic parameters of the iTunes Music Store at this writing:

- Most songs cost $0.99 each (although the record companies keep making noises about implementing "differential pricing"—charging more for hotter properties). The cost of albums varies, but many cost $9.99 or so—around what you'd pay for a discounted CD in many stores. Some CDs are available only as "partial CDs," which typically means that you can't buy the songs you're most likely to want. Extra-long songs (for example, those 13-minute jam sessions used to max out a CD) are sometimes available for purchase only with an entire CD.

- Most videos items cost $1.99 at this writing, but you can also buy them in bulk and save. For example, you might buy a whole season of *Desperate Housewives.*

- You can listen to a 30-second preview of any song, or view a 20-second video clip, to make sure it's what you want. After you buy an item, you download it to your library.

- You can burn songs and videos to CD an unlimited number of times, although you can burn any given playlist only seven times without changing it or re-creating it under another name. (The number of burns was originally 10 but was reduced in early 2005.)

- The songs you buy are encoded in the AAC format (discussed in "AAC" in Chapter 6) and are protected with DRM (discussed in the following section). The videos you buy are in the MPEG-4 video format and are also protected with DRM.

- You can play the songs and videos you buy on up to five "Apple-authorized" computers and devices at a time. You can change which computers are authorized for the songs bought on a particular iTunes Music Store account. Your iPod can contain material from up to five different accounts at the same time.

- You can download each item you buy only once (assuming the download is successful). After that, the item is your responsibility. If you lose the item, you have to buy it again. This means that you must back up the items you buy.

Understand What the iTunes Music Store DRM Means

At this writing, the iTunes Music Store provides a nicely weighted implementation of DRM, known as FairPlay, that's designed to be acceptable both to customers and to the record companies that are providing the songs. The iTunes Music Store started with more than 200,000 songs—an impressive number for the record companies to agree to provide, although only a few drops in the bucket

7

compared to the many millions of songs that music enthusiasts would like to be able to purchase online. By fall 2005, the iTunes Music Store had more than two million different songs available and had sold more than 600 million songs altogether.

For customers, the attraction is being able to find songs easily, acquire them almost instantly for reasonable prices, and use them in enough of the ways they're used to (play the songs on their computer, play them on their iPod, or burn them to CD). For the record companies, the appeal is a largely untapped market that can provide a revenue stream at minimal cost (no physical media are involved) and with an acceptably small potential for abuse. (For example, most people who buy songs won't burn them to CD, rip the CD to MP3, and then distribute the MP3 files.) To the surprise of many analysts, Steve Jobs revealed in late 2003 that Apple makes hardly any money from the iTunes Music Store, which seems to mean that most of the revenue (apart from the overheads of administering the service, running the servers, and providing bandwidth) goes to the record companies.

Being able to download music like this is pretty wonderful: You can get the songs you want, when you want them, and at a price that's more reasonable than buying a whole CD. But it's important to be aware of the following points, even if they don't bother you in the least:

- Even though the AAC format provides relatively high audio quality, the songs sold by the iTunes Music Store are significantly lower quality than CD-quality audio.

- When you buy a CD, you own it. You can't necessarily do what you want with the music—not legally, anyway. But you can play it as often as you want on whichever player, lend it to a friend, and so on.

- When you buy a song from the Apple Music Store, you don't own it. Instead, you have a very limited license. If your computer's hard disk crashes so that you lose your music library, you can't download the songs again from the Apple Music Store without paying for them again.

- The record labels that provide the music reserve the right to change the terms under which they provide the music in the future. Apple has implemented several changes already, reducing the number of computers with which iTunes can share music and the number of CD burns allowed for any given playlist. Like these changes, future changes seem likely to be more restrictive than more liberal.

In October 2005, the iTunes Music Store added a modest selection of video files, and sold one million of them in the first 19 days. As with songs, the convenience of buying via download is wonderful, but some of the same concerns apply: The MPEG format provides good-enough quality, but nothing compared to a DVD; you buy not a tangible object but a license to use the file; you need to back up your purchases to physical media to avoid loss; and the terms of service may change.

NOTE   *The success of the iTunes Music Store has greatly increased consumers' acceptance of DRM. The iTunes Music Store has been successful because it enables people to find and buy music with minimal fuss, and the DRM on iTunes, the iTunes Music Store, and the iPod is implemented in a slick and effective package. Several other online music stores have taken their lead from the iTunes Music Store, even though they use different—and mostly Windows-only—types of DRM.*

Set Up an Account with the iTunes Music Store

To use the iTunes Music Store, you need a PC or a Mac running iTunes 4 or later as well as a .Mac account, an Apple ID, or an AOL screen name. (An Apple ID is essentially an account with the iTunes Music Store and takes the form of an e-mail address. The .Mac service is Apple's online service.) To use the video features, you need iTunes 6.0 or later.

To get started with the iTunes Music Store, click the Music Store item in the Source pane in iTunes. (Alternatively, double-click the Music Store item to display a separate Music Store window.) iTunes accesses the iTunes Music Store and displays its home page, of which Figure 7-1 shows an example on the Mac.

FIGURE 7-1   The iTunes Music Store home page.

FIGURE 7-2   From the Sign In dialog box, you can sign in to an existing account or create
a new account.

To sign in or to create an account, click the Sign In button. iTunes displays the Sign In To
Download Music From The iTunes Music Store dialog box (see Figure 7-2, above).

If you have a .Mac account or an Apple ID, enter it in the Apple ID text box, enter your
password in the Password text box, and click the Sign In button. Likewise, if you have an AOL
screen name, select the AOL option button, enter your screen name and password, and click the
Sign In button.

   *Remember that your Apple ID is the full e-mail address, including the domain—not
just the first part of the address. For example, if your Apple ID is a .Mac address, enter*
yourname@mac.com *rather than just* **yourname**.

The first time you sign on to the iTunes Music Store, iTunes displays a dialog box pointing
out that your Apple ID or AOL screen name hasn't been used with the iTunes Music Store and
suggesting that you review your account information:

Click the Review button to review your account information. (This is a compulsory step. Clicking the Cancel button doesn't skip the review process, as you might hope—instead, it cancels the creation of your account.)

To create a new account, click the Create New Account button and then click the Continue button on the Welcome To The iTunes Music Store page. The subsequent screens then walk you through the process of creating an account. You have to provide your credit card details and billing address. Beyond this, you get a little homily on what you may and may not legally do with the music you download, and you have to agree to the terms of service of the iTunes Music Store.

Understand the Terms of Service

Almost no one ever reads the details of software licenses, which is why the software companies have been able to establish as normal the sales model in which you buy not software itself but a limited license to use it, and you have no recourse if it corrupts your data or reduces your computer to a puddle of silicon and steel. But you'd do well to read the terms and conditions of the iTunes Music Store before you buy music from it, because you should understand what you're getting into.

7

TIP   *The iTunes window doesn't give you the greatest view of the terms of service. To get a better view, click the Printable Version link at the very bottom of the scroll box or direct your browser to www.info.apple.com/usen/musicstore/terms.html.*

The following are the key points of the terms of service:

- You can play songs and videos that you download on five computers at any time. You can authorize and deauthorize computers, so you can (for example) transfer your songs and videos from your old computer to a new computer you buy.

- You can use, export, copy, and burn items for "personal, noncommercial use."

- After you buy and download items, they're your responsibility. If you lose them or destroy them, Apple won't replace them. (You have to buy new copies of the items if you want to get them back.)

- You agree not to violate the Usage Rules imposed by the agreement.

- You agree that Apple may disclose your registration data and account information to "law enforcement authorities, government officials, and/or a third party, as Apple believes is reasonably necessary or appropriate to enforce and/or verify compliance with any part of this Agreement." The implication is that if a copyright holder claims that you're infringing their copyright, Apple may disclose your details without your knowledge, let alone your agreement. This seems to mean that, say, Sony Music or the RIAA can get the details of your e-mail address, physical address, credit card, and listening habits by claiming a suspicion of copyright violation.

- Apple and its licensors can remove or prevent you from accessing "products, content, or other materials."

- Apple reserves the right to modify the Agreement at any time. If you continue using the iTunes Music Store, you're deemed to have accepted whatever additional terms Apple imposes.

- Apple can terminate your account for failing to "comply with any of the provisions" in the Agreement—or for being suspected of such failure. Terminating your account prevents you from buying any more items immediately, but you might be able to set up another account. More seriously, termination might prevent you from playing songs and videos you've already bought—for example, if you need to authorize a computer to play them.

Configure iTunes Music Store Settings

By default, iTunes is configured to display the iTunes Music Store icon in the Source pane and to use 1-Click buying and downloading. You may want to remove the iTunes Music Store icon or use the shopping basket. To change your preferences, follow these steps:

1. Display the iTunes dialog box or the Preferences dialog box:

   - In Windows, choose Edit | Preferences or press CTRL-COMMA or CTRL-Y to display the iTunes dialog box.

   - On the Mac, choose iTunes | Preferences or press either ⌘-COMMA or ⌘-Y to display the Preferences dialog box.

2. Click the Store tab to display its contents. Figure 7-3 shows the Store tab on the Mac. The Store tab in Windows has the same controls.

3. To prevent the iTunes Music Store item from appearing in the Source pane, clear the Show iTunes Music Store check box. Doing this disables all the other controls on the Store sheet or tab, so you've nothing left to do but click the OK button to close the dialog box.

4. If you choose to use the iTunes Music Store, select the Buy And Download Using 1-Click option button or the Buy Using A Shopping Cart option button, as appropriate. 1-Click is great for impulse shopping and instant gratification, whereas the shopping cart enables you to round up a collection of songs and videos, weigh their merits against each other, and decide which ones you feel you must have. (In other words, using the shopping cart is the more sensible approach—so Apple has made 1-Click the default setting.)

   > **TIP**   *If you have a slow connection, consider using the Buy Using A Shopping Cart option to queue up a stack of items to download overnight when the download won't compete with your other online activities for your meager bandwidth.*

5. Select or clear the Play Songs After Downloading check box. This setting lets you hear a song the instant you've downloaded it. If you usually listen to music while downloading, you may prefer to keep this check box cleared, as it is by default.

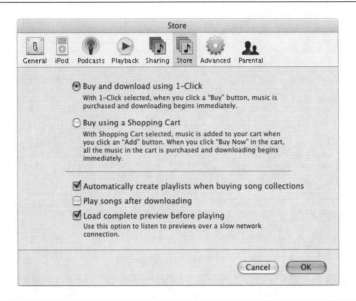

FIGURE 7-3   Configure the settings on the Store tab of the iTunes dialog box or the Preferences
dialog box before you buy any songs unexpectedly.

6. If you're using a slow Internet connection (for example, dial-up or ISDN), select the
Load Complete Preview Before Playing check box. Otherwise, the download stream may
be too slow to sustain play through the preview without interruptions. (Faster Internet
connections should be able to stream the previews without breaking a sweat.)

7. Click the OK button to apply your choices and close the dialog box.

Find the Songs and Videos You Want

You can find songs and videos in the iTunes Music Store in several ways that will seem familiar
if you've used other online stores:

- You can meander through the interface looking for items by clicking links from the
home page.

- You can browse by genre, subgenre, artist, and album. Click the Browse button, choose Edit |
Show Browser, or press CTRL-B (Windows) or ⌘-B (Mac) to display the Browse interface.

- You can search for specific items either by entering the terms in the Search Music Store box
and using the Search bar to restrict the results to the categories you want, or by clicking the
Power Search link on the home page and using the Power Search page to specify multiple
criteria. Figure 7-4 shows the Power Search page with some results found. You can sort
the search results by a column heading by clicking it. Click the column heading again to
reverse the sort order.

FIGURE 7-4   Use the Power Search feature to search for songs by song title, artist, album, genre, and composer.

Preview Songs and Videos

One of the most attractive features of the iTunes Music Store is that it lets you preview an item before you buy it. This feature helps you ensure both that you've found the right item and that you like it.

For some songs, the previews are of the first 30 seconds. For most songs, the previews feature one of the most distinctive parts of the song (for example, the chorus or a catchy line). For videos, the previews are 20 seconds of the most identifiable highlights.

A typical download of a 30-second audio clip involves around 600KB of data; 20 seconds of video takes considerably more. If you have a slow Internet connection, downloading the previews will take a while. It's best to select the Load Complete Preview Before Playing check box on the Store tab of the iTunes dialog box or the Preferences dialog box.

Double-click an item's listing to start the preview playing (or downloading, if you choose to load complete previews before playing).

Understand A*****s and "Explicit"

The iTunes Music Store censors supposedly offensive words to help minimize offense:

■   Songs deemed to have potentially offensive lyrics are marked EXPLICIT in the Song Name column. Where a sanitized version of the same song is available, it's marked CLEAN in the Song Name column. Some of the supposedly explicit songs contain words no more offensive than "love." Some others are instrumentals.

- Strangely, other songs that contain words that are offensive to most people aren't flagged as being explicit. So if you worry about what you and yours hear, don't trust the iTunes Music Store ratings too far.

- Any word deemed offensive is censored with asterisks (**), at least in theory. (In practice, some words sneak through.) When searching, use the real word rather than censoring it yourself.

TIP *To prevent your children from downloading explicit songs, select the Restrict Explicit Content check box on the Parental tab of the iTunes dialog box (Windows) or the Preferences dialog box (Mac). Click the lock icon and enter your system password to effect the change.*

Request Music You Can't Find

Two million songs sounds like an impressive number, but it's a mere cupful in the bucket of all the songs that have ever been recorded (and that music enthusiasts would like to buy). As a result, the iTunes Music Store's selection of music pleases some users more than others. Not surprisingly, Apple and the record companies seem to be concentrating first on the songs that are most likely to please (and to be bought by) the most people. If you want the biggest hits—either the latest ones or longtime favorites—chances are that the iTunes Music Store has you covered. But if your tastes run to the esoteric, you may not find the songs you're looking for on the iTunes Music Store.

If you can't find a song you're looking for in the iTunes Music Store, you can submit a request for it. If a search produces no results, the iTunes Music Store offers you a Request link that you can click to display the Make A Request form for requesting music by song name, artist name, album, composer, or genre. You can also display this form by clicking the Requests & Feedback link on the home page.

Beyond the immediate thank-you-for-your-input screen that the iTunes Music Store displays, requesting songs feels unrewarding at present. Apple doesn't respond directly to song requests, so unless you keep checking for the songs you've requested, you won't know that they've been posted. Nor will you learn if the songs will ever be made available. Besides, given the complexities involved in licensing songs, it seems highly unlikely that Apple will make special efforts to license any particular song unless a truly phenomenal number of people request it. Instead, Apple seems likely to continue doing what makes much more sense—licensing as many songs as possible that are as certain as possible to appeal to plenty of people.

Navigate the iTunes Music Store

To navigate from page to page in the iTunes Music Store, click the buttons in the toolbar. Alternatively, use these keyboard shortcuts:

- In Windows, press CTRL-[to return to the previous page and CTRL-] to go to the next page.

- On the Mac, press ⌘-[to return to the previous page and ⌘-] to go to the next page.

Buy a Song or Video from the iTunes Music Store

To buy a song from the iTunes Music Store, click the Buy Song button. To buy a video, click the Buy Video button.

If you're not currently signed in, iTunes displays the Sign In To Download Music From The iTunes Music Store dialog box. This dialog box is like the dialog box shown in Figure 7-2, but includes a Remember Password For Purchasing check box that you can select if you want iTunes to remember your password so that you don't need to enter it in future. Enter your ID and password and then click the Buy button. iTunes then displays a confirmation message box like this:

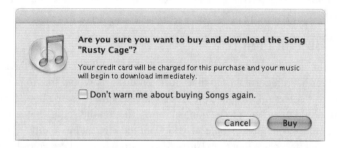

Click the Buy button to make the purchase. Select the Don't Warn Me About Buying Songs Again check box if appropriate. Some people prefer to have this double-check in place to slow down the pace at which they assault their credit cards. For others, even having to confirm the purchase is an annoyance.

iTunes then downloads the song (or video) to your library and adds an entry for it to your Purchased playlist.

Listen to Songs and Watch Videos You've Purchased

When you download an item from the iTunes Music Store, iTunes adds it to the playlist named Purchased in the Source pane. The Purchased playlist is there to provide a quick-and-easy way to get to all the songs and videos you buy. Otherwise, if you purchase items on impulse without keeping a list, they might vanish into your huge library.

To delete the entry for an item in the Purchased playlist, right-click it, choose Clear from the shortcut menu, and click the Yes button in the confirmation message box. However, unlike for regular files, iTunes doesn't offer you the opportunity to delete the file itself—the file remains in your library on the basis that, having paid for it, you don't actually want to delete it.

You can drag songs and videos that you haven't purchased to the Purchased playlist as well.

Restart a Failed Download

If a download fails, you may see an error message that invites you to try again later. If this happens, iTunes terminates the download but doesn't roll back the purchase.

To restart a failed download, choose Advanced | Check For Purchases. Enter your password in the Enter Account Name And Password dialog box and click the Check button. iTunes attempts to restart the failed download.

Review What You've Purchased from the iTunes Music Store

To see what you've purchased from the iTunes Music Store, follow these steps:

1. Click the Account button (the button that displays your account name), enter your password, and then click the View Account button to display the Account Information window.

2. Click the Purchase History button to display details of the songs you've purchased.

3. Click the arrow to the left or an order date to display details of the purchases on that date.

4. Click the Done button when you've finished examining your purchases. iTunes returns you to your Apple Account Information page.

7

TIP

From the Apple Account Information page, you can also access the iTunes Music Store's features for setting up allowances for users to buy music and for buying gift certificates.

(Try to) Fix Problems with Your iTunes Music Store Bill

If something seems to have gone wrong with your iTunes Music Store bill—for example, you seem to have been billed for songs you didn't buy—choose Help | iTunes And Music Store Service And Support, click the iTunes Music Store Customer Service Site link, and use the form on the resulting web page.

Authorize and Deauthorize Computers for the iTunes Music Store

When you buy a song from the iTunes Music Store, you're allowed to play it on up to five different computers at a time. iTunes implements this limitation through a form of license that Apple calls *authorization*. Essentially, iTunes tracks which computers are authorized to play songs you've purchased and stops you from playing the songs when you're out of authorizations.

If you want to play songs you've purchased on a sixth computer, you need to *deauthorize* one of the first five computers so as to free up an authorization for use on the sixth computer. You may also need to specifically deauthorize a computer to prevent it from listening to the songs you've bought. For example, if you sell or give away your Mac, you'd probably want to deauthorize it. You might also need to deauthorize a computer if you're planning to rebuild it.

NOTE

Your computer must be connected to the Internet in order to authorize and deauthorize computers.

Authorize a Computer to Use the iTunes Music Store

To authorize a computer, simply try to play a song purchased from the iTunes Music Store. For example, access a shared computer's Purchased Music playlist and double-click one of the songs. iTunes displays the Authorize Computer dialog box. Enter your Apple ID and password and then click the Authorize button. iTunes accesses the iTunes Music Store and (all being well) authorizes the computer. iTunes displays a message box telling you that authorization was successful and letting you know how many computers you've authorized:

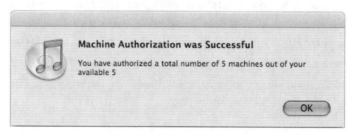

Deauthorize a Computer from Using iTunes Music Store

To deauthorize a computer so that it can no longer play the songs you've purchased from the iTunes Music Store, follow these steps:

1. Choose Advanced | Deauthorize Computer to display the Deauthorize Computer dialog box.

2. Select the Deauthorize Computer For Music Store Account option button if it's not already selected.

3. Click the OK button. iTunes displays the next Deauthorize Computer dialog box.

4. Enter the appropriate Apple ID and password and then click the OK button. iTunes accesses the iTunes Music Store, performs the deauthorization, and then tells you the deed is done.

Buy Music from Other Online Music Stores

If you use an iPod, the iTunes Music Store is the best of the large online music stores, because it sells songs in a format that the iPod can play, whereas most other online music stores use incompatible formats (such as WMA). But you may want to use other online music stores for a couple of reasons:

■ Some sell songs that the iTunes Music Store doesn't have.

■ Some offer subscription pricing that lets you download and listen to as much music as you want for a monthly fee.

■ Some sell music in formats that the iPod can play—and even without DRM restrictions on what you can do with the songs.

This section discusses the leading online music stores at this writing.

Most Other Online Music Stores Work Only with Windows

Most of the online music services work only with Windows at the time of writing. To complicate things still more for anyone using an iPod, most of the online music services use WMA files protected with DRM for their songs. Some services are also tied to specific hardware players, some to their own software players, and some to Windows Media Player.

To use protected WMA files with an iPod, you must burn them to CD and then rip and encode the CD to AAC files or MP3 files. You could also use Apple Lossless Encoding, but because the WMA files are lower quality than Apple Lossless Encoding, doing so makes little sense.

Most of the online music services permit you to burn songs to CD, but creating further copies of the songs could be interpreted to be against the terms and conditions of some services.

7

Napster 2.0

Napster 2.0 (www.napster.com) offers more than a million songs at this writing. Napster 2.0 is run by Roxio, Inc., and has nothing to do with the pioneering file-sharing application Napster except the name and logo, which Roxio acquired via a tortuous path of other companies. Napster uses the WMA format protected with DRM and works only on the PC—there is no Mac client at this writing.

A standard Napster subscription costs $9.95 per month and allows you to download as much music as you want to your PC, where you can play it as often as you like using the Napster player. You can use up to three PCs for the same Napster account, but the terms and conditions specify that the account is for one person only, so you're not allowed to share it with your friends. If you discontinue your subscription, you lose access to all songs you've downloaded except for those you've bought.

If you want to burn a song to CD, you must pay; you must also pay if you want to transfer the song to a music player that supports WMA DRM. At this writing, Napster charges $0.99 per song or around $9.95 for a full album.

Even if you pay, you can't transfer songs to an iPod. You can put songs on the iPod in only two ways:

- Buy the songs, burn them to CD, and then rip the CD to a format that the iPod can play (for example, use iTunes to rip the CD to AAC files).

- Use an audio-grabbing utility (such as Total Recorder, discussed in Chapter 6) that captures the audio stream from the PC's sound card, or route the output from your sound card to an input that you can capture with a conventional audio application (such as Sound Recorder). These maneuvers are against the Napster terms and conditions and are illegal in most circumstances.

The Napster To Go service costs $14.95 a month and enables you to transfer as many songs as you want to a portable player that supports Windows Media Player 10 DRM. (The Napster website lists supported players.)

Napster's restrictions may appear to be onerous, but Napster can be a great way to listen to a wide variety of music for a fixed fee. Being able to "try before you buy" takes the gamble out of buying CDs (or individual songs) that you're not sure you'll like.

> NOTE   *Napster has been marketing its services aggressively to colleges and universities, which pay reduced fees for providing Napster access to all their students. Mac users are out of luck.*

RealPlayer Music Store and Real Rhapsody

The RealPlayer Music Store (www.real.com/musicstore/) provides 192 Kbps AAC files, which give very high audio quality. To access the RealPlayer Music Store, you must use RealPlayer 10, which is free and runs on Windows and Mac OS X. Songs cost $0.99 each, and most albums cost $9.99 each. You can burn songs to CD and download them to some Creative players and some Palm devices.

Of more interest to iPod users is Rhapsody, an application and service started by Listen.com but taken over by Real Networks. Rhapsody provides unlimited streaming access to more than a million songs for $9.99 a month. You can buy songs for $0.79 apiece and put them on a variety of devices, including the iPod.

Like Napster, Rhapsody provides a good way to listen to a wide variety of music for a fixed fee.

Walmart.com

Wal-Mart's website (www.walmart.com) includes a Music Downloads section that offers songs for $0.88 and albums from $8.80 and up. Songs from Walmart.com come as protected WMA files and work only with Windows Media Player and hardware players that Windows Media Player supports. You can use either Windows Media Player or Internet Explorer to buy and download music.

With an easy-to-use interface, 500,000 songs available, and low prices, Walmart.com is an attractive option for anyone using Windows Media Player. For iTunes and iPod users, Walmart .com has little appeal. You can put songs on the iPod in only two ways:

- ■ Buy the songs, burn them to CD, and then rip the CD to a format that the iPod can play (for example, use iTunes to rip the CD to AAC files).

- ■ Use an audio-grabbing utility (such as Total Recorder, discussed in Chapter 6) that captures the audio stream from the PC's sound card, or route the output from your sound card to an input that you can capture with a conventional audio application (such as Sound Recorder). These maneuvers are against the Walmart.com terms and conditions and are illegal in most circumstances.

BuyMusic.com

BuyMusic.com (www.buymusic.com) claims to be the "world's largest download music store." It is a Windows-only service that supplies files in the protected WMA format for its custom music player. Most songs cost $0.99, and most albums $9.99, but some songs are less expensive. Some songs are available encoded at the 256 Kbps bitrate. These songs have higher audio quality but larger file sizes and therefore take longer to download.

On BuyMusic.com, different songs have different licensing terms setting out the number of computers you can play them on, the number of transfers to SDMI-compliant digital audio players, and the number of times you can burn them to CD. Check the licensing terms for any song or CD before buying it.

As with other WMA services, the only ways to put songs from BuyMusic.com onto an iPod are to burn a CD and rip it, to use an audio-grabber utility, or to reroute the output from your sound card to an input that you can capture with an audio application.

Yahoo! Music

Yahoo! Music (http://music.yahoo.com) offers more than 1 million songs that you can access via the Yahoo! Music Unlimited subscription service. Yahoo! Music Unlimited costs $4.99 a month if you buy a yearly subscription, or $6.99 a month if you pay by the month. You can burn downloaded songs to CD for $0.79 each.

Yahoo! Music Unlimited lets you transfer the music to a supported portable device without extra charge, so it offers great value for anyone with one of these devices, which include various models of Dell DJ, RCA Lycra, iRiver players, and the Creative Labs Zen Portable Media Player and the Samsung YH-999 Portable Media Center. Unfortunately, Yahoo! Music Unlimited doesn't support the iPod directly from its subscription, although you can use the Yahoo! Music Engine to transfer songs that you have bought from the service to your iPod.

Sony Connect

Sony's Connect services (http://musicstore.connect.com) offers more than 500,000 songs at $0.99 each. At this writing, Connect works only with some Sony music players, although Sony has announced that it will support other players in the future.

Musicmatch Downloads

Musicmatch, Inc., has been one of the leading names for Internet music on Windows-based PCs with its Musicmatch Jukebox Basic and Musicmatch Jukebox Plus applications. The latest versions of Musicmatch Jukebox integrate with the Musicmatch Downloads service (www.musicmatch.com) and deliver similar features to iTunes, except they work only on Windows. (In the past, Musicmatch has released Mac versions of Musicmatch Jukebox, but these don't support Musicmatch Downloads.)

At the time of writing, Musicmatch Downloads (run Musicmatch Jukebox or Musicmatch Jukebox Plus and then click the Music Store button) offers more than 360,000 songs at $0.99 each and albums starting at $9.99. Musicmatch Downloads provides songs in WMA format with DRM that allows you to burn them to CD and transfer them to some portable devices, but not to an iPod. To put songs from Musicmatch onto an iPod, you can burn a CD and rip it, use an audio-grabber utility, or reroute the output from your sound card to an input that you can capture with an audio application.

NOTE   *You can use Musicmatch Jukebox to manage some iPod models on Windows if you prefer not to use iTunes. See "Musicmatch Jukebox Works with Third-Generation and Earlier iPods Only" in Chapter 15 for details.*

Wippit and Warp

Wippit (www.wippit.com) uses a P2P network to provide a variety of tracks for download in a mixture of unprotected MP3 and protected WMA formats. Unlike the music services mentioned earlier, Wippit uses a subscription model for access to its music: for $89.99 per year, you get all-you-can-eat access to Wippit's catalog. At this point, Wippit offers more than 200,000 songs from more than 200 record labels, including EMI and BMG. The unprotected MP3 files work in iTunes and on the iPod without further ado, whereas the protected WMA files need to be either burned and reripped or captured, like the protected WMA files discussed earlier in this chapter.

You'll also find independent record companies selling music online. Some, such as the British electronic label Warp Records (www.warprecords.com/bleep/), sell songs without DRM restrictions—so once you've bought a song, you can do what you want with it, pretty much.

Find Free Songs Online

Beyond the iTunes Music Store and the other online music stores discussed so far in this chapter, you'll find many sources of free music online. Some of this free music is legal, but much of it is illegal.

Find Free Songs on the Online Music Stores

Most of the major online music stores provide some free songs, usually to promote either up-and-coming artists or major releases from established artists. For example, the iTunes Music Store provides a single for free download each week. The stores typically make you create an account before you can download such free songs as they're offering.

Find Free Songs for Legal Download

The Internet still contains some sources of songs that are distributed for free by the artists who created them. Although many sites that initially provided free songs have been taken over by commercial interests, one of the Internet's longest-running audio sites, the Internet Underground Musical Archive (IUMA; www.iuma.com), is still going strong.

IUMA's banner—"discover unsigned artists, independent bands, local talent"—neatly summarizes what IUMA is about. Artists who use IUMA are typically looking to distribute their music as widely as possible in the hope of increasing their audience, so IUMA offers MP3 downloads as well as MP3 and RealAudio streams. That means you can download music and listen to it as often as you want, burn it to CDs, share it with friends, and so on. This approach makes IUMA a great place for exploring new artists and different kinds of music. If you're looking for established artists, however, look elsewhere.

Many artists also provide some free songs for download on their own websites.

Find Free Songs for Illegal Download

Beyond the legal offerings of the online music stores and the free (and legal) sites, you can find pretty much any song for illegal download on the Internet. Finding a song that you can't find anywhere else can be wonderful, and getting the song for free is even more so. But before you download music illegally, you should be aware of possible repercussions to your computer, your wallet, and even your future.

7

Threats to Your Computer

Downloading files illegally may pose several threats to your computer:

- Many companies that produce P2P software include other applications with their products. Some of these applications are shareware and can be tolerably useful; others are adware that are useless and an irritant; still others are spyware that report users' sharing and downloading habits.

> **TIP** *To detect and remove spyware from your computer, use an application such as the free Ad-aware from LavaSoft (www.lavasoft.de) or Spybot Search & Destroy (www .safer-networking.org/).*

- Many of the files shared on P2P networks contain only the songs they claim to contain. Others are fake files provided by companies working for the RIAA and the record companies to "poison" the P2P networks and discourage people from downloading files by wasting their time.

- Other files *are* songs but also harbor a virus, worm, or Trojan horse. Even apparently harmless files can have a sting in the tail. For example, the tags in music files can contain URLs to which your player's browser component automatically connects. The site can then run a script on your computer, doing anything from opening some irritating advertisement windows, to harvesting any sensitive information it can locate, to deleting vital files or destroying the firmware on your computer.

> **TIP** *Whether you're downloading songs illegally or not, use virus-checking software to scan all incoming files to your computer, no matter whom they come from—friends, family, coworkers, or the Internet.*

Threats to Your Wallet, Your ID, and Your Future

Even if your computer remains in rude health, downloading files illegally poses several threats. Unless you use a service (such as Anonymizer, www.anonymizer.com) that masks your computer's IP address, any action that you take on the Internet can be tracked back to your computer.

Sharing digital files of other people's copyrighted content without permission is illegal. So is receiving such illegal files. The No Electronic Theft Act (NET Act) of 1997 and the Digital Millennium Copyright Act (DMCA) of 1998 provide savage penalties for people caught distributing copyrighted materials illegally. Under the DMCA, you can face fines of up to $500,000 and five years' imprisonment for a first offense, and double those for a second offense.

P2P networks also expose users to social-engineering attacks through the chat features that most P2P tools include. However friendly other users are, and however attractive the files they provide, it can be a severe mistake to divulge personal information. A favored gambit of malefactors is to provide a quantity of "good" (malware-free) files followed by one or more files that include a Trojan horse or keystroke logger to capture sensitive information from your computer.

Find P2P Software

At this writing, there are a large number of P2P networks, some of which interoperate with each other. Here are three starting points:

- **Gnutella (www.gnutella.com)**   A P2P protocol used by a wide variety of clients. At this writing, the leading Gnutella clients include BearShare (Windows only), Morpheus (Windows only), LimeWire (Windows and Mac), and Phex (Windows, Mac, and Linux).

- **Kazaa (www.kazaa.com)**   A P2P network based on the FastTrack engine and organized by Sharman Networks, Ltd. Kazaa provides the Windows-only Kazaa Media Desktop application, which puts a slick graphical interface on searching the Kazaa network. Kazaa routes searches through *supernodes* (users with fast connections) to make searching more efficient than searching through only peer nodes.

- **Freenet (freenetproject.org)**   A P2P network designed to allow "anybody to publish and read information with complete anonymity" and to prevent the network from being shut down. Freenet requires users to make space available to the network, automatically distributes files so no computer knows which files it's hosting, and encrypts the files placed on each computer for security. You can get Freenet clients for Windows, Mac OS X, and Linux.

NOTE   *At this writing, the RIAA, the Motion Picture Association of America, and other content providers are trying to close the P2P networks down by direct legal action against the networks and some of their users and by lobbying Congress to pass more restrictive legislation. By the time you read this, some of the P2P networks may have gone out of business—or may have metamorphosed themselves into legal content-distribution services.*

Chapter 8

Burn CDs and DVDs from iTunes

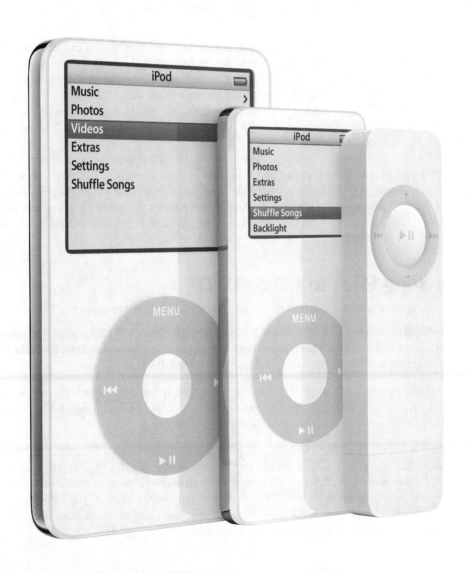

How to...

- Understand why you should burn your music and videos to CD or DVD
- Understand the basics of burning CDs and DVDs
- Configure iTunes for burning CDs and DVDs
- Burn CDs and DVDs
- Print CD covers and playlist listings
- Troubleshoot the problems you run into when burning CDs

iTunes makes it as easy as possible to burn playlists to CD, enabling you to create either regular audio CDs that will work in any CD player or MP3 CDs that will work only in MP3-capable CD players. You can also burn a playlist to a data CD or data DVD for backup or portability—for example, to back up your music library or your videos. Such data DVDs work in computer DVD drives but not in commercial DVD players. However, because each DVD can store around 150 CDs' worth of audio compressed at 128 Kbps or about 20 hours of compressed video, they're great for backup.

Burning with iTunes works in the same way in Windows and on the Mac, so this chapter discusses both operating systems together, showing some screens from each. The chapter starts by quickly running through the basics of burning. You'll then learn how to choose suitable settings for burning, how to burn CDs and DVDs, and how to print covers and playlist listings for the discs. You'll also learn how to minimize avoidable problems and how to troubleshoot common problems you may run into.

Why Burn Song Files to CD or DVD?

Typically, you'll want to burn song files to CD or DVD for one of three reasons:

- You want to create an audio CD that will play either on a regular CD player or on a computer. An *audio CD* is a CD that contains uncompressed audio: up to 74 minutes for a 650MB CD, 80 minutes for a 700MB CD, and 90 minutes for an 800MB CD.

> **NOTE** *You can play audio CDs on CD players (for example, a boom box or a hi-fi component) as well as on CD drives. Audio CDs created on recordable CDs are compatible with all CD players and with most (but not all) DVD players.*

- You want to create an MP3 CD that will play on a computer or on a CD player that can handle MP3 CDs. MP3 CDs can store far more music than audio CDs. For example, if you encode your MP3 files at 128 Kbps, you can fit about 12 hours of music on a CD. The disadvantages are that most CD players can't play MP3 CDs, and you can't burn protected AAC files to an MP3 CD—at least, not without burning them to an audio CD, ripping the CD to MP3 files, and then burning those files to the CD.

NOTE   *An MP3 CD can contain only MP3 files—not AAC, Apple Lossless Encoding, WAV, or AIFF files. If you've encoded your entire CD collection to AAC files, you won't be able to burn them to MP3 CDs without reencoding them. Because iTunes doesn't distinguish visibly among file types in your music library and in playlists, it's easy to trip up on this limitation: You happily queue a hundred or so files for burning to an MP3 CD, but iTunes burns only 20 or so files to the CD, because the rest are in AAC or other non-MP3 formats.*

■   You want to back up part of your music library to CD or DVD to protect it against loss. For example, you'll probably want to back up your Purchased playlist to CD or DVD, because if you lose those songs and videos, you'll need to buy them again. A backup disc is called a *data CD* or *data DVD*. Data discs won't play on most audio CD players, regular DVD players, or even most MP3-capable CD players; essentially, data discs are for computers only, but the occasional sophisticated CD player or DVD player may also be able to handle them.

Understand the Basics of Burning CDs and DVDs

At this writing, most new PCs and all new Macs sold include CD burners. Many also include DVD burners or drives that burn both DVDs and CDs.

To burn CDs with iTunes, your computer must have a CD burner or DVD burner. If your computer has a CD burner, it can be either a CD recorder (CD-R) drive or a CD rewriter (CD-RW) drive.

NOTE   *A CD-R burner can burn only CD-recordable discs—discs that can be burned only one time. A CD-RW burner can burn both CD-recordable discs and CD-rewritable discs; the latter can be burned, erased, and burned again multiple times. Similarly, DVD-R discs can be burned only once, but DVD-RW discs can be rewritten multiple times.*

If your computer doesn't have a burner, you can add a compatible internal CD-R or CD-RW drive (to most desktop PCs or to a PowerMac) or a compatible external USB or FireWire CD-R or CD-RW drive (to a PC notebook, PC desktop, PowerBook, iBook, iMac, eMac, or PowerMac).

TIP   *Before buying a burner for a Mac, consult the Apple Support website (www.apple.com/ support/) for the latest list of compatible drives.*

To burn DVDs (either DVD-R discs or DVD-RW discs), your PC must have a DVD burner that's compatible with iTunes. Your Mac must have either an internal SuperDrive or another compatible DVD burner, and it must be running Mac OS X 10.2.4 or later.

NOTE   *You can burn a playlist to a DVD-R disc or a DVD-RW disc, but not to a DVD-Audio disc.*

Burn CDs and DVDs

iTunes makes the process of burning CDs and DVDs straightforward. You can burn only a playlist to CD or DVD; you can't burn any other subdivision of your music library, such as an album or an artist's entire works, unless you add it to a custom playlist. That means you need to arrange your music files into suitable playlists before attempting to burn them to CD or DVD.

Typically, you'll want to start by choosing burning options, as described first in this section. Then you'll be ready to burn a disc, as described second.

Choose Burning Options

To choose burning options for iTunes, display the iTunes dialog box or the Preferences dialog box:

- In Windows, choose Edit | Preferences or press CTRL-COMMA or CTRL-Y to display the iTunes dialog box.

- On the Mac, choose iTunes | Preferences or press either ⌘-COMMA or ⌘-Y to display the Preferences dialog box.

Click the Advanced tab, and then click the Burning subtab to display its contents. Figure 8-1 shows the Burning subtab for iTunes on the Mac. The Burning subtab for iTunes on Windows has the same controls.

Next, choose options as follows:

- **CD Burner label or list**   If you have multiple CD or DVD burners, make sure iTunes has chosen the right burner. If you have only one burner, there's no decision to make here.

- **Preferred Speed drop-down list**   Choose the Maximum Possible setting to burn discs at the fastest speed iTunes and the drive can manage. If you don't get good results from the maximum possible speed, reduce the speed by choosing one of the other settings in the list. Test the setting and reduce the speed further if necessary.

- **Disc Format options**   To create an audio CD, select the Audio CD option button (the default). Use the Gap Between Songs drop-down list to specify whether to include a gap between the tracks on the CD (you can choose from one second to two seconds; the default is two seconds) or not (choose None). Select the Use Sound Check check box to make iTunes use Sound Check to normalize the volume on the tracks. Using Sound Check should produce CDs with much more consistent volume across their tracks than CDs created without Sound Check. To create an MP3 CD, select the MP3 CD option button. To create a data CD or DVD, select the Data CD Or DVD option button. (If you don't have a compatible DVD burner, this option button is named Data CD.)

Click the OK button to close the dialog box.

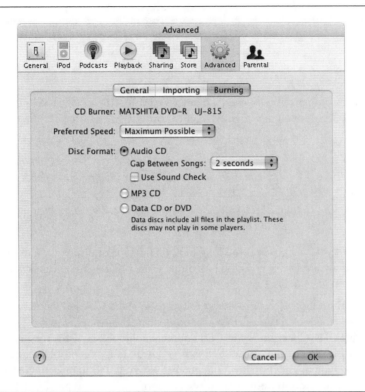

FIGURE 8-1   On the Burning subtab of the Advanced tab of the iTunes dialog box or the Preferences dialog box, configure options for burning CDs and DVDs.

Burn a CD or DVD

To burn a CD or DVD with iTunes, follow these steps:

1. Decide which type of CD or DVD—an audio CD, an MP3 CD, a data CD, or a data DVD—you want to create. If necessary, change your iTunes preferences as discussed in the previous section.

2. Add to a playlist the songs and videos that you want to have on the CD or DVD. Alternatively, open an existing playlist. For example, select your Purchased playlist so that you can burn the songs and videos you've purchased from the iTunes Music Store.

3. If necessary, change the name of the playlist to the name you want the CD to have. To do so, double-click the name, type the new name, and then press ENTER (Windows) or RETURN (Mac).

4. Click the Burn Disc button in the upper-right corner of the iTunes window. (The Burn Disc button replaces the Browse button when you select a playlist in the Source pane.)

5. When iTunes prompts you to insert a blank CD, do so. (If you take too long inserting the disc, iTunes decides you don't really want to burn a disc and stops flashing the message at you.)

NOTE

If you insert a blank recordable CD in your CD-RW drive before clicking the Burn button in iTunes, Mac OS X may display a dialog box inviting you to choose what to do with the CD. Select the Open iTunes item in the Action drop-down list. Select the Make This Action The Default check box if you always want to launch iTunes when you insert a blank CD. Then click the OK button to close the dialog box.

6. If the playlist you've chosen is too long to fit on the type of disc you've inserted in the format set in the Preferences dialog box or the iTunes dialog box, iTunes warns you and asks what you want to do:

  ■ If your Burning preferences are set to create an audio CD, and the playlist you've chosen is too long, iTunes lets you choose whether to split the playlist across multiple CDs. Click the Audio CDs button to split the playlist across as many CDs as necessary. Click the Cancel button if you want to fix the problem yourself. For example, you might slim down the playlist so that it will fit on a single CD, or you might change your burning preferences to burn a different type of CD.

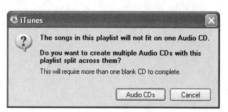

  ■ If your Burning preferences are set to create an MP3 CD, and the playlist you've chosen is too long, iTunes warns you that some of the tracks won't fit, and lets you choose whether to proceed:

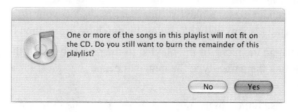

■ If your Burning preferences are set to create a data disc, and the playlist you've chosen is too long, iTunes lets you choose whether to split the playlist across multiple discs. Click the Data Discs button to have iTunes split the playlist automatically, or click the Cancel button if you want to change the playlist or the type of disc you're burning.

When you cancel a burn like this, you'll need to eject the unburned disc manually. If your drive has an Eject button, press it to eject the disc. If not, in Windows, choose Start | My Computer to display a My Computer window. Right-click the drive letter that represents the burner and then choose Eject from the shortcut menu to eject the disc. On the Mac, quit iTunes to force Mac OS X to eject the disc.

■ If the playlist contains a video file, and you've set iTunes to create an audio CD or an MP3 CD, iTunes will object with one of the dialog boxes shown here. Open the iTunes dialog box or the Preferences dialog box, click the Advanced tab, click the Burning subtab, select the Data CD Or DVD option button (if you have a DVD burner) or the Data CD option button (if you don't), click the OK button, and then restart the burn.

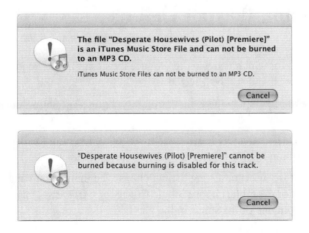

7. Click the Burn Disc button to start burning the CD:

8. When iTunes has finished burning the disc, or the last disc, it plays a notification sound. Eject the disc by right-clicking its entry in the Source pane and choosing Eject Disc from the shortcut menu. Then label the disc carefully, test it to make sure it's playable, and store it safely.

9. If you're burning multiple CDs, iTunes ejects each completed CD in turn and prompts you to insert a blank disc. Insert the disc and then click the Burn Disc button when iTunes prompts you to do so.

Print CD Covers and Playlist Listings

Follow these steps to print a CD jewel case insert, a song listing, or an album listing:

1. Select the playlist for which you want to produce the item. (If you've just burned a playlist to CD, the playlist should still be selected.)

2. Choose File | Print to display the Print dialog box. Figure 8-2 shows the Mac version of the Print Options dialog box.

3. In the Print area, select the CD Jewel Case Insert option button, the Song Listing option button, or the Album Listing option button, as appropriate.

4. For a CD jewel case insert or a song listing, choose the theme you want in the Theme drop-down list. For example, choose Single Cover for a CD jewel case insert to create a single cover from one of the songs in the playlist.

5. Click the Print button to print the item you've chosen.

FIGURE 8-2   iTunes makes it easy to print out a CD jewel case insert, a song listing, or an album listing for a disc you've burned.

Troubleshoot Burning CDs and DVDs

Despite impressive progress in CD and DVD burning, many things can still go wrong, wasting your time, effort, and media. This section discusses how to avoid causing your burner problems and how to solve problems when they nonetheless occur.

Avoid Causing Your Burner Problems

First, avoid avoidable problems with burning CDs and DVDs. To do so, balance quality, speed, and cost sensibly; devote as many processor cycles as possible to the burning; make sure your computer has plenty of memory; and prevent your computer from going to sleep during a burn.

Balance Quality, Speed, and Cost

To get good results, you must select a sensible balance for the classic choice of quality, speed, and cost, in which you are allowed to choose any two of the three but not all three. In the context of burning, this means consider the following:

- *Buy only high-quality recordable media.* (Low-quality media isn't worth using: There's no upside to losing your data—at least, unless the Department of Justice is on your case.) Expect to pay a market price for this media. If anyone offers you recordable media at bargain-basement prices, be duly suspicious. (Remember: Once badly burnt, forever shy.)

■ *In burning, speed is worthless without accuracy.* If your options are to record a CD at 60× with errors or 1× without errors, choose the 1× speed. Otherwise, your data will be useless.

■ *If you're buying a CD burner, get a good one.* Rather than buying the latest, fastest, and sexiest drive, consider buying a somewhat older model—you may be able to get good speed and reliability at a bargain price.

■ *If you're buying a DVD burner for a Mac, your best bet is to buy an internal SuperDrive so that you can use it fully with the iLife applications.* If you must buy an external drive, double-check beforehand that it'll work with the relevant iLife applications.

NOTE   *Different brands of recordable discs use different colors of dye: some green, some blue, some a faint shade of yellowy-brown. In theory, the color doesn't matter, although you'll hear some people claim that some colors are inferior to others—but in practice, it sometimes can make the difference between a burner being able to burn a disc or not, or between a player being able to play a disc back or not. So if you find your burner or player seems to prefer one color of recordable media to another, you're not necessarily imagining things. Stick with the brand and color that give the best results. One other thing: Discs that are made in Japan seem generally to perform better than discs made elsewhere, even when the manufacturer is the same.*

Give the Burner as Many Processor Cycles as Possible

Windows XP and Mac OS X are multitasking operating systems in which you can have multiple applications working actively at the same time. But because burning CDs or DVDs is a processor-intensive activity, it's a good idea not to multitask actively while burning unless you've established that your PC or Mac can comfortably handle the demands of burning and of whatever other work you're doing.

To get the very best burning performance, quit any unnecessary applications, reduce other tasks to a minimum, leave the burner as the foreground application (in other words, don't move the focus to another application window), and take your hands off the keyboard and mouse until the burn is complete.

NOTE   *Because the mouse can do so much in a graphical user interface, mouse-enabled operating systems squander many processor cycles on tracking exactly what the mouse is doing at any given moment if it's moving.*

Get More Memory if You Don't Have Enough

Modern applications are memory hungry, modern operating systems doubly so. And burning CDs or DVDs is a demanding task.

Both Windows XP and Mac OS X Jaguar and Panther will run with 128MB RAM (Tiger requires 256MB), but that's a bare minimum—not a sensible choice in the real world. You'll get significantly better performance with 256MB, much better performance with 512MB, and great performance with around 1GB. Given that RAM prices are at historic low levels (at the time of writing), now is a good time to add RAM to your computer.

Prevent Your PC from Using Screen Savers or Powering Down During a Burn

Processor-intensive screen savers (in other words, most of the visually interesting screen savers) can cause problems with burns by diverting processor cycles from the burn at a critical moment. To avoid this, configure a long wait on your screen saver. Similarly, configure Windows so that it doesn't try to power down the computer during a burn. To do so, follow these steps:

1. Right-click the desktop and choose Properties from the shortcut menu to display the Display Properties dialog box.

2. On the Screen Saver tab, increase the time shown in the Wait text box so it's far longer than even the slowest burn your CD recorder will ever perform. (Better yet, choose None in the Screen Saver drop-down list to turn off your screen saver altogether.) Click the Apply button to apply your choices.

3. Click the Screen Saver tab's Power button to prevent your computer from going to sleep during a burn. Windows displays the Power Options Properties dialog box.

4. On the Power Schemes tab, specify suitably lengthy times (or choose the Never item) in the Turn Off Monitor, Turn Off Hard Disks, System Standby, and System Hibernates drop-down lists to prevent these events from occurring during a burn.

5. Click the Apply button to apply your choices.

Prevent Your Mac from Starting a Screen Saver or Going to Sleep During a Burn

Configure the sleep timing settings in the Energy Saver pane of System Preferences to ensure that neither your Mac nor its display goes to sleep during a burn. Even with modern burners, your Mac's going to sleep during a burn may cause errors on the disc. Having the display go to sleep during a burn shouldn't affect the burn in many cases, but in other cases it may—particularly if you press the wrong keys or buttons when reawakening the display. Unless you care to experiment with having your display go to sleep and checking the resulting discs, you may prefer to be safe than sorry.

To change your Mac's sleep timing settings, follow these steps:

1. Choose Apple | System Preferences to display the System Preferences window.

2. Click the Energy Saver item in the Hardware category to display the Energy Saver pane.

3. If the Energy Saver pane is in its small format, which hides the details, click the Show Details button to display the full pane.

8

4. For a desktop Mac, or for a PowerBook or iBook running on the power adapter (rather than the battery), the easiest option is to choose the Automatic item in the Optimize Energy Settings drop-down list. This item puts the Mac to sleep after one hour of inactivity, which should be plenty long enough for burning any recordable CD—even at 2× speed. For burning a full DVD with one of the slower models of SuperDrive, however, you may need to allow a longer period of inactivity. Alternatively, you may prefer the Highest Performance item, which prevents the Mac from ever going to sleep without your putting it to sleep manually.

5. For a PowerBook or iBook running on battery power, you may find that the Automatic item in the Optimize Energy Settings drop-down list works okay for burning if your 'Book has a fast CD-RW drive or SuperDrive; the Automatic item puts the display to sleep after nine minutes and the computer to sleep after 25 minutes. On older 'Books, or with a slow SuperDrive, you may find these sleep settings too aggressive for comfort. In this case, you can choose the Highest Performance item if you don't care about exhausting your batteries quickly. Or you can choose the Custom item and then choose custom settings as follows:

   ■ Drag the Put The Computer To Sleep When It Is Inactive For slider to a setting that will allow plenty of time for the burn to complete.

   ■ To configure a sleep setting for the display that is different from the setting for the computer, select the Put The Display To Sleep When The Computer Is Inactive For check box and drag the slider to a setting that will allow the burn to complete. For obvious reasons, you can't set a longer sleep delay for the display than for the computer.

   ■ Select the Put the Hard Disk(s) to Sleep When Possible check box if you want Mac OS X to shut down the hard disk whenever possible. Because the hard disk is used extensively (though not quite continuously) during a burn, Mac OS X shouldn't try to shut down the hard disk while the burn is happening.

To prevent further changes to the Energy Saver configuration, click the lock icon at the lower-left corner of the Energy Saver pane. This will prevent anyone from shortening the sleep settings and throwing a monkey wrench into your burns. To unlock the Energy Saver pane, click the lock icon again, and enter your account name and password in the resulting Authenticate dialog box.

   ■ Press ⌘-Q or choose System Preferences | Quit System Preferences to quit System Preferences.

Troubleshoot Specific Problems

This section discusses how to troubleshoot problems in burning CDs and DVDs with iTunes. The section starts with the basics and then moves on to more challenging problems.

iTunes Doesn't List Your Burner on the Burning Subtab of the Advanced Tab

If iTunes doesn't list your burner on the Burning subtab of the Advanced tab of the iTunes dialog box (Windows) or the Preferences dialog box (Mac), the problem is most likely that iTunes doesn't support your burner.

<table>
<tr><td>TIP</td><td>If you need to get a new drive for a Mac, check the list of FireWire, USB, and internal CD burners at www.apple.com/macosx/upgrade/storage.html first.</td></tr>
</table>

Here's how to view the CD Burner readout:

- In Windows, press CTRL-COMMA or CTRL-Y or choose Edit | Preferences to display the iTunes dialog box.
- On the Mac, press ⌘-COMMA or ⌘-Y or choose iTunes | Preferences to display the Preferences dialog box.

Click the Advanced tab, and then click the Burning subtab to display its contents. If the CD Burner readout lists your CD or DVD burner by name or by model number, the drive works with iTunes.

8

Reset an External Burner

If you're using an external burner and you find that the drive stops responding after a burn fails, reset the drive by powering it down and then powering it back up—in lay terms, switching the drive off and then on again. If that doesn't work, you may need to restart your computer to regain control of the drive.

Give an External USB CD Burner a Better Chance

If you're having problems with an external CD burner connected via USB, try the following actions to reduce the problems:

- Disconnect all nonessential USB devices (in other words, don't disconnect a USB keyboard or mouse).
- If the CD burner is connected to the Mac through a USB hub, try removing the hub and plugging the burner directly into the Mac's USB port.
- Reduce the burn speed to 2× and see if that works. If so, increase the burn speed and test again.

Mac: Unable to Eject an Optical Disc

Sometimes Mac OS X doesn't eject a CD or DVD the first time you issue a command to eject it. For example, if you drag the CD's icon to the Trash, Mac OS X sometimes fails to eject it.

In iTunes, click the Eject button to eject the CD. You may need to click the button more than once. Allow a few seconds after each click to allow iTunes to respond.

External CD-RW Drive Stutters or Skips During Playback

Some external CD-RW drives don't play back CDs correctly, and you may hear stutters or apparent skips. To check whether the CD or the drive is the problem, try playing the CD in a CD player or in an internal CD drive (if you have one). If you don't have another CD player or CD drive, try playing another CD in the external CD-RW drive and see if that works.

"None of the Items in This List Can Be Burned to CD" Error Message

iTunes displays the error message "None of the items in this list can be burned to CD" in three cases:

- You try to burn a CD containing a playlist, but you've cleared the check boxes for all the songs on the playlist. To solve the problem, select the check boxes for the songs you want to burn to the CD.

- You try to burn a CD, but iTunes discovers that it can't locate any of the songs on the playlist. This is most likely to happen if you move your music library to a different folder. You may need to change the iTunes Music Folder Location setting on the General subtab of the Advanced tab of the iTunes dialog box or the Preferences dialog to show iTunes where your song files are.

- You try to burn a playlist that contains only protected AAC files that you've purchased from the iTunes Music Store, but iTunes is set to burn an MP3 CD rather than an audio CD or data CD. To solve the problem, choose a different CD type in the Preferences dialog box.

A Long Gap Between Songs Prevents Playlist from Burning

Choosing a Gap Between Songs setting of five seconds may prevent iTunes from burning a playlist successfully. If this happens, choose a shorter setting for Gap Between Songs. Two or three seconds should be adequate for most purposes.

"Songs in the Playlist Are Not Authorized" Error Message

The error message "One or more of the songs in this playlist are not authorized for use on this machine" means that you're trying to burn one or more songs that this computer isn't authorized to play. Click the OK button to close the message box.

The easiest way to fix this problem is to play each song on the playlist and go through the process of authorizing each song for which iTunes prompts you for authorization. (See Chapter 7 for details on authorization.) After doing this, start the burning process again.

"There Was a Problem with the Target Device" Error Message

The error message "There was a problem with the target device. Error code - 7932" means that iTunes can't successfully write to the CD media you're using at the speed you're trying to use. Take one of the following actions to solve the problem:

■ Reduce the burn speed to a lower setting on the Burning tab of the iTunes dialog box or the Preferences dialog box.

■ Use a different type of recordable CD—preferably a better-quality kind.

■ If you're using CD-RW discs (rather than CD-R discs), don't use discs rated faster than 4×, because iTunes may not be able to write to them successfully.

"You Have Inserted a Blank DVD" Error Message

The error message "You have inserted a blank DVD but originally selected a CD format. Are you sure you wish to create a data DVD instead?" occurs when your Burning preferences specify an audio CD but you insert a blank DVD instead. When you see this error message, you'll usually want to click the Cancel button, eject the DVD, and insert a blank CD-R or CD-RW disc instead. If you decide that you do want to burn a data DVD instead of an audio CD, click the Data DVD button.

8

Remember that a data DVD has a huge capacity (typically more than 4.5GB) and that iTunes will store the songs on the DVD in their current format (for example, as AAC files or MP3 files) rather than writing them out to uncompressed audio files, so the DVD will probably end up with most of its capacity unused.

On the Mac, if you click the Cancel button, you may need to quit iTunes (press ⌘-Q) to force Mac OS X to eject the DVD.

iTunes Persistently Rejects a Blank Recordable Disc

If iTunes puzzles over a blank disc for a while and then ejects it without comment, chances are that the disc is either upside down or that it's not usable. Try the disc the other way up and see if iTunes accepts it. If not, try another disc.

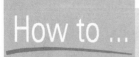

Get the Highest Possible Audio Quality on the CDs You Burn

AAC and MP3 deliver high-quality compressed audio, especially when you use a high bitrate and other appropriate settings. But both AAC and MP3 use lossy compression, losing some of the data required to deliver a perfect audio signal.

If you need to burn CDs with the highest possible audio quality, make sure that your source files are either Apple Lossless Encoding or uncompressed, high-quality audio. If you rip song files from CD, rip them to Apple Lossless Encoding files, AIFF files, or WAV files rather than to AAC or MP3. If you record audio from your own sources, record it to Apple Lossless Encoding, AIFF, or WAV instead of recording it to a compressed format.

Arrange the uncompressed audio files into a playlist and then burn the playlist to CD.

If the CD turns out satisfactorily (as it should), you'll probably want to delete the Apple Lossless Encoding files or uncompressed source files from your hard disk to reclaim the space they take up.

Troubleshoot
Battery Problems and
Replace Batteries

The section "Recharge Your iPod's Battery to Keep the Songs Coming" in Chapter 3 ran you through the basics of recharging your iPod's battery. But if you're reading this Special Project, you probably want to know how the battery works, what you can do to shoehorn in as much power as possible, and how you can squeeze out as much battery life as possible. And if your iPod's battery fails, or if its life grows too short, you may need to have it replaced—or replace it yourself. This section shows you how to:

- Maximize your iPod's battery life
- Extend your iPod's playing time
- Replace the battery in a first- or second-generation iPod
- Replace the battery in a third-generation iPod
- Replace the battery in an iPod mini
- Replace the battery in a fourth-generation iPod

Maximize Your iPod's Battery Life

Your iPod's battery is a lithium polymer that's rated for 500 or more charging cycles. (A *charging cycle* is a full discharge—running the battery all the way down until it has no charge left—followed by a full charge.) Lithium polymer batteries have no memory effect, so you don't need to discharge them fully before recharging them. That means you can recharge your iPod at any time that's convenient.

If you recharge your iPod's battery every other day, 500 charges should last you the best part of three years. If you recharge your iPod's battery less frequently than that, there's a good chance the battery will outlast the hard drive.

NOTE

Memory effect is a phenomenon that occurs with older battery technologies. If you don't fully discharge a battery based on such a technology, when you start charging the battery, it may figure that it *was* fully discharged at that point after all. In other words, the battery resets its zero-charge level to the level at which you started charging it. By doing so, it squanders that part of its capacity that's below the new zero-charge level, thus reducing the amount of power it can provide.

Understand How the Battery Charges

You plug in the iPod, and the battery charges—right? Not exactly. The iPod's lithium-ion battery splits the charging into two stages:

- **Fast Charge**   The battery charges at full speed until it is about 80 percent charged. The first 80 percent takes between one and three hours, depending on the model of iPod. Apple stresses this 80-percent figure in the iPod manuals and marketing literature—and indeed it's great to be able to charge your iPod most of the way very quickly.

- **Trickle Charge**   From the 80-percent level, the battery charges very gradually until it is fully charged. Depending on the model of iPod, the trickle-charge phase can take up to two hours.

Each iPod gives you an indication that the battery is charging:

- The regular iPod, iPod nano, and iPod mini display either the Charging screen or an icon indicating that charging is taking place. The Charging screen changes to "Charged" when the battery is fully charged.

- The iPod shuffle's status light shows amber while the battery is charging. When the battery is fully charged, the status light shows green.

NOTE

If the iPod shuffle's status light doesn't show amber or green when it's plugged into a USB port, the port probably doesn't have enough power to recharge the battery. Try another port.

Understand Battery Life and Battery Lifespan

The *battery life* is the length of time your iPod will run on a single battery charge. With a new, fully charged battery, the iPod mini and third-generation regular iPod should manage nearly eight hours; the iPod shuffle and early fourth-generation iPods should manage nearly 12 hours. The photo-capable fourth-generation iPod and the iPod nano can manage up to 15 hours of playback with a fresh battery. The fifth-generation iPod's battery life depends on how much video you play back, as both the color LCD and the intensive hard-disk access for playing video consume considerable amounts of power. Apple tends to use new battery types in each new generation of iPod, usually improving the battery life.

The *battery lifespan* is the amount of time that a rechargeable battery lasts before you have to replace it. An iPod's battery lifespan is typically two to three years, depending on how and how much you use the battery. Battery lifespan is measured as a minimum number of charge cycles that the battery is expected to manage without significant deterioration. A *charge cycle* means using the entire charge in the battery, either in a single session of battery use (charge the battery and then use it until it is fully discharged) or by using part of the charge, recharging the battery, using more of the charge, recharging again, and so on, until you have used the equivalent of a full charge.

Battery life declines by a small amount with each charge cycle. It also declines gradually over

> **NOTE**
>
> The battery indicator gives only a rough idea of how much power the battery contains. An 85-percent charge has four bars, just as a 100-percent charge does; and a single bar may indicate that your iPod has enough power left to play for a couple of hours or so little power that it will grind to a halt after a minute. Interpret the battery indicator pessimistically, and when in doubt, recharge.

the battery's lifespan, so even if you don't use the battery, the battery gradually loses life. (In fact, *not* using the battery at all is the fastest way to kill it off other than physically damaging it.) Near the end of the battery's lifespan, the decline accelerates from gradual to precipitous.

With an iPod, this means that battery life may decline by a few minutes each month for several years. Unless you regularly measure how long your iPod will play a set of songs encoded at the same bitrate, you're unlikely to notice this gradual decline until you've lost several hours of battery life. But you're certain to notice the steep decline at the end of the battery's lifespan.

> **NOTE**
>
> This Special Project doesn't show you how to replace the battery on a fifth-generation iPod or an iPod nano because, should the battery fail, you should be able to get it replaced under warranty until fall 2006 (or later; a year from purchase) or under AppleCare for a year beyond that.

Check Whether the Battery Is Working Correctly

The easiest way to check whether the battery is working correctly is to load a playlist of 128 Kbps AAC files, charge the battery until it refuses any more, disconnect the iPod, set it to repeat, and allow it to play until it stops. Note the start time, and wait for the music to stop.

Don't Let the Battery Discharge Fully

To get the most life out of your battery, don't let it discharge fully. However little you use your iPod, recharge it fully at least once every three weeks to prevent the battery from going flat. This means if you go on vacation for a month, you should take your iPod with you and recharge it during that time. (But you were going to take your iPod with you on your vacation anyway, weren't you?)

Make Your iPod Wake Up after It Has Been Baked or Frozen

Much like you, your iPod's battery prefers to live at room temperature rather than be baked or frozen. If you leave your iPod somewhere where it hits an extreme temperature, give it a chance to come back up or down to room temperature before you use it.

If your iPod is still comatose when it's back to room temperature, connect the power adapter and hold down the Menu button and the Play button together for a few seconds until the screen displays

the Apple logo. If this problem occurs when you don't have the power adapter, try performing this maneuver without the adapter, but be warned that it doesn't always work.

Reduce Demands on the Battery

To get the longest possible playback time from your iPod, reduce the demand on the battery as much as possible. Here are four ways to do so:

- Play your music by album or by playlist rather than hopping from one track to another. Remember that your iPod can cache ahead on an album or playlist to minimize the time the hard disk is spinning. But when you ask your iPod to produce another track it hasn't cached, it has to spin up the hard disk and access the song.

- Use AAC files or MP3 files on your iPod rather than Apple Lossless Encoding files, WAV files, or AIFF files. Because they're uncompressed and therefore much bigger than compressed files, WAVs and AIFFs prevent your iPod from using its cache effectively, so the hard disk has to work much harder. This chews through battery life. Apple Lossless Encoding files fall in the middle—they're compressed somewhat, but not much, so the hard disk has to work enough to cut down your battery life significantly.

- Minimize your use of the backlight.

- On a fifth-generation iPod, play less video.

Understand Apple's Battery-Replacement Policy

Batteries have proved such a weak chink in the iPod's armor that Apple has reversed its initial policy of not replacing iPod batteries at all. Apple's policy for most of the time since it started releasing iPods is that Apple will replace defective iPod batteries for free if the iPod is still under warranty, and for $59 (plus $6.95 shipping and handling) if the iPod is out of warranty—but only if neither you nor anyone else unqualified has messed with it. (If anyone *has* messed with your iPod, Apple has reserved the right to refuse to repair it.)

The $59 is kinda steep, especially because you get only a 90-day warranty on the materials and workmanship, but it's better than the $99 that it used to be till summer 2005, and it pales in comparison with the $249 that Apple charges for other repairs to the iPod. Many people figure that

if you're paying that much, you might as well get a brand-new iPod instead—and in case anyone asks for repairs without having that thought pop into their head, the Apple staff has been known to suggest it unprompted.

In June 2005, Apple agreed to a settlement in a class-action lawsuit brought by iPod users disappointed by poor battery performance. If you bought a first-, second-, or third-generation iPod before May 31, 2004, you may be able to get the iPod's battery replaced for free or get a credit toward a replacement iPod. See the Apple iPod Settlement website (www.appleipodsettlement.com) for details.

If you choose not to have Apple replace your iPod's battery, you can either do the replacement yourself (as discussed in the next section) or use one of the many companies that offer a replacement service (again, see the next section).

Replace the Battery Yourself

If your iPod is out of warranty, you don't have the AppleCare Protection Plan for iPod for it, and you're sure that you won't want to send the iPod to Apple for a battery replacement, you can find replacement batteries for less money elsewhere. (Make sure your iPod is out of warranty, because opening it voids the warranty.)

CAUTION

Don't even order a replacement battery, let alone start opening your iPod, before verifying that your iPod is out of warranty, out of AppleCare, and not covered by the iPod battery settlement.

Get a Replacement Battery

Now that many millions of iPods have been sold, and that the batteries in millions of them have lost some or all of their life, replacement batteries are big business. The following list mentions some of the major sources of batteries at this writing.

Consult your favorite search engine for "iPod replacement battery" to find other sources.

Here are some of your options at this writing:

- Laptops for Less (www.ipodbattery.com) offers iPod batteries from $29 upward, together with a delicate screwdriver and instructions for fitting the batteries yourself.

- PDASmart (www.pdasmart.com/ ipodpartscenter.htm) offers a DIY battery kit for $59.00 and mail-in service for $68.00.

- ipodminibattery (www.ipodminibattery .com) offers batteries for second-generation and third-generation iPods and the iPod mini from $29 upward.

- OtherWorldComputing.com (http://eshop .macsales.com) sells not only batteries for all generations of regular iPods but also high-capacity replacement batteries for first-generation and second-generation iPods that offer substantially better battery life than the original ones—up to 20 hours of continuous play.

NOTE

When ordering a replacement battery, get the right type for your iPod. The first- and second-generation iPods use different batteries from the third-generation iPods, and the fourth-generation iPod uses another battery yet. The iPod mini uses a smaller battery than the regular iPods, the iPod nano uses an even smaller battery, and the iPod shuffle uses a minute battery.

NOTE

A Word of Encouragement: No matter which model you have, starting to open the iPod's case is the worst part of the procedure. It may take you several tries and several minutes to get the screwdriver in. Be patient and persevere. Once you've accomplished this, things get much easier…apart from a couple of steps that you'll meet in due course, that is.

As the iPod market matures and continues to expand, expect to see more companies offering replacement batteries and installation. At this writing, no replacement battery is available for the iPod nano—which is probably just as well, given that all iPod nanos will be in warranty for almost another year.

Replace the Battery in a First- or Second-Generation iPod

To replace the battery in a first- or second-generation iPod, you'll need a suitable battery and a flat-head screwdriver with a thin but strong blade.

To replace the battery, follow these steps:

1. Turn the iPod off and then move the Hold switch to the On position.

2. Insert your flat-head screwdriver between the clear plastic faceplate and the chrome case at the top corner by the FireWire port at a steep downward angle. Lever the faceplate away from the chrome case. There'll be an uncomfortable-feeling crunch as the first of the retaining clips comes loose.

3. Keep the screwdriver wedged between the case and the faceplate, and work it along the long side of the iPod, undoing each clip in turn.

4. The next step is different for a first-generation iPod than for a second-generation iPod:

   ■ On a first-generation iPod, once you've unclipped all the way from the top to the bottom of the iPod, lift the faceplate and the iPod's insides away from the case.

   ■ On a second-generation iPod, continue unclipping around the bottom and all the way up the other side of the iPod. Then carefully lift the iPod's faceplate and insides from the bottom end. Once you've got the bottom end clear of the case, pull the faceplate and insides downward so that the FireWire port and the headphone and remote connectors clear the metal case. Then lift the faceplate and the insides out.

5. Put the faceplate and the insides down on a flat surface, then:

■ On a first-generation iPod, use the screwdriver to lever the battery away from the insides of the iPod. Work slowly and carefully to unstick each patch of glue in turn. When you finish unsticking the glue, the battery is connected to the iPod only by its power cable.

■ On a second-generation iPod, undo the two top tapes and then unstick the lower tape from the battery. The battery is then connected to the iPod only by its power cable.

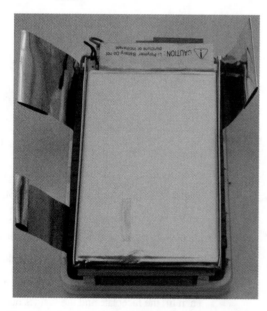

6. Note how the battery is connected. Disconnect the power cable from the iPod by pulling it carefully. Then plug in the new battery in the same orientation.

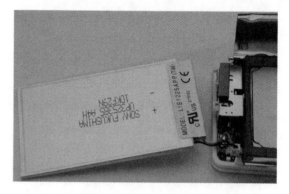

7. Align the new battery correctly and then:

■ On a first-generation iPod, press the battery gently into place to stick it to the glue spots.

■ On a second-generation iPod, stick the lower tape to the battery and fold the other two tapes across the battery.

8. Put the iPod's insides back into the case at an angle and then snap the clips into place.

9. Connect your iPod to a power source and let the battery charge until it is full—about three hours.

Replace the Battery in a Third-Generation iPod

To replace the battery in a third-generation iPod, you'll need a suitable battery and the following:

■ A flat-head screwdriver with a very thin blade

- Either a flat-head screwdriver with a regular small blade or a credit card or similar plastic card that you don't care about

- A ruler

To replace the battery, follow these steps:

1. Turn the iPod off and then move the Hold switch to the On position.

2. Measure 2¼ inches from the top-left corner of the iPod down the left side and then work in the thin-bladed screwdriver there at a steep downward angle.

3. Insert the corner of the credit card next to the screwdriver blade and then remove the screwdriver blade.

4. Work the corner of the credit card up and down the side seam of the iPod until the side pops loose. (It may feel as though the side will never pop loose, but persevere until it does.)

5. Use the credit card to unclip the rest of the clips around the iPod and then lift the faceplate and insides out carefully. The insides are still attached to the case by a ribbon cable.

6. You need to remove the hard drive, which is sandwiched between two layers of blue rubber. Pick up the two layers of blue rubber, with the hard drive between them, and lift the whole lot toward the bottom end of the iPod. You'll see a copper colored foil tab about the size of the top joint of your thumb. Underneath this tab is the connector that attaches the hard drive to the motherboard. Peel the tab up carefully until the connector pops open, leaving the hard

drive free. Put the hard drive sandwich aside for the moment.

7. Lift the battery out of its recess using the screwdriver. You may need to gently unstick the black tape from the top edge of the battery. The battery cable is usually wound around the top of the circuit board. If so, push it around the corner to free it and then disconnect the battery connector.

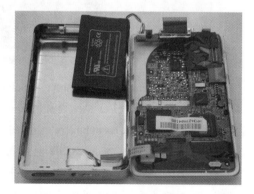

8. Connect the new battery to the battery connector. Wrap the battery's cable around the top corner of the motherboard, pushing it into place with the screwdriver. Then put the battery into its recess.

9. Pick up the hard drive in its sandwich of blue rubber layers and position it carefully so that the copper-colored foil tab to which the drive's connector is attached is exactly over the corresponding connector on the motherboard. Push down gently until you feel the two connectors lock together. Pull back very gently to verify that they are connected properly.

10. Settle the hard drive sandwich in its correct position.

11. Slide one side of the front plate and insides back into the case and then gently clip the other side together. If there's any resistance,

verify that you've got the insides straight. You shouldn't need to use much pressure to do the clips up once everything is in the right place.

12. Connect your iPod to a power source and charge the battery until it is full—about three hours.

Replace the Battery in an iPod mini

To replace the battery in an iPod mini, you'll need a suitable battery and the following:

- A flat-head screwdriver with a really thin blade

- A Phillips screwdriver with a very small head

To replace the battery in an iPod mini, follow these steps:

1. Turn the iPod mini off and then move the Hold switch to the On position.

2. Insert the tip of the flat-head screwdriver carefully between the white plastic cover at the top of the iPod mini and the rim of the

CAUTION

Because of the way the iPod mini is tightly packed inside its metal sleeve, it's more of a challenge to open than the regular iPods. Make sure you have plenty of time and patience before you tackle your iPod mini.

case, starting about halfway along one of the long sides. Working around the iPod mini, pry the cover off. The cover is glued to the case, so removing it will probably feel as though you're doing some damage.

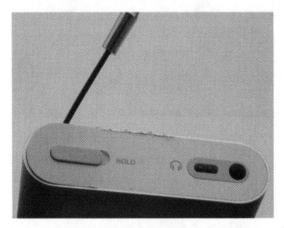

3. Once you've removed the white plastic cover, you'll see two cross-head screws, one at each side of the top of the iPod. Unscrew these screws with the Phillips screwdriver, remove them, and put them somewhere safe.

4. Switch back to the flat-head screwdriver. Insert its tip carefully between the white plastic cover at the bottom of the iPod mini and the rim of the case, again starting about halfway along one of the long sides. Work around the iPod mini again, gradually prying

the cover off. This cover is attached to the iPod with some tiny patches of glue but also with plastic clips that you must unclip before you can remove it.

5. Underneath the white plastic cover at the bottom of the iPod mini lies a metal clip that covers the connector between the motherboard and the bottom of the iPod. You need to remove the clip to get at the connector. The clip has a spring-loaded arm in each corner that nestles in a groove on the inside of the iPod mini. Insert the flat-head screwdriver behind the first arm and lever it inward and toward you until it pops loose. Repeat the process for the arm at the opposite end of the same side of the iPod—for example, if you first opened the arm at the left side of the front of the iPod mini, open the arm at the right side of the front next. With those two loose, tilt the clip toward you so that it pops out of the clips on the other side too. Remove the clip and put it somewhere safe.

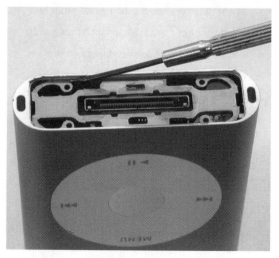

6. Put the tip of the flat-head screwdriver under the connector and wiggle it gently from its socket. You'll probably need to work from all three open sides to get it out.

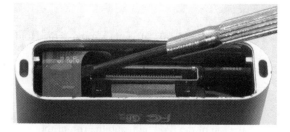

7. The insides of the iPod mini are now free. Push gently on the Dock Connector at the bottom of the iPod mini with your finger so that the insides start sliding out of the top of the case. Then grasp the metal plate at the top and pull the insides the rest of the way out of the case.

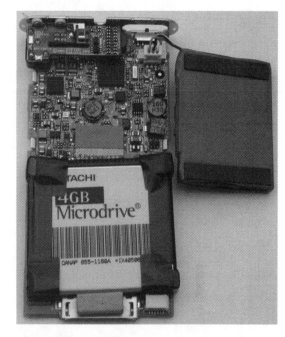

8. Turn the iPod mini over so that you can see its back.

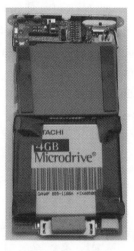

9. Lift the battery off its place on the motherboard. If you need to use a screwdriver to release the battery from the sticky pad that secures it, work very gently and be careful not to touch the motherboard with the screwdriver.

10. Work the battery's white plastic connector from its socket.

11. Unwrap your new battery and connect it to the white plastic connector, then place the battery in its position on the motherboard and press down lightly to secure it to the sticky pad.

12. Slide the insides of the iPod mini carefully back into its case. Make sure the motherboard is resting on the ledges inside the case. If the motherboard gets stuck as you're sliding it back in, double-check its alignment. When it's at the right angle, you'll be able to slide it in all the way. Whatever you do, don't force it.

13. Connect the motherboard connector at the bottom of the iPod by pushing it in gently with your finger.

14. Replace the metal clip at the bottom of the iPod, making sure that the residual glue is toward you. With the clip at an angle, settle the two arms on one side and then use a flat-head screwdriver to lever each of the clips on the opposite side into place.

15. Replace the screws at the top of the iPod.

16. Clip and stick the white plastic cover back into place on the bottom of the iPod. You need to get this cover the right way around: There are no clips on the corner next to the iPod's Click wheel connector.

17. Stick the white plastic cover back into place on the top of the iPod mini. Verify that the Hold switch on the plastic cover is in the right position for the Hold switch on the inside of the iPod and then press this side into place first, followed by the side with the headphone and remote connectors.

18. Connect your iPod mini to a power source and let the battery charge until it is full—about four hours.

Replace the Battery in a Fourth-Generation iPod

To replace the battery in a fourth-generation iPod, you'll need a suitable battery and the following:

- A flat-head screwdriver with a very thin blade

- A torx wrench

To replace the battery, follow these steps:

1. Turn the iPod off and then move the Hold switch to the On position.

2. Work the thin-bladed flat screwdriver into the seam at the right side of the iPod, just alongside the Fast-Forward/Next button, at a downward angle. Lever gently to pop the case clips open.

3. Work the screwdriver along the side of the case until you have opened all of the clips.

4. Hold the iPod face downward, and with your fingers gently wiggle the chrome case until it comes off the faceplate and insides of the iPod. The case and the insides are still connected via a narrow brown cable at the top of the iPod. Open the case carefully, making sure that you don't damage this brown cable.

5. Disconnect the power connector from its socket.

6. Use the torx wrench to undo the two screws at the Dock Connector end of the iPod that secure the motherboard to the case. (The screws are hard to see in the photo. The screws are just behind the two white plastic clips toward the bottom of the picture.) Once you've taken the screws out, move the power cable around the corner of the motherboard.

7. Pick up the hard drive, sandwiched in its layers of protective rubber, in one hand so that you can access the battery. (If you've got a helper, have them pick up the hard drive and hold it.)

8. Using your fingertips, unstick the battery from the glue spots that secure it, starting at the corner of the battery and working around.

9. Remove the battery, replace it with the new battery, and press down gently to secure the new battery to the glue spots. Route the power cable around the corner of the motherboard and then connect it to the power connector.

10. Replace the two screws that secure the motherboard to the case.

11. Put the drive back down in its correct position.

12. Slide one side of the front plate and insides back into the case and then gently clip the other side together. If there's any resistance, verify that you've got the insides straight. You shouldn't need to use much pressure to do the clips up once everything is in the right place.

13. Connect your iPod to a power source and charge the battery until it is full—about three hours.

Chapter 9

Enjoy Music with iTunes and Manage Your Music Library

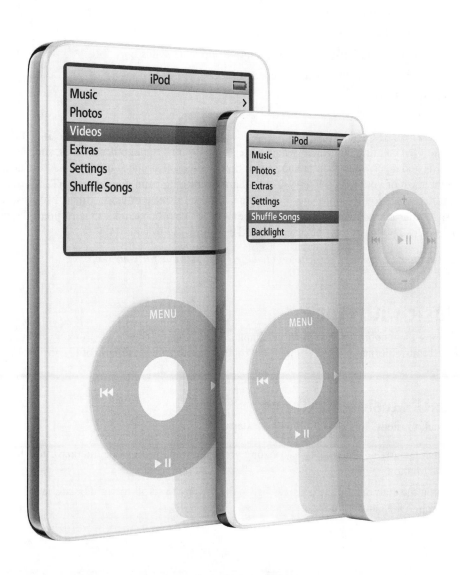

How to...

- ■ Enjoy music with iTunes
- ■ Make iTunes run automatically when you log on
- ■ Improve the sound that iTunes produces
- ■ Change the iTunes interface to suit your preferences
- ■ Enjoy visualizations as you listen to music
- ■ Manage your music library
- ■ Create regular playlists and Smart Playlists
- ■ Consolidate your music library and remove duplicate songs
- ■ Share music with other iTunes users and access their shared music
- ■ Enjoy podcasts

In Chapter 2, you learned how to rip CDs and create playlists; in Chapter 6, you learned the ins and outs of creating high-quality audio files from both CDs and other sources, such as your records and tapes. This chapter shows you how to enjoy that music using iTunes and how to make the most of your music library. You'll learn everything from how to make iTunes run automatically when you log onto your PC or Mac, to how to create effective Smart Playlists, to how to share music effectively with the other members of your household. Finally, you'll learn how to download podcasts to your computer and transfer them to your iPod.

 Chapter 12 discusses how to create video files suitable for your iPod.

Enjoy Music with iTunes

By following the techniques described in Chapter 2 and Chapter 6, you've probably created a fair-sized music library. Now it's time to enjoy that music, using as many of iTunes' features as you need.

Play Back Music with iTunes

To play back music with iTunes, follow these steps:

1. Navigate to the album, playlist, or song you want to play, select it, and then click the Play button.

2. Drag the diamond on the progress bar in the display to scroll forward or backward through the current track.

3. Use the Shuffle button to shuffle the order of the tracks in the current album or playlist. (To change whether iTunes shuffles by song or by album, select the Song option button or the Album option button on the Advanced sheet of the Preferences dialog box.)

To reshuffle the current playlist on the Mac, OPTION-click the Shuffle button.

4. Use the Repeat button to repeat the current song or the current playlist.

5. If you've scrolled the Song list so that the current song isn't visible, press CTRL-L (Windows) or ⌘-L (Mac) to quickly scroll back to where the current song is.

6. To open a Windows Explorer window (Windows) or a Finder window (Mac) to the folder that contains the selected song file, press CTRL-R (Windows) or ⌘-R (Mac).

7. To toggle the display of the artwork, click the Show Or Hide Song Artwork button, press CTRL-G (Windows) or ⌘-G (Mac), or choose Edit | Show Artwork or Edit | Hide Artwork.

8. On the Mac, you can also control iTunes by right-clicking or CTRL-clicking its Dock icon and making the appropriate choice from the shortcut menu, as shown here. In Windows, if you've chosen to display an iTunes icon in the notification area, you can control iTunes from there.

9

You can change the information shown in the display window by clicking the items in it. Click the top line to move among the song title, the artist's name, and the album title. Click the Play icon at the left of the display window to toggle between the track information and the equalization graph. Click the time readout to move among Elapsed Time, Remaining Time, and Total Time.

 **Run iTunes Frequently—or Always on Startup**

Running iTunes from the iTunes icon on your desktop, from the Windows Start menu, or from the Dock works well enough for occasional use, but if you intend to run iTunes frequently, or always, you can do better.

In Windows, you can pin iTunes to the fixed part of the Start menu so that it always appears. To do so, navigate to the iTunes icon on the Start menu in Windows XP, right-click it, and choose Pin To Start Menu from the shortcut menu. If you keep the Quick Launch toolbar displayed, consider dragging an iTunes icon to the Quick Launch toolbar so that it's present there too.

To run iTunes even more quickly, configure a CTRL-ALT keyboard shortcut for it so that you can start iTunes by pressing the keyboard shortcut either from the desktop or from within an application. Here's how to create the shortcut:

1. Right-click the iTunes icon on your desktop or on your Start menu and choose Properties from the shortcut menu to display the iTunes Properties dialog box.

2. On the Shortcut tab, click in the Shortcut Key text box and then press the letter you want to use in the CTRL-ALT shortcut. For example, press I to create the shortcut CTRL-ALT-I.

3. Click the OK button to close the Properties dialog box.

But if you use iTunes whenever you're using your computer, the best solution is to make iTunes start automatically whenever you log on. To do so, follow these steps in Windows:

1. Right-click the iTunes icon on your desktop or on your Start menu and choose Copy from the shortcut menu to copy the shortcut to the Clipboard.

2. Choose Start | Run to display the Run dialog box.

3. Type **%userprofile%\Start Menu\Programs\Startup**. (%userprofile% is a system variable that returns the path to your user profile folder—the folder that contains your My Documents folder and the folders in which your settings are stored.) As you type the path, Windows will try to help you complete it. Press DOWN ARROW to accept a suggestion and then press ENTER to enter it in the text box.

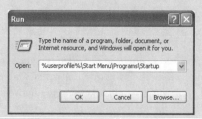

4. Click the OK button. Windows opens the Startup folder, which contains shortcuts to applications that run when you log onto Windows. (This folder may be empty when you open it.)

5. Right-click in the Startup folder and choose Paste from the shortcut menu to paste a copy of the iTunes shortcut into the folder.

6. Click the Close button (the X button), press ALT-F4, or choose File | Close to close the Windows Explorer window.

To make iTunes start automatically on the Mac when you log into Tiger, simply right-click the iTunes icon on the Dock and then select the Open At Login item from the shortcut menu. In earlier versions of Mac OS X, or in Tiger, follow these steps:

1. Choose Apple | System Preferences to open the System Preferences window.

2. Click the Accounts item to display the Accounts sheet.

3. Select your account in the left-hand list box.

4. Click the Login Items tab (in Tiger) or the Startup Items tab (in earlier versions of Mac OS X).

5. Click the + button beneath the These Items Will Open Automatically When You Log In list box.

6. In the resulting dialog box, select iTunes and then click the Add button.

7. Choose System Preferences | Quit System Preferences to close System Preferences.

Join Tracks Together Without Gaps

iTunes' default settings are to create a separate file (AAC, MP3, Apple Lossless Encoding, AIFF, or WAV, depending on your preferences) from each song on CDs you rip. For most CDs, this works well. But sometimes you'll want to rip multiple tracks from a CD into a single file so they play back without a break. For example, some CDs are produced so one song runs into the next, either to execute the artist's concept or to give more conviction to a live album.

(continued)

To rip two or more tracks from a CD into a single file, select the tracks and then choose Advanced | Join CD Tracks. iTunes brackets the tracks, as shown here. These tracks then rip to a single file.

If you made a mistake with the tracks you joined, select one or more of the joined tracks and then choose Advanced | Unjoin CD Tracks to separate the tracks again.

Listen to Audible.com Spoken-Word Files on Your iPod

Even if your iPod is laden nearly to the gunwales with songs, you may be able to cram on a good amount of spoken-word audio. This is because spoken-word audio can sound fine at much lower bitrates than music.

Audible.com provides a wide variety of content—such as audio books, magazines, and plays—in a selection of different subscription types and accounts. To get started, go to the Audible.com website (www.audible.com) and set up an account.

Audible is an interesting service, but read the terms and conditions carefully for the account type you choose. Otherwise, Audible policies such as canceling any unused book credits at the end of each subscription month may give you an unpleasant surprise.

After setting up an account, you can download files to up to three different computers for that account. The first time you download Audible.com content to a particular computer, you need to enter your Audible.com account information on it, as shown here. After that, you can simply drag an Audible file to the iTunes window to add it to your music library.

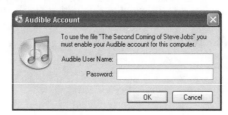

When playing an Audible file, you can press CTRL-SHIFT-RIGHT ARROW (Windows) or ⌘-SHIFT-RIGHT ARROW (Mac) to go to the next chapter. Press CTRL-SHIFT-LEFT ARROW (Windows) or ⌘-SHIFT-LEFT ARROW (Mac) to go to the previous chapter.

If you need to transfer one of the three manifestations of your Audible.com account from one Mac to another, follow these steps:

1.   Establish an Internet connection if you need to do so manually.

2.   In iTunes, choose Advanced | Deauthorize Computer to display the Deauthorize Computer dialog box.

3.   Select the Deauthorize Computer For Audible Account option button.

4.   Click the OK button to display the Remove Audible Account dialog box.

5.   Type your Audible user account and password.

6.   Click the OK button.

Improve the Sound of Music

To make music sound as good as possible, you should apply suitable equalizations using iTunes' graphical equalizer. You can also crossfade one song into another, add automatic sound enhancement, and skip the beginning or end of a song.

Use the Graphical Equalizer to Make the Music Sound Great

iTunes includes a graphical equalizer that you can use to change the sound of the music (or other audio) you're playing. You can apply an equalization directly to the playlist you're currently playing, much as you would apply an equalization manually to a physical amplifier or receiver.

You can also apply a specific equalization to each song in your iTunes music library. Once you've done this, iTunes always uses that equalization when playing that song, no matter which equalization is currently applied to iTunes itself.

After playing a song that has an equalization specified, iTunes switches back to the previous equalization for the next song that doesn't have an equalization specified.

Apply an Equalization to What's Currently Playing

To apply an equalization to the songs you're currently playing, display the Equalizer window (see Figure 9-1) by clicking the Equalizer button at the lower-right corner of the iTunes window. Select the equalization from the drop-down list. If you're playing music, you'll hear the effect of the new equalization in a second or two.

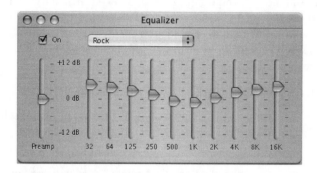

FIGURE 9-1   iTunes's Equalizer window offers preset equalizations, but you can also create custom equalizations.

Specify an Equalization for an Individual Song

To specify the equalization iTunes should use for a particular song, follow these steps:

1. Select the song in your music library or in a playlist.

> **NOTE** *It doesn't matter whether you apply the equalization to the song in the music library or in a playlist, because applying the equalization even in a playlist affects the song in the music library. So if you can access a song more easily through a playlist than through your music library, start from the playlist.*

2. Press CTRL-I (Windows) or ⌘-I (Mac), or choose Get Info from the File menu or the shortcut menu, to display the Song Information dialog box.

3. Click the Options tab to display its contents. Figure 9-2 shows the Options tab for iTunes for Windows. The Options tab for iTunes for the Mac has the same controls.

4. Select the equalization for the song in the Equalizer Preset drop-down list.

5. Choose other options as necessary (for example, set iTunes to remember the song's playback position or to skip the song when shuffling) and then click the OK button to close the Song Information dialog box. Alternatively, click the Prev Song button or the Next Song button to display the information for the previous song or next song in the Song Information dialog box.

> **NOTE** *If the equalization you apply to a song is one of the equalizations built into your iPod, the iPod also automatically uses the equalization for playing back the track. But if the equalization is a custom one your iPod doesn't have, your iPod can't use it. Your iPod doesn't pick up custom equalizations you create in iTunes. The iPod shuffle doesn't use equalizations.*

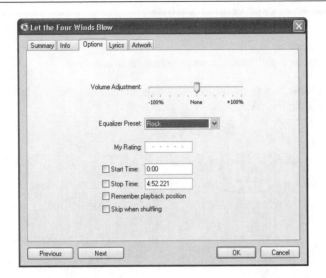

FIGURE 9-2   You can specify the equalization for a particular song on the Options tab of the Song Information dialog box.

9

Create a Custom Equalization That Sounds Good to You

The preset equalizations in iTunes span a wide range of musical types—but even if there's one named after the type of music you're currently listening to, you may not like the effects it produces. When this happens, try all the other equalizations, however unsuitable their names may make them seem, to see if any of them just happens to sound great with this type of music. (For example, some people swear the Classical equalization is perfect for many Grateful Dead tracks.) If none of them suits you, create a custom equalization that delivers the goods.

To create a new custom equalization, follow these steps:

1. Drag the frequency sliders to the appropriate positions for the sound you want the equalization to deliver. When you change the first slider in the current preset, the drop-down list displays Manual.

2. If appropriate, drag the Preamp slider to a different level. For example, you might want to boost the preamp level on all the songs to which you apply a certain equalization.

3. Choose Make Preset from the drop-down list to display the Make Preset dialog box.

4. Type the name for the equalization and then click the OK button.

You can then apply your equalization from the drop-down list as you would any other preset equalization.

Delete and Rename Preset Equalizations

If you don't like a preset equalization, you can delete it. If you find an equalization's name unsuitable, you can rename it.

To delete or rename an equalization, start by following these steps:

1. Select the Edit List item from the drop-down list in the Equalizer window. iTunes displays the Edit Presets dialog box:

2. Select the preset equalization you want to affect.

To rename the equalization, follow these steps:

1. Click the Rename button to display the Rename dialog box.

2. Type the new name in the New Preset Name text box.

3. Click the OK button. iTunes displays a dialog box like this, asking whether you want to change all songs currently set to use this equalization under its current name to use the equalization under the new name you've just specified:

4. Click the Yes button or the No button as appropriate.

To delete a preset equalization, click the Delete button, click the Yes button in the confirmation dialog box, and specify whether to remove the equalization from all songs that are set to use it. Select the Do Not Warn Me Again check box first if you want to turn off confirmation for deleting presets.

Choose Crossfading, Sound Enhancer, and Smart Shuffle Settings

The Playback tab of the iTunes dialog box or the Preferences dialog box offers options for crossfading playback, changing the Sound Enhancer, and configuring how iTunes shuffles songs. Figure 9-3 shows the Playback tab of iTunes for the Mac. The Playback tab for iTunes for Windows has the same controls.

- **Crossfade Playback** Makes iTunes fade in the start of the next track as the current track is about to end. This option lets you eliminate gaps between songs the way most DJs do. Drag the slider to increase or decrease the length of time that's crossfaded. This check box is selected by default. Turn off crossfading if you don't like it.

- **Sound Enhancer** Applies iTunes' sound enhancement to the music being played back. Experiment with different settings on the Low-High scale by dragging the slider to see which setting sounds best to you—or turn off sound enhancement if you don't like it (this check box is selected by default). Sound enhancement can make treble sounds appear brighter and can add to the effect of stereo separation, but the results don't suit everybody. You may prefer to adjust the sound manually by using the graphical equalizer, as described in the next section.

9

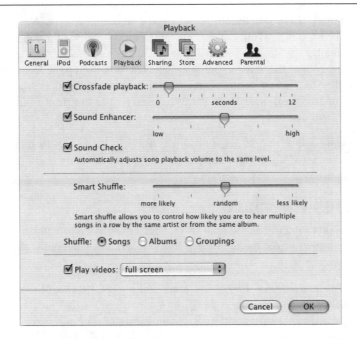

FIGURE 9-3   Choose crossfading, Sound Enhancer, and Sound Check options on the Playback sheet of the Preferences dialog box.

- ■ **Sound Check**   Controls whether iTunes uses its Sound Check feature to normalize the volume of different songs so that you don't experience widely varying audio levels in different songs. Sound Check is turned on by default and is useful for many music libraries. If you don't like Sound Check, or if you find that the extra processing power it requires makes your computer struggle to play music back satisfactorily, turn it off.

- ■ **Smart Shuffle**   Specifies, depending on the position of the slider on its axis, whether iTunes shuffles songs randomly or makes it either more likely or less likely that you will hear songs by the same artist or from the same album in a row. You can also select the Songs option button, the Albums option button, or the Groupings option button to specify the unit of shuffling. The default setting is Songs.

- ■ **Play Videos**   Enables you watch videos when the Play Videos check box is selected. You can then choose the appropriate option in the drop-down list: In The Main Window, In A Separate Window, or Full Screen.

Skip the Boring Intro or Outro on a Song

If you disagree with the producer of a song about when the song should begin or end, use the Start Time and Stop Time controls on the Options tab of the Song Information dialog box (shown in Figure 9-2, earlier in this chapter) to specify how much of the track to lop off. This trimming works both in iTunes and on your iPod.

To trim the intro, enter in the Start Time text box the point at which you want the song to start. For example, enter **1:15** to skip the first minute and a quarter of a song. When you start typing in the Start Time text box, iTunes selects the Start Time check box for you, so you don't need to select it manually.

Similarly, you can change the value in the Stop Time text box to stop the song playing before its end. By default, the Stop Time text box contains a time showing when the song ends, down to thousandths of a second—for example, 4:56:769. When you reduce this time, iTunes selects the Stop Time check box automatically.

When skipping an intro or outro isn't enough, you can edit a song file down to only that part you want. See Chapter 6 for details.

Tweak the iTunes Interface

You can change the iTunes interface in several ways, which include resizing the window, turning off the display of the arrows linked to the iTunes Music Store, and changing the columns of data displayed.

For an extreme makeover of iTunes—and other applications—on the Mac, try ShapeShifter (www.unsanity.com/haxies/shapeshifter), which allows you to apply either existing themes that other people have created or design custom themes of your own.

This section also shows you how to control iTunes by using keyboard shortcuts, how to use iTunes' visualizations, and how to control iTunes with the iTunes widget on Mac OS X Tiger.

Resize the iTunes Window to the Size You Need

iTunes offers various window sizes to suit the amount of space you're prepared to dedicate to it:

■ In Windows, iTunes has four sizes: normal, maximized, small, and minute. The small and minute sizes are considered mini mode.

■ On the Mac, iTunes has three sizes: normal, small, and minute. The small and minute sizes are considered mini mode. Mac OS X Tiger also offers an iTunes widget that you can use to control iTunes from the Dashboard instead of using the main iTunes window.

By default, iTunes opens in a normal window that you can resize by dragging any of its borders or corners. In Windows, you can click the Maximize button to maximize the window so that it occupies all the space on your screen (apart from the taskbar, if you have it displayed), and you can click the Restore Down button to restore the maximized window to its previous size. You can also toggle the iTunes window between its maximized and normal states by double-clicking the title bar.

Once you've set the music playing, you'll often want to reduce the iTunes window to its essentials so that you can get on with your work (or play). To do so, in Windows, press CTRL-M or choose Advanced | Switch To Mini Player to display iTunes in mini mode.

On the Mac, there's no way of maximizing the iTunes window. You can click the Zoom button (the green button on the title bar) to toggle between normal mode and mini mode. You can minimize the iTunes window by double-clicking the title bar, by clicking the Minimize button, or by pressing ⌘-M.

From here, you can drag the sizing handle in the lower-right corner to shrink iTunes down even further to its minute size. This can be handy when you're pushed for space, but it isn't very informative.

Here's how to restore iTunes to its normal size from mini mode:

■ In Windows, press CTRL-M or click the Restore button.

■ On the Mac, click the Zoom button or choose Window | Zoom.

9

In Windows, you can also run iTunes as a desktop toolbar by clicking the Minimize button. If the toolbar doesn't appear, right-click the notification area at the end of the taskbar and choose Toolbars | iTunes.

To restore iTunes to its previous size, click the Restore button at the upper-right corner of the iTunes toolbar.

Remove the Music Store Link Arrows

Unless you're desperate to buy music from the iTunes Music Store at a moment's notice, you'll probably find the arrows that iTunes displays in the Song Name, Artist, Album, and Composer columns an irritant rather than a boon. You can click an arrow to search the iTunes Music Store for related songs.

To remove the arrows, follow these steps:

1. Display the iTunes dialog box or the Preferences dialog box:

   - In Windows, choose Edit | Preferences or press CTRL-COMMA or CTRL-Y to display the iTunes dialog box.

   - On the Mac, choose iTunes | Preferences or press either ⌘-COMMA or ⌘-Y to display the Preferences dialog box.

2. Click the General tab if it's not already displayed.

3. Clear the Show Links To Music Store check box.

4. Click the OK button to close the dialog box.

Change the Columns Displayed to Show the Information You Need

By default, iTunes displays the following columns: Song Name, Time, Artist, Album, Genre, My Rating, Play Count, and Last Played. You can change the columns displayed for the current item (for example, your music library or a playlist) by using either of two techniques.

To change the display of multiple columns in the same operation, press CTRL-J (Windows) or ⌘-J (Mac), or choose Edit | View Options, to display the View Options dialog box. Figure 9-4 shows the View Options dialog box for Windows; the View Options dialog box for the Mac has the same controls. The icon and label in the upper-left corner of the dialog box indicate which item's view you're customizing—for example, Library or Music Store. Select the check boxes for the columns you want to display and then click the OK button to close the dialog box and apply your choices.

To change the display of a single column in the current item, right-click (or CTRL-click on the Mac) the heading of one of the columns currently displayed. iTunes displays a menu of the available columns, showing a check mark next to those currently displayed. Select an unchecked column to display it. Select a checked column to remove it from the display.

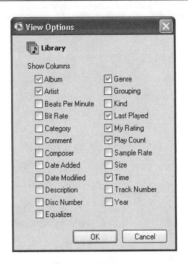

FIGURE 9-4 Use the View Options dialog box to specify which columns iTunes displays for the current item.

9

NOTE *The Play Count item stores the number of times you've played the song in iTunes. iTunes uses this information to determine your favorite tracks—for example, to decide which tracks Smart Playlist should add to a playlist. You can also use this information yourself if you so choose.*

From the context menu, you can also select the Auto Size Column command to automatically resize the column whose heading you clicked so the column's width best fits its contents. Select the Auto Size All Columns command to automatically resize all columns like this.

TIP *You can change the column width by dragging the border of a column heading to the left or right.*

Control iTunes via Keyboard Shortcuts

Controlling iTunes via the mouse is easy enough, but you can also control most of iTunes' features by using the keyboard. This can be useful both when your mouse is temporarily out of reach and when you've reduced the iTunes window to its small size or minute size, and thus hidden some of the controls.

Table 9-1 lists the keyboard shortcuts you can use to control iTunes. Most of these shortcuts work in any of iTunes' four display modes in Windows (normal, maximized, small, and mini) and iTunes' three display modes on the Mac (maximized, small, and mini), but the table notes the shortcuts that work only in some modes.

Action	Windows Keystroke	Mac Keystroke
Play or pause the selected song.	SPACEBAR	SPACEBAR
Increase the volume (mini player only).	UP ARROW	UP ARROW
Decrease the volume (mini player only).	DOWN ARROW	DOWN ARROW
Toggle the display of the iTunes main window.	n/a	⌘-1
Toggle the display of the Equalizer window.	n/a	⌘-2
Skip to the next song.	RIGHT ARROW CTRL–RIGHT ARROW	RIGHT ARROW ⌘–RIGHT ARROW
Skip to the previous song.	LEFT ARROW CTRL–LEFT ARROW	LEFT ARROW ⌘–LEFT ARROW
Rewind the song.	CTRL-ALT–LEFT ARROW	⌘-OPTION–LEFT ARROW
Fast forward the song.	CTRL-ALT–RIGHT ARROW	⌘-OPTION–RIGHT ARROW
Skip to the next album in the list.	ALT–RIGHT ARROW	OPTION–RIGHT ARROW
Skip to the previous album in the list.	ALT–LEFT ARROW	OPTION–LEFT ARROW
Turn the iTunes volume to maximum (mini player only).	SHIFT–UP ARROW	SHIFT–UP ARROW
Turn the iTunes volume down to minimum (mini player only).	SHIFT–DOWN ARROW	SHIFT–DOWN ARROW
Toggle muting.	CTRL-ALT–UP ARROW CTRL-ALT–DOWN ARROW	⌘-OPTION–UP ARROW ⌘-OPTION–DOWN ARROW
Windows: Toggle between the mini player and full player. Mac: Minimize iTunes.	CTRL-M	⌘-M
Display the Open Stream dialog box.	CTRL-U	⌘-U
Toggle the Visualizer on and off.	CTRL-T	⌘-T
Toggle full-screen mode on the Visualizer.	CTRL-F	⌘-F

TABLE 9-1   Keyboard Shortcuts for iTunes

Accompany Your Music with Visualizations

Like many music applications, iTunes can produce stunning visualizations to accompany your music. You can display visualizations at any of three sizes within the iTunes window (which can provide visual distraction while you work or play) or display them full-screen to make your PC or Mac the life of the party.

Here's how to use visualizations:

■ Set the size to use by choosing Visualizer | Small, Visualizer | Medium, or Visualizer | Large. If you want the visualizations to start in full-screen mode, choose Visualizer | Full Screen.

■ To start a visualization of the size you specified, press CTRL-T (Windows) or ⌘-T (Mac) or choose Visualizer | Turn Visualizer On.

■ To turn a windowed visualization off, press CTRL-T (Windows) or ⌘-T (Mac) or choose Visualizer | Turn Visualizer Off.

■ To launch full-screen visualizations, press CTRL-F (Windows) or ⌘-F (Mac) or choose Visualizer | Full Screen.

■ To stop full-screen visualizations, click your mouse button anywhere or press ESC or CTRL-T (Windows) or ⌘-T (Mac)

Configure Visualizations to Get the Best Results

iTunes even lets you configure visualizations to make them look as good as possible on your computer. To configure visualizations, follow these steps:

1. If iTunes is displayed at its small or minute size, click the Restore button (Windows) or the green button on the window frame (Mac) to return iTunes to a normal window.

2. Start a song playing.

3. Press CTRL-T (Windows) or ⌘-T (Mac) or choose Visualizer | Turn Visualizer On to start a visualization running (unless you have one running already).

4. Click the Options button in the upper-right corner of the maximized iTunes window to display the Visualizer Options dialog box. Figure 9-5 shows the Visualizer Options dialog box for Windows on the left and the Visualizer Options dialog box for the Mac on the right.

9

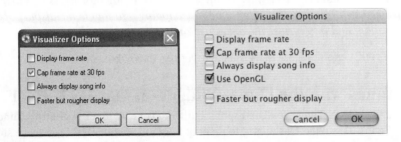

FIGURE 9-5   Use the Visualizer dialog box to configure visualizations for Windows (left) and the Mac (right).

5. Select and clear the check boxes to specify the options you want:

■ **Display Frame Rate**   Controls whether iTunes displays the frame rate (the number of frames being generated each second) superimposed on the upper-left corner of the visualization. This check box is cleared by default. The frame rate is useless information that adds nothing to the visualization, but it can be useful as a point of reference. For example, you may want to compare the visualization frame rates generated by different computers, or you might want to try the Faster But Rougher Display option (discussed in a moment) to see how much difference it produces. The frame rate will vary depending on the size of the visualization window, the complexity of the visualization, and what other tasks your computer is working on at the time.

■ **Cap Frame Rate At 30 fps**   Controls whether iTunes stops the frame from exceeding 30 frames per second. This check box is selected by default. iTunes is configured to cap the frame rate to reduce the demands on the visualization on your computer's graphics card and processor. The cap is at 30 fps because most people find 30 fps provides smooth and wonderful visualizations—so there's no point in trying to crank out extra frames.

■ **Always Display Song Info**   Controls whether iTunes displays the song information overlaid on the visualization all the time or just at the beginning of a song and when you change the Visualizer size while playing a song. This check box is cleared by default.

■ **Use OpenGL**   (Mac only.) Controls whether iTunes uses OpenGL, a graphics-rendering system, to create the visualizations. This check box is selected by default. Leave it selected for best results.

■ **Faster But Rougher Display**   Lets you tell iTunes to lower the quality of the visualizations to increase the frame rate. This check box is cleared by default. You may want to try selecting this check box on a less powerful computer if you find the visualizations are too slow.

TIP   *You can also trigger most of these options from the keyboard while a visualization is playing, without displaying the Visualizer Options dialog box. Press F to toggle the frame rate display, T to toggle frame rate capping, I to toggle the display of song information, and D to restore the default settings.*

6. Click the OK button to close the Visualizer Options dialog box.

Control iTunes with the iTunes Widget on Mac OS X Tiger

If you're using Mac OS X Tiger, you can use the built-in iTunes widget to control iTunes from the Dashboard. To set the Dashboard to display the iTunes widget, follow these steps:

1. Click the Dashboard button on the Dock to display the Dashboard.
2. Click the + button superimposed on the left end of the Dock to display the bar showing the available widgets.
3. Click the iTunes widget, as shown here, to display it.

4. Click the X button superimposed on the left end of the Dock to close the widget bar.

You can then control iTunes by displaying the Dashboard and using the iTunes widget. Figure 9-6 shows the controls on the widget.

TIP   *Apart from clicking the Dashboard button on the Dock, you can display the Dashboard by pressing the hot key assigned it on the Dashboard & Exposé sheet of System Preferences (choose Apple | System Preferences and then click the Dashboard & Exposé icon). On this sheet, you can also set an active screen corner for the Dashboard so that Mac OS X displays the Dashboard when you move the mouse pointer into that corner of the screen.*

To open a playlist, click the Flip Widget button (the button showing the lowercase *i*). The iTunes widget rotates to show its other side. Select the playlist in the drop-down list and then click the Done button to flip the widget back to its regular position.

TIP   *If you use Konfabulator ($19.95, www.konfabulator.com), you can use similar widgets to run iTunes in both earlier versions of Mac OS X and Windows.*

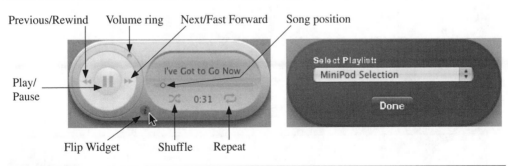

FIGURE 9-6   The iTunes widget lets you control your music from the Dashboard. Flip the widget (right) to select another playlist.

Manage Your Music Library

This section shows you how to use iTunes to manage your music library. You'll learn how to browse quickly by using the Browser panes, how to search for songs, how to create playlists and Smart Playlists, and how to mix up your music with the Party Shuffle feature. After that, you'll meet iTunes' features for applying ratings and artwork to songs, for consolidating your music library so that it contains all your song files, and for removing any duplicate files that are wasting space.

Finally, you'll see how to export playlists so that you can share them with other people and import the playlists they share with you, and how to export your music library to an XML file to store details of your playlists and ratings.

Browse Quickly by Using the Browser Panes

iTunes provides the Browser panes (see Figure 9-7) to browse quickly by artist, album, or (if you choose) genre. You can toggle the display of the Browser panes by clicking the Browse button in the upper-right corner of the iTunes window, pressing CTRL-B (Windows) or ⌘-B (Mac), or using the Edit | Show Browser and Edit | Hide Browser commands. Once the Browser panes are displayed, click an item in the Artist column to display the albums by that artist in the Album column. Then click an item in the Albums column to display that album in the lower pane.

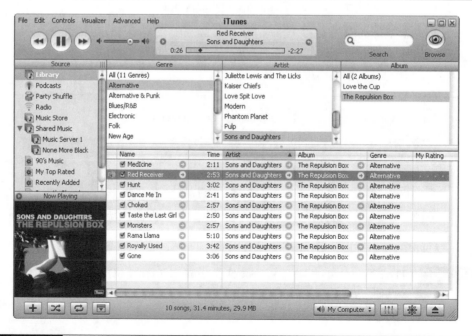

FIGURE 9-7   iTunes' Browser panes let you browse by artist, album, and genre.

9

TIP

When you have the Genre pane displayed but you don't want to restrict the view by genre, select the All item at the top of the Genre pane so that you see all genres at once.

To control whether iTunes displays the Genre pane in the Browser, follow these steps:

1. Display the iTunes dialog box or the Preferences dialog box:

   ◾ In Windows, choose Edit | Preferences or press CTRL-COMMA or CTRL-Y to display the iTunes dialog box.

   ◾ On the Mac, choose iTunes | Preferences or press either ⌘-COMMA or ⌘-Y to display the Preferences dialog box.

2. Click the General tab if it isn't already displayed.

3. Select or clear the Show Genre When Browsing check box, as appropriate.

4. Click the OK button to close the dialog box.

NOTE

The line of text at the bottom of the full iTunes window shows you how many songs are in the current selection and how long they last. This readout has two formats: 5738 songs, 17.4 days, 22.98 GB, and 5738 songs, 17:10:06:58 total time, 22.98 GB. To toggle between the two formats, click the songs-and-time display.

Search for Particular Songs

Browsing for songs works well, but sometimes you may need to search for particular songs. You can also turn up interesting collections of unrelated songs by searching on a word that appears somewhere in the artist name, song name, or album name.

To search all categories of information, type the search text in the Search box and press ENTER (Windows) or RETURN (Mac).

iTunes also lets you constrain the search to different categories of content and different items of information. Choose Edit | Show Search Bar or press CTRL-SHIFT-B (Windows) or ⌘-SHIFT-B (Mac) to display the Search bar:

 ◄── Search bar

Click the appropriate category button on the left (Music, Audiobooks, Podcasts, Videos, or Booklets), and then click the appropriate item button on the right. The buttons change to suit the category; for the Music category, the buttons are All, Artist, Album, Composer, and Song.

Then type the search text and press ENTER (Windows) or RETURN (Mac). To clear the Search box after searching, click the X button:

Create Playlists and Smart Playlists

Typically, a CD presents its songs in the order the artist or the producer thought best, but often you'll want to rearrange the songs into a different order—or mix the songs from different CDs and files in a way that suits only you. To do so, you create playlists in iTunes, and iTunes automatically shares them with your iPod so that you can use them there as well. You can create playlists manually or use iTunes' Smart Playlist feature to create playlists automatically based on criteria you specify.

Create a Playlist Manually

To create a standard playlist, follow these steps:

1. Click the + button in the Source pane, choose File | New Playlist, or press CTRL-N (Windows) or ⌘-N (Mac). iTunes adds a new playlist to the Source pane, names it *untitled playlist* (or the next available name, such as *untitled playlist 2*), and displays an edit box around it.

2. Type the name for the playlist and then press ENTER (Windows) or RETURN (Mac), or click elsewhere, to apply the name.

3. Select the Library item in the Source pane to display your songs. If you want to work by artist and album, press CTRL-B (Windows) or ⌘-B (Mac), or choose Edit | Show Browser, to display the Browser pane.

4. Select the songs you want to add to the playlist and then drag them to the playlist's name. You can drag one song at a time, multiple songs, a whole artist, or a whole CD—whatever you find easiest. You can also drag an existing playlist to the new playlist.

5. Click the playlist's name in the Source pane to display the playlist.

6. Drag the tracks into the order in which you want them to play.

> **NOTE** *For you to be able to drag the tracks around in the playlist, the playlist must be sorted by the track-number column. If any other column heading is selected, you won't be able to rearrange the order of the tracks in the playlist.*

You can also create a playlist by selecting the tracks you want to include and then pressing CTRL-SHIFT-N (Windows) or ⌘-SHIFT-N (Mac) or choosing File | New Playlist From Selection. iTunes organizes the songs into a new playlist provisionally named *untitled playlist* and displays an edit box around the title so that you can change it immediately. Type the new name and press ENTER (Windows) or RETURN (Mac), or click elsewhere to apply the name.

To delete a playlist, select it in the Source pane and press DELETE (Windows) or BACKSPACE (Mac). Alternatively, right-click the playlist (or CTRL-click it on the Mac) and choose Clear from the shortcut menu. Then click the Yes button in the confirmation message box that iTunes displays. If you want to turn off the confirmation for playlists you delete from now on, select the Do Not Ask Me Again check box before clicking the Yes button.

iTunes also offers more complex ways of deleting playlists and their contents:

- If you choose not to turn off confirmation of deleting playlists, you can override confirmation by pressing CTRL-DELETE (Windows) or ⌘-DELETE (Mac) when deleting a playlist.

■ On the Mac, to delete a playlist *and the songs it contains* from your library, select the playlist and press OPTION-BACKSPACE. iTunes displays a confirmation dialog box for the deletion. Click the Yes button. As before, you can select the Do Not Ask Me Again check box to suppress this confirmation dialog box in future, but because you're removing song files from your library, it's best not to do so.

■ On the Mac, to delete a playlist and the songs it contains from your library *and* to temporarily suppress the confirmation dialog box while doing so, select the playlist and press ⌘-OPTION-DELETE.

Automatically Create Smart Playlists Based on Your Ratings and Preferences

The Smart Playlist feature lets you instruct iTunes about how to build a list of songs automatically for you. You can tell Smart Playlist to build playlists by artist, composer, or genre; to select up to a specific number of songs at random, by artist, by most played, by last player, or by song name; and to automatically update a playlist as you add tracks to or remove tracks from your music library. For example, if you tell Smart Playlist to make you a playlist of songs by Ashlee Simpson, Smart Playlist can update the list with new Ashlee tracks after you import them into your music library.

By using Smart Playlist's advanced features, you can even specify multiple conditions. For example, you might choose to include songs tagged with the genre Gothic Rock but exclude certain artists by name that you didn't want to hear.

> NOTE *Smart Playlist maintains playlists such as the My Top Rated playlist, the Recently Played playlist, and the Top 25 Most Played playlist, which iTunes creates by default.*

Here's how to create a Smart Playlist:

1. Press CTRL-ALT-N (Windows) or ⌘-ALT-N (Mac), or choose File | New Smart Playlist, to display the Smart Playlist dialog box (see Figure 9-8). On the Mac, you can also OPTION-click the Add button.

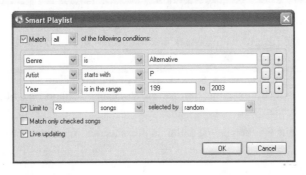

FIGURE 9-8   Smart Playlists are playlists that iTunes automatically populates with songs that match the criteria you specify.

2. Make sure the Match The Following Condition check box is selected so that you can specify criteria. (The other option is to create a random Smart Playlist, which can sometimes be entertaining.) If you create multiple conditions, this check box offers the choices Match All Of The Following Conditions and Match Any Of The Following Conditions. Choose the appropriate one.

3. Use the controls in the first line to specify the first condition. The first drop-down list offers an extensive range of choices: Album, Artist, Bit Rate, Comment, Compilation, Composer, Date Added, Date Modified, Genre, Kind, Last Played, My Rating, Play Count, Playlist, Sample Rate, Size, Song Name, Time, Track Number, and Year. The second drop-down list offers options suitable to the item you chose in the first drop-down list—for example, Contains, Does Not Contain, Is, Is Not, Starts With, or Ends With for a text field, or Is, Is Not, Is Greater Than, Is Less Than, or Is In The Range for the bitrate.

TIP *The Playlist item in the first drop-down list in the Smart Playlist dialog box lets you specify a relationship between the Smart Playlist you're creating and an existing playlist (Smart or regular). For example, you might specify in a Smart Playlist the criterion "Playlist Is Not Recently Played" to prevent any songs that appear in your Recently Played playlist from appearing in the Smart Playlist. Similarly, you could create a Smart Playlist called, say, "Rock Types" that uses several conditions to define all the types of music you consider "rock": Genre Contains Rock, Genre Is Alternative, Genre Contains Gothic, and so on. (Don't dispute these classifications—they're just examples.) You could then use the criterion Playlist Is Rock Types in a Smart Playlist to create a subset of your rock music—for example, 90s rock or rock by artists not named Bryan or Brian.*

4. To create multiple conditions, click the + button at the end of the line. iTunes adds another line of condition controls, which you can then set as described in step 3. To remove a condition, click the − button at the end of the line.

5. To limit the playlist to a maximum number of tracks, time, or disk space, select the Limit To check box and then specify the limit and how iTunes should select the songs. For example, you could specify Limit To 30 Songs Selected By Least Often Played or Limit To 8 Hours Selected By Random.

6. To make iTunes omit songs whose check boxes you've cleared, select the Match Only Checked Songs check box.

7. Select or clear the Live Updating check box to specify whether iTunes should update the playlist periodically according to your listening patterns.

8. Click the OK button to close the Smart Playlist dialog box. iTunes creates the playlist, assigns a name to it (for example, *untitled playlist*), and displays an edit box around the name so you can change it.

9. Type the new name for the playlist and then press ENTER (Windows) or RETURN (Mac).

A Smart Playlist limited by size can be a good way of selecting songs for an iPod shuffle or ROKR, an iPod nano, or even a regular iPod whose capacity is substantially less than the size of your music library. For example, you might create a Smart Playlist with the parameter Limit To 950 MB for loading on an iPod shuffle.

Mix Up Your Music with Party Shuffle

If you like having someone else choose music for you, you may well love iTunes' Party Shuffle feature. Party Shuffle (see Figure 9-9) automatically selects music for you based on four parameters that you specify.

To use Party Shuffle, follow these steps:

1. Click the Party Shuffle item in the Source pane.

If the Source pane doesn't include Party Shuffle, press CTRL-COMMA (Windows) to display the iTunes dialog box or ⌘-COMMA (Mac) to display the Preferences dialog box. On the General tab, select the Party Shuffle check box and then click the OK button to close the dialog box.

FIGURE 9-9   Party Shuffle is like a giant Smart Playlist.

2. Choose options at the bottom of the pane:

- Select the source for the Party Shuffle: your music library or a playlist.
- Select the Play Higher Rated Songs More Often check box if you want iTunes to weight the selection toward songs that you've given a higher rating.
- Choose how many recently played songs and how many upcoming songs to display. The display of recently played songs can be useful for finding out the song details of songs you didn't recognize when Party Shuffle chose them.

3. Click the Play button to start the songs playing.

4. If you don't like the selection, click the Refresh button to display a new selection of songs.

If you find that Party Shuffle dredges up many songs you don't like, you can use it as a means of finding songs for playlists. From the songs that Party Shuffle picks, select those you want to hear, and drag them to a playlist. Click the Refresh button to find more songs, add those you want to hear to the playlist, and repeat the process until you've got a long enough playlist. Then start that playlist playing.

Apply Ratings to Songs

iTunes' My Rating feature lets you assign a rating of no stars to five stars to each song in your music library. You can then sort the songs by rating or tell Smart Playlist to add only songs of a certain ranking or better to a playlist. (See "Automatically Create Smart Playlists Based on Your Ratings and Preferences," earlier in this chapter, for a discussion of Smart Playlist.)

You can apply a rating in either of two ways:

- Right-click a song (or CTRL-click it on the Mac), choose My Rating from the shortcut menu, and select the appropriate number of stars from the submenu.
- Use the My Rating box on the Options tab of the Song Information dialog box (press CTRL-I in Windows or ⌘-I on the Mac, or choose Get Info from the File menu or the shortcut menu) to specify the number of stars.

You can also rate a song on a regular iPod or an iPod nano. To do so, press the Select button twice from the Now Playing screen while the song is playing, scroll left or right to select the appropriate number of stars, and then press the Select button again. iTunes picks up the rating the next time you synchronize your iPod.

Add Artwork to Songs

iTunes lets you add artwork to songs and then display the artwork while the song is playing or is selected.

Most songs you buy from the iTunes Music Store include the appropriate artwork—for example, the cover of the single, EP, album, or CD that includes the song. For other songs, you can add artwork either manually, via a semi-automated process (Windows), or automatically (Mac).

You can apply any image you want to a song, provided that it is in a format that QuickTime supports. (QuickTime's supported formats include JPG, GIF, TIFF, PNG, BMP, and PhotoShop.) For example, you might download album art or other pictures from an artist's website and then apply those to the song files you ripped from the artist's CDs. Or you might prefer to add images of your own to favorite songs or to songs you've composed yourself.

> TIP
>
> *Amazon.com (www.amazon.com) has cover images for millions of CDs and records. For most music items, you can click the small picture on the item's main page to display a larger version of the image. Another source is Allmusic (www.allmusic.com), a service that requires registration.*

Add Artwork to Songs Manually

You can add artwork to songs manually by using either the artwork pane in the iTunes window or the Artwork box in the Song Information dialog box or the Multiple Song Information dialog box. The artwork pane is usually easiest.

Add Artwork to Songs by Using the Artwork Pane   To add an image by using the artwork pane, follow these steps:

1. Open iTunes and select the song or songs you want to affect.

2. If the artwork pane isn't displayed (below the Source pane), display it in one of these ways:

   - Click the Show Or Hide Song Artwork button.
   - Press CTRL-G (Windows) or ⌘-G (Mac).
   - Choose Edit | Show Artwork.

3. If the title bar of the artwork pane says Now Playing, click the title bar to change it to Selected Song.

4. Open a Windows Explorer window or a Finder window to the folder that contains the image you want to use for the artwork, or open a browser window to a URL that contains the image. For example, open an Internet Explorer window to Amazon.com and navigate to the image you want.

5. Arrange iTunes and the Windows Explorer window, Finder window, or browser window so that you can see them both.

6. Drag the image to the artwork pane and drop it there.

7. Add further images to the song or songs if you want while you have them selected.

> NOTE
>
> *Most CD cover images are relatively small in dimensions and are compressed, so their file size is fairly small. Adding an image to a song increases its file size a little, but not normally enough to cause a problem. If you add a large image to a song, iTunes uses a compressed version of the image rather than the full image.*

9

Add Artwork to Songs by Using the Song Information Dialog Box or the Multiple Song Information Dialog Box   Follow these steps to add artwork by using the Song Information dialog box (for a single song) or the Multiple Song Information dialog box:

1. Select the songs, right-click (or CTRL-click on the Mac), and choose Get Info from the shortcut menu to display the dialog box. (You can also choose File | Get Info or press CTRL-I in Windows or ⌘-I on the Mac to display the dialog box.)

2. If you've opened the Song Information dialog box, click the Artwork tab to display it.

3. Open a Windows Explorer window or a Finder window to the folder that contains the picture you want to use for the artwork, or open a browser window to a URL that contains the picture.

4. Drag the image to the Artwork box in the Multiple Song Information dialog box or the open area on the Artwork tab of the Song Information dialog box.

5. If you're using the Song Information dialog box, add further images as needed. To change the order of the images, drag them about in the open area. You may need to reduce the zoom by dragging the slider to get the pictures small enough to rearrange.

When you've added two or more pictures to the same song, the artwork pane displays a Previous button and a Next button for browsing from picture to picture.

You can display the current picture at full size by clicking it in the artwork pane. Click the Close button (the X button) to close the artwork window.

Adding artwork to your songs can be not only esthetic but also practical. For a way of selecting music by cover art, see "Improve the iTunes Interface with Clutter (Mac)" in Chapter 15.

To remove the artwork from a song, right-click (or CTRL-click on the Mac) the song and choose Get Info from the shortcut menu. Click the Artwork tab of the Song Information dialog box, click the picture, and then click the Remove button.

Add Artwork to Songs Semi-Automatically on Windows or the Mac

At this writing, there's no automatic mechanism for adding artwork to songs in iTunes for Windows as there is for the Mac (see the next section), but the art4itunes.com website (www.art4itunes.com) can search for as many artwork items as are available for your music library. You then must add the artwork items manually to the songs. This works on either Windows or the Mac.

To use art4itunes.com, follow these steps:

1. In iTunes, select your music library in the Source pane. If you want to get art for only some songs, create a playlist containing those songs and then select the playlist in the Source pane.

2. Choose File | Export Song List to display the Save As dialog box (Windows) or the Save: iTunes dialog box (Mac).

3. Specify the file name for the list and then choose the folder in which to store it.

4. Make sure iTunes is set to save the file as text:

    ■ In Windows, verify that Text Files is selected in the Save As Type drop-down list.

    ■ On the Mac, verify that Plain Text is selected in the Format drop-down list.

5. Click the Save button to save the file.

6. Open a web browser window to the art4itunes website (www.art4itunes.com) and follow the instructions to upload your library listing, choose an image size, and start the search.

7. From the resulting page, drag an image to iTunes to apply it to songs:

    ■ In Windows, select the songs you want to affect, display the artwork pane, and drop the image in the artwork pane.

    ■ On either Windows or the Mac, select the songs you want to affect, choose File | Get Info to display the Multiple Song Information dialog box, and then drag the image to the Artwork box. Click the OK button to close the Multiple Song Information dialog box.

Add Artwork to Songs Automatically on the Mac

If you're using the Mac and you're prepared to pay a few dollars, you can add artwork to your songs automatically by using iTunes Catalog from KavaSoft ($9.95; www.kavasoft.com). You can use the trial edition to see how well iTunes Catalog finds the images for artists with names starting A, B, C, D, and E. Figure 9-10 shows iTunes Catalog applying artwork to a music library.

9

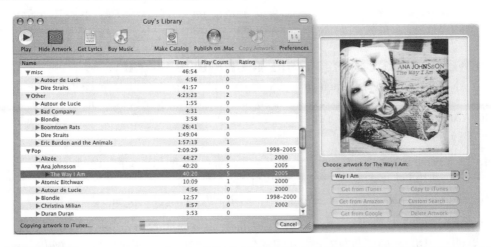

FIGURE 9-10   iTunes Catalog can automatically download art and apply it to the songs in iTunes.

Consolidate Your Music Library So You Can Always Access All Its Songs

As you saw earlier in this book, if you clear the Copy Files To iTunes Music Folder When Adding To Library check box on the Advanced sheet of the iTunes Preferences dialog box, iTunes places in the music library only a reference to the file. When your external drives, network drives, or removable media aren't available (for example, when you grab your laptop and head over to a friend's house for a night of gaming), the songs stored on those drives or media won't be available.

To make sure you can play the music you want wherever you want, you can *consolidate* your music library, making iTunes copy all the files currently outside your iTunes music folder to the music folder.

Understand the implications before you consolidate your music library:

- Consolidation can take a long time, depending on the number of files to be copied and the speed of the network connection you're using. Don't consolidate your library just as the airport shuttle is about to arrive.

- The drive that holds your music library must have enough space free to hold all your songs. If lack of space was the reason you didn't copy the songs to your music library in the first place, you probably don't want to consolidate your library.

- Songs on removable media such as CDs or Zip disks won't be copied unless the medium is in the drive at the time.

To consolidate your music library, follow these steps, choose Advanced | Consolidate Library, and then click the Consolidate button in the confirmation dialog box. iTunes displays the Copying Files dialog box as it copies the files to your music library.

If consolidation goes wrong, see the "iTunes Runs You Out of Hard-Disk Space" sections for Windows and Mac in Chapter 18 for help.

Remove Duplicate Songs from Your Music Library

Even if your music library isn't huge, it's easy to get duplicate songs in it, especially if you add folders of existing song files as well as rip and encode your CDs and other audio sources. Duplicate songs waste disk space, particularly on your iPod, so iTunes offers a command to help you identify them:

1. In the Source pane, click your library. If you want to confine the duplicate-checking to a playlist, click that playlist in the Source pane.

2. Choose Edit | Show Duplicate Songs. iTunes displays a list of duplicate songs.

NOTE   *iTunes identifies duplicate songs by artist and song name, not by album, length, or other often-useful details. Before deleting any duplicate songs, check that they're actually duplicates, not just different versions or mixes of the same song.*

3. Decide which copy of each song you want to keep. To find out where a song is stored, right-click it (or CTRL-click it on the Mac) and choose Show Song File from the shortcut menu.

You'll see a Windows Explorer window or a Finder window that shows the contents of the folder that includes the song file.

TIP
If your music library contains various file formats, you may find it helpful to display the file type in iTunes so that you can see which song is which format. For example, when you have duplicate files, you might want to delete the MP3 files rather than the AAC files. Right-click (or CTRL-click on the Mac) the heading of the column after which you want the Kind column to appear and then select the Kind item from the shortcut menu.

4. To delete a song, select it and press DELETE (Windows) or BACKSPACE (Mac). Click the Yes button in the confirmation dialog box; select the Do Not Ask Me Again check box first if you want to turn off the confirmation.

5. If the song file is stored in your iTunes Music folder, iTunes prompts you to move it to the Recycle Bin (Windows) or to the Trash (Mac). Click the Yes button or the No button as appropriate.

To display all songs again, click the Show All Songs button at the bottom of the iTunes window or choose Edit | Show All Songs.

Import and Export Playlists

If you create a great playlist, chances are that you'll want to share it with others. You can do so by exporting the playlist:

1. Select the playlist in the Source pane.

2. Choose File | Export Song List to display the Save As dialog box (Windows) or the Save: iTunes dialog box (Mac).

3. Specify the file name for the list and then choose the folder in which to store it.

4. Choose the format for the file. Windows lets you choose between Text Files and XML Files. Mac OS X lets you choose among Plain Text, Unicode Text, and XML. Text Files or Plain Text is usually the best choice.

5. Click the Save button to save the playlist.

You can then share the playlist with someone else—for example, by sending it via e-mail. When you receive a playlist, you can import it by choosing File | Import, selecting the file in the Import dialog box (change the Files Of Type setting in Windows if necessary), and then clicking the Open button. iTunes checks the playlist against your library and creates a playlist that contains as many of the songs as you have available. If one or more songs are unavailable, iTunes warns you, as shown here.

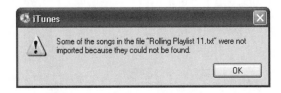

Export Your Music Library

You can export the details of your entire music library and all your playlists as a backup in case your computer suffers data loss or damage. To export the music library, choose File | Export Library, specify the name and folder in the Save As dialog box (Windows) or the Save: iTunes dialog box (Mac), and then click the Save button.

As well as your playlists, your exported music library contains details of your play count, song ratings, equalizations, and other song-specific settings you've applied, such as start times and stop times.

Share Music and Access Shared Music

Listening to your own music collection is great, but it's often even better to be able to share your music with your friends or family—and to enjoy as much of their music as you can stand. iTunes provides features for sharing your music (but not your videos) with other iTunes users on your network and for playing the music they're sharing. You may also want to share music with other users of your computer—which, interestingly, requires a little more effort.

Share Your Music with Other Local iTunes Users

To share your music with other local iTunes users, you must have either Windows 2000 or Windows XP (or a later version of Windows) or Mac OS X 10.2.4 or later. (If you don't have one of these versions, it's probably time to upgrade.) The computers with which you're sharing the music, or whose music you're sharing, must have these versions of Windows or Mac OS X as well.

You can share either your entire music library or selected playlists with other users on your network. You can share MP3 files, AAC files, AIFF files, WAV files, and links to radio stations. You can't share Audible files or QuickTime sound files.

NOTE   *Technically, iTunes' music sharing is limited to computers on the same TCP/IP subnet as your computer is on. (A subnet is a logical division of a network.) If your computer connects to a medium-sized network, and you're unable to find a computer that you know is connected to the same network somewhere, it may be on a different subnet.*

At this writing, you can share your music with up to five other computers per day, and your computer can be one of up to five computers accessing the shared music on another computer on any given day. (The sharing used to be more generous: five concurrent computers at any time. See the sidebar "Apple May Change the Details of Music Sharing" for details.)

Shared music remains on the computer that's sharing it, and when a participating computer goes to play a song, the song is streamed across the network. This means that the song isn't copied from the computer that's sharing it to the computer that's playing it in a way that leaves a usable file on the playing computer.

Apple May Change the Details of Music Sharing

If you read through the license agreements for iTunes and the iTunes Music Store, you'll notice that Apple reserves the right to change the details of what you can and can't do with iTunes and the music files you buy. This isn't unusual, but it's worth taking a moment to consider.

At this writing, Apple has made several changes. Some changes are no big deal. For example, Apple has reduced the number of times you can burn an individual playlist to CD from ten times to seven times. (You can create another playlist with the same songs and burn that seven times too, and then create another.)

More of a big deal are the changes Apple has made to sharing songs on the network. The first versions of iTunes 4 could share songs not only on the computer's local network but also across the Internet. Apple quickly reduced this to the local network only, which seemed fair enough. iTunes could share music with five other computers at a time—enough to reach a good number of people, especially in a dorm situation with many people sharing music and listening to shared music.

But in iTunes 4.7.1, Apple reduced the sharing from five computers at a time to five computers *per day* total. This still works fine for most homes, but on bigger networks, it's very restrictive. Once a computer has shared songs with its five computers for the day, you'll see a "The shared music library '*music library name*' is not accepting connections at this time. Please try again later." message if you try to connect.

All the changes so far have been restrictive and have benefited the music providers (the record companies) rather than iTunes users. Further changes seem likely, so if iTunes doesn't behave as described here, check the latest license agreement on the Apple website.

9

When a computer goes offline or is shut down, any music it has been sharing stops being available to other users. Participating computers can play the shared music but can't do anything else with it; they can't burn the shared music to CD or DVD, download it to an iPod, or copy it to their own libraries.

To share some or all of your music, follow these steps:

1. Display the iTunes dialog box or the Preferences dialog box:

   ■ In Windows, choose Edit | Preferences or press CTRL-COMMA or CTRL-Y to display the iTunes dialog box.

   ■ On the Mac, choose iTunes | Preferences or press either ⌘-COMMA or ⌘-Y to display the Preferences dialog box.

2. Click the Sharing tab to display it. Figure 9-11 shows the Sharing tab of the iTunes dialog box with settings chosen.

3. Select the Share My Music check box. (This check box is cleared by default.) By default, iTunes then selects the Share Entire Library option button. If you want to share only some playlists, select the Share Selected Playlists option button and then select the check boxes in the list box for the playlists.

4. The Shared Name text box controls the name that other users trying to access your music will see. The default name is *username*'s music, where *username* is your username—for example, Anna Connor's Music. You might choose to enter a more descriptive name, especially if your computer is part of a well-populated network (for example, in a dorm).

5. By default, your music is available to any other user on the network. To restrict access to people with whom you share a password, select the Require Password check box and enter a strong (unguessable) password in the text box.

FIGURE 9-11 On the Sharing tab of the iTunes dialog box or the Preferences dialog box, choose whether to look for shared music and whether to share part or all of your music library.

9

TIP

If there are many computers on your network, use a sharing password to help avoid running up against the five-users-per-day limit. If your network has only a few computers, you may not need a password to avoid reaching this limit.

6. Click the OK button to apply your choices and close the dialog box.

NOTE

When you set iTunes to share your music, iTunes displays a message reminding you that "Sharing music is for personal use only"—in other words, remember not to violate copyright law. Select the Do Not Show This Message Again check box if you want to prevent this message from appearing again.

Disconnect Other Users from Your Shared Music

To disconnect other users from your shared music library, follow these steps:

1. Display the iTunes dialog box or the Preferences dialog box:

- In Windows, choose Edit | Preferences or press CTRL-COMMA or CTRL-Y to display the iTunes dialog box.

- On the Mac, choose iTunes | Preferences or press either ⌘-COMMA or ⌘-Y to display the Preferences dialog box.

2. Click the Sharing tab to display it.

3. Clear the Share My Music check box.

4. Click the OK button. If any other user is connected to your shared music library, iTunes displays this message box to warn you:

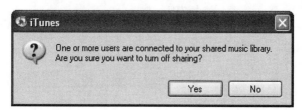

Click the Yes button or the No button, as appropriate. If you click the Yes button, anyone playing music from it will be cut off abruptly without notice.

Access and Play Another Local iTunes User's Shared Music

To access another person's shared music, your computer must be running iTunes 4 on either Windows 2000 or Windows XP (or a later version of Windows) or Mac OS X 10.2.4 or later.

Set Your Computer to Look for Shared Music

First, set your computer to look for shared music. Follow these steps:

1. Display the iTunes dialog box or the Preferences dialog box:

   ◼ In Windows, choose Edit | Preferences or press CTRL-COMMA or CTRL-Y to display the iTunes dialog box.

   ◼ On the Mac, choose iTunes | Preferences or press either ⌘-COMMA or ⌘-Y to display the Preferences dialog box.

2. Click the Sharing tab to display its contents.

3. Select the Look For Shared Music check box.

4. Click the OK button to close the dialog box.

Access Shared Music on the Same TCP/IP Subnet

Once you've selected the Look For Shared Music check box on the Sharing tab of the iTunes dialog box or the Preferences dialog box, iTunes automatically detects shared music when you launch it while your computer is connected to a network. If iTunes finds shared music libraries or playlists, it displays them in the Source pane. Figure 9-12 shows an example of browsing the music shared by another computer.

FIGURE 9-12   Computers sharing music appear in the iTunes Source pane, allowing you to quickly browse the music that's being shared.

If a shared music source has a password, iTunes displays the Music Library Password dialog box. Type the password and click the OK button to access the library. Select the Remember Password check box before clicking the OK button if you want iTunes to save the password to speed up future access to the music library.

TIP   *Double-click the entry for a shared music library in the Source pane to open a separate window that shows its contents.*

Disconnect a Shared Music Library

To disconnect shared music you've connected to, click the Eject icon next to the music library in the Source pane. You can also click the music library in the Source pane and then press CTRL-E (Windows) or ⌘-E (Mac) or choose Controls | Disconnect "*Library*" from the shortcut menu (where *Library* is the name of the shared music library). Alternatively, right-click the music library in the Source pane (or CTRL-click on the Mac) and choose Disconnect from the shortcut menu.

Share Your Music More Effectively with Other Local Users

As you saw in the previous section, iTunes makes it easy for you to share either your music library or specific playlists with other iTunes users on your local area network (LAN). You can share with up to five different computers per day, and of course your computer must be attached to the network and powered on for them to be able to access your music.

You may also want to share your music with other users of your computer. The security features built into Windows and Mac OS X mean that you have to do a little work to share it.

Share Your Music Library with Other Users of Your PC

Windows XP (and Windows 2000, but we'll focus on Windows XP here) automatically prevents other users from accessing your personal files, assigning each user a user account and keeping them out of other users' accounts. The result of this is that your iTunes music library, which is stored in your My Music\iTunes\iTunes Music folder by default, is securely protected from other users of your computer. That's great if you want to keep your music to yourself, but not so great if you want to share it with your friends, family, or coworkers.

The easiest way to give other users access to your music library is to move it to the Shared Music folder. This is a folder created automatically when Windows XP is installed, and which Windows XP automatically shares with other users of your computer but not with other computers on the network. The Shared Music folder is located in the \Documents and Settings\All Users\ Documents\My Music folder.

Alternatively, you can put the music library in another shared folder. This example uses the Shared Music folder. If you're using another folder, substitute it where appropriate.

Moving your music library to the Shared Music folder involves two steps: moving the files, and telling iTunes where you've moved them to.

To move your music library files to the Shared Music folder, follow these steps:

1. Close iTunes if it's running. (For example, press ALT-F4 or choose File | Exit.)

2. Choose Start | My Music to open a Windows Explorer window showing your My Music folder.

3. Double-click the iTunes folder to open it. You'll see an iTunes Music Library.xml file, an iTunes Music Library.itl file, and an iTunes Music folder. The first two files must stay in your My Music folder. If you remove them, iTunes won't be able to find your music, and it will create these files again from scratch.

4. Right-click the iTunes Music folder and choose Cut from the shortcut menu to cut it to the Clipboard.

5. In the Other Places task pane, click the Shared Music link to display the Shared Music folder. (If the Shared Music folder doesn't appear in the Other Places task pane, click the My Computer link, click the Shared Documents link, and then double-click the Shared Music folder.)

6. Right-click in open space in the Shared Music folder and choose Paste from the shortcut menu to paste the iTunes Music folder into the Shared Music folder.

7. Close the Windows Explorer window. (For example, press ALT-F4 or choose File | Close.)

Next, you need to tell iTunes where the song files are. Follow these steps:

1. Start iTunes. (For example, double-click the iTunes icon on your desktop.)

2. Press CTRL-COMMA or choose Edit | Preferences to display the iTunes dialog box.

3. Click the Advanced tab to display its contents, then click the General subtab.

4. Click the Change button to display the Browse For Folder dialog box.

5. Navigate to the Shared Music folder (for example, click the My Computer item, click the Shared Documents item, click the Shared Music item, and then click the iTunes Music item) and then click the OK button.

6. Click the OK button to close the iTunes dialog box.

After you've done this, iTunes knows where the song files are, and you can play them back as usual. When you rip further song files from CD or import files, iTunes will store them in the Shared Music folder.

You're all set. The other users of your PC can do either of two things:

◼ Move their music library to the Shared Music folder, using the techniques described here, so that all music is stored centrally. Instead of moving the iTunes Music folder itself, move the folders it contains. Users can then add songs they import to the shared music library, and all users can access them.

■ Keep their music library separate, but add the contents of the shared music library folder to it. Here's how:

1. Choose File | Add Folder To Library to display the Browse For Folder dialog box.

2. Navigate to the Shared Music folder.

3. Select the iTunes Music folder.

4. Click the Open button. iTunes adds all the latest songs to your music library.

Whichever approach the other users of your PC choose, the songs that they add to the shared music library don't appear automatically in your music library. To add all the latest tracks, use the Add To Library dialog box, as described in the previous list.

Share Your Music Library with Other Users of Your Mac

Mac OS X's security system prevents other users from accessing your Home folder or its contents—which by default includes your music library. So if you want to share your music library with other users of your Mac, you need to change permissions to allow others to access your Home folder (or parts of it) or move your music library to a folder they can access.

The easiest way to give other users access to your music is to put your music library in the Users/Shared folder and put an alias to it in its default location. To do so, follow these steps:

1. Use the Finder to move the iTunes Music folder from your ~/Music/iTunes folder to the /Users/Shared folder.

2. Press ⌘-COMMA (or ⌘-Y) or choose iTunes | Preferences to display the Preferences dialog box.

3. Click the Advanced button to display the Advanced tab, then click the General subtab to display its contents.

4. Click the Change button and use the resulting Change Music Folder Location dialog box to navigate to and select the /Users/Shared/iTunes Music folder.

5. Click the Choose button to close the Change Music Folder Location dialog box and enter the new path in the iTunes Music Folder Location text box on the Advanced sheet.

6. Make sure the Keep iTunes Music Folder Organized check box is selected.

7. Click the OK button to close the Advanced sheet. iTunes displays the Changing The Location Of The iTunes Music Folder dialog box.

8. Click the OK button. iTunes displays the Updating Song Locations dialog box as it updates the locations in its database. iTunes then displays the dialog box asking whether you want to let it organize your music preferences.

9. Click the Yes button to move the music files in your library to the new, shared music library.

9

If you want other users to be able to put song files in the shared music library (for example, if they import them from CD), you need to give them Write permission for it. To do so, follow these steps:

1. Open a Finder window to the /Users/Shared folder.

2. CTRL-click or right-click the iTunes Music folder and then choose Get Info from the shortcut menu to display the iTunes Music Info window.

3. In the Ownership & Permissions area, click the Details arrow to expand its display, if necessary.

4. In the Others drop-down list, select the Read & Write item instead of the Read Only item.

5. Click the Apply To Enclosed Items button. Mac OS X displays this dialog box:

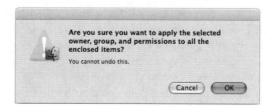

6. Click the OK button.

7. Click the Close button (the X button) to close the Info window.

After you move your music library to the /Users/Shared folder, the other users of your Mac can do one of two things:

- Move their music library to the /Users/Shared folder, using the technique described here, so that all music is stored centrally. Users can then add songs they import to the shared music library, and all users can access them.

- Keep their music library separate, but add the contents of the shared music library folder to it. Here's how:

  1. Press ⌘-Q or choose File | Add To Library to display the Add To Library dialog box.

  2. Navigate to the /Users/Shared/iTunes Music folder.

  3. Click the Open button. iTunes adds all the latest songs to your music library.

Whichever approach the other users of your Mac choose, the songs that they add to the shared music library don't appear automatically in your music library. To add all the latest tracks, use the Add To Library dialog box, as described in the previous list.

If you find that trying to play songs stored in music libraries that keep disappearing off the network is too tedious, another option is to build a music server for your household. You can either build a server from scratch on a new computer or change the role of one of your existing computers—even a pensioned-off computer that's too old to run Mac OS X or Windows XP at a decent speed.

Enjoy Podcasts

A *podcast* is a downloadable show that you can play in iTunes or transfer to your iPod. Some podcasts are versions of professional broadcast radio shows, while others are put together by enthusiasts.

If you want to create your own podcasts, you can find plenty of suitable software online— but you may already have all you need on your Mac. GarageBand, the music-composition tool that comes as part of the iLife suite, is quite capable of creating podcasts. Use the File | Export To iTunes command to export the resulting file to iTunes, select it in iTunes, and then use the Advanced | Convert Selection To command to convert it to the format in which you want to distribute it (for example, AAC using the Podcast quality).

Apple makes selected podcasts available through the iTunes Music Store, which is an easy way to get started listening to podcasts. You can also find many more podcasts on the Internet.

9

Configure Podcast Preferences

Before you start working with podcasts, you should configure podcast preferences. These preferences cover how iTunes handles podcasts and which podcasts are synchronized with your iPod. Follow these steps:

1. Display the iTunes dialog box or the Preferences dialog box:

   ■ In Windows, choose Edit | Preferences or press CTRL-COMMA or CTRL-Y to display the iTunes dialog box.

   ■ On the Mac, choose iTunes | Preferences or press either ⌘-COMMA or ⌘-Y to display the Preferences dialog box.

2. Click the Podcasts tab. Figure 9-13 shows the Podcasts tab for iTunes on the Mac. The Windows version has the same controls.

3. In the Check for New Episodes drop-down list, choose the appropriate frequency: Every Hour, Every Day, Every Week, or Manually.

4. In the When New Episodes Are Available drop-down list, choose what to do: Download All, Download the Most Recent One, or Do Nothing.

5. In the Keep drop-down list, choose which episodes of the podcasts to keep: All Episodes, All Unplayed Episodes, Most Recent Episodes, or the last 2, 3, 4, 5, or 10 episodes.

FIGURE 9-13 Choose podcast settings on the Podcasts tab in iTunes.

6. Click the iPod Preferences button to switch to the Podcasts subtab of the iPod tab of the dialog box. Figure 9-14 shows the Mac version of the Podcasts subtab with several podcasts already added. (If you're just starting with podcasts, you won't see any podcasts listed yet.)

7. Specify how to update the podcasts by selecting the Automatically Update All Podcasts option button, the Automatically Update Selected Podcasts Only option button (and then select the check box for each podcast that you want to have updated), or the Do Not Update Podcasts option button.

8. If you select either the Automatically Update All Podcasts option button or the Automatically Update Selected Podcasts Only option button, choose which episodes to update in the Update drop-down list: All Episodes, Only Checked Episodes, Only Most Recent Episode, or Only Unplayed Episodes.

9. Click the OK button to close the dialog box.

Explore Podcasts on the iTunes Music Store

To explore podcasts on the iTunes Music Store, click the Music Store item in the Source pane (or double-click the Music Store item to open a new window showing the iTunes Music Store). Then either click the Podcasts link or select the Podcasts item in the Choose Genre drop-down list to display the Podcasts page.

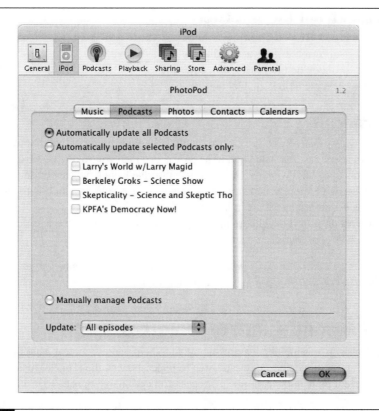

FIGURE 9-14   On the Podcasts subtab of the iPod tab, choose which podcasts you want to transfer to your iPod and how to transfer them.

From here, you can follow the links to the various podcasts. When you find a podcast that interests you, you can either click a Get Episode button to download a particular episode or click a Subscribe button to subscribe to the podcast. When you click the Subscribe button, iTunes displays a confirmation dialog box, as shown here. Select the Do Not Ask About Subscribing Again check box if you want to suppress confirmation in the future, and click the Subscribe button to proceed with the subscription.

Add Podcasts from the Internet

To add a podcast whose URL you know from the Internet, choose Advanced | Subscribe to Podcast to display the Subscribe to Podcast dialog box (shown here), enter the URL of the podcast, and then click the OK button.

Listen to Podcasts

To listen to the podcasts that you've subscribed to, click the Podcasts item in the Source pane, and then double-click the podcast that you want to hear. You can then control the podcast by using the iTunes play controls as usual. From here, you can unsubscribe from a podcast by selecting it and clicking the Unsubscribe button. When you do so, iTunes adds a Subscribe button to the podcast, so that you can easily subscribe to it again if you choose.

To play a podcast on your iPod, choose the Podcasts item on the Music menu, select the podcast, and then use the iPod's play controls as usual.

 *iTunes doesn't automatically add podcasts to your music library, but you can add a podcast to the music library by dragging it there.*

Use iTunes' Parental-Control Features

iTunes 5.0 and later versions include features intended to help parents control what their children are able to do with iTunes: whether they can listen to podcasts, visit the iTunes Music Store and access explicit content on it, and share music or access others' shared music. To use these features:

1. Display the iTunes dialog box or the Preferences dialog box:

   ■ In Windows, choose Edit | Preferences or press CTRL-COMMA or CTRL-Y to display the iTunes dialog box.

   ■ On the Mac, choose iTunes | Preferences or press either ⌘-COMMA or ⌘-Y to display the Preferences dialog box.

2. Click the Parental Control tab (Windows) or the Parental tab (Mac).

 *If the lock icon is closed, you must click it and enter your password before you can make changes.*

3. Select the Disable Podcasts check box, the Disable Music Store check box, the Disable Shared Music check box, or the Restrict Explicit Content check box as appropriate.

4. Click the lock icon, type your system password in the resulting dialog box, and then click the OK button.

5. Click the OK button to close the iTunes dialog box or the Preferences dialog box. iTunes applies the restrictions you chose.

Part III

Put Text, Photos, and Videos on Your iPod

Chapter 10

Put Your Contacts and Calendars on Your iPod

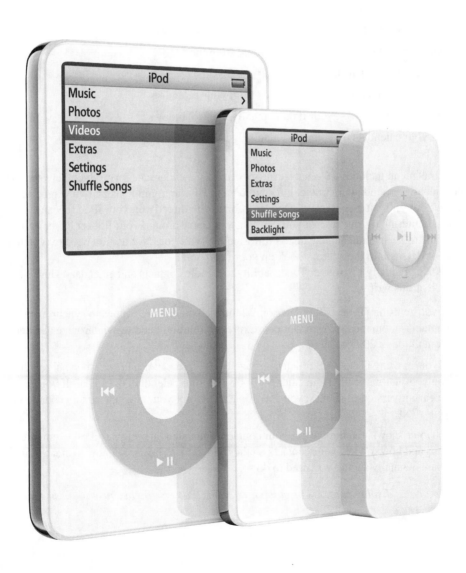

How to...

- Put your contacts and calendars on your iPod automatically from Windows
- Put your contacts and calendars on your iPod automatically from the Mac
- View your contacts on your iPod
- View your calendars on your iPod
- Understand what vCards are and what they're for
- Create vCards from your contacts
- Put your contacts on your iPod manually from Windows
- Put your contacts on your iPod manually from the Mac
- Understand vCalendar and iCalendar
- Create iCalendar and vCalendar files from your calendars
- Put your calendars on your iPod manually using Windows
- Put your calendars on your iPod manually using a Mac

The Extras menu includes a Contacts category and a Calendar category, which between them let you carry around your contact information and your appointments and view records as necessary. You can't enter contact or calendar information directly on your iPod (because there's no means of entering it), but at least you don't have to carry around your Pocket PC or Palm handheld just to keep contact and calendar information with you. Nor do you need to type long addresses or details into the address book on your cell phone.

Apple has gradually improved iTunes' ability to handle contacts and calendars. Here's how things stand at this writing:

- If you're using iTunes 5.0 or later on Windows, you can use iTunes to synchronize your contacts automatically from Outlook Express or Outlook and to synchronize calendars from Outlook 2003 or later.

- If you're using iTunes 4.8 or later on Mac OS X, you can use iTunes to synchronize your contacts automatically from Address Book and your calendars from iCal. If you're using an earlier version of iTunes, you can use iSync to put your contacts and calendars on your iPod.

This chapter shows you how to put your contacts and calendars on your iPod automatically using iTunes and how to view your contacts on the iPod. It also shows you how to create contacts and calendars manually should you need to do so.

NOTE   *You can't display contacts or calendars on an iPod shuffle because it doesn't have a screen.*

Put Your Contacts and Calendars on Your iPod Automatically from Windows

If you keep your contacts in Outlook Express (in other words, in the Windows Address Book) or in Outlook, iTunes can transfer them automatically to your iPod for you. If you use Outlook 2003 or a later version, iTunes can also transfer your calendar information to your iPod automatically.

To configure contact and calendar synchronization, follow these steps:

1. Connect your iPod to your computer as usual.

2. Right-click the iPod and choose iPod Options from the shortcut menu to display the iPod tab of the iTunes dialog box. (Alternatively, click the iPod in the Source pane, and then click the iPod Options button on the right side of the iTunes status bar.)

3. Click the Contacts subtab to display its contents (see Figure 10-1).

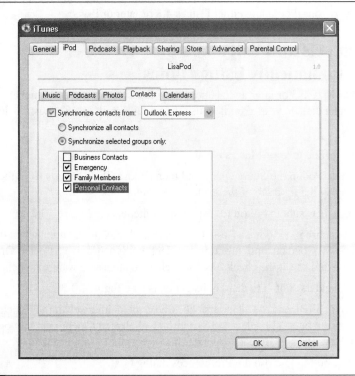

10

FIGURE 10-1   On the Contacts subtab of the iPod tab of the iTunes dialog box, choose which application will supply the contacts, and then specify the groups to synchronize.

4. Select the Synchronize Contacts From check box, and then select Outlook Express or Outlook in the drop-down list, as appropriate.

5. If you want to synchronize all contacts, leave the Synchronize All Contacts option button selected. Otherwise, select the Synchronize Selected Groups Only option button, and then select the check box for each group you want to include.

6. If you want to synchronize calendars as well, click the Calendars subtab to display its contents, then select the Synchronize Calendars From Microsoft Outlook check box.

7. Click the OK button to close the iTunes dialog box.

Now, when you update your iPod, iTunes transfers the contacts and calendars you specified.

Put Your Contacts and Calendars on Your iPod Automatically from the Mac

If you keep your contacts in Address Book and your calendar information in iCal, you can copy them automatically to your iPod using either iTunes 4.8 or later or iSync.

Put Your Contacts and Calendars on Your iPod Automatically Using iTunes

If you have Mac OS X 10.2.3 or later and iTunes 4.8 or later, the easiest and quickest way to put your contacts and calendars on your iPod is to use the features built into iTunes. To do so, follow these steps:

1. Connect your iPod to your Mac as usual.

2. CTRL-click the iPod in the Source pane and then choose iPod Options from the shortcut menu to display the iPod tab of the Preferences dialog box.

3. Click the Contacts subtab button to display its contents (see Figure 10-2).

4. Select the Synchronize Address Book Contacts check box, then either select the Synchronize All Contacts option button or select the Synchronize Selected Groups Only option button and select the check box for each group that you want to synchronize.

5. Click the Calendars subtab to display its contents (see Figure 10-3).

6. Select the Synchronize iCal Calendars check box, then either select the Synchronize All Calendars option button or select the Synchronize Selected Calendars Only option button and select the check box for each calendar that you want to synchronize.

7. Click the OK button to close the Preferences dialog box.

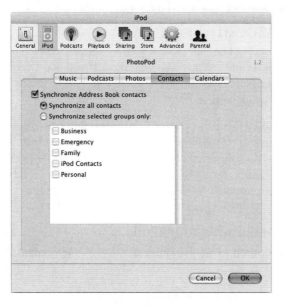

FIGURE 10-2 On the Contacts subtab of the iPod tab of the Preferences dialog box, select the contacts you want to put on your iPod.

10

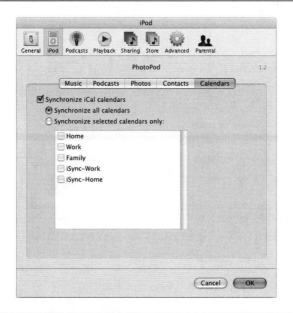

FIGURE 10-3 On the Calendars subtab of the iPod tab of the Preferences dialog box, select the calendars you want to put on your iPod.

Put Your Contacts and Calendars on Your iPod Automatically Using iSync

If you have Mac OS X 10.2.3 or later but are using an earlier version of iTunes than 4.8, you can use iSync to put your contacts and calendars on your iPod. If you don't yet have iSync, download it from the iSync area of the Apple website (www.apple.com/isync). Install iSync and then work your way through the following sections.

Apple keeps updating iSync and iCal, so if you're trying to use them for the first time, check the requirements. If you're using Jaguar, you'll probably do best to update to the latest version of Jaguar available. If you're using Tiger or Panther, you should be in good shape for using iSync and iCal—but updating to the latest version of Tiger or Panther available is unlikely to hurt.

Set iSync to Synchronize with Your iPod

First, you need to add your iPod to the list of devices iSync synchronizes. To do so, follow these steps:

1. Connect your iPod to your Mac as usual.

2. Run iSync by whichever means you prefer.

3. If iSync doesn't automatically detect your iPod and add it to its list, press ⌘-N or choose Devices | Add Device to display the Add Device dialog box (shown here with a device already identified):

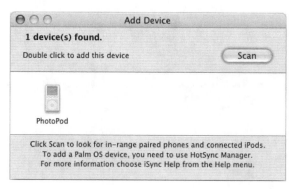

4. If iSync doesn't scan automatically for devices, click the Scan button to force a scan.

5. Double-click the icon for your iPod to add it to the iSync window.

6. Click the close button on the Add Device window.

Figure 10-4 shows an iPod added to the iSync window.

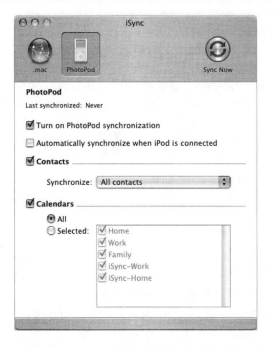

FIGURE 10-4   After adding your iPod to the iSync list of devices, you're ready to choose synchronization options.

Choose Synchronization Options for Your iPod

Once you've added your iPod to the list of devices that iSync can synchronize with, choose the appropriate synchronization options (shown in Figure 10-4):

- **Turn On *iPod* Synchronization**   Controls whether iSync synchronizes with your iPod (where *iPod* is the name of your iPod). Normally, you'll want to keep this check box selected, as it is by default.

- **Automatically Synchronize When iPod Is Connected**   Controls whether iSync automatically synchronizes your contacts and calendar (as appropriate) whenever you plug your iPod into your Mac. If you don't select this check box, you can force a synchronization by clicking the Sync Now button.

- **Contacts**   Controls whether iSync synchronizes your contacts.

- **Synchronize**   Controls which of your contacts iSync synchronizes. The default setting for the iPod is All Contacts.

- **Calendars**   Controls whether iSync synchronizes your calendars. Select the All option button (the default) to synchronize all your calendars. To synchronize only some of your calendars (for example, just your Home calendar, not your Work calendar), select the Selected option button and then select the check boxes for the calendars you want to synchronize.

 **Synchronize Only Some Contacts with Your iPod**

If you keep a lot of contacts in your Address Book, synchronizing them all to your iPod can make the Contacts folder on your iPod difficult to navigate because you have to scroll endlessly to find the people you're interested in.

To get around this problem, you can synchronize only some of your contacts from Address Book to your iPod. To do so, follow these steps:

1. In Address Book, create a new group by clicking the Add New Group button (the + button below the Group pane), pressing ⌘-SHIFT-N, or choosing File | New Group.

2. Type the name for the group and press RETURN.

3. Select the All group (or whichever group contains the contacts you want to add to the group you'll synchronize) to display its contents.

4. Select the contacts and then drag them to the new group you created.

5. In iSync, select the new group in the Synchronize drop-down list.

6. Synchronize your iPod as usual.

Synchronize Your Contacts and Calendar

If you chose to have iSync automatically synchronize your iPod when you connect it, all you need do to start a synchronization is connect your iPod. If you opted for manual synchronization, connect your iPod, run iSync, and then click the Sync Now button.

 To synchronize quickly, or run iSync easily, you can add an iSync icon to the menu bar. To do so, choose iSync | Preferences or press ⌘-COMMA and then select the Show iSync In Menu Bar check box in the Preferences dialog box. You can then click the icon and choose Open iSync (to open iSync so that you can synchronize) or simply select Sync Now from the menu (to synchronize immediately).

iSync displays the Data Change Alert dialog box (see Figure 10-5) or the Safeguard dialog box (the Jaguar incarnation of the same feature) to make sure you understand how the synchronization will affect the data on your iPod. Click the Proceed button if you want to go ahead with the synchronization. Select the Do Not Show This Dialog Again check box first if you want iSync to skip alerting you in the future.

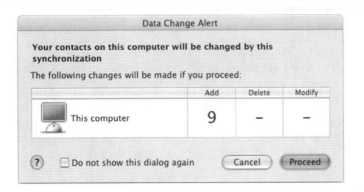

FIGURE 10-5   The Data Change Alert dialog box warns you of the extent of changes that synchronization will cause.

> **TIP** *To turn off the Data Change Alert warnings or Safeguard warnings, choose iSync | Preferences and then clear the Show Data Change Alert check box in the Preferences dialog box. To change the threshold for which the warnings appear, leave this check box selected, but choose Any, More Than 1%, More Than 5%, or More Than 10% in the drop-down list. When the specified amount of data will be changed, iSync displays the warning to make sure you know the changes will occur.*

10

Revert to Last Sync

If synchronizing your data with iSync gives you an undesirable result (for example, you lose contacts or calendar information you weren't intending to get rid of), you should be able to repair the damage by reverting to the last synchronization. To do so, choose Devices | Revert To Last Sync and then click the Revert To Last Sync button in the confirmation dialog box that iSync displays:

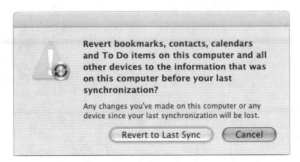

iSync then restores the data from a copy it made of your data at the last synchronization.

> **TIP** *You can also force iSync to make a backup of your data at any time by choosing Devices | Back Up My Data.*

Stop Synchronizing Your iPod

You can stop synchronizing your iPod either temporarily or permanently. Here's how:

- ■ To stop synchronization temporarily, select your iPod in the iSync window and then clear the Turn On *iPod* Synchronization check box (where *iPod* is the name of your iPod).

- ■ To stop synchronization permanently, select your iPod in the iSync window, choose Devices | Remove Device, and then click the Remove button in the confirmation dialog box that appears. To make your iPod synchronize again, add your iPod once more as described in the section "Set iSync to Synchronize with Your iPod," earlier in this chapter.

Prevent Your iPod from Showing Duplicate Contacts and Calendar Information

If you use iSync to put contacts and calendar information on your iPod automatically, you can get duplicate entries for contacts and calendar information you've already copied to your iPod manually (or that you subsequently copy to your iPod manually).

This happens because iSync doesn't delete any data from the iPod that iSync itself hasn't put there. So if you want to synchronize your contacts and calendar information automatically, you need to commit fully to iSync. To do so, follow these steps:

1. Connect your iPod to your Mac.

2. Enable disk mode if it's not currently enabled. (In iTunes, select the icon for your iPod in the Source pane, click the Display Options For Player button, select the Enable Disk Use check box on the General subtab or the Music subtab of the iPod tab in the Preferences dialog box, and click the OK button.)

3. From the Contacts folder on your iPod, import into Address Book the vCards for any contacts it doesn't yet contain. Make sure you don't add existing contacts to Address Book—it'll happily create duplicate entries that you'll then need to weed out manually.

4. From the Calendars folder on your iPod, import into iCal any calendar information it doesn't already contain.

5. Drag the Contacts folder and the Calendars folder on your iPod to the Trash. iSync will automatically create these folders if they don't exist. Alternatively, drag the contents of each folder to the Trash.

6. Run iSync and synchronize your calendars and contacts.

View Your Contacts on Your iPod

To view your contacts on your iPod, follow these steps:

1. Choose Extras | Contacts from the main menu to display the Contacts submenu (shown on the left in Figure 10-6).

2. Scroll to the contact you want to view and then press the Select button. Your iPod displays the contact's information. The right screen in Figure 10-6 shows an example. You may need to scroll down to view all the data about the contact.

NOTE *The fifth-generation and color-screen fourth-generation regular iPods display more contact information per screen than the regular iPods that have monochrome screens, and more than the iPod nano and iPod mini (which have smaller screens).*

3. To display the previous contact, press the Previous button. To display the next contact, press the Next button.

To specify how your iPod should sort your contacts' names and display them onscreen, scroll to the Contacts item on the Settings screen and then press the Select button to display the Contacts screen.

To change the sort order, scroll (if necessary) to the Sort item and then press the Select button to toggle between the First Last setting (for example, "Joe Public") and the Last, First setting (for example, "Public, Joe").

To change the display format, scroll (if necessary) to the Display item and then press the Select button to toggle between the First Last setting and the Last, First setting.

Most people find using the same sort order and display format best, but you may prefer otherwise. For example, you might sort by Last, First but display by First Last.

10

FIGURE 10-6   In the Contacts submenu (left), select the contact you want to view and then press the Select button to display the contact's information (right).

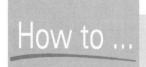

Force a Contact Missing from the Contacts List to Appear on Your iPod

If a contact fails to appear in the Contacts list on your iPod even if you're sure it has been copied to the iPod's Contacts folder, the vCard may be incorrectly formatted. (The vCard must be formatted using either the vCard 2.1 format or the vCard 3.0 format for it to appear on your iPod.)

The easiest way to make sure the vCard is correctly formatted is to export it from a compatible application, as described later in this chapter.

View Your Calendars on Your iPod

To view your calendars on your iPod, follow these steps:

1. Choose Extras | Calendar to display the Calendars screen.

2. If you synchronize multiple calendars, the first Calendars screen contains a list of available calendars, as shown here. Scroll down to the calendar you want (or to your To Do list) and then press the Select button to display it.

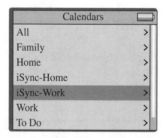

3. If you synchronize only one calendar, your iPod automatically displays the calendar for the current month (the first time you access the calendar) or the last month you accessed (thereafter):

4. Scroll backward or forward to the day you're interested in:

    ■ To access the next month or the previous month, press the Next button or the Previous button, respectively.

    ■ If you're happier scrolling, you can scroll back past the beginning of the month to access the previous month, or you can scroll forward past the end of the month to access the next month.

5. Press the Select button to display your schedule for that day:

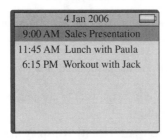

6. To view the details for an appointment, scroll to it and press the Select button. The following illustration shows a sample appointment. From there, you can press the Next button to display the next appointment or the Previous button to display the previous appointment.

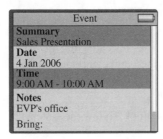

7. Once you've accessed a day, you can press the Next button to access the next day or the Previous button to access the previous day.

Put Contacts on Your iPod Manually

As you saw earlier in this chapter, iTunes can put your contacts on your iPod automatically—as long as you're using the right version of iTunes and your contacts are stored in Outlook Express or Outlook (Windows) or the Address Book (Mac). If you're using an earlier version of iTunes or a different contact management application, you may need to put your contacts on your iPod manually.

Create vCards in Windows

This section discusses how to create vCards from the most widely used sources in Windows: Address Book, Outlook Express, Outlook, and Palm Desktop.

Create a vCard from Address Book

Address Book, an applet that comes built into Windows, is the default location for storing contact information in Windows. You can launch Address Book by choosing Start | Programs | Accessories | Address Book or by clicking the Address Book button in an application such as Outlook Express, Outlook, or Microsoft Word.

You can create vCards from Address Book in two ways. The easier and faster way is to select the contacts you want to export to vCards, drag them to the desktop or the folder in which you want to create the vCards, and drop them there. This technique lets you create multiple vCards at once.

For speed, open a window to display the Contacts folder on your iPod. Then drag the vCards directly into it from Address Book.

To create a vCard from Address Book the harder and slower way, follow these steps:

1. Select the contact from whose entry you want to create a vCard. (You can export only one contact at a time to a vCard.)

2. Choose File | Export | Business Card (vCard) to display the Export As Business Card (vCard) dialog box. (This is a Save As dialog box in disguise.)

3. Specify the file name and location for the file and then click the Save button.

Create a vCard from Outlook Express

The contacts in the Windows Address Book appear in the Contacts pane in Outlook Express, but you can't export them directly from there. Instead, click the Addresses button to display Address Book and then create vCards as described in the previous section.

Create a vCard from Outlook

To create one or more vCards from Outlook, follow these steps:

1. Click the Contacts button, choose Go | Contacts, or press CTRL-3 to display your contacts.

2. Select the contact or contacts for which you want to create vCards.

3. Choose File | Save As to display the Save As dialog box.

4. Select the vCard Files item in the Save As Type drop-down list.

5. Enter the file name in the File Name text box, specify the folder, and then click the Save button.

Create a vCard from Palm Desktop

To create one or more vCards from Palm Desktop, follow these steps:

1. Click the Contacts button or choose View | Contacts to display the Contacts pane.

2. Select the contact or contacts from which you want to create vCards. If necessary, select the appropriate category of contacts in the Category drop-down list, or choose the All item to display all your contacts.

3. Choose File | Export vCard to display the Export As dialog box.

4. Enter the file name in the File Name text box, specify the destination, and then click the Export button.

Put Contacts on Your iPod from Windows Manually

To put contacts on your Windows iPod, you must enable your iPod for use as an external disk and assign a drive letter to it. (In many cases, you may find that Windows treats your iPod as an external disk and assigns it a drive letter without your intervention.) If you've already done this, you're set to go; if not, follow these steps:

1. Connect your iPod to your PC as usual. If you have your iPod set to synchronize automatically, let it do so.

2. In iTunes, right-click the iPod's entry in the Source pane and choose iPod Options from the shortcut menu to display the iPod tab of the iTunes dialog box. Click the General subtab or Music subtab to display its contents (see Figure 10-7).

10

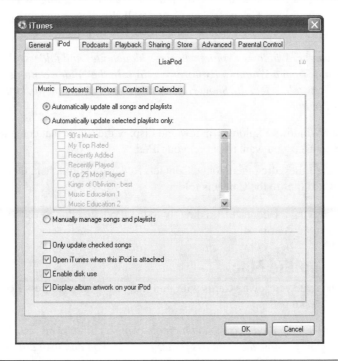

You may need to enable disk use on your iPod before you can put contacts on it.

3. Select the Enable Disk Use check box. iTunes displays a dialog box warning you that you'll need to unmount your iPod manually before disconnecting it:

4. Click the OK button. iTunes returns you to the iTunes dialog box.

5. Click the OK button to close the iTunes dialog box.

Once you've enabled disk mode, you can copy the contact files directly onto your iPod. To do so, follow these steps:

1. Choose Start | My Computer to open a My Computer window that lists the drives on your computer. Your iPod should now appear as a drive with its own drive letter in the Devices With Removable Storage category.

2. Double-click the icon for your iPod to open it in a Windows Explorer window. You'll see it contains the folders Calendars and Contacts. If Windows Explorer is set to display hidden files and folders as well, you'll see an iPod_Control folder too.

To control whether Windows Explorer displays hidden files and folders, choose Tools | Folder Options from a Windows Explorer window. In the Folder Options dialog box, display the View tab, select the Show Hidden Files And Folders option button, and then click the OK button.

3. Open another Windows Explorer window and display the folder that contains the vCard files for the contacts you want to put on your iPod.

4. Select the vCard files, drag them to the Contacts folder, and drop them there. Windows copies the vCard files to the Contacts folder.

Because you're copying the contact files directly to the iPod, you don't need to synchronize to make the files appear on your iPod.

Create vCards on the Mac

On the Mac, you can create your own vCards with minimal effort from Address Book, Entourage, and Palm Desktop.

With each of these applications, you can create contacts directly on your iPod. Open a Finder window to show the Contacts folder on your iPod and then drag the contacts to that folder to create vCards from them.

Create a vCard from Address Book

To create a vCard from Address Book, drag an item from the Address Book to another application or location. For example, to create a vCard on the desktop, drag a vCard to the desktop. Address Book names the vCard using the contact's name and applies the .vcf extension.

> TIP
>
> *Normally, a vCard contains the data for one person or organization. But the Mac OS X Address Book can create a single vCard that contains multiple entries. To create such a vCard, select multiple cards and then export them. Alternatively, export an entire group. You can drag any group to the desktop except for the All group. Alternatively, you can export any group (including the All group) by selecting it, issuing an Export Group vCard command from the File menu or the shortcut menu, specifying the file name and location in the Save dialog box, and then clicking the Save button.*

Create a vCard from Entourage

To create a vCard from Entourage, follow these steps:

1. Click the Address button in the upper-left pane to display your address book.

> CAUTION
>
> *You can export all your Entourage contacts to a tab-delimited text file by opening the Address Book, choosing File | Export Contacts, using the Save dialog box to specify the file name and location, and then clicking the Save button. But the resulting file isn't vCard compatible.*

2. Select the contact or contacts from which you want to create vCards.

3. Drag the selected contact or contacts to the folder in which you want to create the vCards, or to the desktop.

> TIP
>
> *To export all your Entourage information to your iPod, use the iPod It utility. See "iPod It" in Chapter 11 for details.*

Create a vCard from Palm Desktop

You can create a vCard from Palm Desktop by dragging a contact to the folder in which you want to create the vCard. But you can also create vCards by using the Export: Palm Desktop dialog box. To do so, follow these steps:

1. In the Address List window, select the contact from which you want to create a vCard.

2. Choose File | Export to display the Export: Palm Desktop dialog box (shown in Figure 10-8 with settings chosen). The Addresses item will be selected in the Modules drop-down list by default.

3. Use the Save As text box to specify the file name and the Where drop-down list to specify the location under which to save the file.

Export: Palm Desktop

Choose a name and location to export to.

Save As: Contacts for iPod

Where: ☐ Documents

Module: Addresses

Items: All 486 Addresses   Columns...

Format: vCard

Cancel   Export

FIGURE 10-8   You can export one or more contacts as vCards easily from Palm Desktop for the Mac.

4. In the Items drop-down list, select the appropriate item—for example, All *NN* Addresses.

5. In the Format drop-down list, select the vCard item.

6. Click the Export button to export the contacts to the specified file.

How to ...   Create vCards from CSV Files

All these means of creating vCards are fine—provided your addresses are stored in one of those applications. But if the application in which your addresses are stored can't export them as vCards, you'll need to take a couple of extra steps to get the addresses onto your iPod. For example, if you use the Yahoo! address book, you won't be able to create vCards directly from it.

The first step is to export the addresses from the application into a text file. Most applications can create a CSV file, so that's usually the best format to use. Other applications create tab-separated values (TSV) files, which will usually work as well.

Once you've created the CSV or TSV file, import it into an address book that can handle CSV or TSV files *and* can create vCards. On Windows XP, both Address Book and Palm Desktop can handle CSV imports, so use whichever you prefer.

On the Mac, the news isn't so good. The Address Book in Mac OS X can import only vCards and LDAP Interchange Format (LDIF) files. (LDAP is the abbreviation for *Lightweight Directory Access Protocol*, a standard protocol for accessing directory information.) Palm Desktop can't import CSV or TSV files either, but Entourage can import just about anything in sight.

Once you've found the appropriate Import command (usually File | Import), the tricky part of importing is assigning each field in the CSV or TSV file to the corresponding field in the address book. The following illustration shows examples of the dialog boxes used for mapping data to fields. The Specify Import Fields dialog box (on the left) is from Palm Desktop for Windows; the Import Contacts dialog box (on the right) is from Entourage, which can usually map some of the fields automatically.

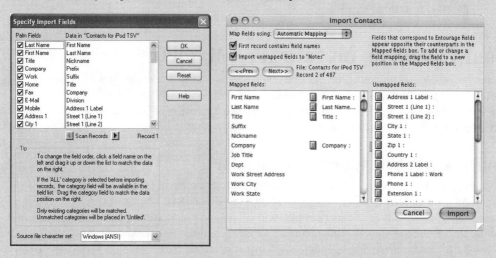

The second step is to export the vCards from the address application, as described earlier in the chapter.

Put Your Contacts on Your iPod Manually Using the Mac

To transfer contacts to your Mac manually, follow these steps:

1. Export your contacts to vCard files.

2. Connect your iPod to your Mac (if it's not currently connected). If iTunes is set to synchronize automatically on connection, let synchronization take place.

3. If disk mode isn't enabled on your iPod, enable it. (In iTunes, select the icon for your iPod in the Source pane, click the Display Options For Player button, select the Enable Disk Use check box on the General subtab or the Music subtab of the iPod tab in the Preferences dialog box, and click the OK button.)

4. Double-click the desktop icon for your iPod to display a Finder window of its contents.

5. Drag the vCard files to the Contacts folder and drop them there.

 *The first time you put contacts on your iPod manually, you may want to get rid of the Instructions and Sample vCards that come preinstalled on your iPod. To do so, delete the files ipod_created_instructions.vcf and ipod_created_sample.vcf. Alternatively, you might want to store the samples in a folder on your Mac as templates in case you ever want to create vCards manually.*

6. Close the Contacts folder.

7. Eject your iPod by selecting it and pressing ⌘-E, issuing an Eject *iPod* command (where *iPod* is the name of your iPod) from the Controls menu or the shortcut menu, or dragging the iPod icon to the Trash.

Put Your Calendars on Your iPod Manually

To put your calendars on your iPod manually, you need to create iCalendar files or vCalendar files and then transfer them to the iPod. The following sections walk you through the process of doing so on Windows and Mac OS X, starting with an explanation of what the iCalendar files and vCalendar files are.

Understand vCalendar and iCalendar

vCalendar and iCalendar are standards for storing information about calendar events and to-do items, and for transferring this information from one vCalendar/iCalendar-aware application to another. vCalendar and iCalendar are platform independent, so a Mac calendaring application can use the vCalendar and iCalendar formats to schedule meetings or other events with vCalendar/iCalendar-aware applications on other platforms, such as Windows, Linux, and Unix.

Typically, calendaring applications (such as iCal, Microsoft Outlook, and Microsoft Entourage) use vCalendar and iCalendar files in the background to transmit the details of events, appointments, and invitations. Under normal circumstances, you won't need to work directly with vCalendar or iCalendar files yourself. But sometimes, when you need to put your calendar on an iPod, you'll need to create vCalendar files or iCalendar files by exporting them from your calendaring software.

 *The iCalendar format was developed after the vCalendar format and contains more data, so if your calendaring application offers a choice of formats, choose iCalendar over vCalendar. However, both formats work fine for transferring basic calendar data.*

Create vCalendar Files in Windows

This section shows you how to create vCalendar files from Palm Desktop for Windows as well as iCalendar and vCalendar files from Microsoft Outlook.

Create vCalendar Files from Palm Desktop

To create a vCalendar file from Palm Desktop, follow these steps:

1. Click the Calendar button or choose View | Calendar to display your calendar.

2. If your calendar isn't already displayed in Day view or Week view, click the Day tab or the Week tab to display the calendar in one of those views.

3. Select the event you want to export.

4. Choose File | Export vCal to display the Export As dialog box.

5. In the File Name text box, enter the file name under which you want to save the file.

6. Specify the folder in which to save the file.

7. Click the Export button to export the event.

Create vCalendar or iCalendar Files from Microsoft Outlook

To create a vCalendar or iCalendar file from Microsoft Outlook, follow these steps:

1. Click the Calendar button in the Outlook bar, choose Go | Calendar, or press CTRL-2 to display your calendar if it's not already displayed.

2. Select the appointment from which you want to create the vCalendar file or iCalendar file.

3. Choose File | Save As to display the Save As dialog box.

4. Specify the location in which to save the iCalendar file or vCalendar file.

> **TIP**
> *If your iPod is currently connected to your computer and disk mode is enabled, you can save the file directly into your iPod's Calendars folder. Otherwise, save your calendar files to a folder from which you can then copy them to your iPod's Calendars folder once you connect your iPod.*

5. In the Save As type drop-down list, select the iCalendar Format item or the vCalendar Format item, as appropriate. (iCalendar is preferable.)

6. Click the Save button to save the appointment to a file.

Create iCalendar and vCalendar Files on the Mac

The following sections show you how to create iCalendar and vCalendar files from iCal, Microsoft Entourage, and Palm Desktop for the Mac.

Create iCalendar Files from iCal

Unlike many other applications, iCal doesn't support creating calendars by dragging to the desktop or another location. Instead, to create iCalendar files from iCal, follow these steps:

1. In the Calendars pane, select the calendar you want to export.

2. Choose File | Export to display the iCal: Export dialog box.

3. Enter the file name in the Save As text box.

4. Use the Where drop-down list to specify the folder in which to save the calendar. If your iPod is docked and mounted, you could save the file directly to your iPod's Calendars folder.

5. Click the Export button.

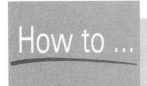

Export Multiple (or All) Appointments from Outlook

As you saw in "Create vCalendar or iCalendar Files from Microsoft Outlook," Outlook lets you export only one appointment at a time to a vCalendar or iCalendar file. Unless your calendar is very sparsely populated or you're very patient, exporting your appointments will be a time-consuming and tedious process.

Good news: Other people have run into this problem before you, and some of them decided to fix it. The following are three of the utilities you can use to export multiple appointments from Outlook:

■   **iPodSync**   iPodSync ($14.95; www.ipod-sync.com) is a powerful shareware application that can export contacts to vCard files and appointment information to iCalendar files. You can choose a wide variety of options, such as whether to synchronize only certain fields, whether to include notes, and even whether to add birthday and anniversary dates to notes. The following illustration shows iPodSync's Calendar page, on which you can choose which appointments to synchronize. You can download a 15-day trial version of iPodSync from the preceding URL. iPodSync works with Outlook XP and Outlook 2000 on Windows XP, Windows 2000, and Windows Me.

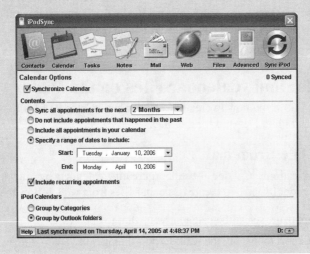

■ **iAppoint**   iAppoint (freeware; www.xs4all.nl/~hagemans/) has a simple interface, shown here, that lets you choose the calendar to work with, specify the range of dates from which you want to export appointments, and tell iAppoint where to store the file. (If your iPod is connected and disk mode is enabled, you can save the file directly to the Calendars folder.) The Contacts button displays a window with controls for exporting your contacts. iAppoint is currently at version 0.5 but seems stable.

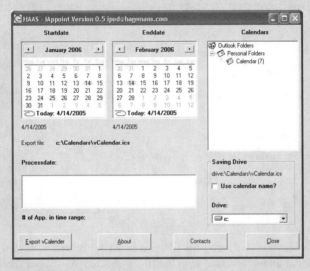

■ **OutPod**   OutPod (freeware; www.stoer.de/ipod/ipod_en.htm) lets you export multiple appointments into a single vCalendar or iCalendar file. OutPod, shown here, also can export multiple contacts at once:

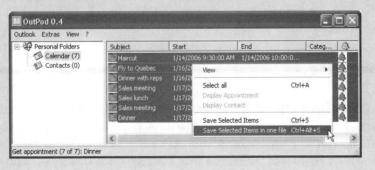

Create iCalendar Files from Microsoft Entourage

To create iCalendar files from Microsoft Entourage, select the appointment or event you want to export, drag it to the desktop or the folder in which you want to create the file, and then drop it there.

To export all your Entourage information to your iPod, use iPod It. See "iPod It" in Chapter 11.

Create vCalendar Files from Palm Desktop

Palm Desktop makes it easy to export the entire contents of your Date Book to a vCalendar file. Follow these steps:

1. Choose File | Export to display the Export: Palm Desktop dialog box:

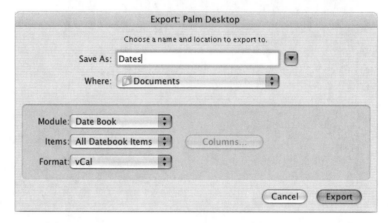

2. Use the Save As text box to specify the file name and the Where drop-down list to specify the location under which to save the file. For example, if your iPod is mounted, you could save the file directly to your iPod's Calendars folder.

3. Ignore the Items drop-down list. It appears to offer you the choice of exporting some Date Book items or all of them, but in fact the only choice is All Datebook Items. Similarly, ignore the Columns button, because Palm Desktop makes this unavailable when you select the vCal format.

4. In the Format drop-down list, select the vCal item.

5. Click the Export button.

Put Your Calendars on Your iPod from Windows Manually

If you can't use iTunes to put Outlook 2003 calendars on your iPod or use iPodSync (discussed in the "Export Multiple (or All) Appointments from Outlook" sidebar, earlier in this chapter) to put calendars from other versions of Outlook on your iPod, you can do things the hard way, as described in this section.

First, check whether you need to enable disk mode on your iPod. Connect the iPod as usual, and allow synchronization to take place if it's configured to do so. Then choose Start | My Computer to open a My Computer window, and see if the window shows a drive for the iPod. The drive will normally bear the name you have assigned to the iPod. If the drive is present, double-click it to display its contents and then double-click the Calendars folder. If you can open the iPod as a drive, you do not need to enable disk mode.

If you do need to enable disk mode, follow these steps:

1. Open iTunes if it's not already running, or activate it.
2. Right-click the iPod's entry in the Source pane and choose iPod Options from the shortcut menu to display the iPod tab of the iTunes dialog box.
3. Click the General subtab or the Music subtab to display its contents.
4. Select the Enable Disk Use check box. iTunes displays a dialog box warning that you'll need to unmount your iPod manually before disconnecting it.
5. Click the OK button. iTunes returns you to the iTunes dialog box.
6. Click the OK button to close the iTunes dialog box.

Once you can access your iPod through Windows Explorer, you can copy the calendar files directly onto your iPod. To do so, follow these steps:

1. Choose Start | My Computer to open a My Computer window and then double-click the drive that represents your iPod.
2. Double-click the icon for your iPod and then double-click the Calendar icon to open that folder.
3. Open another Windows Explorer window to the folder that contains the iCalendar files for the events you want to put onto your iPod.
4. Select the calendar files, drag them to the Calendars folder, and drop them there. Windows copies the calendar files to the Calendars folder.

Because you're copying the calendar files directly to the iPod, you don't need to synchronize to make the files appear on your iPod.

Put Your Calendars on Your iPod Manually from Mac OS X

To transfer contacts manually, disk use must be enabled on your iPod. Here's how to start:

1. Launch or activate iTunes.
2. CTRL-click or right-click the entry for your iPod in the Source pane and choose iPod Options from the shortcut menu to display the iPod tab of the Preferences dialog box.
3. Click the General subtab or the Music subtab to display its contents.
4. Select the Enable Disk Use check box.
5. Click the OK button to close the Preferences dialog box.

Once you've enabled disk mode, you can put the calendar files directly onto your iPod. Connect your iPod to your Mac as usual and then double-click the icon for your iPod to display a Finder window of its contents. You can also use the following techniques:

■ If you haven't yet created the calendar files, you can simply create them in your iPod's Calendars folder. For example, select the Calendars folder in the iCal: Export dialog box or the Export: Palm Desktop dialog box. Or drag an event from Microsoft Entourage or Palm Desktop directly to the Calendars folder.

■ Alternatively, export your contacts to vCalendar or iCalendar files in another folder and then copy them from there to your iPod's Calendars folder. Using this method, you can export the contacts when your iPod isn't connected to your Mac.

After adding your calendar files to your iPod, eject your iPod in any of these ways: Select it and press ⌘-E, issue an Eject command from the File menu or the shortcut menu, or drag the iPod icon to the Trash.

Chapter 11

Put Text and Books on Your iPod

How to…

- Understand the basics of putting text on your iPod
- Use the Notes feature to put text on your iPod from a Mac or Windows
- Put text on your iPod from Windows
- Put text on your iPod from a Mac

In the previous chapter, you learned how to store your contacts and calendars on your iPod. This chapter discusses how to store other text on your iPod so you can display it on the screen. The next chapter shows you how to put pictures on photo-capable iPods, and video on video-capable iPods, and how to use a regular iPod as extra storage for a digital camera.

By using your iPod as a hard drive (as discussed in Chapter 16), you can store any type of file on your iPod. But unless the file is in a text format that your iPod's software can handle, you won't be able to display the file on the iPod's interface—you'll be able to work with the file only when you've connected your iPod to your computer.

Your iPod includes a Notes feature specifically designed for putting text files on your iPod in a readable format, and for accessing and reading those files. To create suitable text files, you can use applications created by developers for first- and second-generation iPods, which lacked the Notes feature.

 *Two great places for finding utilities such as those discussed in this chapter are VersionTracker.com (www.versiontracker.com) and iPodLounge.com (www.ipodlounge.com). You'll also find Mac-related utilities at Apple's Mac OS X Downloads page (www.apple.com/macosx/downloads).*

Limitations to Putting Information on Your iPod

Assuming it's not completely full of music, your iPod has plenty of space to store text, but its screen can only display a small amount of text at a time. You can scroll to see more text, but scrolling a great deal soon becomes tedious.

A fifth-generation iPod can display a heading plus nine or ten lines of text of up to about 40 characters each—enough to be useful for compact information such as recipes, memos, driving directions, or even winsome love poetry, but so small as to make reading any lengthy document feel like hard work. You can see why Apple hasn't yet chosen to incorporate an e-book reader in the iPod. The iPod nano can display substantially less text at a time.

Still, if you've been reading Tolstoy on the bus using your mobile phone's display, reading text on your iPod may appeal to you. Besides, the iPod has enough battery power to let you read for a while in the dark; you can play music at the same time; and putting the text on your iPod can save you from needing to tote multiple devices.

What Text Can You Put on Your iPod?

With the right utilities, you can put on your iPod any text file you have on your computer. That text could be anything from a parts list to part of a novel, from a thesis to a section of a thesaurus. You can store notes of any length on your iPod, but the iPod can display only the first 4KB of a text file. That's roughly 4,000 characters, or about 600-700 words of average length. Various utilities let you split up longer files into iPod-size bites automatically. The iPod can hold up to 1,000 notes at a time, and the notes can be linked together to make them easy to navigate.

> **NOTE**   *The first time you access the Notes category after adding the notes, your iPod has to build an index of the notes it contains. If there are nearly 1,000 notes, building the index takes several minutes. Once the index is built, accessing the notes is quick.*

As you'll see in the following sections, apart from text files, utility designers have concentrated on types of text that are widely useful and can be downloaded easily from sources on the Internet. Here are some examples:

- **News headlines**   Various iPod utilities can download news headlines from news sites. Most of these utilities let you choose the sites, whereas other utilities are limited to a single site. Some utilities can download the stories attached to the headlines, which tends to be more useful than the headlines alone.

- **Weather reports**   Various iPod utilities can download weather reports from online sites. You specify the city (or ZIP code) and the type of weather reports (for example, today's forecast or a five-day report), and the utility downloads the relevant information.

- **Stock quotes**   Several utilities can download stock quotes. You specify the stock symbols and (in some cases) choose the frequency of updates.

- **Lyrics**   Some utilities can look up the lyrics to songs you specify.

- **Horoscopes**   Some utilities can download horoscopes.

- **Driving directions**   Some utilities can download driving directions from mapping services.

Because first- and second-generation iPods didn't have a Notes feature, some utilities create these items as contacts, so the Contacts folder on your iPod can get jammed. But apart from your needing to scroll further than usual, accessing the information is easy. Other utilities create these items as notes, which lets recent, notes-capable iPods keep them in a separate category. This is much preferable, as both notes and contacts remain easy to access.

Use the Notes Feature

Your iPod's built-in Notes feature lets you load text files on your iPod and read them on its screen. This feature works effectively only with plain-text files. You *can* transfer other documents, such as rich-text format documents or Word documents, by using the Notes feature, but the text displayed on the iPod then includes formatting codes and extended characters. These make the text nearly impossible to read, especially given the small size of the iPod's screen.

To put notes on your iPod, connect your iPod and enable disk mode if it's not currently enabled:

1. Open iTunes if it's not already running, or activate it.

2. Right-click (or CTRL-click on the Mac) the iPod's entry in the Source pane and choose iPod Options from the shortcut menu to display the iPod tab of the iTunes dialog box (Windows) or the Preferences dialog box (Mac).

3. Click the Music subtab to display its contents.

4. Select the Enable Disk Use check box. iTunes displays a dialog box warning you that you'll need to unmount your iPod manually before disconnecting it.

5. Click the OK button to close the message box and then click the OK button to close the dialog box.

Once disk mode is enabled, you can copy or move the note files to the Notes folder on your iPod using Windows Explorer (Windows) or the Finder (Mac OS X).

The Notes folder on your iPod contains a note called Instructions that tells you how to use notes. The first time you open the Notes folder on your iPod, you may want to delete this note to prevent it from appearing further in your listings.

On your iPod, you can then read your notes by choosing Extras | Notes, scrolling down to the file, and pressing the Select button.

Use iPod Scripts to Create and Manage Text Notes on the Mac

If you use the Notes feature extensively on the Mac, consider downloading the iPod Scripts collection that Apple provides for creating and managing text notes. These scripts require Mac OS X 10.2 or later.

At this writing, the iPod Scripts collection contains the following scripts:

- **List Notes** This script provides an easy way of opening one of the scripts stored on your iPod for editing on your Mac. This script displays a dialog box that lists the notes stored on your iPod. You select the appropriate script and click the Open button to open it:

- ■ **Clear All Notes**   This script deletes all the notes in the Notes folder on your iPod and lets you choose whether to delete subfolders in the Notes folder as well.

- ■ **Eject iPod**   This script checks that you want to eject the currently mounted iPod and then ejects it if you click the Continue button. In normal use, you'll find it easier to eject the iPod using either iTunes or the desktop icon (if the iPod is in disk mode) rather than running this script.

- ■ **Clipboard To Note**   This script creates a note from the current contents of the Clipboard. This script is great for quickly grabbing part of a document or a web page and generating a note from it. Select the text, issue a Copy command, and then run the script. Click the Continue button in the first dialog box (shown on the left in the next illustration), enter the name for the note in the dialog box shown on the right in the next illustration, and click OK. The script then displays a message box telling you that it has created the note.

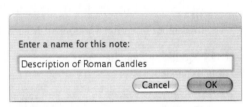

- ■ **MacCentral and Printer Friendly**   The MacCentral and Printer Friendly scripts appear in the Note From Webpages folder. The MacCentral script is for extracting an article from the MacCentral website from the foremost browser window. The Printer Friendly script follows the same theme but is less specialized, extracting the contents of the foremost browser window to a note. For best effect, set the foremost window ready to print without ads and without other HTML items that will otherwise mess up the text of the note.

To use the iPod Scripts collection, follow these steps:

1. Download the iPod Scripts collection from www.apple.com/applescript/ipod/.

2. Move the downloaded file to your ~/Library/Scripts folder and then expand the disk image.

If you haven't used any scripts before, you'll need to create the Scripts folder manually under the ~/Library folder.

3. Connect your iPod to your computer.

4. Use the Script menu to run the script. If you haven't installed the Script menu, do so as described next.

Put the Script Menu on the Mac OS X Menu Bar

You can run the iPod scripts directly from the Scripts folder, but doing so is slower and more awkward than it needs to be. The better way to run scripts is from the Scripts menu that Mac OS X can display on your menu bar.

If you haven't used scripts before, you'll probably need to add the Script menu to the menu bar. To do so, follow these steps:

1. From the Finder, choose Go | Applications to display your Applications folder.

2. Double-click the AppleScript folder to open it in the window.

3. The next step is different in Tiger than in earlier versions of Mac OS X:

   ■ In Tiger, double-click the AppleScript Utility item to run AppleScript Utility. Select the Show Script Menu In Menu Bar check box, and then press ⌘-Q or choose AppleScript Utility | Quit AppleScript Utility.

   ■ In Panther or earlier versions of Mac OS X, double-click the Install Script Menu item.

Mac OS X adds an icon that you can click to display the Script menu, shown here with the iPod scripts expanded:

You can then run scripts easily from the desktop by using the Script menu.

Windows Utilities for Putting Information on Your iPod

The Notes feature is easy to use, but if you have other requirements or a first- or second-generation iPod (these models don't support notes), you need to use third-party utilities. This section discusses Windows utilities for putting text on your iPod. The next section discusses Mac utilities.

EphPod

EphPod (freeware; www.ephpod.com) is a mature utility originally designed, in the days before Windows iPods were released, to enable Windows users to use Mac-formatted iPods. EphPod still performs that function (for which you need to have the non-freeware application MacOpener installed on your PC), but it also works without MacOpener for Windows-formatted iPods.

Among its other features, discussed in "EphPod" in Chapter 15, EphPod lets you download news feeds.

GoogleGet

GoogleGet (freeware; www.markwheeler.net/projects/googleget/) is a compact utility for downloading news from www.google.com. At this writing, you may find you have to download and install Visual Basic component files from the GoogleGet website before GoogleGet (see Figure 11-1) will run—but once it's running, it's straightforward to use.

iPod Agent

iPod Agent (donationware; www.ipodsoft.com/index.php?/software/ipodagent) is a powerful utility that can put text, news, weather, Outlook items, and movie listings on your iPod. iPod

11

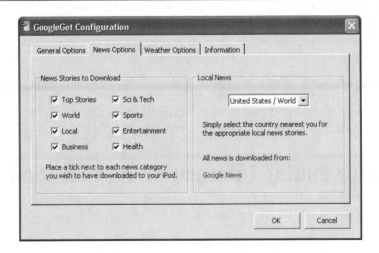

FIGURE 11-1   GoogleGet lets you download news from www.google.com.

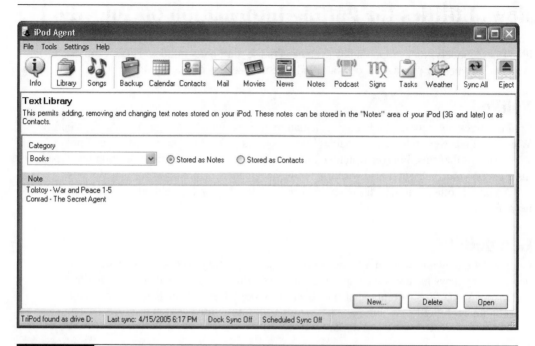

FIGURE 11-2   iPod Agent's many features include transferring news feeds, weather, and text files to your iPod.

Agent (see Figure 11-2, above) can also back up files from your PC to your iPod and retrieve music files from the iPod's music database. (See Chapter 15 for details on other utilities that can retrieve music files from the iPod.)

iPod Library

iPod Library (freeware; www25.brinkster.com/carmagt/ipodlibrary/) is a utility for dividing text files, HTML text files, and PDF files into note-sized sections and loading them on the iPod (see Figure 11-3). You may have to download and install extra Windows DLL (dynamic link library) files from the iPod Library website in order to get iPod Library running.

Mac Utilities for Putting Information on Your iPod

The previous section discussed some utilities for putting information on your iPod from Windows. This section discusses utilities for putting information on your iPod from a Mac, starting with the most useful.

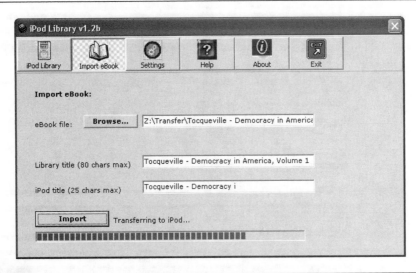

FIGURE 11-3   iPod Library is a freeware tool for managing text notes on your iPod.

iSpeakIt

iSpeakIt ($14.95; www.zapptek.com/ispeak-it/) is a versatile utility that enables you to load news headlines and summaries (from Google), weather forecasts, web pages, and text onto your iPod. iSpeakIt can load not only plain-text files but also the text from other applications installed on your Mac. To transfer the text, choose *Application* | Services | Add Book To iPod (where *Application* is the application's name).

iSpeakIt's name comes from its other leading capability—it lets you use your Mac's text-to-speech capability to "read" text files and create audio files that it loads into iTunes (and thus onto your iPod). You can have iSpeakIt make audio files of the information it downloads from the Internet.

If you have severe sight problems, the Mac's text-to-speech capability can be a great boon. But for most people, the computerized delivery (even of the clearest voices, such as Vicki) lies somewhere between a curiosity and a perversion. You'll know if you want to make audio files from text files—and if you do, iSpeakIt is the application to use.

iPod It

iPod It ($14.95; www.zapptek.com) is a utility that enables you to copy contacts, notes, tasks, e-mail, and calendar information from Microsoft Entourage, or from Mail, Stickies, Address Book, or iCal, to your iPod (see Figure 11-4). iPod It also supports downloading news headlines from Google, weather forecasts, and directions.

11

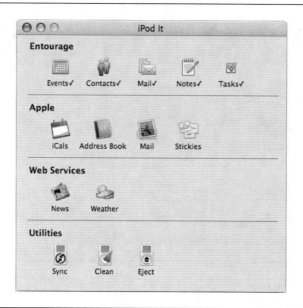

FIGURE 11-4   iPod It can copy a wide variety of text items—including news, weather forecasts, directions, and Entourage items—to your iPod.

Pod2Go

Pod2Go ($12; www.kainjow.com/pod2go/website) lets you put a wide variety of items on your iPod, from news, weather, stock quotes, text files, horoscopes, and driving directions to podcasts (see Figure 11-5). Once you've specified the details of the information you want, Pod2Go downloads the information automatically when you synchronize. Pod2Go can also put your Address Book contacts, Safari bookmarks, Stickies, and iCal calendars onto your iPod. You can even specify files that you want to back up to the iPod.

If you have iPod Software 2.0 or later, Pod2Go lets you choose whether to put the text on your iPod as contacts or as notes. If you're using an earlier version of iPod Software, you can use contacts only.

Book2Pod

Book2Pod (freeware; www.tomsci.com/book2pod or www.ipodlounge.com) is a tool for splitting up a text file into pieces the right size for iPod notes. Book2Pod embeds links at the start and end of each note-size section so that you can navigate to the next section by pressing the Select button. Book2Pod enables you to get around the 1,000-note limitation by letting you load and unload books even after you've split them up into pieces. Book2Pod requires Mac OS X 10.2 or later and iPod firmware 2.0 or higher.

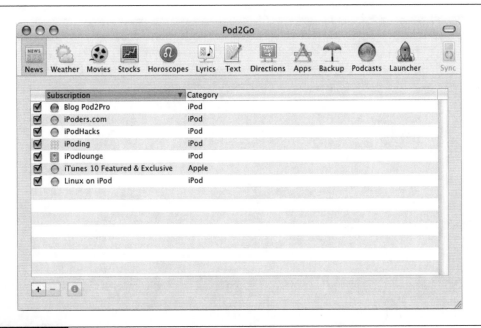

FIGURE 11-5   Apart from text, Pod2Go can also back up specified files to your iPod.

11

iPodMemo

iPodMemo (freeware; various sites including www.versiontracker.com and www.ipodlounge.com) is a text editor with which you can create memos of up to 1,000 characters and put them on your iPod as contacts. iPodMemo is basic but functional—and the price is right.

PodWriter

PodWriter (freeware; www.steigerworld.com/doug/podwriter.php) is a small text editor that you can use to put text files on your iPod. PodWriter has a straightforward interface and works well for creating memos and other short notes.

Chapter 12

Put Photos and Videos on Your iPod

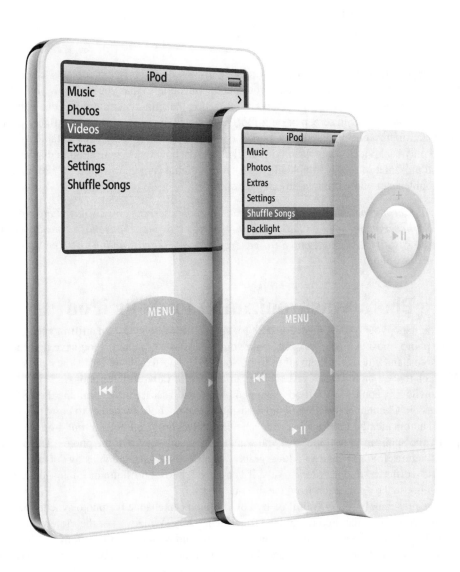

How to…

- Configure photo synchronization for your iPod
- View photos on your iPod
- Configure and view a slide show
- Upload photos from a digital camera to your photo-capable iPod or regular iPod
- Troubleshoot photo-related issues
- Put videos on your iPod
- Create video files suitable for your iPod

Not content with being your music player and a display device for your contacts, calendars, and notes, your iPod can also house your photo collection so that you can view your photos on the screen, one-by-one or as slide shows. Even better, the fifth-generation iPod can play back videos, either on its built-in screen or on a TV. This chapter shows you how to configure photo synchronization for your iPod and view photos on its screen, create video files suitable for your iPod, and play back videos on your iPod. You'll also learn how to use your iPod to display slide shows and presentations, how to upload photos from a digital camera to supported iPods, and how to troubleshoot photo- and video-related issues.

 *All fourth-generation regular iPods that have color screens can display photos too. Earlier iPod models—including fourth-generation regular iPods that have monochrome screens; first-, second-, and third-generation regular iPods; and the iPod mini—cannot display photos.*

Configure Photo Synchronization for Your iPod

On an iPod nano, your photos must compete for space with your songs; on a fifth-generation iPod, the photos must compete for space with your videos as well. Unless you have few enough songs, photos, and videos for them all to fit on your iPod, you'll have to make some choices about which to load on it. iTunes gives you a fair amount of flexibility for photos.

When you first connect your iPod to your computer, (as discussed in "Install the iPod Software and iTunes" in Chapter 2) the iPod Setup Assistant lets you choose whether to copy photos to your iPod automatically. In Windows, you can use the Synchronize Photos From drop-down list to specify the application or folder that you want to use as the source of the photos. The default is your My Pictures folder, where Windows graphics applications save graphics by default, but you can choose a different folder. Alternatively, if you have Photoshop Album or Photoshop Elements installed, choose the application from the drop-down list.

You've presumably set up your iPod by now, but you can change the photo synchronization options by working on the iPod tab of the iTunes dialog box (Windows) or the Preferences dialog box (Mac). Right-click the iPod in the Source pane and choose iPod Options from the shortcut menu to display the dialog box. (Alternatively, choose Edit | Preferences or press CTRL-COMMA in

Windows, or choose iTunes | Preferences or press ⌘-COMMA on the Mac.) Then work through the following sections.

Control Which Pictures iTunes Puts on Your iPod

To control which pictures iTunes puts on your iPod, click the Photos subtab button to display the Photos subtab. Figure 12-1 shows the Photos subtab on iTunes for the Mac. The Photos subtab on iTunes for Windows has similar controls.

If you want to use the photo-synchronization options at all, select the Synchronize Photos From check box. In the drop-down list, make the appropriate choice:

- In Windows, if you have Photoshop Album or Photoshop Elements, select the appropriate application in the Synchronize Photos From drop-down list. Otherwise, select the appropriate folder.

- On the Mac, choose iPhoto in the Synchronize Photos From drop-down list if you want to use your iPhoto library. If not, click the Choose Folder item, use the Change Photos Folder Location dialog box to navigate to and select a different folder, and then click the Choose button; or select another folder that already appears on the drop-down list.

12

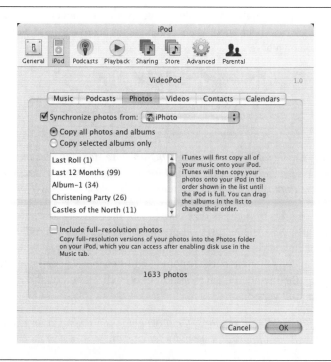

FIGURE 12-1   Configure photo-synchronization options for your iPod on the Photos subtab of the iPod tab of the iTunes dialog box or the Preferences dialog box.

If you want to copy all your photos to your iPod, select the Copy All Photos option button (Windows) or the Copy All Photos And Albums option button (Mac). If you want to control which photos are copied, select the Copy Selected Folders Only option button (Windows) or the Copy Selected Albums Only option button (Mac) and then select the check boxes for the folders or albums in the list box.

> **NOTE** *In Windows, the Copy Selected Folders Only option button isn't available if the folder you choose contains no subfolders.*

Choose Whether to Include Full-Resolution Pictures on Your iPod

When you use iTunes's features to put photos on your iPod, iTunes doesn't simply copy the photo files across to your iPod. Instead, it creates different-sized versions of the photos:

- A miniature version suitable for viewing 30 at a time in thumbnail mode (on a regular iPod) or 12 at a time (on an iPod nano)
- A small version suitable for full-screen viewing on the iPod's screen
- A larger version suitable for full-screen viewing on a television (from a regular iPod)

These three versions are as small as possible for their purposes and are optimized to look as good as possible at the sizes mentioned. When you synchronize your iPod, you'll see iTunes optimizing the files, as shown here:

> **NOTE** *In your iPhoto Cache folder, the optimized pictures are stored in files that use the ithmb format. The iPod itself also uses the ithmb format for the pictures it stores in the Thumbs folder inside the Photos folder (Photos\Thumbs in Windows; Photos/Thumbs on the Mac).*

Normally, these three sizes of pictures take care of all you're likely to want to do with your iPod: view the thumbnails, view the pictures onscreen, or (from a regular iPod) view the pictures on a television. But sometimes you may want to take your actual picture files with you—for example, so that you can copy them to another computer, or so that you can manipulate them at work. In this case, select the Include Full-Resolution Photos check box on the Photos subtab to make iTunes include the full versions.

> **CAUTION** *Including the full-resolution versions of many photos can take up a large amount of space, especially if you have a high-resolution digital camera.*

iTunes stores the full-resolution photos in the Full Resolution folder inside the Photos folder (Photos\Full Resolution as seen by Windows; Photos/Full Resolution as seen by the Mac).

Within this folder, the pictures are divided into subfolders by year, month, and date. For example, pictures you load on May 31, 2006 go into the 2006\05\31 folder (as seen by Windows) or the 2006/05/31 folder (as seen by the Mac). This naming convention ensures that photos are grouped together suitably for sorting by date in either ascending or descending order.

> **TIP** *Selecting the Include Full-Resolution Photos check box on the Photos subtab of the iPod tab is an easy way to get your full-resolution pictures onto your iPod automatically, but you can access them only from a PC or Mac after connecting your iPod to it: you can't display the full-resolution pictures on your iPod's screen or directly on a TV from the iPod. Because of this limitation, you may find it easier to mount your iPod in disk mode and copy the full-resolution versions of photos to the iPod manually. By doing so, you can control the folder in which the photos are stored on the iPod rather than having iTunes create complex folder structures based on the year, month, and day.*

Choose Whether to Display Album Artwork on Your iPod

The iPod can also display any album artwork associated with the songs you load on your iPod. These artwork files take up some space, but not usually a significant amount compared to the songs themselves. This is because the artwork files are relatively compact.

When you have a photo-capable iPod connected, the Music subtab of the iPod tab of the iTunes dialog box or the Preferences dialog box includes the Display Album Artwork On Your iPod check box. Select this check box to display the artwork; clear the check box to prevent your iPod from displaying the artwork. After you finish choosing options for photos and artwork, click the OK button to close the dialog box.

View Photos on Your iPod

To view photos on your iPod, follow these steps:

1. Press the Menu button as many times as necessary to get to the Main menu.

2. Scroll down to highlight Photos and then press the Select button.

3. Scroll down to select your Photo Library or the album you want and then press the Select button. The iPod displays thumbnails of the photos.

4. Scroll to select the thumbnail of the photo you want (scroll clockwise to go forward; scroll counterclockwise to go backward) and then press the Select button to display it.

5. Navigate from photo to photo:

- Press the Previous button to move to the previous photo.

- Press the Next button to move to the next photo.

- Scroll forward or back to move quickly through the photos.

6. To exit the album, press the Menu button.

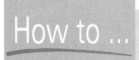 **Delete Unneeded Photo Cache Folders**

iTunes caches the photos it puts on your iPod in a folder named iPod Photo Cache that it creates in the folder that contains your photos. This folder contains all the photos you put on your iPod, so it typically takes up about as much space on your computer's hard disk as on your iPod. (Depending on the file systems used, there may be a minor difference in size.) If you put a lot of photos on your iPod, the cache can take a fair bite out of your hard disk capacity. If you're short of disk space anyway, this bite may cause problems.

When you set iTunes to synchronize a new folder of photos, you can delete your old iPod Photo Cache folder to reclaim space. (iTunes doesn't delete the cache folder for you.) Open the parent folder and then delete the iPod Photo Cache folder:

- In Windows, click the iPod Photo Cache folder, press the DELETE key, and then click the Yes button in the Confirm Folder Delete dialog box that checks whether you want to move the folder to the Recycle Bin. You'll need to empty the Recycle Bin to actually recover the disk space. (Alternatively, click the iPod Photo Cache folder, hold down the SHIFT key, press the DELETE key, and then click the Yes button in the Confirm Folder Delete dialog box to bypass the Recycle Bin.)

- On the Mac, drag the iPod Photo Cache folder to the Trash. You'll need to empty the Trash to actually get the space back.

Configure and View a Slide Show

Before starting a slide show, choose suitable slide show settings. To do so, follow these steps:

1. Press the Menu button as many times as necessary to get to the Main menu.

2. Scroll down to highlight Photos and then press the Select button.

3. Select the Slideshow Settings item and then press the Select button to display the Slideshow Settings screen (see Figure 12-2). This is the Slideshow Settings screen for a fifth-generation iPod; the iPod nano does not have the TV Out option or the TV Signal option.

4. Scroll to the Time Per Slide item, press the Select button, and use the Next Slide screen (see Figure 12-3) to choose either manual advancing or a specific time interval. Press the Menu button to return to the Slideshow Settings screen.

5. Scroll to the Music item, press the Select button, and use the Slideshow Music Screen (see Figure 12-4) to select the music you want for the slide show. (Choose the Off item if you don't want any music.) Press the Menu button to return to the Slideshow Settings screen.

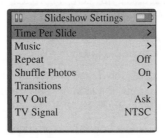

FIGURE 12-2   Use the options on the Slideshow Settings screen to set up your slide show.

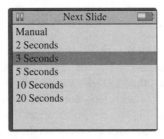

FIGURE 12-3   You can set your iPod to advance the slides automatically or advance them manually yourself.

12

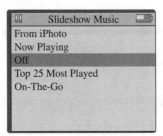

FIGURE 12-4   Use the Slideshow Music screen to add music to your iPod slide show. If you don't have a suitable playlist, create an On-the-Go playlist for your slide show, and then assign it.

6. Change the Repeat setting if necessary by scrolling to it and then pressing the Select button. Repeat can be either On or Off.

7. Change the Shuffle Photos setting if necessary by scrolling to it and then pressing the Select button. Shuffle Photos can be either On or Off.

8. Scroll to the Transitions item, press the Select button, and use the Transitions screen (see Figure 12-5) to choose the transition to apply between slides. Press the Menu button to return to the Slideshow Settings screen.

9. For a regular iPod, scroll to the TV Out setting and then press the Select button to choose the setting you need: Off to display the slide show on the iPod's screen, On to send the output via the cable to a TV, or Ask to have your iPod prompt you when you start a slide show.

10. If you're using a TV with a regular iPod, scroll to the TV Signal setting and press the Select button to choose the appropriate standard: NTSC (which is used in North America, Japan, and some other countries) or PAL (which is used in most Europe countries and some others).

11. Press the Menu button to return to the Photos screen.

If you're using a regular iPod to display the slide show on a TV, connect the iPod to the TV with an Apple iPod AV Cable (http://store.apple.com; $19). This cable has an overlong miniplug at one end and three RCA plugs at the other. Connect the miniplug to your iPod's headphone socket, and the RCA plugs to the appropriate, color-coded RCA jacks on your TV. The S-video plug is colored yellow, and the two audio plugs are colored white and red.

To start a slide show, navigate to the album that contains the pictures and then select the picture at which you want the show to start. Press the Select button to start the show running. If you chose Ask for the TV Out setting on a regular iPod, scroll to select TV Off or TV On from the resulting screen and then press the Select button.

When the iPod is outputting the slide show to a TV, on the iPod's screen you see the current slide, together with miniatures of the previous slide and the next slide as well as a countdown of the seconds to the next slide (if you're using automatic advancement).

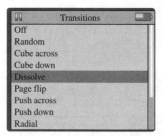

FIGURE 12-5   The iPod offers a modest number of transitions between slides. Avoid the Random setting for formal presentations, because many people find it distracting.

Give a Presentation Using Your Regular iPod

If you're forced to travel light, you can use a photo-capable fourth- or fifth-generation iPod's slideshow feature to give a straightforward presentation direct from your iPod. To do so, follow these steps:

1. Create the slides in your presentation software—for example, PowerPoint or Keynote—as usual and then save the presentation. Don't include transitions, animations, or audio in the slides because they won't be transferred to your iPod. (If you must show a slide that appears one element at a time, create it as a sequence of partial slides: the first slide containing the first element, the second slide adding the second element, and so on until the final slide contains all the elements.)

2. Export the slides as graphics. Here are two examples:

   ■ From PowerPoint, choose File | Save As, select JPEG File Interchange Format in the Save As Type drop-down list, and then click the Save button. When PowerPoint prompts you with the dialog box shown here, click the Every Slide button to export every slide in the presentation.

   ■ From Keynote, choose File | Export, select the Images option button, and then select the JPEG item in the Format drop-down list.

3. Put the slides in a photo album of their own and then synchronize them with your iPod.

4. Navigate to that album on your iPod and then play it as a slide show. At this writing, you'll have to use the buttons on your iPod to control the slide show—even if you have a remote control, the iPod's slideshow feature won't recognize it.

Upload Photos from a Digital Camera to Your Regular iPod

The photo and slideshow features on the iPod are impressive, but you may also want to use your iPod for another purpose: as extra storage for your digital camera when you're away from your computer. Instead of having to download the pictures you've taken from your digital camera to

12

your PC or Mac once you've filled your camera's memory, you can download them to a regular iPod and store them there—and then continue shooting freely.

These days, digital cameras are increasing rapidly in resolution, which means that they're creating ever-larger picture files. Given the modest amount of storage in many digital cameras, and given the expense of buying a larger memory card, using your iPod for temporary storage for your pictures makes a lot of sense. An iPod can hold thousands of pictures comfortably as well as thousands of song files (provided that you haven't packed it full of songs, video, or other files).

Upload Photos from Your Digital Camera to Your Photo-Capable iPod

If you have a fifth-generation iPod or a photo-capable fourth-generation iPod, all you need is the Apple iPod Camera Connector ($29.00, http://store.apple.com), which is a short flattened barrel with a Dock Connector at one end and a USB socket at the other end. You connect the Dock Connector to your iPod and the USB socket to your digital camera or a media reader (for example, a CompactFlash or SD card reader). The iPod switches automatically to Import Photos mode and walks you through the process of importing the photos, which it stores in a folder named Roll #1, Roll #2, or the next available number.

When the import is done, you can erase the memory card directly from the iPod, but it's usually best to check your photos before doing so. You can view the photos on the iPod's screen, but you can't view them on a TV. To do so, you must import the photos to your PC or Mac, as described later in this section, and then use iTunes to put them back on the iPod, as described earlier in this chapter.

Transfer Photos from Your iPod to Your Computer

When you return to your computer, you can transfer the photos from your iPod to your computer so that you can work with them. You'll find the photos in subfolders of your iPod's DCIM folder. (DCIM is the industry standard abbreviation for *digital camera images.*)

Transfer Photos from Your iPod to Your Mac

To transfer photos from your iPod to your Mac, follow these steps:

1. Connect your iPod to your Mac. If your iPod is set to synchronize with iTunes, allow it to do so.

2. Enable disk mode on your iPod (see "Enable Disk Mode," in Chapter 16, for details).

3. Double-click your iPod's icon on the desktop to open a Finder window to view its contents.

4. Double-click the DCIM folder to open it. Depending on the photo-transfer tool you're using, you'll see one or more subfolders containing photos.

5. To load your photos into iPhoto, drag each folder in turn into the iPhoto window and drop it there:

   ■ To add the photos to your Photo Library, select your Photo Library in the Source pane and then drop the photos in the viewing area.

   ■ To add the photos to an existing album, select the album in the Source pane and then drop the photos in the viewing area.

   ■ To create a new album and put the pictures of a folder into it, drag the folder to the Source pane in iPhoto and drop it in open space. iPhoto creates a new album with the name of the folder.

6. To copy the photos to a folder on your hard disk, use normal Finder techniques.

7. After importing or copying all the photos to your Mac, delete the photos from your iPod if appropriate. (You might also choose to keep the photos on your iPod as a backup in case you do something horrible to the photos on your Mac.)

Transfer Photos from Your iPod to Your PC

To transfer photos from your iPod to your PC, follow these steps:

1. Connect your iPod to your PC. If your iPod is set to synchronize with iTunes, allow it to do so.

2. Choose Start | My Computer to open a My Computer window.

3. Double-click the drive allocated to your iPod to display its contents in a window.

4. Double-click the DCIM folder to open it. Depending on the photo-transfer tool you're using, you'll see one or more subfolders containing photos.

5. Copy or move the folders to your hard disk by using standard Windows Explorer techniques.

6. After importing or copying all the photos to your PC, delete the photos from your iPod if appropriate. (You might also choose to keep the photos on your iPod as a backup in case you damage or lose the pictures you've transferred to your PC.)

Troubleshoot the iPod's Photo-Related Features

This section discusses how to troubleshoot common problems that occur with the iPod's photo-related features. For advice on troubleshooting other problems with iPods, see Chapter 17.

Some of the Album Covers Have Gone Missing

If some of the album covers appear on your iPod but others don't, the reason is most likely that you have copied some songs to the iPod manually and then set your iPod to update automatically. If you do this, the album covers for the songs you copy manually tend not to get transferred to the iPod.

12

The fix for this problem is (arguably) counterintuitive and (unarguably) tedious. Connect the iPod and take the following actions:

1. Right-click the iPod in the Source pane, choose iPod Options from the shortcut menu to display the iPod tab of the iTunes dialog box (Windows) or the Preferences dialog box (Mac), click the Music button to display the Music subtab, and select the Manually Manage Songs And Playlists option button. In the message box warning you that you'll need to manually unmount the iPod before each disconnect, click the OK button. Click the OK button to close the iTunes dialog box or the Preferences dialog box.

2. If iTunes displays the "Updating iPod" message, wait until it disappears. Then, with the iPod still selected in the Source pane, click the Date Added column to produce a sort by the last date on which you added songs. (The black arrow on the Date Added column points downward when you select this type of sort.) Click the first of the songs you added manually, hold down SHIFT and click the last, and then press DELETE or BACKSPACE to delete the songs. If iTunes prompts you to confirm the deletion, do so.

3. Right-click the iPod in the Source pane, choose iPod Options from the shortcut menu to display the iTunes dialog box (Windows) or the Preferences dialog box (Mac), click the Music button, and select either the Automatically Update All Songs And Playlists option button or the Automatically Update Selected Playlists Only option button (whichever button was selected before you selected the Manually Manage Songs And Playlists option button in step 1). Then click the OK button to close the iTunes dialog box or the Preferences dialog box.

iTunes Displays a Message Saying That iPhoto 4.0.3 or Later Is Required

If you see the message shown here when using your iPod with your Mac, it means that your version of iPhoto is too old and ignorant to put photos on your iPod. Choose Apple | Software Update and use Software Update to download the latest updates to iPhoto so that it can put photos on your iPod.

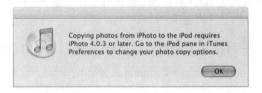

"iTunes Could Not Locate a Supported Photo Application" Message

The error message "iTunes could not locate a supported photo application. Would you like to change your photo copy options?" (shown next) occurs on the Mac when you connect an iPod that is set to synchronize photos with one Mac to another Mac that doesn't have iPhoto installed (or that has a version of iPhoto that's too old for the iPod to work with).

Click the Yes button to display the iPod tab of the Preferences dialog box. Click the Photos button and then clear the Synchronize Photos From check box.

"An Unknown Error -2003 Has Occurred"

The error "The iPod *iPod's name* cannot be updated. An unknown error -2003 has occurred" happens sometimes with the iPod. If this error occurs, restore your iPod as described in "Restore Your iPod" in Chapter 17 and then synchronize your iPod again.

"Permissions Error" when You Try to Synchronize Photos

If you see an error message box saying "Permissions error" the first time you try to synchronize photos to your iPod, the problem is that you don't have write access to the drive or folder on which the photos are stored.

This problem is most likely to arise when you're trying to load photos that are stored on a network drive—for example, in a folder that a family member is sharing—on your iPod. You need write access to the folder or drive because iTunes needs to create a cache folder for the smaller versions of the pictures. If you don't have write access to the folder or drive, iTunes can't create the cache folder and therefore can't copy the photos to your iPod. You'll get the same problem if the photos are stored on a read-only optical disk—for example, on a CD-ROM or on a DVD.

To fix this problem, copy the photos to a folder for which you do have write access—for example, a folder in your My Pictures folder on a Windows PC or a folder in your Home folder on a Mac. Then synchronize the photos from that folder.

The Photos Weren't Copied to the iPod

If your photos don't get copied to the iPod, first check that iTunes is set to copy them:

1. Connect your iPod to your computer.

2. Right-click the iPod in the Source pane and choose iPod Options from the shortcut menu to display the iPod tab of the iTunes dialog box (Windows) or the Preferences dialog box (Mac).

3. Click the Photos subtab and verify that the Synchronize Photos From check box is selected. If not, select it and then choose the appropriate source for the photos.

4. Click the OK button to close the dialog box.

12

If the Synchronize Photos From check box was already selected, the problem is most likely to have been that you stopped an update before it finished, changed the iPod's settings, and then finished the update. If you did this, try synchronizing your iPod again. If you don't interfere with the update, the photos should transfer properly.

Windows Takes Ages to Eject the iPod

If you find that Windows takes ages to eject your iPod, try turning disk mode on:

1. Connect your iPod to your PC and launch iTunes if it doesn't launch itself.
2. Choose Edit | Preferences in iTunes to display the iTunes dialog box.
3. Click the iPod tab and then click the Music subtab.
4. Select the Enable Disk Use check box.
5. Click the OK button to close the iTunes dialog box.

When you need to eject your iPod, eject it manually by clicking the Eject button on the device's entry in the Source pane or by right-clicking the entry in the Source pane and then choosing Eject from the shortcut menu.

Put Video Files on Your iPod

The fifth-generation iPod, with its brilliant 2.5-inch screen, is great for viewing photos and even better for viewing videos. Apple has made the process of loading video files onto your iPod and playing them back as easy as possible, so this section covers this topic only briefly. What generally needs more effort is creating video files suitable for putting on your iPod, which is the subject of the last section in this chapter.

Buy Video Files from the iTunes Music Store

The easiest way to get video files that are suitable for the iPod is to buy them from the iTunes Music Store. At this writing, the iTunes Music Store sells a good selection of music videos, a handful of Pixar movies, and episodes of some TV shows, including *Desperate Housewives* and *Lost*. You can also download movie trailers for free.

When you download videos from the iTunes Music Store, iTunes adds them to your Purchased playlist. You can play the videos from there, or by browsing to them, and you can add them to other playlists using the same techniques as for song files. As discussed in Chapter 2, you can control which videos iTunes synchronizes with your iPod by using the controls on the Videos subtab of the iPod tab of the iTunes dialog box (Windows) or the Preferences dialog box (Mac).

Play Videos on Your iPod

To play videos on your iPod, scroll to the Videos entry on the main menu, and then press the Select button to access the Videos screen (see Figure 12-6). Scroll to the appropriate category,

FIGURE 12-6 The Videos screen gives you access to your video playlists, video files, and the Video Settings screen.

and then press the Select button to access it. Scroll to the item you want, and then press the Select button to access it and start it playing.

You can fast-forward through the video file by pressing the Fast Forward button, and rewind by pressing the Rewind button, but these controls are comfortable only for moving short distances. To move farther, press the Select button to display the scrub bar, and then scroll to scrub forward or backward. When you reach the point you want, press the Select button to hide the scrub bar again.

To play a video file through a television rather than on the iPod's built-in screen, scroll to the Video Settings item on the Videos screen, and then press the Select button to display the Settings screen (see Figure 12-7). Set the TV Out setting to On if you want the iPod always to output the video to TV, or to Ask if you want the iPod to prompt you first (Ask is often more convenient). Set the TV Signal setting to NTSC or PAL, as appropriate for your TV. (NTSC is primarily used in North America and Japan; PAL is used in most European countries.) For the Widescreen setting, choose On or Off to suit your TV or your tastes.

12

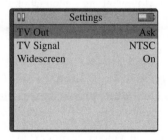

FIGURE 12-7 On the Settings screen, choose whether to output to a TV and, if so, which format to use.

Press the Menu button to return to the Videos screen, and connect the iPod to the TV using an Apple iPod AV Cable. Connect the miniplug to your iPod's headphone socket, and the RCA plugs to the appropriate, color-coded RCA jacks on your TV. The S-video plug is colored yellow, and the two audio plugs are colored white and red.

Set the video playing, and enjoy.

Create Video Files Suitable for Your iPod

Buying video files from the iTunes Music Store is easy, but the selection is limited at this writing—and you probably already have video content that you'd like to put on your iPod. This section discusses the main options for doing so.

Get Videos Files That You Can Convert

The first step is to get the video file you plan to convert for the iPod. Possible sources of video files include your digital video camera, your DVDs, video files you download, and video files that you record from a TV, VCR, or similar source.

Create iPod Video Files from Your Digital Video Camera

If you make your own movies with a digital video camera, you can easily put them on your iPod. Use an application such as Windows Movie Maker (Windows) or iMovie (Mac) to capture the video from your digital video camera and turn it into a portable home movie.

Create iPod Video Files Using Windows Movie Maker At this writing, Windows Movie Maker can't export video files in an iPod-friendly format, so getting video from Windows Movie Maker to your iPod is a two-stage process:

1. After creating your movie in Windows Movie Maker, choose File | Save Movie File. Select the My Computer item on the Movie Location screen and click the Next button. On the Saved Movie File screen, enter the name and choose the folder for the movie, and then click the Next button. On the Movie Setting screen, click the Show More Choices link (unless you see the Show Fewer Choices link), select the Other Settings option button, and then select the DV-AVI item in the drop-down list. Click the Next button to save the movie in this format.

The DV-AVI item appears as DV-AVI (NTSC) or DV-AVI (PAL), depending on whether you've chosen the NTSC option button or the PAL option button on the Advanced tab of the Options dialog box.

2. Use an application such as Xilisoft Video Converter (www.xilisoft.com; $35 shareware) to convert the AVI file to a MOV file.

Create iPod Video Files Using iMovie   To create iPod-friendly video files from iMovie, follow these steps:

1. With the movie open in iMovie, choose File | Share to display the Sharing sheet.

2. Click the QuickTime button to display its tab.

3. In the Compress Movie For drop-down list, choose Expert Settings, and then click the Share button to display the Save Exported File As dialog box.

4. Type the name for the file in the Save As text box, and specify the folder in which to save it.

5. In the Export drop-down list, select the Movie To iPod (320×240) item.

6. Click the Save button, and then wait while iMovie creates the compressed file.

Create iPod Video Files from Your Existing Video Files

There are several ways of converting your existing video files so that they'll work on your iPod. The Apple approved and recommended way is to use QuickTime Pro, which you can purchase from the Apple Store (http://store.apple.com) for around $30. You can also use third-party software if you prefer. This section shows you how to create iPod-friendly video files using QuickTime and also using the third-party application Podner, which runs only on the Mac.

Create iPod Video Files Using QuickTime   QuickTime, Apple's multimedia software for Mac OS X and Windows, comes in two versions: QuickTime Player (the free version) and QuickTime Pro, which costs $29.99. On Mac OS X, QuickTime Player is included in a standard installation of the operating system; and if you've somehow managed to uninstall it, it'll automatically install itself again if you install iTunes. Likewise, on the PC, you install QuickTime Player when you install iTunes, because QuickTime provides much of the multimedia functionality for iTunes. The "Player" name isn't entirely accurate, because QuickTime provides encoding, as well as decoding, services to iTunes—but QuickTime Player does prevent you from creating most formats of video files until you buy QuickTime Pro.

QuickTime Player is a crippled version of QuickTime Pro, so when you buy QuickTime Pro from the Apple Store, all you get is a registration code to unlock the hidden functionality. To apply the registration code, choose Edit | Preferences | Register in Windows to display the Register tab of the QuickTime Settings dialog box. On the Mac, choose QuickTime Player | Registration to display the Register tab of the QuickTime dialog box.

CAUTION

When you register QuickTime, you must enter your registration name in the Registered To text box in exactly the same format as Apple has decided to use it. For example, if you've used the name John P. Smith to register QuickTime, and Apple has decided to address the registration to Mr. John P. Smith, *you must use **Mr. John P. Smith** as the registration name. If you try to use **John P. Smith**, registration will fail, even if this is exactly the way you gave your name when registering.*

12

To create an iPod video file from QuickTime, follow these steps:

1. Open the file in QuickTime, and then choose File | Export to display the Save Exported File As dialog box.

2. Specify the file name and folder as usual, and then choose Movie To iPod (320×240) in the Export drop-down list. Leave the Default Settings item selected in the Use drop-down list—at this writing, there's no alternative.

3. Click the Save button to start exporting the video file.

Create Video Files with Podner on Mac OS X Podner from Splasm Software (www.splasm.com; $9.99) is a video-transformation application focused directly at creating files suitable for the iPod and transferring them automatically to iTunes. To transform video files, Podner uses QuickTime's capabilities, which means that if your video file is in a format that QuickTime Player can play, Podner should be able to convert it to an iPod-friendly format for you. Splasm offers an evaluation version of Podner that's limited to converting the first two-and-a-half minutes of any video file—plenty for you to see whether Podner will work with your files.

When you run Podner, you see a window that invites you to drag a file to it. To convert a video file:

1. Drag a movie file to the window. Podner displays its control panel.

2. Drag the video slider, or simply play the video, to the frame that you want to use as the poster frame, the picture used as the still image for the file's thumbnail.

3. Click the Action button and choose Set Poster Frame from the shortcut menu (see Figure 12-8).

4. In the Encoding drop-down list, choose the appropriate iPod option:

   - **iPod, 320×240, MPEG-4** This format gives fast encoding, moderate picture quality, and a relatively large file size.

   - **iPod, 480×480, MPEG-4** This format gives fast encoding and good picture quality, but has a 1:1 aspect ratio (the other three choices have a 1.5:1 aspect ratio) that uses more pixels. The file size is correspondingly larger.

   - **iPod, 320×240, H.264** This format gives better picture quality and a smaller file size than MPEG encoding, but the encoding takes longer.

   - **iPod, 320×240, H.264, Multipass** This format gives you the highest-quality movie with the smallest possible file size, but it requires much more processing and takes the longest.

5. Drag the Quality slider to the Good, Better, or Best position, depending on the results you want. The higher the quality, the longer the processing will take.

6. Choose the appropriate genre in the Genre drop-down list: Movies, Music Videos, Sports, or TV Shows.

FIGURE 12-8   In Podner, set the poster frame, then choose suitable encoding options for the video.

7. Enter the name for the movie in the Name text box. Podner enters the file's name (minus the extension) by default.

8. Click the Continue button to start processing the movie. Podner displays a Processing readout showing you the elapsed time and remaining time as it works, then displays a Process Complete message that tells you that Podner has put the video inside the Podner playlist in iTunes.

9. Click the Go To iTunes button if you want to go directly to iTunes, or click the OK button if you just want to dismiss the Process Complete message so that you can drag another movie file to the Podner window.

Create iPod Video Files from Your TiVo

If you have a TiVo, chances are that it contains content you'd like to transfer to your iPod. To do so:

- On the PC, use DirectShow Dump (http://prish.com/etivo/tbr.htm; freeware) to convert the shows from the TiVo format to MPEG. Then use another application (for example, QuickTime) to convert the MPEG file to iPod video format.

- On the Mac, if you have a hacked TiVo, use TivoTool (www.tivotool.com; donationware) to create iPod video files from TiVo content.

Create iPod Video Files from Your DVDs

Another possibility is to rip your DVDs to files that you can put on your iPod. Ripping DVDs is usually considered to be a violation of copyright unless you have specific permission to do so (or you hold the copyright to the DVD—for example, if it's one you've created yourself).

- In Windows, you can use an application such as DVDx (http://sourceforge.net; freeware) to rip the DVD to an AVI file. You can then use an application such as Xilisoft Video Converter (www.xilisoft.com; $35 shareware) or QuickTime to convert the AVI file to a MOV file.

- On the Mac, you can use an application such as HandBrake (http://handbrake.m0k.org; freeware) to rip a DVD to one or more MPEG files that you can then put on your iPod.

Part IV

Learn Advanced iPod Use

Chapter 13

Use Multiple iPods, Multiple Computers, or Both

How to...

- Move your iPod from Windows to the Mac or from Mac to Windows
- Change the computer to which your iPod is linked
- Synchronize several iPods with the same computer
- Load your iPod from two or more computers

The chapter starts by walking you through the processes of moving an iPod from a Mac to a PC, and vice versa. Then it shows you how to change the computer to which your iPod is linked—a useful skill when you upgrade your computer. The chapter explains the nuances of synchronizing several iPods with the same computer, and it walks you through loading your iPod from two or more computers at the same time.

Move Your iPod from Mac to Windows—and Back

The first generation of iPod worked only with the Mac. Enough Windows users craved the iPod for EphPod (discussed in Chapter 15) to be created. Apple then released second-generation iPods in separate versions for the Mac and for Windows; the iPods for the two platforms started off separate, but you could convert them from one platform to the other. All current iPods—fifth-generation regular iPods, the iPod nano, and the iPod shuffle—come in a single version for both the Mac and Windows.

 *If you reformat your iPod, you'll lose all its contents—every file you've stored on it. If your iPod contains valuable files, back them up to your PC or Mac before reformatting your iPod.*

Move Your iPod from the Mac to Windows

If you've used your regular iPod, iPod nano, or iPod mini only with a Mac, and you move it to Windows, you must reformat the hard disk (or, in an iPod nano, the flash memory). This permanently removes all the contents of the iPod. Follow the procedure described in the upcoming section "Move a Mac-Formatted Regular iPod, iPod nano, or iPod mini to Windows."

If you've used your regular iPod, iPod nano, or iPod mini with Windows, and then moved it to the Mac without reformatting it, and you then move it back to Windows, you won't need to reformat it. Follow the procedure described in "Move a FAT32-Formatted iPod from the Mac Back to Windows."

If you have an iPod shuffle, use the procedure described in "Move a FAT32-Formatted iPod from the Mac Back to Windows."

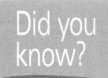

Which File System Does Your iPod Use?

That bit about iPods coming in a single version for both the Mac and Windows isn't entirely true. At this writing, regular iPods and the iPod nano all ship with their disks partitioned using the Mac OS Extended file system. When you connect a new regular iPod or iPod nano to a Windows PC, the iPod Software on the PC detects that the iPod needs to be reformatted, and it reformats using the FAT32 file system without notifying you. If the iPod contains files, the iPod Software warns you before reformatting the iPod. More on this topic later in this chapter.

The Mac OS Extended file system works better for the Mac than FAT32 does, but Windows can't read it; so the iPod uses FAT32 for Windows instead. FAT32 works with Mac OS X as well as with Windows, so once you've formatted an iPod for Windows, you don't necessarily need to reformat it if you need to use it with a Mac again.

The iPod shuffle uses the FAT32 file system for both Windows and the Mac, so there's no need to convert it from one format to another.

Move a Mac-Formatted Regular iPod, iPod nano, or iPod mini to Windows

To move an iPod from the Mac to Windows, follow these steps:

1. Make sure the PC has iTunes installed and the iPod Software—preferably the latest version of each.

TIP

For the first three generations of regular iPods and the first generation of the iPod mini, Apple provided different versions of the iPod Updater for different models. Apple has now wrapped all the different versions into one iPod Updater package that you can download from www.apple.com/ipod/download. This single package makes for a bigger download, but it eliminates the chance of your downloading the wrong item.

13

2. If nobody has used iTunes on that computer, run iTunes and complete the iTunes Setup Assistant.

3. Connect the iPod to the PC. If the iPod's hard disk or flash memory is formatted with the Mac OS Extended file system, the iPod Software displays the iPod Not Readable dialog box. If so, follow steps 4 and 5. Otherwise, go to step 6.

4. Click the Update button to launch the iPod Updater. If you see a screen showing the various models of iPod that the updater supports, click the OK button.

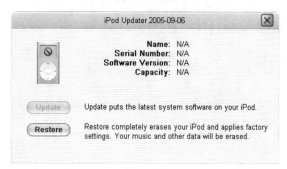

 *If the iPod Software Updater displays the error message "Updater can't install firmware on connected iPod. The iPod's hardware and the Updater firmware are not compatible," refer to "You See the 'Updater Can't Install Firmware on Connected iPod' Message" in Chapter 18.*

5. Click the Restore button to format the iPod using the FAT32 file system and to reinstall the iPod firmware on it. The iPod Updater displays a confirmation dialog box:

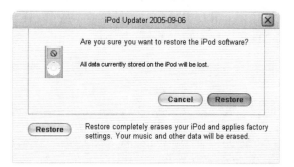

6. Click the blue Restore button and then allow the restore process to continue. Follow the instructions to complete the restore. Depending on the iPod model, you may need to unplug your iPod from the PC when the iPod Software Updater tells you to, plug it into the iPod Power Adapter to complete the firmware reflash, and then plug it back into the PC.

7. iTunes displays the iPod Setup Assistant dialog box (see Figure 13-1). Follow through the steps of assigning your iPod a name, choosing whether to update your iPod automatically, and deciding whether to register it. For a photo-capable iPod, you also get to choose whether to automatically copy photos to your iPod.

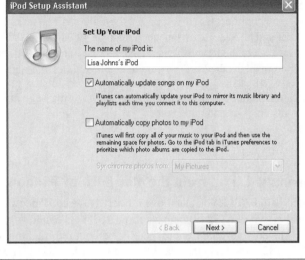

FIGURE 13-1 In the iPod Setup Assistant, specify the name for your iPod and choose how to update it.

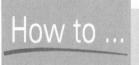

Recover from a Stalled Restore Process on the PC

Some versions of the iPod Software Updater may hang while telling you to wait for the iPod to complete the restore process. It's usually pretty clear when this has happened: The iPod Software Updater tells you to wait, and the iPod tells you not to disconnect it...and several minutes pass without completion occurring.

If you've waited several minutes, recover by taking as many of the following steps as necessary:

1. Disconnect your iPod from your PC.

2. Let your iPod recover from any confusion caused by your unplugging it. If all is well, your iPod displays the Language screen.

3. Select your preferred language and press the Select button. (If the Select button on a third-generation iPod isn't working, move the Hold switch to the On position and then back to the Off position. If that doesn't make the Select button work, connect your iPod to the iPod Power Adapter and then repeat the trick with the Hold switch.)

4. Connect your iPod to your PC again.

(continued)

5. If the iPod Software Updater is still telling you to wait, try to close it by clicking its Close button (the X button). Usually, it then tells you it can't be interrupted. Right-click the taskbar and choose Task Manager to display Windows Task Manager. On the Applications tab, select the iPod Software Updater entry and then click the End Task button. Windows displays the End Program dialog box. Click the End Now button.

If the iPod Software Updater displays the iPod Updater error message box saying that it can't mount the iPod, restart your computer.

Move a FAT32-Formatted iPod from the Mac Back to Windows

If your iPod is formatted with FAT32, you can move it freely between Windows and the Mac. Your iPod will be formatted with FAT32 if you have formatted it on Windows using the iPod Updater. If you've then moved your iPod back to the Mac without reformatting it, the iPod will still be formatted with FAT32 rather than the Mac OS Extended file system. The same applies if your iPod is an iPod shuffle, because the iPod shuffle uses only the FAT32 file system.

To move a FAT32-formatted iPod from the Mac back to Windows:

1. Connect the iPod to the PC. iTunes detects the iPod and displays the dialog box shown here, warning you that the iPod is linked to another music library and asking if you want to change the link and replace all the songs.

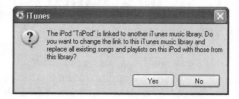

2. Click the Yes button to associate the iPod with the Windows music library and overwrite the Mac music library.

Move Your iPod from Windows to the Mac

To move your iPod from Windows to the Mac, follow these steps:

1. For best results, update iTunes and the iPod Updater to the latest versions available.

TIP

The easiest way to check that iTunes is up to date is to choose Apple | Software Update to check for updates. If Software Update identifies any iTunes updates, or other updates that your Mac requires, install them before moving your iPod to your Mac.

2. Connect the iPod to the Mac. When iTunes detects the iPod, it displays a dialog box such as that shown here, pointing out that the iPod is linked to a different music library and asking if you want to replace that music library:

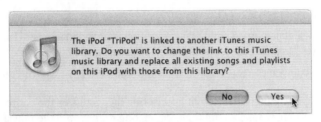

3. Click the Yes button. iTunes replaces the music library on the iPod with the music library on the Mac. This may take some time if the music library is extensive.

At this point, you've set up your iPod to work with your Mac, but you've left it using the FAT32 file system. FAT32 works fine with Mac OS X but is marginally less efficient than the Mac OS Extended file system, so you won't be able to fit quite as many files on your iPod with FAT32 as with Mac OS Extended.

If you intend to use your iPod with the Mac for the long term, and if your iPod doesn't contain any valuable files that you want to keep, you may choose to convert it to Mac OS X Extended to pack on as many songs as possible. To do so, restore your iPod by following the process described in "Restore Your iPod on Mac OS X," in Chapter 17.

If you want to boot your Mac from your iPod, you must reformat the iPod with the Mac OS Extended file system.

Change the Computer to Which Your iPod Is Linked

Apple has designed the iPod so that it can synchronize with only one computer at a time. This computer is known as the *home* computer—home to the iPod, not necessarily in your home. However, you can use two or more Macs, or two or more Windows PCs, to load files onto the same iPod. See the section "Load Your iPod from Two or More Computers at Once," later in this chapter for details.

CAUTION   *Linking your iPod to another computer replaces all the songs and playlists on your iPod with the songs and playlists on the other computer. Be sure you want to change the link before you proceed. You can restore your previous music library by linking again to the first computer, but, even with FireWire or USB 2.0 file-transfer speeds, you'll waste a good deal of time if your music library is large.*

To change your iPod's home computer, follow these steps:

1. Make sure the other computer contains an up-to-date version of iTunes and the latest version of the appropriate iPod Software for the iPod. If necessary, set up iTunes and install any relevant updates.

13

NOTE   *If you're moving an iPod formatted with the Mac OS Extended file system to Windows, you'll need to restore it as described in "Move Your iPod from the Mac to Windows," earlier in this chapter.*

2. Connect your iPod to the other PC or Mac.

3. iTunes displays a dialog box warning that your iPod is linked to another iTunes music library and asking if you want to change the link to that iTunes music library.

4. If you're sure you want to replace your music library, click the Yes button.

Because changing your iPod to a different home computer replaces the entire music library, the initial synchronization may take a long time, depending on how big the music library is and whether it's stored on a local drive or a network drive.

Synchronize Several iPods with the Same Computer

As you've seen earlier in this book, usually a computer and an iPod have a mutually faithful relationship—but, as discussed in the previous section, the iPod can decide to leave its home computer and set up home with another computer. It can even switch to the other platform as well.

Synchronize a Full—Different—Music Library onto Different iPods from the Same Computer

Synchronizing two or more iPods with the same computer works well enough provided that each iPod user is happy using the same music library or the same set of playlists. But if you want to synchronize the full music library for each iPod, yet have a different music library on each, you need to take a different approach.

In most cases, the easiest solution is to have a separate user account for each separate user who uses an iPod with the computer. Separate user accounts are best in any case for keeping files and mail separate.

Place the music files that users will share in a folder that each user can access. In iTunes, make sure that the Copy Files To iTunes Music Folder When Adding To Library check box on the General subtab of the Advanced tab of the iTunes dialog box (Windows) or the Preferences dialog box (Mac) is cleared so iTunes doesn't consolidate the files for the music library.

If you have enough free space on your hard disk, users can set up their own music libraries under their own user accounts and store all their music files in them. But unless your hard disk is truly gigantic, sharing most of the files from a central location is almost always preferable.

For most people, such fidelity (or serial fidelity) works fine. But if you have several iPods and one computer—for example, if several music-lovers in a household share the same computer—what happens? Can one computer load several iPods?

Briefly—yes. Whereas your iPod is wired not to sync around, the computer in the partnership has no such restrictions and can sync with as many iPods as you have. Here are the points to keep in mind:

- Even if your computer has plenty of FireWire or USB ports, it's best not to plug in more than one iPod at once. That way, you don't get confused, and synchronization can take place at full speed.

- Each iPod has a unique ID number that it communicates to your computer on connection, so your computer knows which iPod is connected to it. You can even give two or more iPods the same name if doing so amuses rather than confuses you.

- You can configure different updating for each iPod by choosing options in the iPod Preferences dialog box when the iPod is connected.

Load Your iPod from Two or More Computers at Once

As you read earlier in this chapter, you can synchronize your iPod with only one computer at a time—your iPod's home computer. You can change your iPod's home computer from one computer to another, and even from one platform (Mac or PC) to the other, but you can't actively synchronize your iPod with more than one computer at once.

But you *can* load tracks onto your iPod from computers other than the home computer. If your iPod is formatted using the FAT32 file system, you can use a mixture of Macs and PCs to load files onto your iPod. If your iPod is formatted using the Mac OS Extended file system, you can use only Macs.

All the computers you use must have iTunes and the appropriate iPod Software installed and configured, and you must configure the iPod for manual updating on each computer involved—on the home computer as well as on each other computer. Otherwise, synchronizing the iPod with the home computer after loading tracks from other computers will remove those tracks because they're not in the home computer's music library.

13

TIP   *You can temporarily override automatic updating by holding down CTRL-ALT-SHIFT (Windows) or ⌘-OPTION (Mac) when you connect your iPod to your computer.*

Configure Your iPod for Manual Updating

The first step in loading your iPod from two or more computers is to configure it for manual updating. You'll need to do this on your iPod's home computer first, and then on each of the other computers you plan to use.

To configure your iPod for manual updating, follow these steps:

1. Connect your iPod to your Mac or PC. Allow synchronization to take place.

2. Right-click your iPod in the Source pane and choose iPod Options from the shortcut menu to display the iPod tab of the iTunes dialog box (Windows) or the Preferences dialog box (Mac).

3. Select the Manually Manage Songs And Playlists option button on the Music subtab or the General subtab. iTunes displays the warning dialog box telling you that you'll need to unmount your iPod manually before disconnecting it.

4. Click the OK button to return to the iTunes dialog box or the Preferences dialog box. iTunes selects the Enable Disk Use check box (if it wasn't already selected) and makes it unavailable so that you can't clear it manually.

5. Click the OK button to close the dialog box.

Load Files onto Your iPod Manually

After you've configured your iPod for manual updating, you can load files onto it manually by following these general steps:

1. Connect your iPod to the computer that contains the files you want to load. Your iPod will appear in the Source pane in iTunes.

2. Drag song files from your iTunes library, or from a Finder window or a Windows Explorer window, and then drop them on your iPod or on one of its playlists.

3. After loading all the songs you want from this computer, unmount your iPod by issuing an Eject command before you disconnect it. For example, right-click the iPod's entry in the Source pane and choose Eject.

You can then disconnect your iPod from this computer, move it to the next computer, and then add more song files by using the same technique.

From this point on, to add further song files to your iPod from your home computer, you must add them manually. Don't synchronize your iPod with your home computer, because synchronization will delete from the iPod all the song files your music library doesn't contain.

Chapter 14

Recover Your Songs and Videos from Your iPod

How to...

- Know why your iPod hides its song files and video files from you
- Understand how your iPod stores song files and video files
- Recover your songs and videos from your iPod in Windows
- Recover your songs and videos from your iPod on the Mac

As you saw in Chapter 2, you can copy all or part of your music library onto your iPod almost effortlessly by choosing suitable synchronization settings and then synchronizing the iPod; if your iPod supports video, you can put your video files on your iPod as well. Normally, any songs and videos on your iPod are also in your music library, so you don't need to transfer the songs and videos from your iPod to your computer. But if you have a computer disaster, or if your computer is stolen, you may need to recover the songs and videos from your iPod to your new or repaired computer.

This chapter shows you how to recover songs and videos from your iPod on both Windows and the Mac. The chapter starts by explaining why your iPod hides the files. It then covers where the files are stored on your iPod, how you can access them through conventional file-management utilities (such as the Finder or Windows Explorer), and why copying the files using conventional means yields unsatisfactory results. The chapter ends by showing you the best recovery utilities for Windows and the Mac.

Why Your iPod Hides Its Song Files and Video Files from You

For copyright reasons, your iPod's basic configuration prevents you from copying song and video files from your iPod's library to your computer. This restriction prevents you from loading files onto your iPod on one computer via iTunes and then downloading them onto another computer, which would most likely violate copyright by making unauthorized copies of other people's copyrighted material. But if you turn on disk mode (discussed in detail in Chapter 16), you can use your iPod as a portable drive. In disk mode, you can copy music files onto your iPod from one computer, connect your iPod to another computer, and copy or move the files from the iPod to that computer. The only limitation is that the files you copy this way aren't added to your iPod's music and video database, so you can't play them on the iPod.

Normally, you shouldn't need to copy songs and videos from your iPod to your computer, because your computer will already contain all the songs and videos that your iPod contains. But there may come a time when you need to get the song files and video files out of your iPod's library for legitimate reasons. For example, if you dropped your iBook, or your PC's hard disk died of natural causes, you might need to copy the song and video files from your iPod to a replacement computer or disk. Otherwise, you might risk losing your entire music and video collection.

> **TIP**
> *To avoid losing data, you should back up all your valuable data, including any songs and videos that you can't easily recover by other means (such as ripping your CDs again), especially the songs and videos you've bought from the iTunes Music Store or other online music stores. However, the amount of data—and, in particular, the size of many people's libraries—makes backup difficult, requiring either an external hard drive (preferably USB 2.0 or FireWire) or multiple DVDs.*

To help you avoid this dreadful possibility, iPod enthusiasts have developed various utilities for transferring files from an iPod's hidden music storage to a computer.

Where—and How—Your iPod Stores Song Files and Video Files

When you turn on disk mode (as you did in Chapters 10 and 11 for working with contacts, calendars, and text items), you can access the contents of your iPod's hard drive by using Windows Explorer (Windows) or the Finder (Mac). Until you create other folders there, though, you'll find only the Calendars, Contacts, Notes, and Photos folders—there's no trace of your song files and video files. If you enable disk mode on an iPod shuffle, you'll find no folders at all, because the iPod shuffle can't hold contacts, calendars, notes, or photos.

> **NOTE**
> *You can also use other file-management utilities (if you have them) for manipulating files on your iPod. This chapter assumes that you're using Windows Explorer (Windows) or the Finder (Mac).*

You can't see the song files and video files because the folders that contain them are formatted to be hidden in Windows and to be invisible on the Mac. Before you can see the folders or the files they contain, you need to change the Hidden attribute on the Windows folders or the Visible attribute on the Mac folders.

> **TIP**
> *If you're comfortable with Unix commands, you can open a Terminal window on Mac OS X and use the ls command to list the folders and files on the iPod, even though they're invisible to the Finder. Navigate to /Volumes/ipodname/iPod_Control/Music, where ipodname is the name of your iPod, and then examine the folders named F00, F01, and so on.*

Make the Hidden Folders Visible in Windows

To display hidden files and folders in Windows XP, follow these steps:

1. Choose Start | My Computer to open a My Computer window.
2. Choose Tools | Folder Options to display the Folder Options dialog box.
3. Click the View tab to display it (see Figure 14-1).

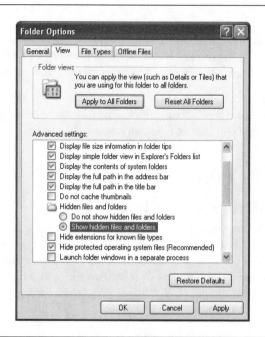

FIGURE 14-1   Use the controls on the View tab of the Folder Options dialog box to make your iPod's hidden folders visible in Windows.

4. Select the Show Hidden Files And Folders option button.

5. Click the OK button to apply the change and to close the Folder Options dialog box. Windows Explorer now displays hidden files and folders as well as normal, unhidden files and folders.

To see the song folders on your iPod, follow these steps:

1. Double-click the icon for your iPod in the My Computer window. Windows Explorer displays the contents of your iPod: the Calendars, Contacts, Notes, and Photos folders, as before, but also an iPod_Control folder that was previously hidden.

2. Double-click the iPod_Control folder to display its contents: a Device folder, an iTunes folder, and a Music folder.

3. Double-click the Music folder to display its contents: a series of folders named F*NN*, where *NN* is a two-digit number (F00, F01, F02, and so on).

4. Double-click one of these F folders to display its contents. Figure 14-2 shows an example.

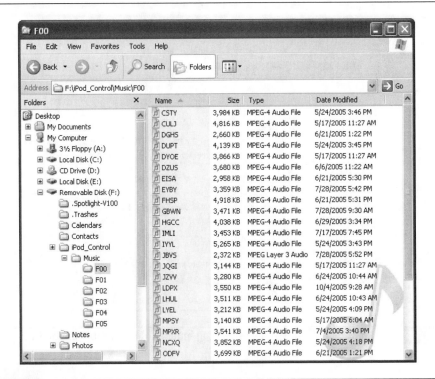

FIGURE 14-2   Your iPod stores songs in folders named F00, F01, F02, and subsequent numbers.

Make the Hidden Folders Visible on the Mac

To make hidden folders visible on Mac OS X, download and install TinkerTool from www.bresink .de/osx/TinkerTool.html. TinkerTool is a free configuration utility that lets you perform a variety of tweaks on Mac OS X, including making hidden folders visible.

After installing TinkerTool, follow these steps to make hidden folders visible:

1. Run TinkerTool from wherever you installed it (for example, your Applications folder).

2. On the Finder tab (see Figure 14-3), select the Show Hidden And System Files check box in the Finder Options area.

3. Click the Relaunch Finder button in TinkerTool to relaunch the Finder. (You need to relaunch the Finder to make it read the now-visible folders.)

4. Navigate back to TinkerTool if necessary (relaunching the Finder may have moved the focus to a Finder window) and then press ⌘-Q or choose TinkerTool | Quit TinkerTool to quit TinkerTool.

14

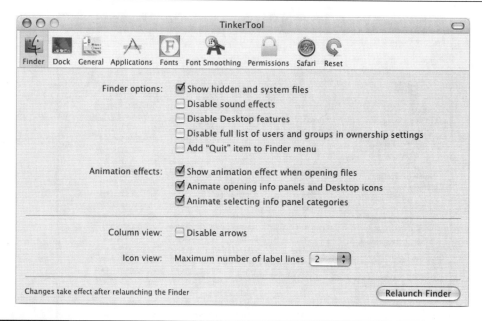

FIGURE 14-3 TinkerTool is the easy way of making hidden folders visible on the Mac.

Turning on the display of hidden and system files makes system files pop out of the woodwork. For example, you'll probably see files named .DS_Store and .localized appear on your desktop.

After the Finder relaunches, you can examine the song folders. To do so, follow these steps:

1. Connect your iPod to your Mac as usual.

2. If you haven't yet enabled disk mode, enable it.

3. Double-click your iPod's icon on the desktop to display its contents in a Finder window. The contents will include the Calendars folder and the Contacts folder, as before, but you'll also be able to see the previously hidden files and folders: the iPod_Control folder, the .Trashes folder, and the .DS_Store, .VolumeIcon.cns, Desktop DB, Desktop DF, and Icon files.

4. Double-click the iPod_Control folder to open it.

5. Double-click the Music folder to open it.

6. Double-click one of the F folders to open it. Figure 14-4 shows an example of the structure of the iPod's music folders in Column view.

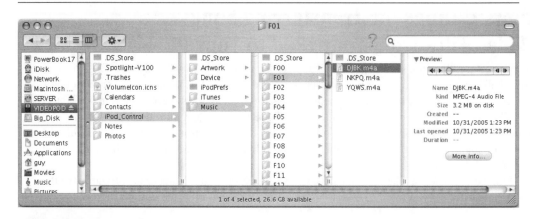

Turn on the display of hidden and system files to reveal your iPod's song folders and files.

Transfer Song and Video Files from Your iPod Using the Finder or Windows Explorer

If you looked closely at the illustrations of the files in the previous two sections, you'll probably have noticed that the way in which your iPod stores the files isn't immediately useful to most humans for two reasons:

■ First, your iPod lumps the files arbitrarily into automatically named folders (F01, F02, and so on) at its convenience. As long as your iPod's internal database knows which folder a particular song or video is in, that's fine. But if you want to find a particular file you'll need to go spelunking for it.

■ Second, your iPod assigns four-letter names to the songs and videos, so you have to a song or video to find out what it is. (In Windows, double-click the file to start play it. On the Mac, use the Preview feature in column view to play a song file, or doub click a video file to start it playing.)

So if you copy or move files from your iPod's library folders to your computer, yo to perform some heavy-duty sorting and renaming afterward. Even this will likely be to losing your entire music and video collection (if you've lost your library on your but you'll probably feel there's got to be a better way.

There is. Read on.

Windows Utilities for Transferring Song and Video Files from Your iPod to Your PC

At this writing, there are several Windows utilities for transferring song and video files from your iPod to your PC. This section also discusses a specialist utility, iPod Access for Windows.

The three heavy-duty iPod-management applications for Windows—EphPod, Anapod Explorer, and XPlay—also enable you to transfer files to, and generally manage, your iPod, and are discussed in detail in the next chapter. See the sections "Recover Song Files from Your iPod with EphPod," "Recover Song Files from Your iPod with Anapod Explorer," and "Recover Songs from Your iPod with XPlay" for details.

EphPod is freeware, whereas Anapod Explorer and XPlay are commercial software—so if you're interested only in rescuing your files from an iPod, EphPod is the best place to start.

iPod Access for Windows

iPod Access for Windows from Findley Designs (www.ipodaccess.com) lets you transfer files from your iPod to your PC. iPod Access for Windows (see Figure 14-5) costs $14.99, but you

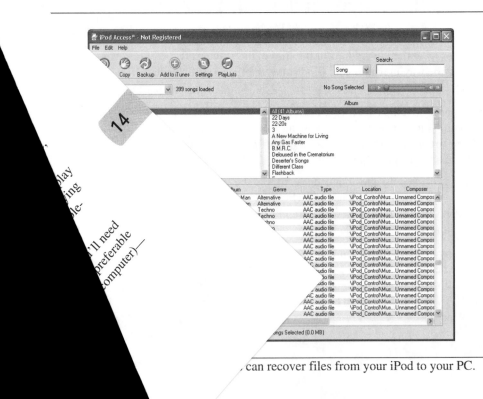

can recover files from your iPod to your PC.

can download a limited evaluation version to see if the application works for you. You can also use iPod Access to play back tracks directly from your iPod.

Mac OS X Utilities for Transferring Song and Video Files from Your iPod to Your Mac

iPod enthusiasts have created an impressive array of utilities for transferring song and video files from an iPod to a Mac. This section discusses some of the leading utilities for doing so.

NOTE *If you don't like the look (or performance) of these utilities, search sites such as iPodLounge.com (www.ipodlounge.com), VersionTracker.com (www.versiontracker .com), MacUpdate (www.macupdate.com), and Apple's Mac OS X Downloads page (www.apple.com/macosx/downloads) for alternatives.*

Different utilities work in different ways. The most basic utilities simply assemble a list of the file names in the iPod's music folders, which leaves you with cryptic file names. The best utilities read the database the iPod maintains of the files it holds, whereas other utilities plow painstakingly through each file on your iPod and extract information from its ID3 tags. Reading the iPod's database gives much faster results than assembling what's essentially the same database from scratch by scouring the tags. But if the database has become corrupted, reading the tags is a good recovery technique.

PodWorks

PodWorks from Sci-Fi Hi-Fi ($8; www.scifihifi.com/podworks) is a neat utility for transferring song and video files from your iPod to your Mac. PodWorks (see Figure 14-6) requires Mac OS X 10.2 or later. You can download an evaluation version that limits you to 30 days, copying 250 items total, and copying one item at a time—enough limitations to persuade you to buy the full version.

iPod Access

iPod Access from Findley Designs (www.ipodaccess.com) also simplifies the process of transferring song and video files from your iPod to your Mac. iPod Access (see Figure 14-7) costs $14.99, but you can download a limited evaluation version to see if the application works for you. You can also use iPod Access to play back songs directly from your iPod.

iPodRip

iPodRip from The Little App Factory PTY Ltd. ($9.00; www.thelittleappfactory.com) integrates with iTunes and enables you to play back songs from either your music library or your iPod.

14

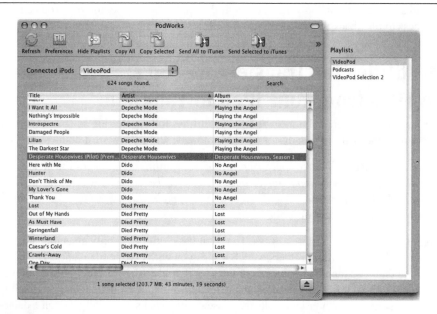

FIGURE 14-6 PodWorks can quickly recover songs from your iPod.

FIGURE 14-7 iPod Access is a commercial application for recovering songs and videos from your iPod.

iPodRip (see Figure 14-8; the application's title bar shows the iPod's name) comes in a trial version that you can use ten times before it cripples itself. iPodRip's SmartSync feature enables you to automatically copy to your music library songs and videos that you've loaded onto your iPod using a different computer.

FIGURE 14-8   iPodRip can recover songs from either an iPod or iTunes.

Chapter 15

Use Your iPod with Software Other Than iTunes

How to...

- Understand why to use software other than iTunes to control your iPod
- Manage your iPod with EphPod on Windows
- Manage your iPod with Musicmatch Jukebox on Windows
- Manage your iPod with Anapod Explorer on Windows
- Manage your iPod with XPlay on Windows
- Use Clutter to give iTunes a super-graphical interface on the Mac

Apple includes iTunes with every iPod, which gives you a strong incentive to use iTunes to manage your iPod. But if you choose not to use iTunes, there are some alternatives, particularly on Windows. This chapter introduces you to those alternatives, starting with the key question—Why use them?

Why Use Software Other Than iTunes to Control Your iPod?

iTunes is one of the core applications that have made Mac OS X such a powerhouse for multimedia, and both iTunes and Mac OS X have been built to work with iPods. As a result, iTunes is by far the best software for managing an iPod on the Mac, unless you need features that iTunes cannot or will not provide, such as recovering song files from the iPod to the computer (see the previous chapter) or the ability to synchronization your Entourage data with your iPod.

At this writing, iTunes for Windows suffers by comparison with iTunes for Mac OS X. This perhaps isn't surprising—iTunes for Windows is still at a relatively early stage of development, having started with version 4.0 to keep pace with iTunes for Mac OS X rather than having made the trek from version 1. iTunes for Windows' current problems include very slow startup, sporadic failure to notice new CDs you've inserted, frequent failure to notice when you've connected an iPod, and generally lethargic behavior. Some of iTunes for Windows' problems may be due to Windows itself, but that doesn't make iPod users any happier.

Also, as with iTunes for Mac OS X, you may require features that iTunes for Windows doesn't provide, such as the ability to recover your music library after your PC has disagreed violently with itself.

NOTE
Another reason to use other software is if iTunes doesn't run on your operating system. For example, iTunes for Windows requires Windows XP or Windows 2000. If you're using an earlier version of Windows, such as Windows 98 or Windows Me, you'll need to use other software.

Control Your iPod with Other Software on Windows

If you find iTunes for Windows slow or balky, or if iTunes doesn't run on your version of Windows, you have several alternatives. This section discusses the three leading contenders: EphPod, Anapod Explorer, and XPlay.

None of these applications can rip and encode audio from CD or burn CDs. iTunes will perform both tasks, as will Windows Media Player, which is included with most versions of Windows XP.

EphPod

EphPod (pronounced *eef*pod rather than *eff*pod, and downloadable from www.ephpod.com and other sites) is a free and very full-featured application for managing iPods on Windows. Technically, EphPod is donationware rather than freeware—the author invites you to contribute to his beer fund, and even allows you to request that a donation be spent on something better than beer.

EphPod was originally built, in the days when the iPod worked only with the Mac, to enable you to use Mac iPods with Windows PCs. Since then, Apple first teamed up with Musicmatch to deliver the version of Musicmatch Jukebox Plus that works with Windows iPods and the Updaters with which you can change Mac iPods to Windows iPods, and then later released iTunes for Windows.

These days, EphPod works with Windows iPods as well as Mac iPods. EphPod still lets you use Mac iPods with Windows, but you need to use MacOpener, a $40 product from DataViz, Inc. (www.dataviz.com), to enable Windows to read an iPod formatted with the Mac OS X Extended file system. Few users want to spend good music money on MacOpener when they can reformat their iPod's hard disk to FAT32 and manage it for free from Windows.

If you're finding iTunes for Windows awkward to use, you may want to try EphPod and see how it suits you. EphPod offers features for downloading news, weather, and RSS (Really Simple Syndication) web feeds to your iPod. EphPod also works on Windows 98 and Windows Me.

NOTE   *Even if you find iTunes fine for managing your iPod, you may need EphPod to recover music from your iPod after your computer has a disaster. EphPod not only makes this process easy, but it allows you to specify the conventions to use for naming the files that it recovers.*

Get and Install EphPod

Download the latest stable version of EphPod from the EphPod website (www.ephpod.com) and double-click the file to install it. Follow through the installation procedure, which is straightforward, and then launch EphPod from the Start menu.

NOTE   *If you're using Windows XP with Service Pack 2 or later, when you double-click the EphPod distribution file, you may see an Open File – Security Warning dialog box warning you that the publisher cannot be verified. This is because EphPod is not signed with a digital signature. But if you've just downloaded the file from the EphPod website, it should be fine.*

15

The first time you run EphPod, it prompts you to select the drive that represents your iPod (see Figure 15-1).

View the Contents of Your iPod

Once you've identified your iPod, EphPod displays the contents of your iPod. You can view them by playlist, by artist, by album, by genre, by song, by contact (if you've added any), or by recent items. Figure 15-2 shows the song database with the Artists category selected.

Add Songs to Your iPod

To add songs to your iPod with EphPod, click the Add Songs button, the Add Directory button, or the Add Playlists button, and then use the resulting dialog box to select the items to add. When you're adding songs, EphPod not only shows you its progress but also the transfer speed to your iPod (see Figure 15-3).

FIGURE 15-1   Identify your iPod to EphPod.

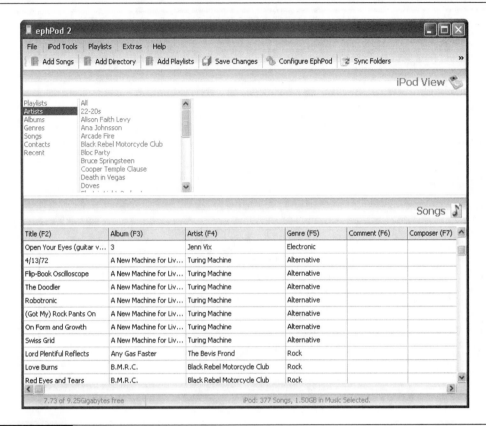

FIGURE 15-2   Viewing the contents of an iPod with EphPod.

NOTE

EphPod can't add songs in the Apple Lossless Encoding or AIFF format to your iPod. If you have songs in these formats, use iTunes to convert them to AAC, MP3, or WAV before loading them onto your iPod.

Recover Song Files from Your iPod with EphPod

One of EphPod's most compelling features is its ability to download song files from your iPod to your computer. This enables you to recover your music library from your iPod if your computer suffers a disaster.

To recover song files, first configure downloading options:

1. Click the Configure EphPod button on the toolbar, or choose Extras | Configuration, to display the Configuration dialog box.

2. Click the Advanced Options tab to display its contents (see Figure 15-4).

15

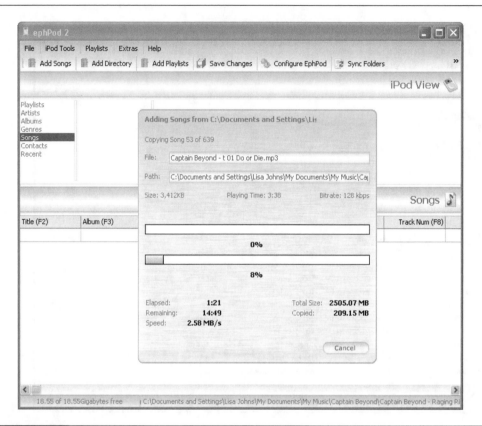

FIGURE 15-3   Transferring songs to an iPod using EphPod.

3. Make sure the Preserve MP3 Filename In Copy check box is cleared.

4. Make sure the Use Internal Copy Routines option button is selected.

5. To improve performance, increase the size of the Internal Copying Buffer Size drop-down list from its default setting of 1024KB to 4096KB.

6. In the Naming Convention For Copied Songs text box, enter the format EphPod should use for creating folders and naming the MP3 files it saves to your hard disk. You can use the variables shown in the following list to use information from the tags on the MP3 files. For example, you might use **%A\%L\%A – %T.mp3** to create folders and files such as Artist\Album\Artist – Song Title.mp3. If you're copying files in formats other than MP3,

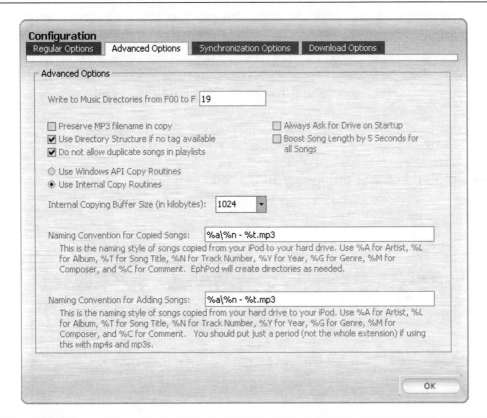

Configuration

| Regular Options | Advanced Options | Synchronization Options | Download Options |

Advanced Options

Write to Music Directories from F00 to F [19]

☐ Preserve MP3 filename in copy   ☐ Always Ask for Drive on Startup
☑ Use Directory Structure if no tag available   ☐ Boost Song Length by 5 Seconds for
☑ Do not allow duplicate songs in playlists   all Songs

○ Use Windows API Copy Routines
◉ Use Internal Copy Routines

Internal Copying Buffer Size (in kilobytes): [1024 ▾]

Naming Convention for Copied Songs: [%a\%n - %t.mp3]
This is the naming style of songs copied from your iPod to your hard drive. Use %A for Artist, %L for Album, %T for Song Title, %N for Track Number, %Y for Year, %G for Genre, %M for Composer, and %C for Comment. EphPod will create directories as needed.

Naming Convention for Adding Songs: [%a\%n - %t.mp3]
This is the naming style of songs copied from your hard drive to your iPod. Use %A for Artist, %L for Album, %T for Song Title, %N for Track Number, %Y for Year, %G for Genre, %M for Composer, and %C for Comment. You should put just a period (not the whole extension) if using this with mp4s and mp3s.

[OK]

FIGURE 15-4   Before downloading song files, check the naming convention that suits your needs.

put a period at the end but don't include the mp3 extension. These are the variables that you can use:

Variable	Explanation
%A	Artist name
%L	Album title
%T	Song title
%N	Track number
%Y	Year
%G	Genre
%C	Comment

7. Click the OK button to close the Configuration dialog box.

15

Once you've chosen the settings, export the song files by following these steps:

1. Navigate through the EphPod interface to the songs you want to export.

2. Select the songs and press CTRL-ALT-C, or right-click, and then choose Copy Songs To Directory from the shortcut menu (see Figure 15-5).

3. In the Browse For Folder dialog box, select the folder in which you want EphPod to create the folders and files.

4. Click the OK button. EphPod copies the files and folders and names them according to the convention you specified.

Close EphPod Before Unplugging Your iPod

At the end of your EphPod session, close EphPod and accept its offer to write the changes to your iPod before you unplug your iPod.

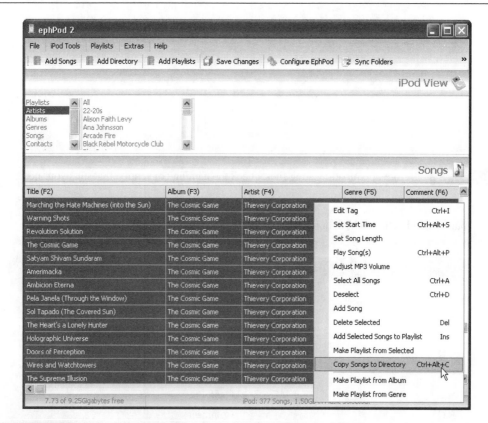

FIGURE 15-5   Recovering song files from an iPod to a computer with EphPod.

TIP *EphPod seems happy enough to work alongside iTunes, but it's a good idea to choose iPod Tools | Make EphPod Default iPod Manager App to make EphPod the default application for managing your iPod.*

Anapod Explorer

Anapod Explorer is a full-fledged utility for managing your iPod or iPods on Windows. Anapod Explorer comes in a Trial Edition that's free but has limited features, and a Full Edition that costs between $20 and $30, depending on how many iPods you use and which model or models they are. For example, the iPod shuffle license for Anapod Explorer is less expensive than those for the iPod nano and the regular iPods. (If you're like most iPod users, further iPods probably lie in your future, so the Universal version is probably the best bet.) Anapod Explorer runs as a plug-in to Windows Explorer, so you work in a largely familiar interface, and you can use drag-and-drop to perform file transfers.

NOTE *Anapod Explorer works with Windows XP, Windows 2000, Windows Me, and Windows 98.*

Get and Install Anapod Explorer

To get Anapod Explorer, go to the Red Chair Software, Inc. website (www.redchairsoftware.com) and either download the trial edition or buy one of the paid versions. Double-click the download file to open it.

NOTE *If you're using Windows XP with Service Pack 2 or later, when you double-click the Anapod Explorer distribution file, you may see an Open File – Security Warning dialog box warning you that the publisher cannot be verified. This is because Anapod Explorer is not signed with a digital signature. But if you've just downloaded the file from the Anapod Explorer website, you can probably be confident that it contains only trustworthy code.*

Anapod Explorer installs easily using a wizard. You can choose whether to create desktop shortcuts and a group on the Start menu. You have to activate Anapod Explorer for each iPod you want to use. The activation process involves generating an ID for the iPod, supplying that ID to Red Chair Software via the company's website, and waiting to receive an activation key via e-mail. The process can take up to 24 hours.

If you're using Windows XP with Service Pack 2 or later, you will probably see a Windows Security Alert dialog box at the end of the Anapod Explorer installation asking if you want Windows Firewall to keep blocking the Red Chair Manager from accepting connections from the Internet or a network (see Figure 15-6). You will need to click the Unblock button to allow Red Chair Manager to accept connections before Anapod Explorer will work correctly. Red Chair Manager manifests itself as a controller named Anapod Manager, which is used to establish communication with and control the iPod. Anapod Manager runs by default when you launch Windows and displays an icon in the notification area. You can right-click this icon to launch Anapod Explorer or configure Anapod Manager.

15

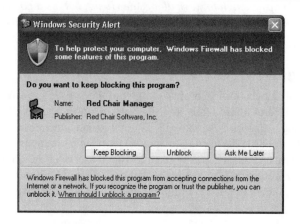

FIGURE 15-6   Windows XP with Service Pack 2 or later automatically blocks Red Chair Manager from accepting connections. You must unblock Red Chair Manager to get Anapod Explorer to work.

When the installation is complete, connect your iPod and then open Anapod Explorer in one of the following ways:

- Right-click the Anapod Manager icon in the notification area and choose Open Anapod Explorer from the shortcut menu. This is usually the easiest way, and it gives you access to the Anapod Manager's other commands.

- Double-click the Anapod Explorer icon on your desktop (if you chose to create one).

- Choose Start | All Programs | Red Chair Software | Anapod Explorer | Anapod Explorer.

You'll see a Windows Explorer window named Anapod Explorer. The window uses Windows Explorer's Folders view, and the Anapod Explorer item is selected in the Folders pane. The right pane shows the message that Anapod Explorer is not yet activated for your iPod and instructs you to double-click to activate it.

Double-click the message and follow through the instructions in the Anapod Activation dialog box. After activating your iPod, you must close the Anapod Activation dialog box, close the Windows Explorer window, disconnect and reconnect your iPod, and then reopen Anapod Explorer.

If the Open Anapod Explorer command on the Anapod Manager shortcut menu is grayed out, choose the Connect iPod item first to establish the connection with your iPod and then choose the Open Anapod Explorer item.

Transfer Songs to Your iPod with Anapod Explorer

To see the songs on your iPod, click the Audio Tracks item under the Anapod Explorer heading (see Figure 15-7).

You can then add songs to your iPod by dragging them or by using SpeedSync:

■ Drag the song files and drop them on the Audio Tracks item. Anapod Explorer displays the Transferring To Device dialog box (see Figure 15-8), which not only lets you see which file Anapod Explorer is working on, the overall progress, and the transfer performance, but also lets you compare the transfer performance to that of other users. You can drop further song files on the Transferring To Device dialog box to include them in the transfer, or you can simply wait until the transfer is complete and then click the Close button.

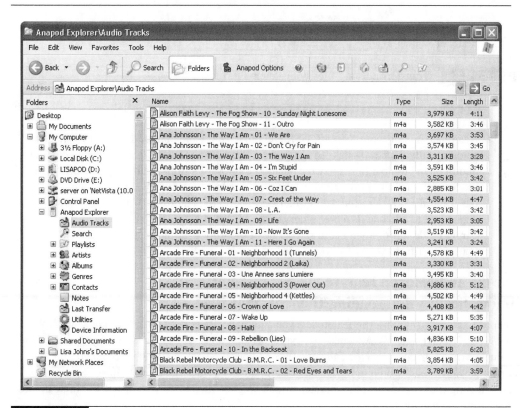

15

FIGURE 15-7   Anapod Explorer uses Windows Explorer as its interface.

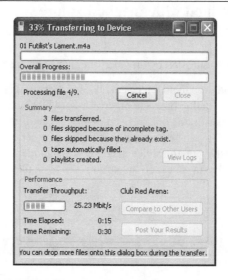

FIGURE 15-8   Transferring song files with Anapod Explorer.

■ Designate one or more SpeedSync folders that you want Anapod Explorer to check automatically for new songs. To designate a SpeedSync folder, click the Anapod Options button on the toolbar to display the Anapod Explorer Options dialog box and then click the SpeedSync item in the iPod category on the left to display the SpeedSync items (see Figure 15-9). Use the Add Folder button and the resulting Browse For Folder dialog box to add one or more folders to the PC Source Folders list. Then use the PC Target Folder drop-down list to select one of the folders as the destination for song files you recover from your iPod to your PC.

Use the AudioMorph Feature to Convert Songs Automatically when Loading Them on Your iPod

Anapod Explorer's AudioMorph feature lets you automatically convert song files in the MP3, WAV, OGG (Ogg Vorbis), and WMA formats to a particular bitrate when loading them on your iPod. For example, you might choose to load all song files on your iPod at the 128 Kbps bitrate if you felt that bitrate delivered the optimum balance of audio quality versus file size. Anapod Explorer then converts song files encoded at other bitrates (usually higher bitrates) to your specified bitrate before transferring them to the iPod.

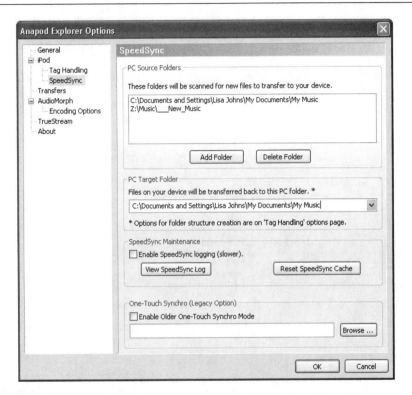

FIGURE 15-9 On the SpeedSync section of the Anapod Explorer Options dialog box, designate one or more PC Source Folders and a PC Target Folder.

Here's how to use AudioMorph:

1. Click the Anapod Options button on the toolbar to display the Anapod Explorer Options dialog box.
2. Click the AudioMorph item in the left column to display its contents (see Figure 15-10).
3. Select the Enable AudioMorph During Transfers check box to turn AudioMorph on.
4. Check the list boxes at the top of the pane to see which plug-ins are installed. To get further plug-ins, click the Help And More Plug-ins button and follow the instructions in the resulting browser window to download and install the plug-ins.

NOTE

If you're using Windows XP with Service Pack 2 or later, when you double-click the distribution file of an Anapod Explorer encoder, you may see an Open File – Security Warning dialog box warning you that the publisher cannot be verified because the file is not signed with a digital signature. But if you've just downloaded the file from the Anapod Explorer website, it should be okay.

15

FIGURE 15-10 You may need to use the Help And More Plug-ins button to get Anapod Explorer's AudioMorph feature working for all the audio file types you want Anapod Explorer to convert automatically when loading songs onto your iPod.

5. To change the transfer rule for a file format, right-click the rule in the lower pane and choose the rule you want from the shortcut menu.

6. To change the encoding rate for creating or reencoding MP3 or WMA files, click the Encoding Options item in the left list and work with the resulting controls (see Figure 15-11).

Recover Songs from Your iPod with Anapod Explorer

Before recovering songs from your iPod with Anapod Explorer, you must designate the PC target folder, as described in the previous section. (If you missed it: Click the Anapod Options button on the toolbar to display the Anapod Explorer Options dialog box, click the SpeedSync item in the iPod category on the left, and then select the folder in the PC Target Folder drop-down list).

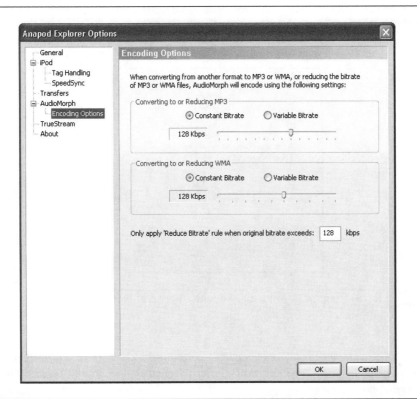

FIGURE 15-11   Anapod Explorer can reduce the bitrate of songs when transferring them to your iPod. This is a great way to maximize the amount of music your iPod can hold.

Once you've designated your PC target folder, proceed as follows:

1. Select the songs you want to recover.

2. Right-click the selection and choose Copy To Computer from the shortcut menu. Anapod Explorer displays the Browse For Folder dialog box.

3. Navigate to and select the target folder and then click the OK button. Anapod Explorer copies the song files, displaying the Transferring To PC dialog box as it does so (see Figure 15-12).

Access Your iPod Remotely Across the Network with Anapod Explorer

Anapod Explorer includes a miniature web server called Anapod Xtreamer that allows you to access your iPod remotely from any computer on the network. You can play songs in formats that your browser's plug-ins can play, or you can download any song to your local hard disk.

15

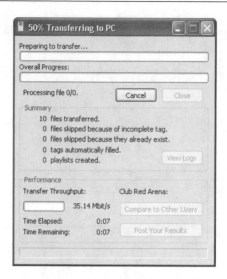

Recovering songs from an iPod with Anapod Explorer.

> **TIP**   *You can also stream music from your iPod to your own computer. To do so, right-click the Anapod Manager icon in the notification area and choose Browse Anapod Xtreamer from the shortcut menu.*

Before using Anapod Xtreamer from another computer, you must set up one or more remote access accounts. Here's how to do so:

1. Right-click the Anapod Manager icon in the notification area and choose Anapod Manager Options from the shortcut menu to display the Anapod Manager Options dialog box.

2. Click the Xtreamer HTTP Options item in the left pane to display the Xtreamer HTTP Options sheet (see Figure 15-13).

3. Click the Add button, type the user name and password in the Remote Access Account dialog box (shown here), and then click the OK button.

4. If necessary, choose other options. For example, you might change the Xtreamer port from its default setting of 8046 if it conflicts with another application or your firewall. Or you could apply a different skin (a different look) to Xtreamer, or configure logging.

5. Click the OK button to close the Anapod Manager Options dialog box.

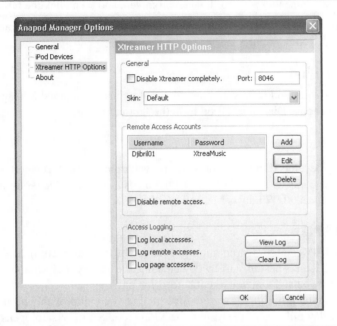

FIGURE 15-13 Set up remote access to Xtreamer on the Xtreamer HTTP Options sheet of the Anapod Manager Options dialog box.

You can then connect to your iPod from another computer by using the user name and password:

1. On the other computer, start the web browser and identify the computer by name or by IP address:

   ■ To identify the computer by name, choose Start | My Computer, click the My Network Places link in the Other Places pane, and then click the View Workgroup Computers link in the Network Tasks pane. Double-click the computer you want to access and then change the entry in the Address Bar from the computer's name (for example, \\KitchenBox) to **http://**, the computer's name, a colon, and the Xtreamer port number, such as **http://KitchenBox:8046**. Press ENTER or click the Go button.

   ■ To learn the computer's IP address, on that computer choose Start | All Programs | Accessories | Command Prompt. In the Command Prompt window, type **ipconfig** and press ENTER. Note the IP Address readout for the network connection—for example, 10.0.0.4 or 192.168.0.1. On the remote computer, type **http://**, the IP address, a colon, and the port number (for example, **http://10.0.0.4:8046**) and then press ENTER or click the Go button.

15

  2. Type your user name and password, when prompted, and then click the OK button.

  3. Use the controls on the Anapod Xtreamer interface to play the music remotely or to download it to your computer.

Disconnect Your iPod

Before disconnecting your iPod from your computer, right-click the Anapod Manager icon in the notification area and choose Disconnect iPod from the shortcut menu.

XPlay

XPlay was originally developed to let Windows users synchronize Mac-formatted iPods with their PCs. XPlay now works with Windows-formatted iPods as well as Mac iPods, and runs on Windows XP, Windows 2000, Windows Me, and Windows 98.

Get and Install XPlay

To get XPlay, go to the Mediafour Corporation website (www.mediafour.com). The full version of XPlay costs $29.95, so it's best to start by downloading the 15-day trial version of XPlay to make sure it works for you and that you like it before you pay.

   The XPlay installation procedure is straightforward, but you will probably need to restart your PC to enable XPlay fully. After the restart, the XPlay iPod Setup Wizard opens and walks you through the process of setting up your iPod to work with XPlay. This includes deciding whether to configure iTunes to work with Mac iPods, as shown here. Unless you have a Mac-formatted iPod, you shouldn't need to do this. Select the Don't Ask This Question Again check box to suppress the warning in the future.

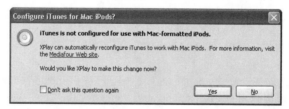

   If you've previously been using iTunes to update either your entire music library or part of it on your iPod, the XPlay iPod Setup Wizard also warns you that your iPod is set to be updated automatically using iTunes, as shown here. Select the Don't Show This Again For This iPod check box if you want to suppress this warning from now on.

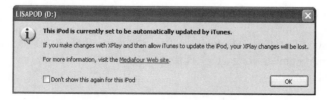

The setup procedure also lets you rename your iPod and choose whether to synchronize it automatically using XPlay.

At the end of the setup procedure, start XPlay in one of these ways:

- Double-click the Explore My iPod With XPlay icon in the notification area.
- Double-click the Explore My iPod With XPlay icon on your desktop.
- Choose Start | All Programs | XPlay | Explore My iPod.

XPlay then opens a Windows Explorer window to the root of the drive that represents your iPod (see Figure 15-14).

Double-click the XPlay Music item to view XPlay's representation of your iPod's music database (see Figure 15-15). Within the XPlay Music folder, you can drill down to view playlists, albums, and artists. You can use the Songs item to view all the songs on your iPod.

Transfer Songs to Your iPod with XPlay

To copy song files to your iPod, drag them and drop them on it.

Recover Songs from Your iPod with XPlay

To copy song files from your iPod to your PC using XPlay, drill down to the appropriate song or folder on the iPod. Then either drag the song or folder to a folder on your PC or click the Copy This Item link in the XPlay Music Tasks pane, use the resulting Browse For Folder dialog box to specify the destination, and then click the OK button.

Prepare Your iPod for Disconnection

Before disconnecting your iPod, click the Stop My iPod button (the button with the Eject icon) on the toolbar in the XPlay window.

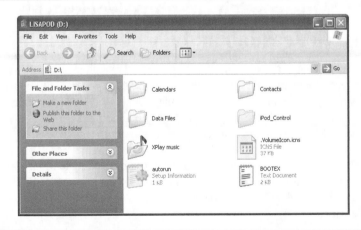

FIGURE 15-14   XPlay displays your iPod as a drive in a Windows Explorer window.

15

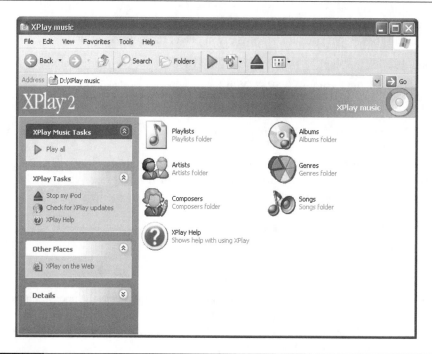

FIGURE 15-15   The XPlay Music item lets you access your music by playlists, albums, artists, genres, composers, or songs.

Did you know?

Musicmatch Jukebox Works with Third-Generation and Earlier iPods Only

Musicmatch Jukebox Plus is the software that Apple included with the Windows-formatted versions of the second-generation iPods and then with the third-generation iPods until it released iTunes for Windows in late 2003. Musicmatch Jukebox Plus and its more limited version, Musicmatch Jukebox Basic, work with third-generation and earlier iPods except for first-generation, Mac-only iPods. Musicmatch Jukebox Plus costs $19.99; Musicmatch Jukebox Basic is free.

Musicmatch Jukebox offers strong features for ripping and encoding to MP3, burning CDs, managing your music library, and tagging files. Unfortunately, in version 10, Musicmatch has discontinued its support for the iPod, so Musicmatch Jukebox is no longer a viable solution, even if you have an earlier iPod.

If you're determined to try Musicmatch Jukebox with an early iPod, visit the MMJB Software Release Archives (http://partners.musicmatch.com/archives/) and download the file mmsetup_7.50.5005-ENU_Apple.exe, the latest version designed to work with the iPod. Once you get this working, you may be able to upgrade to version 8 or version 9 (both available from the MMJB Software Release Archives) and keep Musicmatch Jukebox working with your iPod, but you will not be able to upgrade to version 10.

Improve the iTunes Interface with Clutter (Mac)

Sleek and effective as iTunes' interface is, it could be more visually compelling. If you'd like to be able to navigate your music collection by the covers of the CDs rather than by their names, download the freeware application Clutter (see Figure 15-16) from www.sprote.com/clutter.

15

FIGURE 15-16 Clutter is a free application that enables you to spread your music collection across your desktop and select music by its CD cover.

When you start playing a song in iTunes, Clutter tries to download the cover picture for the CD that contains the song. If Clutter can connect to the Internet and finds the picture at Amazon .com, it displays it in the Now Playing window. You can then drag the picture to your desktop and position it wherever you want it. Each CD cover is a separate window, so you can overlap the covers however you want.

If you started a song playing while your Mac wasn't connected to the Internet, after connecting, you can force Clutter to search Amazon.com for the CD cover by pressing ⌘-F or choosing File | Find Cover On Amazon. If Amazon.com doesn't have the cover, you can search Google by pressing ⌘-G or choosing File | Search Google. Alternatively, you can drag a graphic to the Now Playing window from a browser window or a Finder window, so you can apply any graphic that you have or that you can find.

The main Clutter window shows the details of the song that's currently playing, and it provides a Play/Pause button, a Previous button, and a Next button. You can start any CD playing by double-clicking its cover on your desktop.

To get your desktop back again, quit Clutter (press ⌘-Q). The next time you start Clutter, it places the CD covers across the desktop in the same arrangement as you left them.

Chapter 16

Use Your iPod as an External Drive or Backup Device

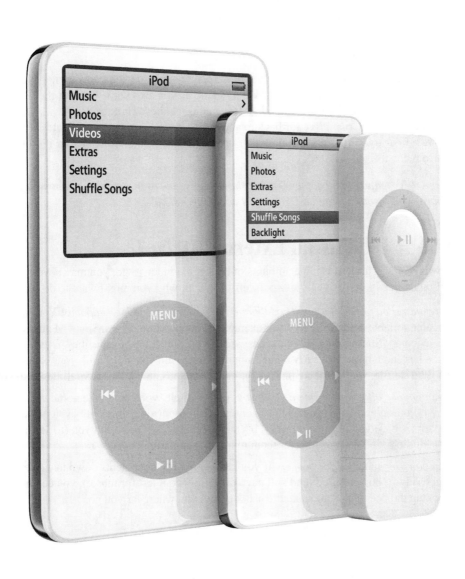

How to...

- Decide whether or not to use your iPod as an external drive
- Enable disk mode on your iPod using Windows
- Enable disk mode on your iPod using a Mac
- Transfer files to and from your iPod
- Start up your Mac from your first- to fourth-generation regular iPod
- Back up your iPod so you don't lose your music or data
- Optimize your iPod's hard disk to improve performance

Apple sells the iPod primarily as a portable music player—and, as you know by now, it's arguably the best portable music player around. But, as you also know by now, the iPod is essentially an external USB drive with sophisticated audio features. This chapter shows you how to use your iPod as an external drive for backup and portable storage. If your computer is a Mac and you have a first- to fourth-generation regular iPod, you can even boot from your iPod for security or to recover from disaster.

 *One drive feature this chapter doesn't show you is how to transfer files from your iPod's library onto your computer. Chapter 14 covers this subject.*

Why Use Your iPod as an External Drive?

If all you want from your iPod is huge amounts of music and video to go, you may never want to use your iPod as an external drive. Even so, briefly consider why you might want to do so:

- *A regular iPod provides a great combination of portability and high capacity.* You can get smaller portable-storage devices (for example, CompactFlash drives, Smart Media cards, and Memory Sticks), but they're expensive and have much lower capacities. Even an iPod nano has enough space to carry a fair amount of data with you along with your songs. On an iPod shuffle, you'll feel the pinch a bit more, but you can take some vital files with you.

- *You can take all your documents with you.* For example, you could take home that large PowerPoint presentation you need to get ready for tomorrow. You could even put several gigabytes of video files on your iPod if you needed to take them with you (for example, to a studio for editing) or transfer them to another computer.

- *You can use your iPod for backup.* If you keep your vital documents down to a size you can easily fit on your iPod (and still have plenty of room left for music), you can quickly back up the documents and take the backup with you wherever you go.

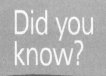

Extreme Examples of Using iPods for Storage

The regular iPod's combination of small size and large storage have led to some surprising uses. Here are a couple:

- Radiologists at the UCLA Medical Center have developed an open-source application running on Mac OS X to put medical imaging data on an iPod so that they can easily transfer it from one place to another. The files tend to be too large to burn to a CD, but they fit easily on an iPod.

- iPods have even been used to steal software from stores. For example, enterprising thieves have plugged iPods into Macs in computer stores such as CompUSA and copied application software (such as Microsoft Office) from the Mac onto the iPod. You can use this same technique legally to move an application from one Mac to another if you don't have a means of connecting them.

- *You can use your iPod for security.* By keeping your documents on your iPod rather than on your computer, and by keeping your iPod with you, you can prevent other people from accessing your documents. If your computer is a Mac (and if it's the right kind of Mac—more on this later), you can even boot your Mac from a first- to fourth-generation regular iPod, thus preventing anyone else from using your computer at all.

The disadvantages to using your iPod as an external disk are straightforward:

- Whatever space you use on your iPod for storing other files isn't available for music and video.

- If you lose or break your iPod, any files stored only on it will be gone forever.

Enable Disk Mode

To use your iPod as an external drive, you must first enable disk mode. In disk mode, your computer uses your iPod as an external disk. You can copy to your iPod any files and folders that will fit on it.

16

NOTE   *You can copy song files, video files, and playlists to your iPod in disk mode, but you won't be able to play them on the iPod. This is because when you copy the files, their information isn't added to the iPod's database the way it's added by iTunes and other applications (for example, EphPod or XPlay) designed to work with the iPod. So your iPod's interface doesn't know the files are there, and you can't play them.*

From the computer's point of view, an external disk connected via USB works in essentially the same way as any other disk. Here are the differences:

■ The disk is external.

■ The disk may draw power across the USB connection (as iPods do) rather than being powered itself (as high-capacity and high-performance external disks tend to be).

■ When you use your iPod as a disk, it draws power from the computer.

■ The USB controller and the USB cable or connection must supply enough power to feed the iPod. All USB connections supply power, but some don't supply enough for an iPod. (Other devices, such as USB keyboards and mice, require much less power than an iPod.) Apple refers to USB ports as "high-powered" (giving enough power for an iPod) and "low-powered" (not giving enough power).

Using a disk-based iPod (for example, a regular iPod) as an external disk with a connection that can't supply power may run down the battery quickly. Part of the problem is that your iPod can't use its caching capabilities when you use it as an external disk. (Caching works only for playlists and albums, when your iPod knows which files are needed next and thus can read them into the cache.) If your iPod isn't receiving power, check the battery status periodically to make sure your iPod doesn't suddenly run out of power.

Enable Disk Mode on Your iPod Using Windows

To use your iPod as an external disk on a PC, enable disk mode. Follow these steps:

1. Connect your iPod to your PC as usual.

2. Launch iTunes if it doesn't launch automatically.

3. In the Source pane, right-click the icon for your iPod and choose iPod Options from the shortcut menu to display the iPod tab of the iTunes dialog box. Alternatively, click the Display iPod Options button in the lower-right corner of the iTunes window.

4. Click the Music subtab if it isn't already displayed. (For an iPod shuffle, skip this step, as there are no subtabs on the iPod tab.)

5. Select the Enable Disk Use check box. iTunes displays the following warning dialog box, telling you that using disk mode requires you to manually unmount the iPod before each disconnect, even when you're automatically updating music:

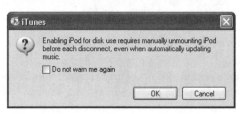

6. Select the Do Not Warn Me Again check box and then click the OK button. iTunes returns you to the iTunes dialog box.

7. For an iPod shuffle, drag the slider along the More Songs-More Data continuum to specify how much space you want to devote to data and how much to songs:

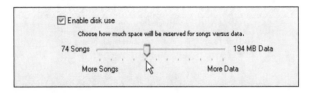

8. Click the OK button to close the iTunes dialog box.

Once you've enabled disk mode, your iPod appears to Windows Explorer as a removable drive. Windows Explorer automatically assigns a drive letter to the drive, so you can access it as you would any other drive connected to your computer.

To eject your iPod, take any of the following actions:

- In the Source pane in iTunes, click the Eject icon next to your iPod's name. (This is by far the easiest means of ejection.)

- In the Source pane in iTunes, right-click the icon for your iPod and then choose Eject.

- In the Source pane in iTunes, select the icon for your iPod and then click the Eject iPod button in the lower-right corner of the iTunes window.

- Choose Start | My Computer to open a Windows Explorer window to My Computer view, right-click the icon for your iPod, and choose Eject from the shortcut menu to eject it.

When your iPod displays the "OK to disconnect" message, you can safely disconnect it.

Enable Disk Mode on Your iPod Using a Mac

To enable disk mode on your iPod using a Mac, follow these steps:

1. Connect your iPod to your Mac as usual.

2. If iTunes doesn't launch automatically, launch it manually. For example, click the iTunes icon in the Dock.

3. In the Source pane, right-click the icon for your iPod and choose iPod Options from the shortcut menu to display the iPod tab of the Preferences dialog box. Alternatively, click the Display iPod Options button in the lower-right corner of the iTunes window.

4. Click the Music subtab if it isn't already displayed. (For an iPod shuffle, skip this step, as there are no subtabs on the iPod tab.)

16

5. Select the Enable Disk Use check box. iTunes displays the following warning dialog box, telling you that using disk mode requires you to unmount the iPod manually before each disconnect, even when synchronizing songs (instead of being able to have iTunes unmount the iPod automatically):

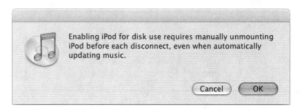

Enabling iPod for disk use requires manually unmounting iPod before each disconnect, even when automatically updating music.

Cancel   OK

6. Click the OK button. iTunes returns you to the Preferences dialog box.

7. For an iPod shuffle, drag the slider along the More Songs-More Data continuum to specify how much space you want to devote to data and how much to songs:

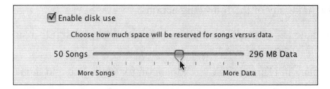

☑ Enable disk use

Choose how much space will be reserved for songs versus data.

50 Songs ——————————————— 296 MB Data

More Songs   More Data

8. Click the OK button to close the Preferences dialog box.

How to ... **Force Disk Mode**

If your USB port is underpowered, you may need to force your iPod to enter disk mode. To do so, follow these steps:

1. Connect your iPod via USB as usual.

2. Toggle the Hold switch on and off, then hold down the Select button and the Menu button for about five seconds to reboot your iPod.

3. When your iPod displays the Apple logo, hold down the Select button and the Play button. Your iPod sends the computer an electronic prod that forces the computer to recognize it.

Once you've enabled disk mode, you'll need to unmount your iPod manually using one of the following methods after synchronizing your music library or transferring files to or from your iPod.

- In the Source pane in iTunes, click the Eject icon next to your iPod's name.

- In the Source pane in iTunes, select the icon for your iPod and then click the Eject iPod button in the lower-right corner of the iTunes window.

- In the Source pane in iTunes, CTRL-click the icon for your iPod and then choose Eject from the shortcut menu.

- Select the icon for your iPod on the desktop and then issue an Eject command from the File menu or the shortcut menu.

- Drag the desktop icon for your iPod to the Trash.

When your iPod displays the "OK to disconnect" message, you can safely disconnect it.

Transfer Files to and from Your iPod

When your iPod is in disk mode, you can transfer files to it by using Windows Explorer (Windows), the Finder (Mac), or another file-management application of your choice. (You can transfer files by using the command prompt, if you so choose.)

CAUTION   *If your iPod appears in the My Computer window as a drive named Removable Drive, and Windows Explorer claims the disk isn't formatted, chances are you've connected a Mac-formatted iPod to your PC. Windows Explorer can't read the HFS Plus disk format that Mac iPods use, so the iPod appears to be unformatted. (HFS Plus is one of the disk formats Mac OS X can use and is also called the Mac OS Extended format.)*

You can create and delete folders on your iPod as you would any other drive. But be sure you don't mess with the iPod's system folders, such as the Calendars folder, the Contacts folder, the Notes folder, the Photos folder, and the iPod_Control folder.

NOTE   *As mentioned earlier, don't transfer music or video files to your iPod by using file-management software if you want to be able to play the files on your iPod. Unless you transfer the files by using iTunes or another application designed to access the iPod's music database, the details about the files won't be added to the iPod. You won't be able to play those files on your iPod because their data hasn't been added to its database of contents.*

The exception to transferring files from your iPod is transferring files that you've put on your iPod by using iTunes or another application that can access the iPod's database. Chapter 14 shows you how to do this.

16

Start Up Your Mac from a First- to Fourth-Generation Regular iPod

If you have a first- to fourth-generation regular iPod, you can start up (boot) your Mac from your iPod. This capability can be useful for backup—you can start your Mac from your iPod even when your Mac hard disk has stopped working—but you may also want to use it for security: By making your iPod the only bootable disk for your Mac, you can prevent other people from booting your Mac when your iPod isn't present. If you carry your iPod with you, you can extend that restriction to any time you're not using your Mac.

Sadly, the fifth-generation (video-capable) iPod doesn't offer booting. Neither do the iPod nano, the iPod mini, nor the iPod shuffle.

Because this topic doesn't apply to current iPod models, there isn't space to cover it in detail in this book. But here's what you need to know to get started:

■ You can make your iPod bootable either by installing Mac OS X (or System 9) on it directly or by cloning an existing installation of Mac OS X (or System 9).

■ You'll need between 1GB and 2GB for Jaguar, between 2GB and 3GB for Panther, and between 2GB and 4.8GB for Tiger, depending on which files you choose to install. For System 9, you'll need a more modest amount of space—from 250MB to 500MB, depending on the options you choose.

■ To install an operating system directly, run the installation routine from your Mac OS X or System 9 installation disc exactly as you would to install the operating system on your Mac, except that you specify your iPod, rather than your Mac's hard disk, as the destination disk for the install. Omit any files you don't need—for example, printer drivers or extra fonts.

■ Installing the operating system directly works fine if you have a version of the operating system that fits on a single CD or a single DVD. The problem with having multiple CDs is that installing to the iPod tends to fail when you switch to the second disc. In practice, this means that you can install Mac OS X versions before 10.2 (for example, 10.1.x) or System 9 from a CD, because those operating systems fit on a single CD. But to install Mac OS X 10.2 or later, you need to have a DVD (and a DVD drive), because these versions take up two or more CDs.

■ Instead of installing the operating system directly, you can use a cloning tool such as Carbon Copy Cloner (CCC; www.bombich.com/software/ccc.html) or SuperDuper! (www.shirtpocket.com/SuperDuper/SuperDuperDescription.html) to clone an existing installation. This is often easier than a clean installation, and you can choose to omit certain parts of the installation to save space on the iPod.

- After installing or cloning the operating system onto your iPod, you may need to designate your iPod as the startup disk to make your Mac boot from it. Choose Apple | System Preferences to display the System Preferences window, click the Startup Disk icon in the System area to display the Startup Disk sheet, select the item that represents your iPod, and then click the Restart button. In the confirmation dialog box, click the Restart button.

- If your Mac fails to boot from your iPod, press ⌘-CONTROL-POWER to force a restart. When your Mac plays the system sound, hold down OPTION to display a graphical screen of the available startup disks. Click the disk from which you want to start the computer, and then click the arrow button on the screen to start your Mac using that startup disk.

Back Up Your iPod So You Don't Lose Your Music or Data

If you synchronize your complete library with your iPod, and perhaps load your contacts, calendar information, and photos on your iPod as well, you shouldn't need to worry about backing up your iPod. That's because your computer contains all the data that's on your iPod. (Effectively, your iPod is a backup of part of your hard disk.) So if you lose your iPod, or it stops functioning, you won't lose any data you don't have on your computer.

If your computer's hard disk stops working, you might need to recover your library, contacts, calendar data, and photos from your iPod onto another computer or a new hard disk. You can transfer contacts, calendars, and full-resolution photos by enabling disk mode and using the Finder (Mac) or Windows Explorer (PC) to access the contents of the Contacts folder, the Calendars folder, and the Photos/Full Resolution folder. For instructions on recovering song and video files from your iPod, see Chapter 14.

So, normally, your iPod will be the vulnerable member of the tag team. But if you store files directly on your iPod, you should back them up to your computer to make sure you don't lose them if your iPod vanishes or its hard disk gives up the ghost.

To back up files, either use a file-management utility (for example, the Finder or Windows Explorer) to simply copy the files or folders to your computer, or use custom backup software to create a more formal backup. For example, you might use the Backup Utility included with Windows XP (Start | All Programs | Accessories | System Tools | Backup) to back up your Windows iPod. On Mac OS X, you might use the Backup application to back up your files to your .Mac iDisk (which you can access via any Internet connection), use iDisk Utility to mount your .Mac iDisk via WebDAV (a protocol for transferring information to web servers), or use a commercial alternative such as Dantz Retrospect (www.dantz.com).

16

Optimize Your iPod's Hard Disk to Improve Performance

If you've been using a Windows computer for a while, you'll know you need to optimize your computer's hard disk every now and again to keep it performing well. This is because each file of any size beyond the smallest files occupies multiple clusters of the sectors into which a hard disk is divided. If the clusters are close to one another, the hard disk's read head can read the clusters without needing to travel back and forth unnecessarily across the disk. But if the clusters are spread out all over the disk, the read head needs to travel farther to do the reading. Traveling farther makes the reading take longer.

Ideally, your operating system writes each file into a nice, neat series of contiguous clusters, so the disk head doesn't have to move far to read them. But when your hard disk grows full, your operating system is forced to break files across whichever clusters are available on the disk rather than being able to put them all together. The disk's read head then has to travel farther, so reads take longer.

Breaking files across various clusters is called *fragmentation*. To reduce fragmentation and improve performance, you can *defragment* (or *defrag*) a drive. The defragmentation utility rearranges and rewrites the data so that files are written onto contiguous clusters wherever possible. As a result, your disk's read head can access any given file more quickly and with less effort, and performance improves.

Defragmenting utilities reshuffle the files on your hard disk so that files are stored on contiguous clusters wherever possible. Depending on the efficiency of the defragmenter, you may need to run it twice or more to get the files arranged as well as possible.

 The iPod nano and iPod shuffle use memory chips rather than a hard disk and don't need defragmentation.

 **Decide Whether to Defragment Your iPod**

If you're not using your iPod as a hard drive, you may not need to defragment it at all. This is for a couple of reasons.

First, under normal use, your iPod's hard disk won't become fragmented quickly or to a severe degree. What will typically happen is that you'll load a relatively large number of song, photo, and video files at first, and then gradually add to them, perhaps removing those you don't like. The files for your contacts, calendars, notes, and so on may change more frequently than your music, photo, and video files, but typically these text files will be fairly small. If you take and load many photos, fragmentation may occur, especially if the photo files are large.

Second, when you're using your iPod only for music, videos, contacts, calendars, and maybe photos, you won't necessarily need the ultimate performance that its hard drive can deliver. Performance is more important when you're using your iPod as an external disk. However, having your song files defragmented may help you squeeze a little more playing time out of your iPod's battery, so this may give you the motive to defragment it.

On the other hand, if you use your iPod extensively as a hard drive, it may become fragmented relatively quickly. If this happens, defragmenting it is a good idea.

Windows XP includes a disk defragmenter called Disk Defragmenter. Mac OS X doesn't include a disk defragmenter, and Apple doesn't specifically recommend any single defragmentation utility, but most people find that utilities such as Norton Utilities for the Mac's Speed Disk from Symantec Corporation (www.norton.com) and PlusOptimizer from Alsoft, Inc. (www.alsoft.com) get the job done.

Before defragmenting a drive, it's always a good idea to back up the data on it just in case anything goes wrong. It's especially important to back up your data if you decide to defragment all your drives at once, including your iPod. If your iPod contains a partial backup of your hard disk, it's a much better idea to defragment them separately (in case you need to recover files from one to the other) than to defragment them at the same time.

Run the Windows XP Disk Defragmenter

To run the Disk Defragmenter included with Windows XP, choose Start | All Programs | Accessories | System Tools | Disk Defragmenter. Alternatively, follow these steps:

1. Choose Start | My Computer to open a My Computer window.

2. In the Devices With Removable Storage area, right-click the drive that represents your iPod and then choose Properties from the shortcut menu to display the Properties dialog box.

3. Click the Tools tab to display it.

4. Click the Defragment Now button to display the Disk Defragmenter window (see Figure 16-1).

The Disk Defragmenter utility is straightforward to use. You select the drive you want to defragment and then click the Analyze button to analyze it or the Defragment button to defragment it. If you click the Analyze button, Disk Defragmenter displays a summary of the state of the drive and tells you whether or not you need to defragment it.

Defragment Your iPod the Cheap and Easy Way

If you prefer not to pay for a defragmenter for your Mac, you don't need to: You can defragment your iPod easily by moving all the files off it, optionally reformatting it, and then putting the files back on it. When you put the files back on your iPod, they're written in contiguous clusters as much as possible.

16

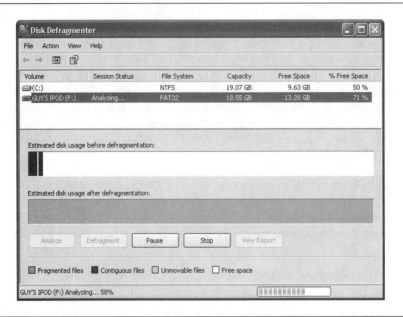

FIGURE 16-1 You can use the Disk Defragmenter utility included with Windows XP to defragment your Windows iPod.

 *You can defragment your iPod by using this technique on Windows, as well. In many cases, it's a toss-up whether to use this technique or to use Disk Defragmenter. Your decision will probably depend on exactly which files you store on your iPod and how difficult it would be to replace them after restoring your iPod.*

The cleanest method of performing defragmentation this way is to restore your iPod's operating system (as described in "Restore Your iPod" in Chapter 17) and then synchronize your iPod with your computer. Restoring the iPod removes all the files, leaving the disk in great shape. This synchronization will take much longer than normal synchronizations because your computer will have to transfer every file to your iPod.

Before you defragment your iPod in this way, make sure you have a copy of all the files on it:

■ If your iPod contains only a copy of your iTunes library and synchronized copies of your contacts, calendars, and photos, you shouldn't need to worry about making copies of the files—your computer already contains copies of them.

■ If your iPod contains files other than your iTunes library, your contacts, your calendars, and your photos, you may need to copy them to (or back them up to) your computer.

■ If you've installed Mac OS X or System 9 on your first- to fourth-generation regular iPod, don't restore your iPod unless you want to lose the operating system. Instead, move the files from your iPod to a different disk and then move them back again.

Part V

Troubleshoot Your iPod and iTunes

Chapter 17

Troubleshoot Your iPod

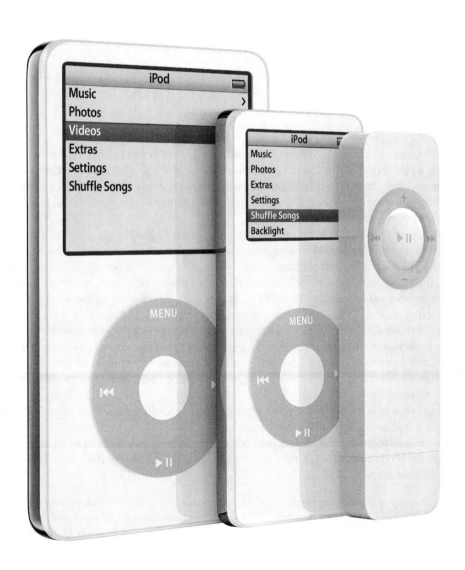

How to…

- Understand what your iPod consists of
- Get the maximum life possible from your iPod's battery
- Avoid doing things that make your iPod unhappy
- Keep your iPod's operating system up to date
- Carry and store your iPod safely
- Clean your iPod
- Avoid voiding your warranty
- Know the best approach for troubleshooting your iPod
- Learn key troubleshooting maneuvers
- Use your iPod's built-in diagnostic tools to pinpoint problems
- Troubleshoot common and less-common problems

Apple designs and builds the various iPod models to be as reliable as possible—after all, Apple would like to sell at least one iPod to everyone in the world who has a computer, and it would much prefer to be thwarted in this aim by economics or competition than by negative feedback. But even so, iPods go wrong sometimes. This chapter shows you what to do when it's *your* iPod that goes wrong.

To identify what's wrong, it helps to understand a bit about what an iPod consists of and what's required to keep your iPod in good working shape. The first part of this chapter tells you what you need to know; points out some avoidable things that can make your iPod unhappy; shows you how to keep your iPod's operating system up to date; and mentions how to carry, store, and clean your iPod.

For when basic care doesn't suffice, this chapter pursues a two-pronged approach to troubleshooting. First, it shows you some standard troubleshooting maneuvers you may need to perform to resuscitate your iPod or rope its operating system back under control, and some diagnostics you may want to try when you think something is really wrong (or you want to see what—if anything—the diagnostic tests do). Second, it presents problems as they'll typically manifest themselves and then walks you through troubleshooting the problems and (with any luck) solving them.

Also, before we get your hands grubby, we'll talk briefly about the warranty your iPod should have included and how you can avoid voiding it.

As in previous chapters, this chapter uses "iPod" as a generic term to refer to regular (full-size) iPods, the iPod nano, the iPod mini, and the iPod shuffle. Where the discussion is specific to a particular model, this chapter tells you.

This chapter focuses on the fifth-generation regular iPod, the iPod nano, and the iPod shuffle, but it also provides essential information about the iPod mini and the fourth-generation regular iPod, because there are plenty of those left in the wild—and you may be having trouble with them.

What's in Your iPod

A regular iPod or iPod mini is based around a hard drive that takes up the bulk of the space inside the case. The hard drive in a regular iPod is similar to those used in the smaller portable PCs; the hard drive in an iPod mini is even smaller, and it's similar to those used in consumer electronics, such as the more ambitious mobile phones.

> NOTE   *The iPod nano and iPod shuffle use flash memory chips rather than a hard disk, which makes them more or less immune to shock. Besides the flash memory, the iPod nano and iPod shuffle contain a battery, a controller chip, and audio-processing circuits.*

Some of the remaining space is occupied by a rechargeable battery that provides between 8 and 20 hours of playback. The length of time the battery provides depends on the model of iPod and on how you use it. Like all rechargeable batteries, the iPod's battery gradually loses its capacity—but if your music collection grows, or if you find the iPod's nonmusic capabilities useful, you'll probably want to upgrade to a higher-capacity model in a couple of years anyway.

> CAUTION   *Your iPod isn't user-upgradeable—in fact, it's designed to be opened only by trained technicians. If you're not such a technician, don't try to open your iPod if your iPod is still under warranty, because opening it voids the warranty. Open your iPod only if it's out of warranty and there's a problem you can fix, such as replacing the battery. See the Special Project insert in this book for advice on installing a replacement battery in the first four generations of regular iPod models and the iPod mini.*

Hard disk–based iPods include a 32MB memory chip that's used for running the iPod's operating system and for caching music from the hard drive. The cache reads up to 20 minutes of data ahead from the hard drive for two purposes:

- Once the cache has read the data, your iPod plays back the music from the cache rather than from the hard disk. This lets the hard disk *spin down* (stop running) until it's needed again. Because hard disks consume relatively large amounts of power, the caching spares the battery on your iPod and prolongs battery life.

> NOTE   *After the hard disk has spun down, it takes a second or so to spin up again—so when you suddenly change the music during a playlist, there's a small delay while your iPod spins the disk up and then accesses the song you've demanded. If you listen closely (put your ear to your iPod), you can hear the disk spin up (there's a "whee" sound) and search (you'll hear the heads clicking).*

- The hard disk can skip if you joggle or shake your iPod hard enough. Modern hard drives can handle G loads that would finish elite fighter pilots, so take this on trust rather than trying it out. If your iPod were playing back audio directly from the hard disk, such skipping would interrupt audio playback, much like bumping the needle on a turntable (or bumping a CD player, if you've tried that). But because the memory chip is solid state and has no moving parts, it's immune to skipping.

17

The length of time for which the caching provides audio depends on the compression ratio you're using and whether you're playing a playlist (or album) or individual songs. If you're playing a list of songs, your iPod can cache as many of the upcoming songs as it has available memory. But when you switch to another song beyond those cached, or to another playlist, your iPod has to start caching once again. This caching involves spinning the hard disk up again and reading from it, which consumes battery power.

The fifth-generation iPod caches video as well, but because video files are much larger than audio files, playing them makes the hard disk work more than does playing songs.

Understand What Makes Your iPod Unhappy

This section discusses four items that are likely to make your iPod unhappy: unexpected disconnections, fire and water (discussed together), and punishment. None of these should come as a surprise, and you should be able to avoid all of them most of the time.

Disconnecting Your iPod at the Wrong Time

If you've ever performed a successful synchronization with your iPod, you'll know the drill for disconnecting your iPod from your computer: Wait until your iPod has stopped displaying the "Do not disconnect" message and is showing the "OK to disconnect" message. Then—and not before—you can safely unplug the cable. (For an iPod shuffle, wait until the green light or amber light stays on steadily before unplugging.)

The main danger in disconnecting your iPod at the wrong time is that you may interrupt data transfer and thus corrupt one or more files. Typically, you'll know when data is being transferred, because iTunes displays status information and progress messages as it updates your iPod and transfers data to it. Similarly, if you're using your iPod in disk mode, you'll know when you're copying or moving data to it, because you'll have put the copy or move operation in process.

In theory, you could scramble the data on your iPod's hard drive badly enough that you'd need to restore your iPod before you could use it. A restoration would lose any data on the iPod that you didn't have on your computer—so a badly timed disconnection could cost you valuable data.

In practice, however, disconnecting your iPod during data transfer is likely to corrupt only those files actually being transferred at the moment you break the connection. If those files are valuable, and if you're moving them to your iPod rather than copying them, corrupting them could cause you problems. But in most cases, you won't need to restore your iPod.

Disconnecting the cable without warning when no data is being transferred should do nothing worse than annoy your computer. If you disconnect your iPod from your Mac at the wrong time, your Mac displays the Device Removal dialog box shown in Figure 17-1, telling you that you should have ejected it properly and that data may have been lost or damaged. If iTunes was transferring data to your iPod when you disconnected it, you may also see another dialog box such as the one that appears at the top of Figure 17-1.

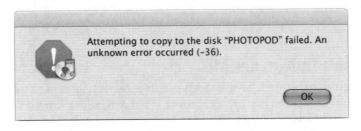

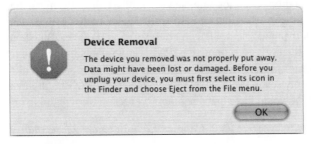

FIGURE 17-1 Mac OS X objects when you disconnect your iPod at the wrong time.

At this writing, iTunes for Windows tends not to notice if you disconnect an iPod when it's telling you not to. If you find your iPod's entry is showing up in the Source pane in iTunes for Windows long after the iPod has bolted, shut the stable door by right-clicking the iPod's entry in the Source pane and choosing Eject iPod from the shortcut menu.

After an unexpected disconnection, your iPod simply figures out there's a problem, dusts itself down, and displays its main screen.

Your iPod Doesn't Like Fire or Water

Apple reckons regular iPods work at temperatures of up to 158 degrees Fahrenheit (70 degrees Celsius). You're unlikely to endure temperatures this high voluntarily outside a hardcore session in a sauna or steam room, so scratch any plans you may have had for using your iPod in such locations. The danger is more that you'll leave your iPod running in a confined space, such as the glove box of a car parked in the sun, which might reach searing temperatures. If you live somewhere sunny, take your iPod with you when you get out of the car.

If your iPod gets much too hot or much too cold, don't use it. Give it time to return to a more normal temperature before trying to find out if it still works.

17

Further, your iPod isn't waterproof, so don't expect to use it for swimming or in the bath. You can get various water-resistant cases for iPods (see Chapter 4), but most are intended to keep out rain and splashes rather than to go deep-sea diving.

The iPod nano is more sensitive to extremes of temperature than the regular iPod. Apple gives 32–95 degrees Fahrenheit as acceptable operating temperatures for the iPod nano, and from –4 up to 113 degrees Fahrenheit as safe storage temperatures.

Your iPod Isn't Indestructible

Apple has built the iPod to be tough, so it'll survive an impressive amount of rough handling. *Macworld* columnist Chris Breen has written about how he eventually destroyed a regular iPod by dropping it from a bicycle traveling at 30 mph. (This was after the iPod survived a 25-mph drop from the bicycle, a drop while jogging, and a stationary drop from waist height—each of which caused some damage to the iPod and probably weakened it.)

More through luck than judgment, I haven't destroyed an iPod yet. But should the need arise, various means suggest themselves: running the iPod over with a Hummer, hitting it squarely with an eight-pound sledgehammer, or playing Sinatra uninterrupted for a couple of days should do the trick. In the meantime, my seven iPods have traveled the equivalent of halfway around the world and taken a few falls that would have damaged me, so I reckon they're doing pretty well.

Use a case to protect your iPod. Chapter 4 outlines some of the many options available.

Keep Your iPod's Operating System Up to Date

To get the best performance from your iPod, it's a good idea to keep its operating system (or *firmware*) up to date. To do so, follow the instructions in this section to update your iPod on Windows or Mac OS X.

In 2005, Apple started to issue iPod Updaters that included updates for all available iPods. Before that, different types and generations of iPods required different updaters, so you had to be careful to download and install the appropriate updater. With the combined iPod Updaters, you no longer need to worry because each Updater detects the iPod type and installs the appropriate updates. The only disadvantage is that the combined iPod Updaters are much larger than the individual updaters used to be, so they take longer to download.

Update Your iPod on Windows

Apple hasn't yet managed to insinuate iPod software updates into Microsoft's Windows Update process, but iTunes does check for updates, and it displays a message box such as that shown here if it finds an update. Click the Run Updater button to run the updater.

NOTE *At this writing, the iPod Updater for Windows doesn't work when two or more iPods are attached to your PC. Even if you unplug all iPods except one, the Updater tends to think multiple iPods are still connected. You may need to restart Windows to force the Updater to read the available iPods properly again.*

Alternatively, you may prefer to check for and download updates manually from the Apple Software Downloads website (www.apple.com/swupdates/). Double-click the distribution file to launch the setup routine and then follow through the installation process. Then choose Start | All Programs | iPod | iPod Updater | iPod Updater to run the iPod Updater.

Whichever way you run the iPod Updater, it looks like Figure 17-2. Click the Update button to update your iPod's software. Depending on the iPod model and how it's connected to your PC, you may need to disconnect it and reconnect it during the update. Some earlier iPod models also require plugging into the iPod Power Adapter, which administers an electric kiss to reawaken your sleeping beauty.

When the update is complete, and when you've reconnected your iPod (if you had to disconnect it), the iPod launches or activates iTunes.

NOTE *Typically, a "Can't lock iPod" message indicates that another application is trying to access the iPod while the iPod Software Updater is attempting to update it. Make sure that iTunes and any other iPod-management applications you're using are closed. Also, close any Windows Explorer windows that are displaying My Computer (because these will show the iPod as a removable drive) and any Windows Explorer windows that are open to the drive letter representing the iPod.*

Update Your iPod on Mac OS X

The easiest way to update your iPod on Mac OS X is to use the Software Update feature: Choose Apple | Software Update to check for updates. Mac OS X checks for iPod updates along with all other updates and presents them to you in the Software Update dialog box.

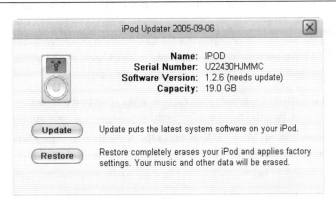

iPod Updater 2005-09-06

Name: IPOD
Serial Number: U22430HJMMC
Software Version: 1.2.6 (needs update)
Capacity: 19.0 GB

Update   Update puts the latest system software on your iPod.

Restore   Restore completely erases your iPod and applies factory settings. Your music and other data will be erased.

17

FIGURE 17-2   The iPod Updater on Windows.

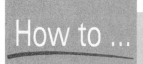 **Restore Your iPod to an Earlier Version of the iPod Software on Windows**

If you install an update that produces an effect you don't like, you can run an earlier updater again to restore your Windows iPod to the previous version of the iPod Software—provided that you have a copy of the earlier updater. You can run the older updaters from the Start | All Programs | iPod | Previous Updaters submenu.

Click the Install button (it's called Install 1 Item, Install 2 Items, and so on, depending on how many updates you're installing) to proceed. You'll need to authenticate yourself by entering an administrative password in the Authenticate dialog box to show the installer that you have authority to install the software. Mac OS X then downloads the update and installs it to your Utilities folder.

If you choose not to use Software Update, you can download the updater from the Apple Software Downloads website (www.apple.com/swupdates/). Double-click the disk-image file to mount the disk image, double-click the disk image to display its contents in a Finder window, double-click the iPod Software Updater folder to display its contents in the Finder window, and then double-click the iPod.pkg file to open it. Follow through the resulting installation routine.

After downloading and installing the update, you need to apply it to your iPod. iTunes may prompt you to apply the update automatically, but usually you'll have to apply it manually. To do so, follow these steps:

1. Connect your iPod to your Mac as usual.
2. With the Finder active, press ⌘-SHIFT-U or choose Go | Utilities to open a Finder window to your Utilities folder.
3. Double-click the folder that contains the Updater that you downloaded. (The folder will be named iPod Updater followed by the date—for example, iPod Updater 2005-10-12.)
4. Double-click the iPod Updater icon to launch the iPod Software.
5. When the iPod Software Updater notices your iPod, it displays its details, as shown in Figure 17-3. Check that the Software Version readout says "needs update."
6. Click the Update button. Mac OS X displays the Authenticate dialog box to check that you have administrative rights.
7. Type your password in the Password text box and then click the OK button.
8. Click the Update button and wait for the update to take place.

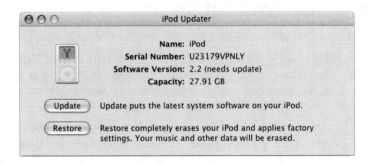

FIGURE 17-3 Use the latest iPod Updater available to update the software on your iPod.

Depending on the type of iPod you're updating and the type of connection you're using, you may have to unplug the iPod from your Mac and then plug it back in. You may also need to plug a USB-connected iPod into its power adapter for part of the update process. One other point: The iPod Updater switches to telling you to "plug in an iPod to update it" while the iPod itself performs the update. Wait for a minute or two, and then your iPod should reestablish communication with the iPod Updater.

9. When the iPod Software Updater displays the details about your iPod again, check that the Software Version readout says "up to date," as shown here:

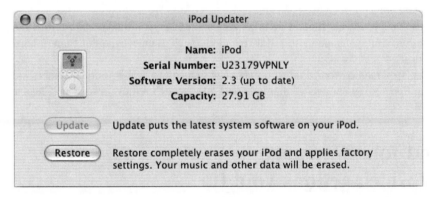

10. Press ⌘-Q or choose iPod Updater | Quit iPod Updater to quit the iPod Updater.

11. If iTunes isn't running, it should launch itself automatically and recognize your iPod.

17

Carry and Store Your iPod Safely

Carrying and storing your iPod safely is largely a matter of common sense:

■ Use a case to protect your iPod from scratches, dings, and falls. A wide variety of cases are available, from svelte-and-stretchy little numbers designed to hug your body during vigorous exercise, to armored cases apparently intended to survive Schwarzenegger movies, to waterproof cases good enough to take sailing. See Chapter 4 for details.

■ If your iPod spends time on your desk or another surface open to children, animals, or moving objects, use a dock or stand to keep it in place. A dock or stand should also make your iPod easier to control with one hand. For example, if you patch your iPod into your stereo, you might use a dock or stand to keep it upright so you can push its buttons with one hand. Some stands can also supply power to your iPod. See Chapter 4 for more information on stands.

Clean Your iPod

To keep a your iPod looking its best, you'll probably need to clean it from time to time. Before doing so, unplug it to reduce the chance of short disagreements with the basic principles of electricity. If it's a second-generation iPod, close the cover of the FireWire port to help avoid getting liquid in the port. If the iPod has a Dock Connector, treat it with due care.

Various people recommend different cleaning products for cleaning iPods. You'll find various recommendations on the Web—but unless you're sure the people know what they're talking about, proceed with great care. In particular, avoid any abrasive cleaner that may mar a regular iPod's acrylic faceplate or its polished back and sides.

Unless you've dipped your iPod in anything very unpleasant, you'll do best to start with Apple's recommendation: simply dampen a soft, lint-free cloth (such as an eyeglass or camera-lens cloth) and wipe your iPod gently with it.

But if you've scratched your iPod, you may need to resort to heavier duty cleaners. Sites such as everythingiPod.com (www.everythingipod.com) offer scratch removers such as iCleaner and iCleaner Pro.

Understand Your Warranty and Know Which Actions Void It

Like most electronics goods, your iPod almost certainly came with a warranty. Unlike with most other electronics goods, your chances of needing to use that warranty are relatively high. This is because you're likely to use your iPod extensively and carry it with you.

Even if you don't sit on your iPod, rain or other water doesn't creep into it, and gravity doesn't dash it sharply against something unforgiving (such as the sidewalk), your iPod may suffer from other problems—anything from critters or debris jamming the Dock Connector port, to its hard drive getting corrupted or its operating system getting scrambled. Perhaps most likely of all is that your iPod's battery will lose its potency, either gradually or dramatically. If any of these misfortunes befalls your iPod, you'll probably want to get it repaired under warranty—provided you haven't voided the warranty.

The first iPods carried a 90-day warranty, which inspired little confidence in their durability. However, Apple then moved to a one-year warranty both for newer iPods and for those already sold. The iPod Service Page (http://depot.info.apple.com/ipod/index.html) contains details of which iPods are still under warranty and the prices you'll pay for repairs if your iPod is out of warranty.

Most of the warranty is pretty straightforward, but the following points are worth noting:

■ You have to make your claim within the warranty period, so if your iPod fails a day short of a year after you bought it, you'll need to make your claim instantly.

■ If your iPod is currently under warranty, you can buy an AppleCare package for it to extend its warranty to two years. Most extended warranties on electrical products are a waste of money, because the extended warranties largely duplicate your existing rights as a consumer to be sold a product that's functional and of merchantable quality. But given the attrition rate among hard-used iPods, AppleCare may be a good idea. Similarly, CompUSA offers a Technology Assurance Program (TAP) for HP iPods that provides two years of service and a one-time replacement of your iPod if you break it.

■ Apple can choose whether to repair your iPod using either new or refurbished parts, exchange it for another iPod that's at least functionally equivalent but may be either new or rebuilt (and may contain used parts), or refund you the purchase price of your iPod. Unless you have valuable data on your iPod, the refund is a great option, because you'll be able to get a new iPod—perhaps even a higher-capacity one.

■ Apple takes no responsibility for getting back any data on your iPod. This isn't surprising because Apple may need to reformat your iPod's hard drive or replace it. But this means that you must back up your iPod if it contains data you value that you don't have copies of elsewhere.

You can void your warranty more or less effortlessly in any of the following easily avoidable ways:

■ Damage your iPod deliberately.

■ Open your iPod or have someone other than Apple open it for you. As discussed in "What's in Your iPod," earlier in this chapter, your iPod isn't designed to be opened by anyone except trained technicians. The only reason to open your iPod is to replace its battery—and you shouldn't do that yourself unless the iPod is out of warranty (and out of AppleCare, if you bought AppleCare for the iPod).

■ Modify your iPod. Modifications such as installing a larger drive in the iPod would necessarily involve opening your iPod anyway, but external modifications can void your warranty, too. For example, if you choose to trepan your iPod so as to screw a holder directly onto it, you would void your warranty. (You'd also stand a great chance of drilling into something sensitive inside the case.)

17

Approach Troubleshooting Your iPod

When something goes wrong with your iPod, take three deep breaths before you do anything. Then take another three deep breaths if you need them. Then try to work out what's wrong.

Remember that a calm and rational approach will always get you further than blind panic. This is easy to say (and if you're reading this when your iPod is running smoothly, easy to nod your head at). But if you've just dropped your iPod onto a hard surface from a significant height, left it on the roof of your car so it fell off and landed in the perfect position for you to reverse over it, or gotten caught in an unexpectedly heavy rainfall, you'll probably be desperate to find out if your iPod is alive or dead.

So take those three deep breaths. You may well *not* have ruined your iPod forever—but if you take some heavy-duty troubleshooting actions without making sure they're necessary, you might lose some data that wasn't already lost or do some damage you'll have trouble repairing.

Things can go wrong with any of the following:

- The iPod's hardware—anything from the Dock Connector port or the FireWire port (which is surprisingly vulnerable) to the battery, the hard disk, or the flash memory
- The iPod's software
- The iPod's power adapter (if it has one)
- The cable you're using to connect your iPod to your computer
- Your computer's USB port or USB controller, or its FireWire port or FireWire controller
- iTunes or the other software you're using to control your iPod

Given all these possibilities, be prepared to spend some time troubleshooting any problem.

Learn Troubleshooting Maneuvers

This section discusses several maneuvers you may need to use to troubleshoot your iPod: resetting your iPod, draining its battery, restoring its operating system on either Mac OS X or Windows, running a disk scan, and using its built-in diagnostic tools to pinpoint problems.

Reset Your iPod

If your iPod freezes so it doesn't respond to the controls, you can reset it:

1. Connect it to a power source—either a computer that's not sleeping or the iPod Power Adapter plugged into an electrical socket.

2. Reset the iPod by moving the Hold switch to the On position and then back to the Off position. Hold down the Menu button and the Select button for about six seconds, until the iPod displays the Apple logo.

3. After you release the buttons, give your iPod a few seconds to finish booting.

If your iPod freezes when you don't have a power source available, try resetting it by using the preceding technique without the power source. Sometimes it works; other times it doesn't. But you've nothing to lose by trying.

To reset an iPod shuffle, move the switch on the back to the Off position and then move it to one of the other two positions.

Drain Your iPod's Battery

If you can't reset your iPod, its battery might have gotten into such a low state that it needs draining. (This supposedly seldom happens—but the planets might have decided that you're due a bad day.) To drain the battery, disconnect your iPod from its power source and leave it for 24 hours. Then try plugging your iPod into a power source. After your iPod has received power for a few seconds, reset the iPod by moving the Hold switch to the On position and then back to the Off position. Hold down the Menu button and the Select button for about six seconds, until the iPod displays the Apple logo.

If draining the battery and recharging it revives your iPod, update your iPod's software with the latest update from Apple Software Updates to try to prevent the problem from occurring again. See the section "Keep Your iPod's Operating System Up to Date," earlier in this chapter, for details on how to update your iPod's operating system.

Restore Your iPod

If your iPod is having severe difficulties, you may need to restore it. Restoring your iPod replaces its operating system with a new copy of the operating system that has Apple's factory settings.

Restoring your iPod deletes all the data on your iPod's hard disk—the operating system, all your songs, photos, videos, contacts, calendar information, and notes—and returns your iPod to its original factory settings. So restoring your iPod is usually a last resort when troubleshooting. Unless your iPod is so messed up that you cannot access its contents, back up all the data you care about that's stored on your iPod before restoring it.

To restore your iPod, you need the iPod Updater. You should have installed a version of it with your iPod, but for best results, download the latest version of the iPod Updater:

- On Windows, go to www.apple.com/swupdates/ and follow the iPod link to find iPod-related updates. If there's a new version of the iPod Updater, download it and then double-click the resulting file to install it.
- On Mac OS X, choose Apple | Software Update to check for the latest version.

When restoring an iPod mini connected to a Windows PC via USB, you may find the iPod mini displaying the "Do not disconnect" screen at the same time that the iPod Updater is telling you to disconnect the iPod mini and plug it into the iPod Power Adapter to complete the restoration. If this happens, disconnect the USB connection and plug the iPod mini into the iPod Power Adapter.

17

Restore Your iPod on Windows XP

To restore your iPod on Windows XP, follow these steps:

1. Connect your iPod to your PC via USB or FireWire as usual. Allow iTunes to synchronize with your iPod if it's set to do so.

2. Choose Start | All Programs | iPod | iPod Updater | iPod Updater to display the iPod Updater window:

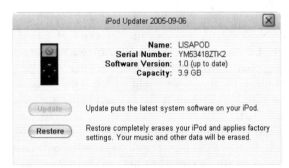

3. Click the Restore button. The iPod Updater warns you that you will lose all the data currently stored on the iPod:

4. Click the Restore button. The iPod Updater formats your iPod's hard disk or flash storage.

5. Depending on the type and generation of iPod you're restoring and how it's connected to your PC, you then need to do the following:

   ■ Simply wait until the restore process is complete.

   ■ Unplug the iPod from your PC for a moment and then plug it back in to the PC.

   ■ Unplug the iPod from your PC and connect it to the iPod Power Adapter to finish the reflashing process. When your iPod displays its normal screen again, connect it to your PC once more.

6. Click the Close button (the X button) in the upper-right corner of the iPod Updater window to close the iPod Updater.

7. iTunes should now launch (or be activated) automatically. (If not, launch iTunes manually from the Start menu or from a shortcut.) When iTunes notices your iPod, it starts the iPod Setup Assistant, which walks you through the process of naming your iPod and choosing how to load it.

After you disconnect your iPod, set the language it uses.

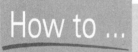

If the iPod Updater hangs after you plug your iPod back in, follow the steps described in "Recover from a Stalled Restore Process on the PC," in Chapter 13, to recover.

How to ... Recover from a "Can't Mount iPod" Error on Windows

If the Restore operation fails, you may find your iPod unable to boot past the Sad iPod icon or the Folders icon (both discussed later in this chapter) and iTunes and the iPod Service unable to recognize it. When you plug your iPod into your PC, you'll see the Can't Mount iPod error (shown here).

This means you're stuck, but don't despair yet. Try the following:

1. Run the iPod Updater and then try the Restore operation again. If you can get the iPod Updater to recognize your iPod, the Restore operation may work.

2. If the iPod Updater can't recognize your iPod, restart Windows and try again.

3. If that doesn't work, try connecting your iPod to a different PC—for example, to a friend's PC. Install the iPod software on the PC if it's not already installed, and then perform the Restore operation from that PC. Don't use a Mac to perform the restoration: even though the restoration is likely to work, you'll end up with a Mac-formatted iPod that will need reformatting to work with your PC.

17

Restore Your iPod on Mac OS X

To restore your iPod on Mac OS X, follow these steps:

1. Connect your iPod to your computer as usual. If your iPod is set to synchronize automatically with iTunes, allow it to do so.

2. Activate the Finder (for example, click the Desktop) and then press ⌘-SHIFT-U or choose Go | Utilities from the Finder menu to display the contents of your Applications/Utilities folder.

3. Open the iPod Software Updater folder and then double-click the latest iPod Updater to run it. Early versions of the iPod Updater used version numbers, but the more recent versions are identified by date, so it's easy to tell which is the most recent. The iPod Updater recognizes your iPod and lists its details:

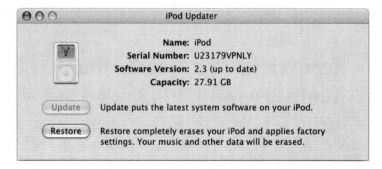

4. Click the Restore button to start the restore process. The iPod Updater warns you that all the data on the iPod will be lost:

5. Click the Restore button if you're absolutely sure you want to proceed. Mac OS X displays the Authenticate dialog box to check that you have administrative rights.

6. Type your password in the Password text box and then click the OK button. The iPod Updater restores your iPod's operating system and deletes the files on it.

7. Depending on the type and generation of iPod you're restoring and how it's connected to your Mac, you then need to do the following:

   ■ Simply wait until the restore process is complete.

   ■ Unplug the iPod from your Mac for a moment and then plug it back in to the Mac.

   ■ Unplug the iPod from your Mac and connect it to the iPod Power Adapter to finish the reflashing process. When your iPod displays its normal screen again, connect it to your Mac once more.

8. Press ⌘-Q or choose iPod Updater | Quit iPod Updater to close the iPod Updater window.

9. Your iPod should then appear on your desktop under the default name "iPod." If it doesn't, you may need to reset it, as described in "Reset Your iPod," earlier in this chapter.

10. When iTunes notices your iPod, it starts the iPod Setup Assistant, which walks you through the process of naming your iPod and choosing how to load it. (If iTunes doesn't notice your iPod, launch iTunes manually.)

After you next disconnect your iPod, you'll need to specify the language for it to use.

How to ... **Recover from a Disk Insertion Error on the Mac**

If something goes wrong while you're restoring your iPod, Mac OS X may display a Disk Insertion error message box such as the one shown here.

The large red exclamation icon makes the problem seem severe, but click the Ignore button rather than the Initialize button. (Clicking the Initialize button launches Disk Utility, the tool used for partitioning, repairing, and initializing regular hard disks, as opposed to the iPod.) Then run the iPod Updater and try the Restore operation again. Usually, you'll be able to make it work after an attempt or two.

Use Your iPod's Diagnostics to Pinpoint Problems

To access your iPod's various diagnostic tools, enter diagnostic mode:

1. Toggle the Hold switch on and off.

 These instructions work for Click-wheel iPods: the fourth- and fifth-generation regular iPods, the iPod nano, and the iPod mini.

2. Hold down the Select button and the Menu button for about six seconds, until the Apple logo appears.

3. Hold down the Previous and Select buttons for a few seconds until the iPod displays a reversed Apple logo.

NOTE *The iPod nano sometimes fails to register your pressing the Previous and Select buttons. If this happens, restart the iPod and try again—and again if necessary.*

4. In a fifth-generation iPod, you'll see the FA Diag Boot screen. Press the Menu button to access the main iPod Diagnostics screen (see Figure 17-4).

CAUTION *Sometimes Apple changes the diagnostic tests in iPod firmware updates, so your iPod may show you different diagnostics than those listed here.*

To use the diagnostic tests, use the following keys:

- Press the Next and Previous buttons to navigate through the list of tests. On a fifth-generation iPod, you can also scroll up and down.
- Press the Select button to run the highlighted test.
- Press the Menu button (on a fourth- or fifth-generation iPod) or the Play button (on other iPods) to return from the results of a test to the diagnostic screen.
- To leave the diagnostic screen, either run the Reset test or reset your iPod again by holding down the Menu button and the Play/Pause button for a few seconds.

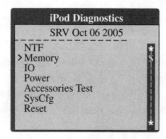

FIGURE 17-4   The initial diagnostic screen for a fifth-generation iPod.

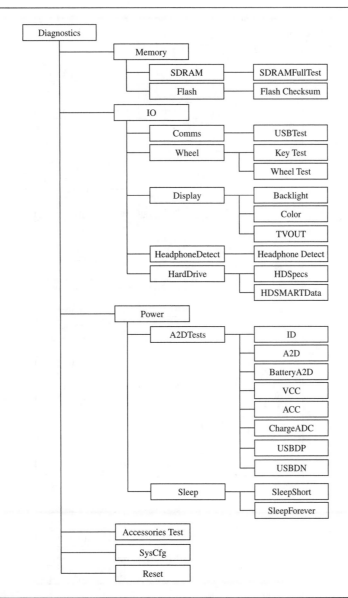

FIGURE 17-5   The hierarchy of diagnostic tests on the fifth-generation iPod.

17

Because they have more extensive features, the fourth- and fifth-generation iPods include more diagnostic tests than earlier iPods. To make the tests more accessible, these iPods arrange the tests in a hierarchy of submenus. Figure 17-5 shows the hierarchy of menus for a fifth-generation iPod. Figure 17-6 shows the hierarchy of menus for a fourth-generation iPod. As you can see, there's a lot of overlap, but there are also some differences.

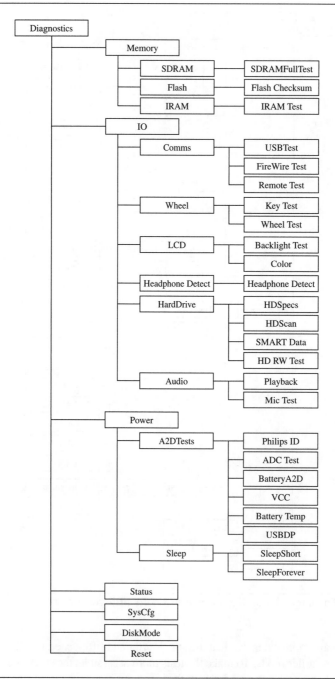

FIGURE 17-6   The hierarchy of diagnostic tests on the fourth-generation iPod.

The following sections discuss the diagnostic tests you'll most likely want to perform.

Run a Disk Scan on a Fourth-Generation iPod

If you think there might be something wrong with your fourth-generation iPod's hard disk, you can run a disk scan to find out. A scan takes anything from 15 minutes to an hour or more, depending on the capacity of your iPod's hard disk, so set aside plenty of time to run the scan.

NOTE *At this writing, you can't run a disk scan for a fifth-generation iPod or an iPod mini using this technique. And because an iPod nano contains flash memory rather than a hard disk, the iPod nano's diagnostics offer a flash scan rather than a disk scan.*

To run a disk scan, follow these steps:

1. Enter diagnostic mode as described previously.
2. At the iPod Diagnostics screen, press the Next button once to scroll down to the IO category. (IO is input and output, not the Hawaiian hawk.) Press the Select button to display the IO menu.
3. Press the Next button several times to select the HardDrive item and then press the Select button to display the HardDrive menu.
4. Press the Next button once to move down to select the HDScan item and then press the Select button.
5. Allow the scan to complete.
6. At the end of the scan, you'll see a message indicating whether the drive passed or failed the scan:

   ```
   After Scan:
   Smart Scan PASS
   Test OK
           MENU to exit
   ```

7. Press the Menu button to return to the HardDrive menu.

NOTE *If your iPod runs a disk scan automatically when you start it, that means your iPod suspects there's a problem with the hard drive. It's best to allow the scan to continue, but in extreme circumstances, you may need to cancel the scan. To cancel it, hold down the Select button for a few seconds. Your iPod then displays a disk icon with a cross mark on it, which means it'll repeat the disk scan the next time you turn it on.*

Run a Flash Scan on an iPod nano

Follow these steps to run a flash scan on an iPod nano:

1. Reset your iPod:
   - First, move the Hold switch to the On position and then move it back to the Off position.
   - Second, hold down the Menu button and the Select button for about six seconds, until the iPod displays the Apple logo.

17

2. When the logo appears, hold down the Select button and the Previous button together for a second or two, until the screen blinks. Release the buttons, and the iPod Diagnostics screen appears.

3. Press the Next button twice to select the FlashScan item, and then press the Select button to access the test. Wait until the test completes, and then read the resulting screen.

Check That a Fourth-Generation iPod or an iPod mini Is Making a FireWire Connection

To check that a fourth-generation iPod or an iPod mini is connecting successfully via FireWire, run the FIREWIRE test. The iPod mini gives a readout such as the following for a successful FireWire connection:

```
FW TEST
CONNECT
SPD S400
CHIP OK
FW PASS
```

If the test diagnoses no connection, the iPod mini displays NOCONECT.

The fourth-generation iPod gives a readout such as the following for a successful FireWire connection:

```
Connection
Rate=s400 OK
FW Chip OK
FireWire OK
```

If the test diagnoses no FireWire connection, the fourth-generation iPod displays No Connection.

Check the USB Connection on a Fourth- or Fifth-Generation iPod or an iPod nano

To check a USB connection on a fourth- or fifth-generation iPod, run the USBTest. If the test returns an ID number, such as ID=0x22FA05, the connection is working. If the test detects no connection, it displays No Cable Connection.

To check the USB connection on an iPod nano, run the Status test and check the USBPWR_Det readout. The value 1 indicates that power is detected; the value 0 indicates no power is detected.

Check the Audio Subsystem on a Fourth-Generation iPod, an iPod nano, or an iPod mini

To check the audio subsystem on a fourth-generation iPod, run the Playback test on the Audio menu. The sound played is a moment of static. The iPod then displays END OF TEST.

On an iPod nano, run the Playback test. The sound is a burst of high-pitched bleeps that continue until you press the Menu button to end the test.

The AUDIO test on the iPod mini is a little different. When you enter the test, your iPod mini displays AD GAIN and a number (for example, 120). You can press the Previous button to decrease the gain or the Next button to increase it. Press the Select button to play the audio test and check that you hear fast-paced electronic beats. The iPod mini then displays END TEST.

Check the RAM

To check the RAM on a fourth- or fifth generation iPod, run the SDRAMFullTest test. If you see the message SDRAM OK, all is well.

On an iPod nano, run the FiveInOne test and look at the SDRAM line. If all is well, your iPod nano displays SDRAM OK.

On an iPod mini, run the ALLSDRAM test. You'll get a PASS message or a FAIL message when the test is complete.

Check the iPod's Buttons

If one of the buttons on your iPod seems to stop working, you'll probably be able to tell without diagnostics. But before you call for backup, you may want to check that your iPod agrees with you that there's a problem. To do so, run the Key Test on the Wheel menu of a fourth- or fifth-generation iPod, the KeyTest on an iPod nano, or the Key test on an iPod mini, and then press the iPod's buttons when prompted:

- If the fourth-generation iPod doesn't register you pressing one of the listed buttons within a few seconds, it displays "Timeout Error," and you can press the Menu button to exit the test (assuming the Menu button is working).

- If the fifth-generation iPod doesn't register you pressing one of the listed buttons, it continues to wait until you reset it by holding down the Select button and the Menu button for a few seconds. (If one or both of these buttons aren't working, you're in trouble here.)

- If the iPod mini doesn't register your pressing one of the buttons within a few seconds, it displays the message "Key Fail." Press the Play button to exit the test.

Check the Remote Control on a Fourth-Generation iPod or an iPod mini

To check the remote control on the iPod mini, run the REMOTE test and press the buttons on the remote. The iPod mini screen displays text for the buttons: + and − for Volume Up and Volume Down, Next and Pre for the Next and Previous buttons, and Play for the Play button. The iPod mini describes the test as UARTTEST and rewards it with UARTPASS or UARTFAIL. (UART is the acronym for *universal asynchronous receiver/transmitter.*)

On a fourth-generation iPod, run the Remote Test on the Comms menu. Press each button on the remote except for the Hold button. If you fail to press a button, or if it fails to register, you'll see an ERROR readout next to the button's listing.

Check the Click Wheel

To test the Click wheel on a fifth-generation iPod, run the WheelTest diagnostic on the Wheel menu. The iPod verifies the wheel's ID, displays WHEEL ID PASS if it's okay, and prompts you

17

to press the Menu button to "exit." When you press the Menu button, the screen displays a list of blocks that represent the touch sensing on the wheel. Scroll around the wheel until the iPod removes each of the block numbers and displays the WHEEL PASS message.

On a fourth-generation iPod, run the WheelTest on the Wheel menu. The iPod first displays the Wheel ID and then prompts you to scroll around the wheel. You'll see WHEEL PASS if all is well, and WHEEL FAIL if something's wrong.

To test the Click wheel on an iPod mini, run the WHEEL test. The iPod mini screen displays WHELTEST and a value that changes as you move your finger around the Click wheel. Reset your iPod to escape from this test.

To test the Click wheel on an iPod nano, run the WheelTest diagnostic. The iPod prompts you to spin the wheel and displays the value of the current reading of your finger position as you spin it. If you want to see the register of Touchwheel values, run the TouchwheelID diagnostic.

Check That Sleep Mode Is Working

To check that Sleep mode is working on your iPod, run the SLEEP test. If the test works, you'll need to reset your iPod to get it working again. If your iPod doesn't go to sleep, the test has failed.

On a fourth- or fifth-generation iPod, run the SleepShort test on the Sleep menu to give the iPod a momentary nap. The iPod then returns to the diagnostics menu. To put the iPod into a full coma, run the SleepForever test on the Sleep menu. You'll then need to wake the iPod up manually.

On an iPod nano, run the SleepShort test. The iPod nano goes to sleep. Press a button to reawaken your sleeping beauty.

The earliest firmware of the iPod mini included a Sleep test, but the November 2004 firmware patch replaced it with another diagnostic test.

Change the Default Contrast on an iPod mini

To change the default contrast on an iPod mini, run the CONTRAST diagnostic but use the Play button to move from screen to screen, and the Previous and Next buttons to increase or decrease the contrast on each screen. Press the Menu button to toggle the backlight. At the end, you reach a screen that invites you to press Action (in other words, the Select button) to quit or Play to continue.

Check How Your iPod Is Receiving Power

To check whether your fifth-generation iPod is receiving power across a USB cable or FireWire cable connected to an iPod Power Adapter, run the Accessories test. On the Accesorize (*sic*) Test screen, connect the FireWire adapter when prompted. If the iPod detects power, it changes the FWPWR: 0 readout to FWPWR:1 and prompts you to plug in the USB. After you plug in a USB cable connected to an iPod Power Adapter, the USBPWR:0 readout changes to USBPWR:1, the screen displays PASS, and the test ends.

 *If you don't have a FireWire cable connected to a FireWire iPod Power Adapter and a USB cable connected to a USB iPod Power adapter, you won't be able to complete the Accessories test. To escape from the test, hold down the Select button and the Menu button for several seconds to reset the iPod.*

To check whether your iPod nano is receiving a charge along a FireWire cable, run the Status test and look at the FW_PWR_GOOD line and the CHRG line. A value of 0 for each of these indicates that the iPod nano is receiving power along a FireWire cable; a value of 1 indicates that the iPod nano is not receiving power.

```
LCD       :   01
SrNm:TM35418ZTK3
MOD#:MA107
HP        :   0
FW_PWR_GOOD    :   0
USBPWB_Det   :  0
CHRG      :   0
```

To check how your fourth-generation iPod is being charged, run the Status test and look at the FWPWR and USBPWR lines. For example, the following entry indicates that the iPod is receiving power via USB:

```
LCD       : sharp
HP        : 1
FWPWR     : 0
USBPWR    : 1
```

To check how your iPod mini is being charged, run the STATUS test and look at the FWPW and USBPW lines. For example, the following entry indicates that the iPod mini is being charged along the FireWire cable:

```
STATUS
WINTKLCD
NO HP
FWPW OK
NO USBPW
NO CHGR
```

Check How Hot Your iPod or iPod mini Is Running

To check the temperature of your fourth- or fifth-generation iPod, run the HDSpecs test on the HardDrive menu and check the Temp: Current readout. The Min and Max readouts give the drive's minimum and maximum operating temperatures.

To check how hot your iPod mini is running, run the DRV TEMP test. You'll see a screen that gives the current temperature, together with minimum and maximum temperatures.

What about the Other Diagnostic Tests?

Table 17-1 briefly explains all the diagnostic tests for the fourth- and fifth-generation iPods, dividing them by menu and submenu so that you can easily access them.

17

Submenu	Test	Description
NTF Menu (Fifth-Generation iPod Only)		
AutoTest	AutoTest	Runs a battery of tests: Graphic Self Test, SDRAMQuickTest, Checksum, RTC, USBTest, KeyTest, WheelTest, HeadphoneDetect, Accessory Test, ChargeADC, Backlight, and Color. You can move to a particular item in the menu to start running that test and those that follow it.
Memory Menu		
SDRAM	SDRAMFullTest	Checks the SDRAM on the iPod. Returns SDRAM OK if all is well.
Flash	Flash Checksum	Checks the flash memory on the iPod. Checksum=0xF354 means the flash memory is okay.
IRAM	IRAM Test	Checks the IRAM (Intelligent Random Access Memory) on the iPod. You see "Waiting" for several minutes, and then the iPod restarts. Fourth-generation iPod only.
IO Menu		
Comms	USBTest	Tests whether the iPod is connected to a computer (not to the iPod Power Adapter) via USB.
Comms	FireWire Test	Tests whether the iPod is connected to a computer (not to the iPod Power Adapter) via FireWire. Fourth-generation iPod only.
Comms	Remote Test	When a remote control is connected, prompts you to press each button on the remote. Displays ERROR for any remote key that is not pressed or detected. Fourth-generation iPod only.
Wheel	Key Test	Prompts you to press each button on the Click wheel.
Wheel	Wheel Test	Returns the Wheel ID and then prompts you to scroll around the wheel.
LCD/Display	Backlight Test	Lets you check that different degrees of backlighting are working.
LCD/Display	Color	Displays a sequence of colors, gradients, and patterns to check that the LCD is working correctly. Press the Select button to move through the sequence.
Display	TVOUT	Lets you press the Select button to toggle between NTSC and PAL TV standards.
Headphone Detect	Headphone Detect	Displays a readout of whether a device is connected to the headphone socket (1) or not (0) and whether the iPod is on hold (1) or not (0).
HardDrive	HDSpecs	Displays information about the hard disk, including its size, model number, serial number, current temperature, and maximum and minimum temperatures.

TABLE 17-1 Diagnostic Tests for the Fourth- and Fifth-Generation iPods

Submenu	Test	Description
HardDrive	HDScan	Scans the hard drive for errors. Fourth-generation iPod only.
HardDrive	SMART Data/ HDSMARTData	Displays information on the Self-Monitoring, Analysis, and Reporting Technology (S.M.A.R.T.) in the drive.
HardDrive	HD RW Test	Tests that the hard drive can read and write data successfully. Displays HDD R/W PASS or HDD R/W FAIL. Fourth-generation iPod only.
Audio	Playback	Plays back a sample sound to check that audio output is working. Fourth-generation iPod only.
Audio	Mic Test	Records a sound through the connected microphone and allows you to play it back. Fourth-generation iPod only.
Power Menu		
A2DTests	Various Tests	These tests display information on the iPod's ID; the analog-to-digital converter; the battery, battery system, and battery temperature; and USB information. The selection of tests differs slightly between the generations of iPod.
Sleep	SleepShort	Puts the iPod to sleep for a few seconds and then wakes it back up to the diagnostic screen.
Sleep	SleepForever	Puts the iPod into deep sleep, like switching it off.
Status Menu (Fourth-Generation iPod Only)		
Status		Displays information on the LCD ("sharp"), headphone socket (HP: 1 indicates a device plugged in, HP: 0 indicates no device), and whether the iPod is receiving power via FireWire (FWPWR: 1 indicates power, FWPWR: 0 indicates no power) or via USB (USBPWR: 1 indicates power, USBPWR: 0 indicates no power).
SysCfg Menu		
SysCfg		Displays information on the iPod's serial number, manufacturer number, and hardware version.
DiskMode Menu (Fourth-Generation iPod Only)		
DiskMode		Forces the iPod into disk mode.
Accessories Test Menu (Fifth-Generation iPod Only)		
Accessories Test		Displays the LCD ID and prompts you to plug in a FireWire power source and then a USB power source.
Reset Menu		
Reset		Resets the iPod. You can use this command to quit diagnostic mode.

TABLE 17-1   Diagnostic Tests for the Fourth- and Fifth-Generation iPods

17

Table 17-2 briefly explains all the diagnostic tests for the iPod nano.

Table 17-3 explains the diagnostic tests briefly for the iPod mini that have not been discussed in detail earlier in this chapter.

Test	Explanation
FiveInOne	Runs five tests and displays the results on a single screen. RTC checks the real-time clock. SDRAM checks the iPod's random access memory. Chksum displays the checksum value (checking the integrity of the memory). ID displays the iPod's ID number. The final line displays the iPod's real capacity—for example, 3.81GB for a "4GB" iPod.
KeyTest	Lets you check the iPod's buttons by pressing them. This test doesn't check the Hold button.
FlashScan	Scans the iPod's flash memory. This test takes several minutes to complete.
PowerTest	Runs a series of power-related tests: Battery A2D, VCC Main, ACC A2D, and Charge Current Test.
WheelTest	Lets you check that the iPod's Click wheel is working by spinning it with your finger.
TouchWheelID	Displays register information about the Click wheel.
Playback	Plays a burst of audio beeps to let you check that the iPod is outputting audio through the headphone socket.
Linein	Checks the iPod's line-in capability (for audio recording). The iPod nano's line-in capability is implemented through the Dock Connector (rather than through the remote-control socket, as on third- and fourth-generation regular iPods). At this writing, the test instructs you to press the Action button (the Select button), but doing so has no effect.
Status	Displays status information about the iPod's LCD, serial number and model number, whether headphones are connected (HP:1) or not (HP:0), whether the iPod is receiving power via FireWire or via USB, and whether the iPod is being charged.
HDSpecs	Displays specification information about the iPod's "hard disk"—in other words, its flash memory. The information includes the model number, the firmware revision, the total number of memory blocks being addressed (Total LBA), the total memory size, and the partition type (FAT32 or HFS).
PatternTest	Displays a series of colors and patterns to let you verify that the screen is working. When you enter this test, the screen goes blank. Press the Select button to display each color or pattern. Press the Menu button to exit the test.
SleepShort	Puts the iPod nano to sleep.
Reset	Resets the iPod nano. Use this "test" to exit diagnostic mode and restart your iPod.

TABLE 17-2   Diagnostic Tests for the iPod nano

Test	Explanation
5 IN 1	Runs the following tests: LCM, RTC, SDRAM, FLASH, and WHEEL A2D. Press the Select button to move through the LCM test; if you don't, your iPod will appear to have hung with a blank screen.
RESET	Resets your iPod.
CHGRCUR	Displays a screen on which you can check and set charging and suspend levels for USB.
HP STAT	Displays a screen that lets you check whether the iPod mini has detected a device plugged into its headphone socket (HP 1) or not (HP 0) and whether the Hold switch is on (HOLD 1) or off (HOLD 0).
IRAM3	Performs a detailed test of the IRAM chip. If all is well, you'll see the message "PASS, HITPLAY CONTINUE." Press the Play button.
BATTA2D and A2D TEST	Test your iPod's battery and power system.
HDD R/W	Performs a read-write test on the hard disk. You must plug the iPod mini into a power source before the scan will start.
SMRT DAT	Displays a readout of drive-related data.
DISK SCAN	Performs a scan of the hard disk. You must plug the iPod mini into a power source before the scan will start.
CLR BLKS	This test clears the blocks of the iPod's memory. You'll see a CLEARBLKS message and a percentage readout as it works. The iPod mini then displays the diagnostics screen.
DISKMODE	Forces disk mode on the iPod mini.
ALLSDRAM	This test performs a comprehensive test of the iPod mini's SDRAM chip. You'll see a PASS or FAIL message at the end.
HDD DROP	This test checks the hard disk's anti-drop protection. Press the Play button to simulate a drop. If the protection is working, the iPod mini displays HDD DROP. Press the Select button to restore the DROPTEST display if you want to try again. Press the Previous button or the Next button to return to the diagnostics screen.

TABLE 17-3   Brief Explanations of the Other Diagnostic Tests for the iPod mini

Troubleshoot Specific Problems

This section discusses how to troubleshoot specific problems with the iPod, starting with the more common problems and moving gradually toward the esoteric end of the spectrum.

17

Your iPod Won't Respond to Keypresses

If your iPod won't respond to keypresses, follow as many of these steps, in order, as are necessary to revive it:

1. Check that neither the Hold switch on your iPod nor the Hold switch on the remote control (if you're using it) is on.

2. Check that the battery is charged. When the battery is too low to run the iPod (for example, for playing back music), your iPod will display a low-battery symbol—a battery icon with an exclamation point—for a few seconds when you press a key. (You may miss this icon if you're using the remote or you're pressing your iPod's buttons without looking at the screen.) Connect the iPod to a power source (either a computer that's not asleep or the iPod Power Adapter, if you have one), give it a few minutes to recharge a little, disconnect it again, and then try turning it on.

3. Reset your iPod (see the section "Reset Your iPod," earlier in this chapter).

4. Enter diagnostic mode and run the Key test (see the section "Check the iPod's Buttons," earlier in this chapter).

Your Remote Control Stops Working

If your iPod's remote control suddenly stops working without having suffered any obvious accident (such as you sitting on it or the dog chewing it into tinsel and confetti), check that its plug is pushed in fully. This is a particular problem on second-generation iPods, on which the remote control connects in a recessed ring around the headphone socket; you may need to twist the plug a little to improve the connection. (Don't twist the plug on a third- or fourth-generation regular iPod or an iPod mini, because you'll stand a good chance of breaking it.)

If the plug is firmly seated, enter diagnostic mode and run the Remote test. See the section "Check the Remote Control on a Fourth-Generation iPod or an iPod mini," earlier in this chapter, for details.

Your Computer Doesn't React when You Plug In Your iPod

If your computer (Mac or PC) doesn't react when you plug in your iPod, any of several things might have gone wrong. Try the actions described in the following subsections.

Unplug Any Other Devices in the USB or FireWire Chain

If there's another device plugged into your computer's USB or FireWire controller, try unplugging it. The problem may be that the controller can't supply power to another unpowered device as well as to your iPod.

If the connection uses a hub, disconnect the hub and try a direct connection.

Check That the Cable Is Working

For any iPod other than an iPod shuffle (which you normally connect directly to a USB port using its built-in connector), make sure that the cable is firmly connected to the iPod and to the

USB port or FireWire port on your computer. If you normally use a dock or connecting stand for your iPod, try the connection without it in case the dock or stand is causing the problem.

If you're not sure the cable is working, and you have an iPod Power Adapter, you can run a partial check by plugging the cable into your iPod and the iPod Power Adapter and then plugging the iPod Power Adapter into an electrical socket. If your iPod starts charging, you'll know that at least the power-carrying wires on the cable are working. It's likely that the data-carrying wires are working as well.

Check That the USB Port or FireWire Port on the Computer Is Working

Check that the USB port or FireWire port on the computer is working. In most cases, the easiest way to check is by plugging in another device that you know is working. For example, you might plug in a USB scanner or a FireWire external CD-ROM drive.

Your iPod Says "Do Not Disconnect" for Ages when Connected to Your Computer

When you connect your iPod to your Mac or PC, your iPod displays the "Do not disconnect" message while it synchronizes with iTunes. When synchronization is complete, your iPod should display the charging indicator for as long as it's taking on power via the FireWire cable or USB cable.

But sometimes it doesn't. If your iPod displays the "Do not disconnect" message for long after synchronization should have finished, first try to remember if you've enabled disk mode on your iPod. If so, you always need to unmount your iPod manually, so this message doesn't mean that there's a problem. You can unmount the iPod in one of these ways:

- Click the Eject button next to the iPod's entry in the Source pane in iTunes.

- Right-click the iPod in the Source pane and choose Eject from the shortcut menu.

- Right-click the iPod's drive icon in a My Computer window in Windows, or right-click the iPod's icon on your Mac desktop, and choose Eject from the shortcut menu.

- On the Mac, from the Finder, drag the iPod to the Trash, or select it and press ⌘-E.

Your iPod should then display the "OK to disconnect" message.

If you haven't enabled disk mode on your iPod, your iPod's hard drive may have gotten stuck spinning. If you pick up your iPod to scrutinize it further, you'll notice it's much hotter than usual if the drive has been spinning for a while. Try unmounting it anyway using one of the methods described in the preceding list. The iPod should then display the "OK to disconnect" message, and you can disconnect it safely.

If that doesn't work, you may need to reset your iPod (see "Reset Your iPod," earlier in this chapter). After your iPod reboots, you should be able to eject it by taking one of the actions listed previously.

17

TIP   *If you experience this problem frequently, try updating your iPod to the latest software version available. If there's no newer software version, or if an update doesn't help, use the AC adapter to recharge your iPod rather than recharging it from your computer.*

Your iPod Displays a Disk Icon with Magnifying Glass, Arrow, Check Mark, X, or Exclamation Point

If your iPod displays a disk icon on startup, it suspects there's a problem with its hard disk. See the section "Run a Disk Scan on a Fourth-Generation iPod," earlier in this chapter, for details.

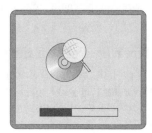

Your iPod Displays Only the Apple Logo When You Turn It On

If, when you turn on your iPod, it displays the Apple logo as usual but goes no further, there's most likely a problem with the iPod software. Try resetting your iPod first to see if that clears the problem. (See "Reset Your iPod," earlier in this chapter.)

If resetting doesn't work, usually you'll need to restore your iPod as described in "Restore Your iPod," earlier in this chapter. Restoring your iPod loses all data stored on it, so try several resets first.

Songs in Your Music Library Aren't Transferred to Your iPod

If songs you've added to your music library aren't transferred to your iPod even though you've synchronized successfully since adding the songs, there are two possibilities:

■ First, check that you haven't configured your iPod for partial synchronization or manual synchronization. For example, if you've chosen to synchronize only selected playlists, your iPod won't synchronize new music files not included on those playlists.

■ Second, check that the songs' tags include the artist's name and song name. Without these two items of information, iTunes won't transfer the songs to your iPod, because your iPod's interface won't be able to display the songs to you. You can force iTunes to transfer song files that lack artist and song name tags by adding the song files to a playlist, but in the long run, you'll benefit from tagging all your song files correctly.

Mac OS X Displays the SBOD and Then Fails to Recognize Your iPod

If, when you connect your iPod, Mac OS X displays the Spinning Beachball of Death (SBOD) for a while (usually several minutes) and then refuses to recognize your iPod even though your iPod is displaying the "Do not disconnect" message, it may mean you've plugged a Windows iPod into your Mac. This problem usually occurs only with first- and second-generation iPods; usually, Mac OS X can read FAT32-formatted iPods without a problem.

iPod nano Restarts when You Press the Select Button

If you find that your iPod nano decides to restart when you scroll down to the Music item on the Main menu and then press the Select button, go to Diagnostic mode and run the Key test to check whether the iPod thinks the Select button (or the "Action" button, as the firmware refers to it) is working correctly. If so, you will probably need to restore the iPod's software to restore normal service.

Fifth-Generation iPod Causes "The iPod Cannot Be Updated" Message

The message "The iPod 'iPod_Name' cannot be updated. The disk could not be read from or written to." (shown here) is a curious one, because the iPod usually seems to be working fine. Even so, you will probably need to restore the iPod's software before your Mac can read it successfully again.

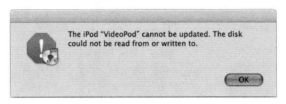

The iPod "VideoPod" cannot be updated. The disk could not be read from or written to.

OK

TIP   *All logic and sanity to the contrary, it's sometimes possible to get completely stuck in diagnostic mode by using some tests on certain iPod models in particular conditions. If you can't reach the Reset test so as to reset the iPod the polite way, and you're not able to reset the iPod by brute force by holding down the Select button and the Menu button for a few seconds, you may have to resort to waiting until the iPod's battery runs out of power before you can regain control of the iPod. When the battery runs out, recharge the iPod as usual, and it should start in normal mode (in other words, not in diagnostic mode).*

17

Chapter 18

Troubleshoot iTunes

How to…

- Deal with iTunes not starting on Windows
- Force Windows and iTunes to recognize your iPod
- Make iTunes on Windows notice that you've inserted a CD
- Solve common iTunes and iPod error messages in Windows
- Deal with iTunes not starting on the Mac
- Make Mac OS X eject a "lost" CD
- Deal with the "not enough access privileges" error on the Mac
- Recover from iTunes running you out of disk space on Windows or the Mac

If you read Chapter 17, you'll have seen that some of the problems with the iPod involve iTunes as well—which is hardly surprising, given how closely they work in partnership. This chapter focuses on problems that are primarily related to iTunes or that manifest themselves on the iTunes side of the partnership.

The chapter starts with a section of Windows-specific problems, including iTunes refusing to start at all, iTunes refusing to recognize your iPod or the CDs you insert, and some of the error messages you may be unlucky enough to encounter. After that, the remainder of the chapter covers Mac-specific problems, ranging from iTunes refusing to start on the Mac to Mac OS X telling you that you don't have enough access privileges. For both operating systems, you'll learn how to recover from an ill-advised consolidation that threatens to run your computer out of disk space.

Troubleshoot iTunes on Windows

This section shows you how to troubleshoot the problems you're most likely to encounter when running iTunes on Windows.

iTunes Won't Start on Windows

If iTunes displays this Cannot Open iTunes dialog box saying that you can't open iTunes because another user currently has it open, it means that Windows XP is using Fast Switching and that someone else is logged on under another account and has iTunes open:

Click the OK button to dismiss the dialog box. If you know the other user's password, or if you know they have no password, you can switch the user to their account by choosing Start | Log Off | Switch User and clicking their entry on the Welcome screen, close iTunes, and then switch back to your own account.

If you don't know the other user's password, either induce them to log on and close iTunes for you, or use Task Manager to close iTunes (right-click the taskbar and choose Task Manager from the shortcut menu to display Windows Task Manager, select the iTunes entry on the Applications tab, and then click the End Task button).

iTunes Won't Recognize Your iPod

If all goes well, your computer recognizes your iPod as soon as you connect it, and the iPod Setup Assistant shepherds you through the process of naming (or renaming) your iPod and deciding how to synchronize it with your music library. But sometimes Windows, iTunes, or both will fail to recognize your iPod. If this happens, work through the following sections.

"USB Device Not Recognized" Warning

When your PC recognizes your iPod connected via USB, it may display a series of Found New Hardware pop-ups announcing that it has found a USB Mass Storage Device, an Apple iPod USB Device, and a couple of other partly accurate descriptions. This is normal. Let Windows complete the installation process.

On some PCs, Windows may claim not to recognize the iPod, as shown here:

After displaying this pop-up, Windows usually recognizes the iPod. So if you see this message, wait for a minute or two, and see if Windows, iTunes, and the iPod Service can work out between them what your iPod is and load the appropriate drivers for it. If they do, you'll see the Safely Remove Hardware icon in the notification area. If you click this icon, it will tell you that it thinks your iPod is a USB Mass Storage Device and the drive letter it has assigned to it:

iTunes Helper Message Box Appears

If you've installed iTunes but you haven't yet installed the iPod Software when you connect your iPod, iTunes displays the iTunes Helper message box telling you that you need to install the iPod Software. Click the OK button to dismiss the message box, install the iPod Software, and then try again:

Your USB Card Doesn't Work with Your iPod

In theory, your iPod should work with any standard USB card. In practice, not all cards are created equal. If everything else seems to be well, but you cannot make Windows recognize your iPod, your USB card may be the problem. If so, the solution is to replace it with a card that'll work with the iPod. Many cards will work, but your first step should be to check the latest list of cards at http://docs.info.apple.com/article.html?artnum=93405. This article also lists FireWire cards, which you may need for connecting an older iPod.

Reinstall the iPod Software

If Windows recognizes your iPod but iTunes still doesn't, you may need to reinstall the iPod Software. After reinstalling it, restart your PC and try again.

iTunes Starts Very Slowly

At this writing, iTunes takes much longer to start on a PC than on a Mac, even if the two computers start other applications (for example, Microsoft Word) at roughly the same speed. The more songs and videos your library contains, the worse this problem is.

Short of switching to the Mac or buying a faster PC, there's not much you can do about this problem. But one thing that makes iTunes start up even slower is having to look up a CD's information across a slow Internet connection—so don't load a CD that iTunes hasn't yet looked up until after iTunes has started. (iTunes caches the data for CDs that it has successfully looked up, so it doesn't need to look them up again.)

iTunes Starts But Doesn't Appear

Sometimes you may find that iTunes doesn't appear after you launch it—even when you give it more than its usual length of time (see the previous section) to get going. When this happens, you'll usually need to track down iTunes and kill it ("kill" is the technical term) so that you can start it again. Follow these steps:

1. Right-click the taskbar and choose Task Manager from the shortcut menu to display Windows Task Manager.

2. Check on the Applications tab (shown on the left in Figure 18-1) whether iTunes is listed. If it is, try selecting it and clicking the Switch To button to display it. If that works, start using iTunes. If not, continue with these steps.

FIGURE 18-1   If iTunes starts but doesn't appear, use Windows Task Manager to shut it down. First, check for iTunes on the Applications tab. If iTunes doesn't appear there, use the Processes tab to shut down iTunes.

3. If iTunes appears on the Applications tab, select it and click the End Task button to close it.

4. If iTunes doesn't appear on the Applications tab, click the Processes tab (shown on the right in Figure 18-1).

5. Click the Image Name heading to sort the processes by name if necessary.

6. Select the iTunes.exe entry.

7. Click the End Process button. Windows displays a Task Manager Warning dialog box like this:

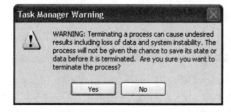

8. Click the Yes button to close iTunes.

9. Press ALT-F4 or choose File | Exit Task Manager to close Windows Task Manager.

Once you've done this, you should be able to start iTunes again as usual. If you're still not able to start iTunes, restart Windows and then try again.

18

iTunes Doesn't Recognize Your iPod

If your iPod doesn't appear in the Source pane in iTunes, take as many of the following steps as necessary to make it appear there:

1. Check that your iPod is okay. If you find it's displaying an exclamation point or the Sad iPod symbol, you'll know iTunes isn't guilty this time.

2. Check that your iPod knows it's connected to your PC. Your iPod should be displaying the Do Not Disconnect message. If it's not, fix the connection so that it does display this message.

3. Check that Windows is recognizing your iPod. Choose Start | My Computer to display a My Computer window that shows all the drives and devices that Windows thinks are connected to your PC. Your iPod should show up as a drive, even if you haven't specifically enabled disk mode.

   - If your iPod doesn't appear as a drive in My Computer, toggle the Hold switch on your iPod, then restart the iPod by holding down the Play button and the Menu button together for several seconds. Wait for a few seconds and then press F5 or choose View | Refresh to refresh the view in the My Computer window.

   - If restarting your iPod doesn't make it appear in My Computer, repeat the process for restarting it. This time, when your iPod displays the Apple symbol, hold down the Select button and the Play button for a moment to force disk mode. Forcing disk mode sends a request to the computer to mount your iPod as a drive.

4. If Windows is recognizing your iPod, but iTunes isn't, restart iTunes.

5. If restarting iTunes doesn't make it recognize your iPod, restart Windows and then restart iTunes.

iTunes Doesn't Notice when You Insert Another CD

If iTunes doesn't notice when you remove one CD and insert another, usually you'll need to quit iTunes and restart it to make it reread the CD.

If your PC has two or more optical drives, try using another drive. iTunes may be better at noticing that you've changed the CD in another drive. If you've turned off AutoRun for the optical drive, turn it back on.

If you're familiar with Windows, you may be disappointed to find that a few maneuvers you might expect to help with this problem don't help:

- First, using the Show Songs Using iTunes item in the AutoPlay dialog box for the CD (which you can display by right-clicking the Audio CD entry in a My Computer window and choosing AutoPlay from the shortcut menu) merely makes iTunes list the CD it thinks is in the drive. (The Play CD Using iTunes item has even less effect—it doesn't even start the CD playing.)

- Second, ejecting the CD from iTunes itself (instead of from Windows Explorer or by using the manual eject button on your CD drive) doesn't make iTunes realize that you've removed the CD and that it should probably check to see whether you've put in another CD.

- Third, choosing Advanced | Get CD Track Names doesn't make iTunes check which CD is in the drive. Instead, this command makes iTunes check CDDB for information on the CD it thinks is in the drive.

Repair iTunes if You've Recently Installed Burning Software

If iTunes used to notice when you inserted CDs, but now no longer notices, one possibility is that you've installed some software recently that is preventing iTunes from monitoring the CD drive correctly. The usual suspects are CD- or DVD-burning software (such as Easy CD and DVD Creator or Nero) and audio applications that support burning (such as Napster and Musicmatch Jukebox). In this case, repair iTunes as follows:

1. If iTunes is running, press ALT-F4 or choose File | Exit to close it.

2. Choose Start | Control Panel to open a Control Panel window. Then click the Add Or Remove Programs icon. (If you're using Classic View rather than Category View, double-click the Add Or Remove Programs icon.) Windows opens the Add Or Remove Programs window with the Change Or Remove Programs tab at the front.

3. In the Currently Installed Programs list, click iTunes and then click the Change/Remove button to launch the InstallShield Wizard.

4. Select the Repair option button and then click the Next button. iTunes Setup repairs the configuration of iTunes and QuickTime.

5. When the Maintenance Successful screen appears, click the Finish button.

6. Click the Close button (the X button) to close the Add Or Remove Programs window.

7. Restart iTunes and then check if it notices when you insert a CD.

Update iTunes to the Latest Version

If you're not already running the latest version of iTunes, update to it. From iTunes, choose Help | Check For iTunes Updates to see if there's a new version. If so, download and install it.

Update the Driver for Your Optical Drive

See if there's a new driver for your optical drive by following these steps:

1. Choose Start | My Computer to open a Windows Explorer window to My Computer.

2. Right-click the icon for your optical drive and choose Properties from the shortcut menu to display the Properties dialog box for the drive.

3. Click the Hardware tab to display its contents.

4. Click the listing for your optical drive in the All Disk Drives list box.

18

5. Click the Properties button to display the detailed Properties dialog box for the drive.

6. Click the Driver tab to display its contents.

7. Click the Update Driver button and then follow through the steps of the Hardware Update Wizard to install any new driver that is available.

8. Click the OK button to close each Properties dialog box in turn and then click the Close button (the X button) to close the My Computer window.

Another possibility is to check for updates to the firmware of your optical drive and your sound card.

If iTunes Recognizes Only the First CD, Prevent Shwicon2k from Running

If iTunes recognizes the first CD you insert during a session, but then won't recognize any other CDs, the culprit may be Shwicon2k.exe, a multimedia card reader program. If you're not using your multimedia reader, you can prevent Shwicon2k.exe from running when you start Windows, which should get rid of this problem with iTunes.

Here's how to prevent Shwicon2k.exe from running when you start Windows:

1. Close iTunes and all other running applications.

2. Choose Start | Run, type **msconfig**, and then press ENTER to start System Configuration Utility.

3. Click the Startup tab to display it.

4. Clear the check box for the Shwicon2k item.

5. Click the OK button. System Configuration Utility exits and displays a System Configuration dialog box telling you that you must restart your computer.

6. Click the Restart button. System Configuration Utility restarts Windows and then displays the System Configuration Utility dialog box shown here:

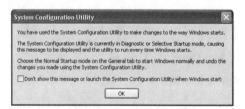

7. Select the Don't Show This Message Or Launch The System Configuration Utility When Windows Starts check box and then click the OK button.

8. Start iTunes.

9. Insert a CD, remove it, and then insert another CD. See if iTunes recognizes the CD.

Run the iTunes CD Diagnostics and Submit the Results to Apple

If you've been through the previous suggestions in this section, and iTunes still refuses to recognize CDs you insert, run the iTunes CD diagnostics and report the results to Apple so that Apple can try to stamp out the problems in future versions of iTunes. Open www.apple.com/support/itunes/windows/cddiagnostics/ in your browser, follow the instructions on the web page for running the CD diagnostics, and then paste the results from the CD Diagnostics window into the box on the web page and submit the form to Apple. Click the Close button to close the CD Diagnostics window.

Give Up in Disgust

If you're still stuck with iTunes refusing to recognize any CD you insert after iTunes starts, you'll need to quit iTunes and restart it to make it notice the new CD. If even that doesn't work, you'll need to restart Windows.

Windows Displays the "iPod Not Readable" Dialog Box

The iPod Not Readable dialog box, shown here, indicates that you've plugged a Mac-formatted iPod into your PC:

If you did so by mistake, click the Cancel button and then disconnect the iPod. If you plugged in the iPod intentionally, you'll need to reformat the iPod before you can use it with Windows. Click the Update button to launch the iPod Software Updater and then follow through the update process to reformat the iPod. See "Keep Your iPod's Operating System Up to Date" in Chapter 17 for details.

You See the "Updater Can't Install Firmware on Connected iPod" Message

The error message "Updater can't install firmware on connected iPod. The iPod's hardware and the Updater firmware are not compatible" indicates that you're trying to use the wrong version of the iPod Software Updater for your iPod. For example, you can't use the iPod Software Updater versions 2.0 and above on first- and second-generation iPods.

18

To solve this problem, get the latest version of the iPod Updater. Since Apple switched from using separate updaters for different iPod firmware versions to providing a single updater that works for all known iPods, getting the right iPod Updater is no longer a problem—but downloading it over a slow connection can take several hours.

Deal with the "Please Reinstall iTunes" or "iPod Service Error" Message on Windows

The most frustrating error you'll encounter at this stage is iTunes' not being able to identify your iPod. There can be several causes for this problem, including a configuration problem with iTunes or a conflict with the iPod Service that runs on Windows to notify iTunes of the iPod and its details. This section shows you the solutions. Try the solutions in the order they're presented, stopping when iTunes recognizes the iPod.

Uninstall and Reinstall iTunes

The error message "The software required for communicating with the iPod is not installed correctly. Please reinstall iTunes to install the iPod's software" usually indicates that you need to reinstall iTunes.

To reinstall iTunes, follow these steps:

1. Choose Start | Control Panel and then click the Add Or Remove Programs link or double-click the Add Or Remove Programs icon to display the Add Or Remove Programs window.

2. In the Currently Installed Programs list, click the iTunes item and then click the Change/Remove button to launch the InstallShield Wizard.

3. Select the Remove option button and then click the Next button.

4. Click the OK button in the Confirm Uninstall dialog box, wait for the wizard to finish uninstalling iTunes, and then click the Finish button.

5. Click the Close button to close the Add Or Remove Programs window.

6. Choose Start | Run, type **%programfiles%** in the Run dialog box, and then click the OK button to open a Windows Explorer window to your Program Files folder.

7. If you see the message "These files are hidden," click the Show The Contents Of This Folder link to display them.

8. If the Program Files folder contains an iTunes folder, click it and then press DELETE. Click the Yes button in the confirmation message box.

9. Double-click the iPod folder to display its contents. Click the bin folder and then press DELETE. Click the Yes button in the confirmation message box.

10. If Windows displays the Error Deleting File Or Folder message box (shown in Figure 18-2), click the OK button. Choose Start | Run, type **services.msc**, and then click the OK button to open the Services window. Right-click the iPod Service item and choose Stop from the

FIGURE 18-2   The Error Deleting File Or Folder message box means that the iPod Service is still running. You'll need to stop the iPod Service before you can reinstall iTunes.

shortcut menu. The Service Control window appears for a moment as Windows stops the service. Choose File | Exit to close the Services window. Again, click the bin folder and then press DELETE. Click the Yes button in the confirmation message box.

11. Choose Start | Turn Off Computer and then click the Restart button to restart Windows.

12. Download the latest version of iTunes from the Apple website (www.apple.com/itunes/download/) and then install it.

Disable System Services That Conflict with the iPod Service

If uninstalling and reinstalling iTunes doesn't enable iTunes and Windows to recognize the iPod, the next most likely problem is that your PC is running a service or a startup item that conflicts with the iPod Service. A *service* is a process that Windows runs automatically, whereas a *startup item* is either a service or an application that is set to start automatically when Windows starts.

If you can't get your iPod working by reinstalling iTunes, you may need to disable some services or startup items. Proceed as follows:

1. Close all running applications.

2. Choose Start | Run, type **msconfig** in the Run dialog box, and then click the OK button to open the System Configuration Utility.

3. Click the General tab if it's not already displayed.

4. The Normal Startup option button will usually be selected. Select the Selective Startup option button instead (see Figure 18-3).

5. Clear the Load Startup Items check box.

6. Click the Startup tab to display its contents (see Figure 18-4) and then select the iTunesHelper check box. Clearing the Load Startup Items check box in the previous step cleared all the check boxes on this tab. You have turned them off because they may conflict with the iPod Service, but you will probably need to restart most of them after you get the iPod Service working.

18

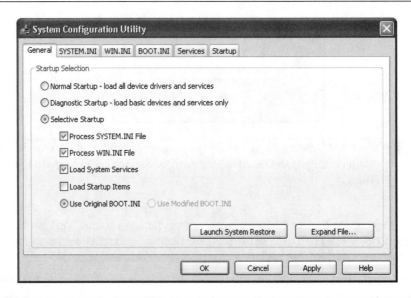

FIGURE 18-3 Choose the Selective Startup option button in System Configuration Utility to enable yourself to disable system services that conflict with the iPod Service.

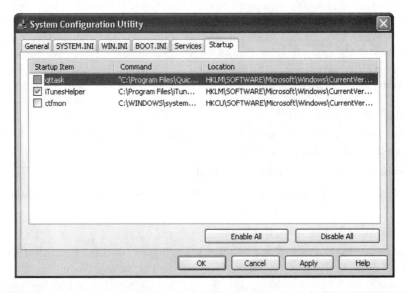

FIGURE 18-4 Select the iTunesHelper check box on the Startup tab to force Windows to start the iTunesHelper service.

7. Click the Services tab to display its contents (see Figure 18-5) and then select the Hide All Microsoft Services check box if it's not already selected.

8. Clear the check box for each service except the iPod Service item. These items, too, may conflict with the iPod Service.

9. Click the OK button to close System Configuration Utility and then click the Restart button in the System Configuration dialog box that tells you that you must restart your computer.

10. When Windows restarts, it displays a System Configuration Utility dialog box reminding you that you've made changes to your Windows configuration.

11. Click the OK button to dismiss it.

12. Connect your iPod to see if Windows detects it and iTunes starts.

If so, all is well. If not, open System Configuration Utility again (step 2 in the previous list), click the Services tab, and clear the iPod Service check box. Download the latest version of iTunes from the Apple website (www.apple.com/itunes/download/), install it, and see if it detects the iPod.

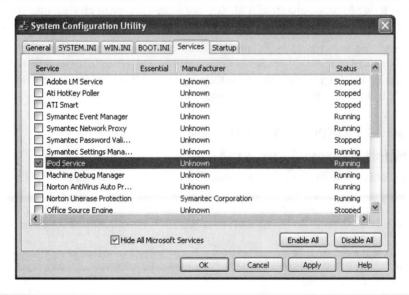

FIGURE 18-5   Select the iPod Service check box on the Services tab to force Windows to start the iPod Service.

Reinstall the iPod Service's COM Interface

If the previous measures don't enable Windows and iTunes to recognize your iPod, try reinstalling the iPod Service's COM interface. (COM is the Component Object Model that enables different computer components to communicate with each other.)

1. Choose Start | Run, type **services.msc**, and then click the OK button to open the Services window.

2. Right-click the iPod Service item and choose Stop from the shortcut menu. The Service Control window appears for a moment as Windows stops the service.

3. Choose File | Exit to close the Services window.

4. Choose Start | Run, type **"%programfiles%\ipod\bin\ipodservice.exe" /service** (including the double quotation marks and the space before the forward slash), and then press ENTER.

5. Choose Start | Turn Off Computer and then click the Restart button to restart Windows.

iTunes Won't Play Some AAC Files

iTunes and AAC go together like bacon and eggs, but you may find that iTunes can't play some AAC files. This can happen for either of two reasons:

- You're trying to play a protected AAC file in a shared library or playlist, and your computer isn't authorized to play the file. In this case, iTunes skips the protected file.

- The AAC file was created by an application other than iTunes that uses a different AAC standard. The AAC file then isn't compatible with iTunes. To play the file, use the application that created the file, or another application that can play the file, to convert the file to another format that iTunes supports—for example, MP3 or WAV.

"The iPod Is Linked to Another iTunes Music Library" Message

If, when you connect your iPod to your computer, iTunes displays the message "The iPod '*iPod_name*' is linked to another iTunes music library," chances are that you've plugged the wrong iPod into your computer. The message box also offers to change this iPod's allegiance from its current computer to this PC. Click the No button and check which iPod this is before synchronizing it.

 For details about moving your iPod from one computer to another, see "Change the Computer to Which Your iPod Is Linked," in Chapter 13.

iTunes Runs You Out of Hard-Disk Space on Windows

As you saw earlier in the book, iTunes lets you choose between copying to your library folder all the files you add to your library and leaving the files in other locations. Adding all the files to your music library means you have all the files available in one place. This can be good, especially if your computer is a laptop and you want to be able to access your music and videos when it's not connected to your external drives or network drives. But if you have a large library, it may not all fit on your laptop's hard disk.

If your files are stored on your hard drive in folders other than your music library folder, you have three choices:

- You can issue the Advanced | Consolidate Library command to make iTunes copy the files to your library folder, doubling the amount of space they take up. In almost all cases, this is the worst possible choice to make. (Rarely, you might want redundant copies of your files in your library so you can experiment with them.)

- You can have iTunes store references to the files rather than copies of them. If you also have files in your library folder, this is the easiest solution. To do this, clear the Copy Files To iTunes Music Folder When Adding To Library check box on the Advanced tab of the iTunes dialog box in Windows.

- You can move your library to the folder that contains your files. This is the easiest solution if your library is empty.

If you choose to consolidate your library, and there's not enough space on your hard disk, you'll see the following message box. "IBM_PRELOAD" is the name of the hard disk on the computer.

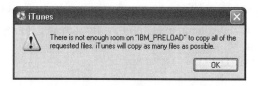

Clearly, this *isn't* okay, but iTunes doesn't let you cancel the operation. Don't let iTunes pack your hard disk as full of files as it can, because that will make Windows severely unhappy. Quit iTunes by pressing ALT-F4 or choosing File | Exit. If iTunes doesn't respond, right-click the taskbar and choose Task Manager to display Windows Task Manager. On the Applications tab, select the iTunes entry and then click the End Task button. If Windows double-checks that you want to end the task, confirm the decision.

Once you've done this, you may need to remove the tracks you've just copied to your music library from the folder. You can do this by using the Date Created information about the files and folders, because Windows treats the copy made by the consolidation as a new file. To search for the new files on Windows XP, follow these steps:

1. Choose Start | Search to display a Search Results window.

2. On the What Do You Want To Search For? screen, click the Pictures, Music, Or Video link. (If Search Companion displays the Search By Any Or All Of The Criteria Below screen instead of the What Do You Want To Search For? screen, click the Other Search Options link to display the What Do You Want To Search For? screen. Then click the Pictures, Music, or Video link.)

18

3. On the resulting screen, select the Music check box in the Search For All Files Of A Certain Type, Or Search By Type And Name area.

4. Click the Use Advanced Search Options link to display the remainder of the Search Companion pane.

5. Display the Look In drop-down list, select the Browse item to display the Browse For Folder dialog box, select your iTunes Music folder, and then click the OK button. (If you're not sure where your iTunes Music is, switch to iTunes, press CTRL-COMMA, and check on the Advanced sheet of the iTunes dialog box.)

6. Click the When Was It Modified? heading to display its controls and then select the Specify Dates option button. Select the Created Date item in the drop-down list and then specify today's date in the From drop-down list and the To drop-down list. (The easiest way to specify the date is to open the From drop-down list and select the Today item. Windows XP then enters it in the To text box as well.)

7. Click the Search button to start the search for music files created in the specified time frame.

8. If the Search Results window is using any view other than Details view, choose View | Details to switch to Details view.

9. Click the Date Created column heading twice to make Windows Explorer sort the files by reverse date. This way, the files created most recently appear at the top of the list.

10. Check the Date Modified column to identify the files created during the consolidation and then delete them without putting them in the Recycle Bin. (For example, select the files and press SHIFT-DELETE.)

After deleting the files (or as many of them as possible), you'll need to remove the references from iTunes and add them again from their preconsolidating location before iTunes can play them. When iTunes discovers that it can't find a file where it's supposed to be, it displays an exclamation point in the first column. Delete the entries with exclamation points and then add them to your music library again.

Troubleshoot iTunes on the Mac

This section shows you how to troubleshoot a handful of problems that you may run into when running iTunes on the Mac.

iTunes Won't Start on the Mac

If iTunes displays the following dialog box, saying that you can't open iTunes because another user currently has it open, it means that your Mac is using Fast User Switching and that someone else is logged on under another account and has iTunes open:

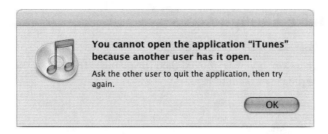

Click the OK button to dismiss the dialog box, then either log on as that user (if you know that user's password, or if they have no password) and quit iTunes, or have the user log on and quit iTunes. When you switch back to your account, you'll be able to run iTunes.

"The iPod Is Linked to Another iTunes Music Library" Message

If, when you connect your iPod to your computer, iTunes displays the message "The iPod '*iPod_name*' is linked to another iTunes music library," chances are that you've plugged the wrong iPod into your computer. The message box also offers to change this iPod's allegiance from its current computer to this Mac. Click the No button and check which iPod this is before synchronizing it.

For details about moving your iPod from one computer to another, see "Change the Computer to Which Your iPod Is Linked," in Chapter 13.

Eject a "Lost" CD

Sometimes Mac OS X seems to lose track of a CD (or DVD) after attempting to eject it. It's as if the eject mechanism fails to get a grip on the CD and push it out, but the commands get executed anyway, so that Mac OS X believes it has ejected the CD even though the CD is still in the drive.

When this happens, you probably won't be able to eject the disc by issuing another Eject command from iTunes, but it's worth trying that first. If that doesn't work, use Disk Utility to eject the disc. Follow these steps:

1. Press ⌘-SHIFT-U or choose Go | Utilities from the Finder menu to display the Utilities folder.

2. Double-click the Disk Utility item to run it.

3. Select the icon for the CD drive or the CD itself in the list box.

4. Click the Eject button.

5. Press ⌘-Q or choose Disk Utility | Quit Disk Utility to quit Disk Utility.

If that doesn't work, you may need to force your Mac to recognize the drive. If it's a hot-pluggable external drive (for example, FireWire or USB), try unplugging the drive, waiting a minute, and then plugging it back in. If the drive is an internal drive, you may need to restart your Mac to force it to recognize the drive.

"You Do Not Have Enough Access Privileges" when Importing Songs

The following error occurs when you've moved the iTunes music folder to a shared location and the user doesn't have Write permission to it:

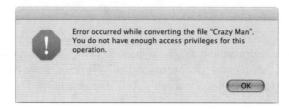

To fix this problem, an administrator needs to assign Write permission for the music folder to whoever received this error.

"The iPod 'iPod Name' Cannot Be Updated"

The message "The iPod 'iPod name' cannot be updated. The disk could not be read from or written to" (see the illustration) seems to indicate that you need to restore your iPod to resume normal service. Before taking this drastic step, check the Apple support site to see if Apple has posted other advice for this problem.

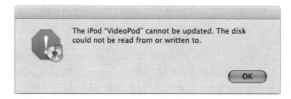

iTunes Runs You Out of Hard-Disk Space on the Mac

As you saw earlier in the book, iTunes can copy to your library folder all the files you add to your library. Adding all the files to your library means you have all the files available in one place. This can be good when (for example) you want your 'Book's hard disk to contain copies of all the song and video files stored on network drives so you can enjoy them when your computer isn't connected to the network. But it can take more disk space than you have.

If your files are stored on your hard drive in folders other than your library folder, you have three choices:

- ■ You can use the Advanced | Consolidate Library command to cause iTunes to copy the files to your library. This doubles the amount of space the files take up and is usually the worst choice. (Rarely, you might want redundant copies of your files in your library so you can experiment with them.)

■ You can have iTunes store references to the files rather than copies of them. If you also have files in your library folder, this is the easiest solution. To do this, clear the Copy Files To iTunes Music Folder When Adding To Library check box on the Advanced sheet of the Preferences dialog box.

■ You can move your library to the folder that contains your files. This is the easiest solution if your library is empty.

If you choose to consolidate your library, and your Mac doesn't have enough disk space, iTunes displays this message box to alert you to the problem:

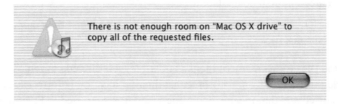

Click the OK button to dismiss this message box—iTunes gives you no other choice. Worse, when you click the OK button, iTunes goes ahead and tries to copy all the files anyway.

This is a bad idea, so stop the copying process as soon as you can. To do so, quit iTunes by pressing ⌘-Q or choosing iTunes | Quit iTunes. If you can't quit iTunes gently, force quit it: OPTION-click the iTunes icon in the Dock and choose Force Quit from the shortcut menu. (Failing that, press ⌘-OPTION-ESC to display the Force Quit dialog box, select the entry for iTunes, and click the Force Quit button.)

Once you've done this, remove the files you've just copied to your music library from the folder. Unfortunately, Mac OS X maintains the Date Created information from the original files on the copies made by the consolidation, so you can't search for the files by date created on the Mac the way you can on Windows.

Your best bet is to search by date created to identify the folders that iTunes has just created in your music library folder so that you can delete them and their contents. This approach will get all of the consolidated songs and videos that iTunes put into new folders, but it will miss any songs and videos that were consolidated into folders that already existed in your music library.

For example, if the song file Blue Orchid.m4a is already stored in your music library with correct tags, your music library will contain a White Stripes/Get Behind Me Satan folder. If you then consolidate your library so that other songs from that album are copied, the files will go straight into the existing folder, and your search will miss it. The date-modified attribute of the Get Behind Me Satan folder will change to the date of the consolidation, but you'll need to drill down into each modified folder to find the song files that were added.

To search for the new folders, follow these steps:

1. Press ⌘-F or choose File | Find from the Finder to display the Find window.

2. In the Search In drop-down list, choose the Specific Places item.

3. Click the Add button and use the resulting Choose A Folder dialog box to specify your iTunes Music folder. (If you're not sure where your iTunes Music folder is, check on the Advanced sheet of the Preferences dialog box in iTunes.)

4. In the list box, make sure the check box for your iTunes Music folder is selected.

5. In the Search For Items Whose group box, specify a first condition of Date Created Is Today and a second condition of Kind Is Folder.

6. Click the Search button. Mac OS X displays a list of the folders created today.

7. Sort the folders by date created, identify those created during the consolidation by the time on the date, and then delete them.

8. Verify that the Trash contains no other files you care about and then empty the Trash to get rid of the surplus files.

After deleting the files (or as many of them as possible), you'll need to remove the references from iTunes and add them again from their preconsolidating location before iTunes can play them. When iTunes discovers that it can't find a file where it's supposed to be, it displays an exclamation point in the first column. Delete the files with exclamation points and then add them to your library again.

Ripping CDs "Takes Too Long"

Ripping a large CD collection takes many hours, even if you have a couple of computers working at the same time—but there's not much alternative. One possibility is to use a utility such as Roxio Toast on Mac OS X to copy entire CDs to your Mac and then rip them all in sequence.

The problem with this approach is that it's seldom any quicker to copy an entire CD to your hard drive than it is to rip it, so you save little time, if any—and you need to have a full CD's worth of space on your hard disk for each CD you copy, rather than just requiring space for the compressed files iTunes creates. But if you do decide to try this, get the "Rip CDs in a Row" script from Doug Adams' website (www.dougscripts.com/itunes/scripts/scripts02.php?page=2#ri pcdsinarow), which speeds up the ripping part of the process.

Index